QUEERING CRIMINOLOGY IN THEORY AND PRAXIS

Reimagining Justice in the Criminal Legal System and Beyond

Edited by
Carrie L. Buist and Lindsay Kahle Semprevivo

BRISTOL
UNIVERSITY
PRESS

First published in Great Britain in 2023 by

Bristol University Press
University of Bristol
1-9 Old Park Hill
Bristol
BS2 8BB
UK
t: +44 (0)117 374 6645
e: bup-info@bristol.ac.uk

Details of international sales and distribution partners are available at bristoluniversitypress.co.uk

British Library Cataloguing in Publication Data
A catalogue record for this book is available from the British Library

ISBN 978-1-5292-1069-9 hardcover
ISBN 978-1-5292-1070-5 paperback
ISBN 978-1-5292-1072-9 ePub
ISBN 978-1-5292-1071-2 ePdf

Cover design: Nicky Borowiec
Front cover image: Brain Light / Alamy Stock Photo

Bristol University Press uses environmentally responsible print partners.

Printed in Great Britain by CPI Group (UK) Ltd, Croydon, CR0 4YY

Carrie:
I dedicate this book to my wife, Cherie – you inspire me
and you make my world complete. Thank you for loving me,
teaching me to live with intention and being my universal
sound. Every day with you is the best day of my life.

Lindsay:
For Danielle. Thank you for continuing to believe
in me no matter what. I would never be where I
am without your endless love and support.

Contents

List of Figures and Tables

Figures

Tables

Notes on Contributors

Laura Agnich Chavez (she/her) currently serves as Chief of Research and Evaluation of the Alameda County Probation Department where she leads a team of research staff working to improve processes and outcomes for justice-involved youth and adults. She received her PhD from Virginia Tech and was formerly an Associate Professor and Chair of the Department of Criminal Justice and Criminology at Georgia Southern University.

Naseem Badiey (she/her) is a political sociologist working in the Research and Evaluation Unit of the Alameda County Probation Department. Prior to joining the probation Department, she was Assistant Professor of International Development and Humanitarian Action at California State University Monterey Bay. She holds a BA from University of California Berkeley, a BFA from San Francisco Art Institute, and MPhil and DPhil (PhD) degrees from Oxford University.

Tusty ten Bensel (she/her) is an Associate Professor and the Director of the School of Criminal Justice and Criminology at the University of Arkansas at Little Rock. Her research interests focus on hate crimes against special populations, sexual violence and victimization, and neighborhoods and re-entry. Dr. ten Bensel has published in journals such as *Criminology, Criminal Justice and Behavior*, and *Journal of Interpersonal Violence*.

Rose M. Buckelew (she/her) is an Assistant Professor, General Faculty, in the Department of Sociology at the University of Virginia. Her research explores the role of race and racism in the social construction of crime and safety. In her teaching, she is committed to an intentionally antiracist pedagogy that decenters whiteness in the classroom and builds course learning centered on Black feminist and Chicanx principles of shared power, collaborative learning, and humility. Her experiences as a mother and Chicana from southeast Los Angeles inform her belief that abolition is loyalty to humanity.

Carrie L. Buist (she/her) is an Associate Professor at Grand Valley State University's School of Criminology, Criminal Justice, and Legal Studies.

Dr. Buist has been published in several notable journals such as *Critical Criminology, University of Richmond Law Review, Crime and Justice*, and *Culture, Health, & Sexuality*. Dr. Buist also co-authored the award-winning *Queer Criminology* which was honored as the book of the year by The American Society of Criminology's Division on Critical Criminology in 2016. Dr. Buist has been recognized for her contributions to the discipline with multiple awards, guest and key note speaking invitations, and in addition to her research she has been recognized for her mentoring and teaching students.

Aisha Canfield (she/her) is the Director at Ceres Policy Research. For almost a decade, she has conducted research on the disproportionate detention of LGBQ/GNCT youth of color and their pathways into the justice system. Ms. Canfield seeks to make her research a useful advocacy tool for youth, their families, communities, and the practitioners working directly with them. In addition, she serves as an evaluation partner to community-based organizations serving as alternatives to traditional system responses for youth of color.

April Carrillo (she/her) is an Assistant Professor at the University of South Dakota who studies social inequity in the criminal legal system, particularly concerning LGBTQ+ folx. She especially focuses on platforming and elevating the voices of trans and Black, Indigenous, and other people of color (BIPOC).

Roddrick A. Colvin (he/him) is a Professor of Public Administration in the School of Public Affairs at San Diego State University, where he teaches courses in public administration and criminal justice. His current research interests include public employment equity, police officers' shared perceptions and decision-making, and lesbian and gay civil rights. His research has appeared in a number of scholarly journals, including the *Review of Public Personnel Administration, Police Quarterly*, and *Women and Criminal Justice*. He is also the author of the book *Gay and Lesbian Cops: Diversity and Effective Policing* (Lynne Rienner, 2012). Dr. Colvin earned undergraduate degrees in political science and philosophy at Indiana University at Bloomington, a graduate degree in public administration at Seattle University, and a doctorate degree in public administration at the University at Albany (SUNY).

Luca Suede Connolly (she/her) is a Southern transfeminine community organizer, facilitator, and writer. She currently serves as the codirector of the Richmond Community Bail Fund and cofounded the Richmond Legal Collaborative. She is working towards an MSW and PhD in Social Welfare at the University of California Berkeley. Her research deploys qualitative methods to understand how community organizers understand and do their work, as well as the histories, tactics, and strategies of the carceral abolition movement. Her work centers the beliefs that everyone should be free and that our communities know how to get there.

Illandra Denysschen (she/her) is an independent researcher from South Africa and resides in Texas. She received a Bachelor's degree in psychology and a Master's degree in criminology and criminal justice, while striving to go back to finish her PhD in Criminology. Her research interests lie in the mental health aspects of the people affected by every aspect of the criminal justice system.

S. Page Dukes (she/her) is a native Atlien, comms staffer for the Southern Center for Human Rights, suffragist, and abolitionist. In 2017, immediately following her release, she helped found the Athens Reentry Collaborative, a support group for released people. Along with Lucilla R. Harrell, she is a founding member of Mourning Our Losses, a space for disenfranchised grief, and Georgia Freedom Letters, a letter-writing project building solidarity and community through pen pals and political education. Her modi operandi include raising awareness about the effects of incarceration and the need for restoration of rights, accurate media representation, and amplification of the active first-person voice.

Angela Dwyer (she/her) is an Associate Professor in Policing and Emergency Management, School of Social Sciences, University of Tasmania. She is the Deputy Director of the Tasmanian Institute of Law Enforcement Studies, the Co-Chair of the Division of Queer Criminology with the American Society of Criminology, and the Secretary of Equality Tasmania and a board member of Just Equal, advocacy bodies working to change legislation to further protect LGBTIQ people. Angela conducts research on the intersection between sexuality, gender diversity, and criminal justice, with a particular focus on frontline policing and service enhancement programs, and she frequently advises police organizations around Australia on their approaches to relationship building with LGBTIQ people. She is lead editor of *Queering Criminology*, edited with Matthew Ball and Thomas Crofts, published with Palgrave (2016).

Rosalind Evans (she/her) is an Assistant Professor at Our Lady of the Lake University. She teaches social work courses at Worden School of Social Service. Her research focuses on LGBTQ+ topics that involve inclusivity, identity development, coming out experiences, campus climate, and violence prevention. Evans's research also focuses on mindfulness and self-care experiences for social work students.

Shanna N. Felix (she/they) is an Assistant Professor in the Department of Sociology and Criminal Justice at the University of Wisconsin at La Crosse. Their research interests are in the areas of victimology, especially queer peoples' patterns of victimization and their experiences with the criminal justice system. Their most recent publication, which appears in *Sexuality Research and Social Policy*, found that LGB victims were more likely to report their victimization to mental health providers than any other organization. Their current research is based on findings from their dissertation, which explores binary and nonbinary trans peoples' experiences with victimization and social support. Their scholarly interests stem from direct experience working with victims of crime, most notably six years as a victims' advocate in southeastern Georgia and a year evaluating Georgia's Victim Legal Assistance Network.

Alexandria Garcia (she/her) is a Probation Specialist in the Research and Evaluation Unit at the Alameda County Probation Department. She holds a BA from the University of California Davis and an MPA from California State University East Bay. Currently, she is a doctoral candidate in Education and Organizational Leadership at the University of the Pacific where her research focuses on the impacts of COVID-19 on probation and organizational change.

Xavier L. Guadalupe-Diaz (he/him) is an Associate Professor and Criminology Coordinator in the Department of Sociology at Framingham State University in Massachusetts. His research examines intimate partner and sexual violence within LGBTQ communities with a focus on transgender victimization. He is the author of *Transgressed: Intimate Partner Violence in Transgender Lives* (New York University Press, 2019) and is co-editor (with Adam Messinger) of *Transgender Intimate Partner Violence: A Comprehensive Introduction* (New York University Press, 2020).

Lucilla R. Harrell (she/her) is a sister, daughter, niece, aunt, jailhouse lawyer, law student, and builder in Atlanta. With a background in journalism, marketing, and music, she spends her down time rooting out lawful 'discriminhatred' and instigating policy change. She is keeping the community safer with Atlanta's Policing Alternatives & Diversion (PAD) Initiative. Through Igniting Hope, she is decriminalizing survivors of intimate partner violence. With S. Page Dukes as her partner, she is continuing graduate research on post-incarceration syndrome and peer-based re-entry support and boosting access to college with the Georgia Coalition for Higher Education in Prison, the two of them navigating a wild living record driven by love and the ever-pressing quest toward liberation.

Chrystina Y. Hoffman (she/her) is an Assistant Professor at the University of West Florida and conducts research, broadly, on victimization. She earned her PhD at Georgia State University and her Master's and Bachelor's degrees at the University of North Carolina at Charlotte. Her research has examined questions such as whether children or adolescents who have been bullied experience greater consequences in adulthood, whether international students face the same victimization risk as domestic students, whether experiencing violent victimization impacts future expectations, and what factors motivate or hinder college students' decisions to intervene. Dr. Hoffman's work has been published in peer-reviewed publications such as *Youth Violence & Juvenile Justice, Journal of Interpersonal Violence, Victims & Offenders, Journal of American College Health,* and *Journal of Ethnicity in Criminal Justice.*

Angela Irvine-Baker (she/her) is the founder and Principal Consultant of Ceres Policy Research. With over 25 years of experience, Dr. Irvine-Baker has studied housing, education, health, and criminal justice policy. With a primary focus on youth incarceration, she aims to understand the links between school discipline and justice involvement. More specifically, she works to gain a deeper understanding about LGBT youth and youth of color regarding their trajectory into the juvenile justice system.

Lindsay Kahle Semprevivo (she/her) is a Teaching Assistant Professor of Criminology in the Department of Sociology and Anthropology. She is also affiliate faculty of the WVU Research Center on Violence, and the Laboratory for Youth Inequality and Justice. Dr. Semprevivo received her BA in Psychology and her MA in Sociology from Indiana University of Pennsylvania, before pursuing her PhD in Sociology at Virginia Tech. Her preliminary areas of specialization are in criminology and women's gender studies. Thus, her areas of teaching include: criminology, gender and crime, race/class/gender and justice, youth violence, and victimology. Her research interests focus primarily on the intersections of gender, sexual orientation, and race and ethnicity in youth violence and victimization. Her dissertation, entitled *Examining Victimization in the Lives of Lesbian, Gay, Bisexual and Questioning Youth,* assessed the effects of bullying, homophobic bullying, dating violence, and sexual assault on school avoidance, substance use and poor mental health outcomes in LGBQ youth. Dr. Semprevivo's research has been published in peer-reviewed journals and books such as: *Criminal Justice Studies, Journal of Child and Family Studies, Victims & Offenders, Sociological Spectrum, Violence and Victims, Gender, Place & Culture, Journal of Interpersonal Violence, Journal of Criminology, Sociology Compass, The Encyclopedia of Research Methods in Criminology and Criminal Justice,* and *The Handbook of Race, Ethnicity, Crime, and Justice.*

Rebecca S. Katz (she/her) is a Professor Emerita and adjunct faculty member at Morehead State University and has been teaching there since 1996. She has published articles in a variety of sociological and criminological journals over the last 20 years. She served in the active US Army from 1978 to 1981. She was a mental health therapist from 1985–1995 and re-initiated this career in 2017. She is currently an MSSW graduate student in Social Work at the Kent School of Social Work where she interns for the Center for Community and Family Wellness and works part time at Best Life Counseling in Louisville, Kentucky. She has a loving partner of 26 years, Ms. Shelley White.

Victoria Kurdyla (she/they) is a doctoral candidate in the Department of Sociology and Anthropology at North Carolina State University. Her research focuses on intimate partner violence in transgender and nonbinary communities.

Dave McDonald (he/him) is a Lecturer in Criminology in the School of Social and Political Sciences at the University of Melbourne, Australia. His research explores social and legal responses to child sexual abuse, with a particular interest in pedophilia as a category of criminality. He has published on topics including queer theory and pedophilia; sex offending and post-sentence preventative detention; child pornography and the visual arts; pedophilia and hate crime; and serial killing and sexual difference. His forthcoming work investigates community-level responses to institutional child sexual abuse in the wake of public inquiries.

Adam M. Messinger (he/him) is an Associate Professor of Justice Studies, as well as Women's, Gender and Sexuality Studies, at Northeastern Illinois University, where he researches intimate partner violence in the relationships of lesbian, gay, bisexual, transgender, and queer people (LGBTQ IPV). He is the co-editor (with Xavier Guadalupe-Diaz) of *Transgender Intimate Partner Violence: A Comprehensive Introduction* (New York University Press, 2020) and author of *LGBTQ Intimate Partner Violence: Lessons for Policy, Practice, and Research* (University of California Press, 2017) – books that offer an in-depth look at the last 40 years of LGBTQ IPV research and provide evidence-based tips for future public policy and service provision.

Rayna E. Momen (they/them) is a Black, trans poet, queer criminologist, and abolitionist from West Virginia. Their research explores the criminalization of transgender people and mass incarceration more broadly. Momen is a long-time volunteer with the Appalachian Prison Book Project and a certified Inside-Out Prison Exchange Program Instructor.

Vanessa R. Panfil (she/her) is an ethnographer, criminologist, sociologist, and advocate. She is the author of *The Gang's All Queer: The Lives of Gay Gang Members* (New York University Press, 2017), co-author of *Sex-Positive Criminology* (Routledge, 2021), and co-editor of the *Handbook of LGBT Communities, Crime, and Justice* (Springer, 2014; second edition forthcoming). Centrally involved in developing the burgeoning field of queer criminology, her research explores how intersections of gender and sexuality shape young people's experiences with gangs, crime, victimization, and the juvenile justice system. She is currently an Associate Professor in the Department of Sociology and Criminal Justice at Old Dominion University.

Trye Mica Price (he/him) is a doctoral student in the School of Criminal Justice and Criminology at the University of Arkansas at Little Rock. His research interests include victimization of LGBTQ+ individuals, homelessness, and queer criminology.

Nayan G. Ramirez (he/him) is an Assistant Professor of Criminology and Justice Studies at California State University, Northridge. He received his MA in Criminology and PhD in Sociology from Pennsylvania State University. Broadly, his interests include gender and sexualities, juvenile delinquency, and social network analysis. His research examines the relationship between sexual orientation and criminal offending from adolescence through adulthood.

Carolyn Reyes (she/her) is the Policy Director at Ceres Policy Research. She has spent the entirety of her professional career as a leader and advocate working on behalf of marginalized children, youth, and families in various capacities. As a national expert on issues related to LGBT youth in out-of-home care, she has coordinated two projects and a campaign with the goal of improving services to and outcomes for LGBT youth in child welfare and juvenile justice systems. Working from the classroom to the courtroom, she shares her working knowledge of these systems and those involved in direct fashion.

Jon Rosenstadt (they/them) is an independent scholar with a background in Women's and Gender Studies. Their research interests include queer experiences in the justice system, queer victimology, and explorations of sex-gender in the horror genre.

Jaclyn A. Siegel (she/her) is a postdoctoral research scholar at San Diego State University. Her research focuses on the intersection of gender, body image, and social justice. Her research interests primarily focus on shedding light on the social contexts and conditions that expand and restrict people's lives in the hopes of creating a better, safer, and more accepting world for all. She received her PhD from Western University in 2021, where she worked closely with Dr. Rachel Calogero.

Danielle C. Slakoff (she/her) is an Assistant Professor of Criminal Justice at California State University, Sacramento. She received her PhD in Criminology and Justice from the University of Nebraska Omaha. Her research interests include media representations of women victims and perpetrators, women's issues within the criminal justice system, race, LGBTQ+ issues, and intimate partner violence. Her work can be found in *Violence Against Women, Feminist Criminology, Race and Justice*, and *Criminology, Criminal Justice, Law, and Society*.

Wendy Still (she/her) is Chief Probation Officer of the Alameda County Probation Department. In her four decades of public service, she has spearheaded major prison and community corrections reform efforts in the California criminal justice system. A criminologist and a peace officer, she earned her Masters' of Advanced Studies, Criminal, Law & Society from the University of California, Irvine.

Michael K. Winters (he/him & they/them) is a PhD candidate at Texas Woman's University. His teaching and research interests include gender and sexuality, juvenile delinquency, digital communities, research methodology, animals and society, and media studies. His particular research interests include feminism in gaming, queer offenders, and animal-based rehabilitation programs in prison. He has co-authored work on the 'final girl' trope in horror movies. His current projects include the intersection of feminist identities and gaming spaces, streaming communities on Twitch, and the treatment of queer offenders in the American criminal justice system.

Aimee Wodda (she/her) is an Assistant Professor of Criminal Justice, Law and Society at Pacific University. Her research focuses on the intersection between institutionalized forms of harm and gender, sexuality, and the law.

Meredith G.F. Worthen (she/her) is a Professor of Sociology and elected faculty member of the Women's and Gender Studies Program at the University of Oklahoma. She is interested in the sociological constructions of deviance and stigma, LGBTQ identities, as well as feminist and queer criminology.

Acknowledgments

We would first like to thank Bristol University Press, and specifically Rebecca Tomlinson for her excitement regarding this project and her support and understanding during a global pandemic. In addition to Rebecca, we thank Freya Trand for her attention and care in assisting us throughout the process, and Alice Greaves and Elizabeth Stone at Bourchier. Next, we are deeply grateful to all the contributors who took the time to make this book what it is – a collective of thoughtful, committed researchers and practitioners, both veterans and rookies. The book wouldn't exist without all of you – your care, your desire and dedication to move forward towards real change, and how hard you work is inspiring and we think that shines through in the chapters presented in this volume.

Queer criminology as a discipline continues to emerge and gain respect in the wider world of criminology and although that is nice, it is not necessary. As queer folx we know just how right good ol' Albert Einstein was when he said 'what is right is not always popular and what is popular is not always right'. (We are looking at you, mainstream criminology.) We thank the folx who have come before us and look forward to the work that awaits. We also hope that scholars who are doing the work will remember the importance of being seen and safe, and welcomed. There's little worse than the cool kids standing in the corner arguing about which one of them is the coolest of the kids. Those who have forged the path must provide accurate directions. We have faith that the new Division on Queer Criminology will be a catalyst for support and positive change within the broader realm of the American Society of Criminology and beyond.

We also want to thank everyone working in the field, supporting real-world change regarding LGBTQ+ people in the United States and abroad. You are the ones who can take the research and theoretical paradigms and apply them to praxis – education, policy, training, resources, and more. The work is hard, the funding is minimal, but you all continue to push forward and we are honestly in awe of the lifelong impact all of you have on so many queer lives.

We have both benefitted from the mentorship of wonderful people who have made a real difference in our personal and professional lives, and for that we are eternally grateful. We hope to pay this care and wisdom forward to our own students who inspire us every day. In particular on this project, we would like to extend our thanks to Kayla Bates and Alyssa McCord, two graduate students who have been exceptionally helpful during this process. Incidentally, these two students are interested in both ends of the spectrum between theory and practice and undoubtedly will move the work into the future.

We would like to express our appreciation to institutions, colleagues and other advocates and allies who promote our work.

Finally, I (Carrie) would like to thank my co-editor for her tireless work on this project, her support, enthusiasm, patience, friendship, and for having my back during a trying year to say the least. You are not only a brilliant scholar but you're a gem of a human being. You're a good egg, Linds.

I (Lindsay) would also like to thank the person who illuminated this path for me back in 2013, as a new graduate student. I am forever indebted to you, Carrie, for taking the time to listen to me and my ideas and believing in the potential contribution that each of us can make to this discipline. To now be co-editing with you is truly a gift I never would have thought possible back then. Thank you for believing in me, and all of us wanting to make the world a better place.

Introduction: Towards Freedom, Empowerment, and Agency: An Introduction to Queering Criminology in Theory and Praxis: Reimagining Justice in the Criminal Legal System and Beyond

Carrie L. Buist and Lindsay Kahle Semprevivo

How can queer criminology, a still developing discipline within the broader world of criminological research, help folx obtain agency? We contend that this question, along with the general yet obviously important question of 'so what?', are inquiries the contributors to this volume will help to answer (or perhaps they will develop more questions). While a full history of queer criminology is not included here, there is utility in highlighting the influence of other disciplines and in very briefly noting that queer criminology focuses on the experiences of LGBTQ+ individuals and groups in the criminal legal system.[1] Queer criminology includes the experiences of victims and offenders as well as the experiences of individuals working within the criminal legal system (see Buist & Lenning, 2016). Additionally, the concept of 'queering' criminology is important in this discussion as well. Criminology as a discipline has traditionally been focused on mainstream explanations of crime by mainstream researchers who contribute to maintaining the status quo. In general, this means there is a preponderance of research conducted *by* white cisgender males *on* white cisgender males. This isn't to say that all of criminology is like this – there have been areas of research that expanded the knowledge base, such as critical criminology, which has long argued for the need to address issues of power, inequality, and a plethora of other intersections as related to crime. Sykes (1974) argued for the dismantling of work that would continue to support the status quo, and Ball (2016), among others, has noted the importance of activism and scholarship (see also Buist, 2020). The editors of this book strongly believe in and propose the importance of research, application, praxis, and activism in queer/ing criminology and more, including dismantling the status quo.

These are some of the many reasons we have worked to bring you this edited volume. The work presented here has been produced by a group of people who have a plethora of experience in the field – whether they work or have worked in the criminal legal system or some component of it, whether they are researchers, teachers, students, whether they establish and implement policy, or do all of the above, we hope this book will contribute to the knowledge we work so hard to share. We do, however, continue to argue that there is a lack of 'real-world' application of queer criminology, and this in turn continually reminds us that when there is lack of recognition, regard, respect, and inclusion in research and professional fields in the criminal legal system, it makes it much easier for our larger social systems to ignore LGBTQ+ populations. This pay-no-mind attitude is evidenced in a seemingly constant lack of resources.

At the time of this writing, the United States has just experienced an incendiary presidential election after four years of a divisive administration that has been no friend to LGBTQ+ people. In fact, with less than two weeks before the 45th president left office, the administration 'finalized a regulation that would permit discrimination against LGBTQ people, religious minorities, and women in programs related to foster care, adoption, HIV and STI prevention, youth homelessness, refugee resettlement, elder care programs and more' (Tran, 2021). What we, in part, argue and highlight in this volume is that the modus operandi in the United States and abroad has been to ignore or criminalize (see Woods, 2015; see also Buist & Lenning, 2016) LGBTQ+ people, which in turn prevents those individuals from developing their human agency. Indeed, instead of humanizing them, society has often villainized marginalized populations. However, in its first week the Biden/Harris administration reversed anti-LGBTQ+ suggestions and policy, such as the previously mentioned regulation and the ban on transgender individuals serving in the military. Perhaps the tides are changing.

It would be remiss to ignore the ongoing violence against the LGBTQ+ community across the globe as well. Human Rights Watch (HRW), an organization that has investigated and produced research on human rights abuses since the late 1970s, is but one resource that continues to bring attention to the inhumane treatment of LGBTQ+ folx. For instance, HRW has documented the injustices suffered by LGBT people in the Northern Triangle of Central America (El Salvador, Guatemala, and Honduras), which includes discrimination and violence experienced in many aspects of their lives, often in their homes from family members, and in public including by law enforcement. The report begins by highlighting the murder of Camila Díaz Córdova, a 29-year-old transgender woman who was murdered by three police officers (all of whom were convicted in 2020). LGBT citizens in these areas indicate their need to flee and seek asylum, for example in the United States, where they have been denied entry (see HRW, 2020a).

HRW has also compiled country profiles related specifically to sexual orientation and gender identity. One can access their website and scroll through an extensive list of harms (because not every deplorable act is considered criminal) against LGBT people. Not all the information is negative – Canada is spotlighted for 'expunge[ing] the records of individuals who were prosecuted because of their sexuality when same-sex conduct was criminalized in Canada' (HRW, 2020b, n.p.). Iran, however, still punishes same-sex conduct with the death penalty or flogging, which is exampled in several countries including Libya, and the punishment in the Maldives involves receiving 100 lashes.

Although we continue to see advancements around the world in recognizing LGBTQ+ folx rights, there are still over 70 countries were identifying as LGBTQ+ is illegal, with 12 of those countries' punishments including the death penalty and many of the countries punishing LGBTQ+ people with prison (Wareham, 2020). There is also a need for investigations regarding the actual legality of being out in certain countries. Russia, for example, may seem to be an ally of LGBTQ+ people, having legalized marriage in the early 1990s, yet Russia continues to be one of the worst places in the world to be LGBTQ+. Russia's anti-propaganda laws consistently threaten the lives and livelihoods of people based on their sexuality and/ or gender identity. The documentary 'Hunted: The War Against Gays in Russia' details how LGBTQ+ people are literally hunted down by hate groups in Russia, and any support of the LGBTQ+ population, whether with words or signs (propaganda), can result in prison (see Steele, 2014).

As we continue to learn of new ways in which LGBTQ+ rights are revoked or ignored, violence against LGBTQ+ people persists around the world. Forty-four transgender and gender non-conforming people were murdered in the United States in 2020, most of whom were women of color (Human Rights Campaign, 2020). Recognizing this violence is of vital importance as we relate this knowledge to structure and agency and how these concepts contribute to each other. As indicated by Cole (2019, n.p.):

> Structure refers to the complex and interconnected set of social forces, relationships, institutions, and elements of social structure that work together to shape the thought, behavior, experiences, choices, and overall life courses of people. In contrast, agency is the power people have to think for themselves and act in ways that shape their experiences and life trajectories. Agency can take individual and collective forms.

The LGBTQ+ community continues to face inequalities; therefore, one goal of this book is to identify the importance of social justice. Structure, agency, justice – all of these are inextricably linked, and in terms of queer criminology, both research and praxis contribute to us expanding our social worlds. Agency looks different for people, that is true, but what is also true is that for marginalized populations agency is even harder to achieve.

Marginalized folx might be considered so based on race, class, gender, sexuality, ability, and more; indeed, the list of identities is long, and individuals who live in these identities have unique perspectives on how the lack of power, for instance, can impede the achievement of personal agency. This leads us to intersectionality. Intersectionality is a concept, credited to Kimberlé Crenshaw (1989), focusing on the multiple identities within which we all operate. Potter (2015, n.p.) notes that intersectionality (and intersectional) are 'concept[s] or conceptualization[s] that each person has an assortment of coalesced socially constructed identities that are ordered into an inequitable social stratum'. Further insight into the concept of intersectionality from Patricia Hill Collins and Sirma Bilge (2020, n.p.) provides a definition that also spotlights the importance of power relations:

> Intersectionality investigates how intersecting power relations influence social relations across diverse societies as well as individual experiences in everyday life. As an analytic tool, intersectionality views categories of race, class, gender, sexuality, class, nation, ability, ethnicity, and age – among others – as interrelated and mutually shaping one another. Intersectionality is a way of understanding and explaining complexity in the world, in people, and in human experiences.

While institutions such as education, religion, family, government, economy, and so on are empowering for many, marginalized groups often experience these institutions as impeding the development of their agency. For instance, education can mean freedom for many, but for people of color and LGBTQ+ folx education can mean judgment, punishment, pain, and a direct line to the criminal legal system. These institutions are often seen as safe places, but for marginalized populations, they can be just as dangerous as a pandemic. As indicated earlier, discussions of power, identity, and the influence of institutions in our application of intersectionality is not unique, but we contend that these topics should move towards a broader interpretation of what agency means and how outside forces often impede the development of agency because of the lack of power. Recall Cole (2019, n.p.), who commented that 'agency refers to the thoughts and actions taken by people that express their individual power'. When we look at this through a social justice lens, marginalized populations are often without power – hence their marginalization. The institutions and individuals with power impact the decisions of every single person with less power than they possess – from what we eat, wear, study, and worship, our every move is often dictated by those with more power than we have and, in many cases, will ever have. This, some would argue, is partially the reason why people protest, riot, loot, or even run and hide, removing themselves from society in any socially acceptable manner. They are outcasts, but only because the ones with power say so. In the midst of a global pandemic, many people finally realize how life looks when you cannot live the way you want to; perhaps as a collective we have never felt so powerless. So how do we move forward? How do we attain agency if we are not in command of the ways in which we achieve it? This is not to say that individuals are without choices, but choices are often limited based on social status. Queer folx are indeed capable of freedom and empowerment on their own terms, whatever that may look like for each person, but it would be remiss to ignore the fact that those with social power can either help to build or to destroy.

In this edited volume we present the work of an array of young scholars, seasoned researchers, and professionals working in the criminal legal system. We sincerely hope that the knowledge this volume has produced will be disseminated and shared with a wide variety of people. We felt the call to include research that can contribute to policy advances as well as the work of professionals who have experience in the field. It is imperative that these professionals are well versed in how to interact with folx who have a history of distrust of all actors within the criminal legal system and their affiliates. As practitioners learn how to navigate the system, LGBTQ+ folx will be better served and ultimately experience a more accurate definition of justice. Conversely, as criminologists, many of whom have no experience working in the criminal legal profession, listen to the professionals and practitioners, we too can learn best practices in informing policy, conducting research, and interacting with professionals in the most effective and supportive ways. We think this is as good a place as any to start, especially because we strongly believe that our work and research can be a form of activism (see Ball, 2016).

We have sought to include a variety of research, including personal narratives, empirical studies, and theoretical chapters that contribute to the field of queer criminology and in general contribute to understanding LGBTQ+ folx and their experiences in the criminal legal system. The contributors to this volume are not limited to the United States nor to the ivory towers of academia. The chapters in this volume address a range of topics, including bail funds, victims' services, juvenile justice, social work, legal concerns, policy suggestions, a personal account of relationships while incarcerated, and more. In our conclusion we highlight the varying themes that emerged while putting this work together – keeping in mind the importance throughout of structure, agency, and justice. Some chapters address queer criminology not in words but in actions. Other chapters specifically address theory development and application, while still others provide us with knowledge that may lead to the empowerment and freedom we have discussed. As one person observed in discussing this volume, we strive for equity and justice. Some may call for equality, for understanding, compassion, and more – none of those calls are wrong; forward movement is what we desire.

Our volume begins with content that we believe advances theoretical paradigms. First, Meredith G.F. Worthen's chapter 'Gender- and Sexuality-Based Violence Among LGBTQ People: An Empirical Test of Norm-Centered Stigma Theory' explores the higher risk of violence experienced by LGBTQ individuals. Worthen's work is couched within an intersectional framework and also explores the impact of social power, which we believe is a foundational element that must be explored in relation to the importance of structure and agency. Worthen's research focuses on centering the voices of queer people and uses survey data to capture her findings. This chapter is also unique in that it applies quantitative measures in queer criminological research, of which we have seen very little published thus far, and Worthen's own norm-centered stigma theory takes important steps to advance theoretical paradigms.

Next, Michael K. Winters's chapter 'Queer Pathways' explores elements of queer criminology coupled with the feminist pathways approach to argue that a pathways approach to crime can provide an understanding of the factors that contribute to queer offending, and further, that this endeavor can lead to the development of a more inclusive criminology that better represents queer folx in the research. As the pathways approach has focused on early trauma and victimization, the impact of social influences, and the role that relationships play in pathways to offending, applying this approach can help to prevent future offending by queer youth and influence policy that addresses the needs of queer people in the criminal legal system and beyond.

Dave McDonald provides a critical discussion on queering criminology that includes theoretical constructions from Foucault and more to examine queer deconstruction and how this can lead to greater understandings of harm and violence. The chapter includes sure-to-be discussion-raising perspectives on child sexual abuse using queer theory, queer criminology, and psychiatry and argues that the latter has been complicit in misconceptions and myths related to the abuse of children. 'Queer Criminology and the Destabilization of Child Sexual Abuse' delves into these questions from the perspective of the institution of the family.

It is important to note that the chapters in this book represent a myriad of topics, research methods, personal and practical experience, and more. In some instances, what we would consider as research that applies theory, others might argue is an exploration of new application and praxis. This is a challenge and a great opportunity to spotlight the interconnectedness of research and praxis. As evidenced earlier, theoretical advancements are achievable and are demanded of us as we continue to advance queer criminology. Part of that progression is understanding that LGBTQ+ criminal legal professionals often experience their professional worlds differently than do others working in the field. Angela Dwyer and Roddrick A. Colvin examine these concerns in 'Queer(y)ing the Experiences of LGBTQ Workers in Criminal Processing Systems'. Their chapter highlights the ongoing challenges of being queer on the job. While there has been some progress and some small victories, gay and lesbian people working in the system continue to experience challenges on the job. Increased and continued visibility is imperative to improving working conditions worldwide.

In considering the importance of policy recommendations and implementation, the Prison Rape Elimination Act (PREA) has long been criticized by scholars and professionals researching and working in corrections. There is continued concern over the lack of proper enactment of PREA policy and standards. April Carrillo's chapter, "PREA Is a Joke': A Case Study of How Trans PREA Standards Are(n't) Enforced', examines just that, the failure of corrections to recognize the needs of transgender individuals who are incarcerated. Carrillo's research focuses on Naomi and her experiences within the system, how vastly different institutions are, and how these differences are an example of the clear disconnect between the federal guidelines and state guidelines in addressing transgender needs.

There continues to be a need to transform the system in order to move forward. This is also discussed in examining the barriers to entry and re-entry that transgender people face in relation to being under state-sanctioned surveillance. 'Queerly Navigating the System: ★Trans Experiences Under State Surveillance' by Rayna Momen uses both queer criminology and intersectionality to uncover the myriad problems associated with the over-criminalization of transgender lives in the criminal legal system in the United States. The ongoing hyper-victimization, discrimination, and social isolation of transgender people contributes to the criminal legal system's failure to recognize marginalized folx as fully human. This is an integral discussion related to the lack of human agency within the structure of institutions both in the United States and abroad. The trans-aid model is applied in Momen's chapter to highlight the lack of support in addressing the aforementioned barriers. The model itself is important in suggesting action to improve the experiences of transgender individuals, including support for those who have experienced trauma, providing employment and education assistance, and providing legal counsel such as help with identification documentation. This leads us to Jon Rosenstadt's chapter, 'Sex-Gender Defining Laws, Birth Certificates, and Identity'. This chapter details the blatant disregard for the humanization of gender non-conforming individuals, as the majority of laws in the United States, especially House Bill 153, prevent transgender people from changing or altering their assigned sex/gender on government documents. The research provided here is essential as courts continue to hear more cases regarding legal documents, and it highlights more generally the importance of language, identity, and human understanding and acceptance.

This volume dedicates much space to areas that are in need of research and policy change. This is true of intimate partner violence (IPV) and the need for policy and practice implementation. Concerns associated with IPV include safety, protection, proper and thorough training of service providers, and access to services, which is particularly challenging for transgender survivors of IPV (the barriers to services will be discussed in great detail in a later chapter). The first IPV-focused chapter, Rosalind Evans and Illandra Denysschen's 'Effects of Intimate Partner Violence in the LGBTQ Community: A Systematic Review', highlights some of the existing research and poses important questions that lead to further exploration of IPV in LGBTQ+ populations. Meanwhile, 'Health Covariates of Intimate Partner Violence in a National Transgender Sample' by Victoria Kurdyla, Adam M. Messinger, and Xavier L. Guadalupe-Diaz examines health-related conditions among transgender survivors of IPV and explores lifelong victimization of transgender individuals and more, which leads to suggestions for intervention and policy. These authors highlight numerous implications for service providers and in doing so address the importance of policies that recognize the need for trauma-informed care and different approaches to service, including assessing and addressing a variety of forms of intimate partner violence.

We have taken care to provide several chapters that focus on juvenile experiences as we continue to see this area as in need of further research and policy recommendations. Alexandria Garcia, Naseem Badiey, Laura Agnich Chavez, and Wendy Still's 'Serving Transgender, Gender Non-Conforming, and Intersex Youth in Alameda County's Juvenile Hall' indicates the need for change management to move towards non-discrimination and in doing so to work towards better planning using a data-driven basis, clear objectives, and policies to support youth. Angela Irvine-Baker, Aisha Canfield, and Carolyn Reyes's chapter, 'Liberating Black Youth Across the Gender Spectrum Through the Deconstruction of the White Femininity/ Black Masculinity Duality', provides a detailed intersectional framework that examines the shortcomings of existing gender-binary programs and provides several suggestions for programmatic improvement based on the authors' own professional experiences. Further, the authors implore us all to recognize privilege and develop an understanding of intersectionality, and in doing so to create intersectional youth programs that allow for gender fluidity, affirm race and gender, and continue to properly and effectively train staff. This chapter speaks to the importance if intersectionality and agency, as we argued previously as well.

Next, Vanessa R. Panfil and Aimee Wodda's '"I Thought They Were Supposed To Be On My Side": What Jane Doe's Experience Teaches Us About Institutional Harm Against Trans Youth' tells the story of the abuses faced by Jane Doe while under the custody of the Department of Children and Family Services. The authors' detailed account provides at least ten policy recommendations that stemmed specifically from this single case. One of their discussions includes the importance of recognizing the impact of institutional harm as we move toward a more practical application of queer criminology. There is an ongoing need to address the oft-ignored transgender juveniles, and it is necessary to understand that in some cases, it's not just a matter of a lack of training, but that professionals within the criminal legal system express transphobia and adopt exclusionary practices on the job.

Nayan G. Ramirez, in 'The Role of Adolescent Friendship Networks in Queer Youth's Delinquency', uses longitudinal data to observe factors that may contribute to offending such as social isolation, sexual orientation, and traditional gender role expectations of femininity and masculinity, while exploring delinquency and substance abuse. The chapter also focuses on the institution of education and how schools need to address the experiences of transgender youth by queering curriculum and developing other supportive programming. This, too, speaks to our previous discussion on structure and agency and the negative impact that education and the school experience can have on marginalized populations.

Policy and practice within courts and corrections is addressed in several chapters, including Luca Suede Connolly and Rose Buckelew's '"At the Very Least": Politics and Praxis of Bail Fund Organizers and the Potential for Queer Liberation', which highlights how bail policy in the United States impacts marginalized populations, namely the poor, people of color, and transgender and gender non-conforming people. This is an issue that has needed to be unpacked for a long time, and the chapter provides important information about how vulnerable populations are affected by the criminal legal system. The chapter also continues the conversation on agency and intersectionality and spotlights an abolitionist framework. Although Luci Harrell and S. Page Dukes's chapter, 'A Conspiracy', does not necessarily address theory, policy, or practice in any specific way, it does apply personal knowledge that few incarcerated and formerly incarcerated folx have the opportunity to share, especially in a platform such as this. The authors' tale of their experiences under state surveillance addresses loss, love, and freedom, to name but a few topics covered in this creative non-fiction piece.

The book ends with a series of chapters that address victim services related to homelessness, trauma, veterans support, and barriers to reporting. First, 'LGBTQ+ Homelessness: Resource Obtainment and Issues With Shelters', by Trye Mica Price and Tusty ten Bensel, identifies the disproportionate impact that homelessness has on the LGBTQ community and the need to train shelter employees in particular in order to combat discrimination and the re-victimization of those experiencing homelessness. The authors note the importance of transitional living options and more LGBTQ-specific resources that are advertised, known, and accessible.

Rebecca Katz's chapter, 'The Color of Queer Theory in Social Work and Criminology Practice: A World Without Empathy', uses the author's own personal experiences working in academia as a professor as well as her ongoing professional experience working in the field as a social worker. The chapter takes a timely walk through the importance of the Black Lives Matter movement and the need for social justice. Katz also applies ACES (Adverse Childhood Experiences) to explore the unique experiences of LGBTQ folx, namely concerns with child welfare, homelessness, and trauma-informed care. The chapter draws attention to empathy and advocating for change within queer criminology.

One topic that is often overlooked or ignored outright in the United States is the care of military veterans regardless of sexual orientation or gender identity. While there is existing research on unique issues that veterans face such as suicide ideation, homelessness, and more, Shanna N. Felix and Chrystina Y. Hoffman dive deeper to provide insight on the specific experiences of LGBTQ+ military members and the dire lack of services available to them in their chapter, aptly titled 'Camouflaged: Tackling the Invisibility of LGBTQ+ Veterans When Accessing Care'.

Finally, the book closes with Danielle C. Slakoff and Jaclyn A. Siegel's chapter, 'Barriers to Reporting, Barriers to Service: Challenges for Transgender Survivors of Intimate Partner Violence and Sexual Victimization', which highlights the risks that transgender individuals face and what must be done in order to keep survivors safe. This chapter is integral and foundational to developing policy suggestions. The authors also make numerous recommendations and encourage research, training, and policy couched within an intersectional framework.

In this book, we have sought to bring together professors and students, researchers and practitioners, practitioners who conduct research – folx from all walks of life with myriad experiences, identities, motivations, commitments, and – luckily for us – a willingness to contribute to creating and sharing knowledge. We hope that in facilitating a much-needed (ongoing) conversation, the book will encourage readers to think deeply about the experiences of the LGBTQ+ community. We also hope that it will get people thinking about policy, activism, and the importance of human agency; to think how equality, equity, and empathy can contribute to the personhood and agency of marginalized communities who continue to fight to be seen, heard, protected, and empowered.

We strongly believe the contributors have provided important work that may lead us in new directions and encourage and inspire folx to think critically and promote change and activism, and while some of this might anger you (as it should, quite frankly), we hope it leads you toward compassion. We sincerely thank all the authors for contributing to this book and we thank you for reading it.

Note

[1] There are myriad different uses of acronyms throughout the book; these vary based on author and/or research design, and/or previous research that the author is citing. The intent is to address both broadly and specifically members of the LGBTQ+ and queer community.

References

Ball, M. (2016) 'Queer criminology as activism', *Critical Criminology*, 24: 473–487.

Buist, C.L. (2020) 'LGBTQ rights in the fields of criminal law and law enforcement', *University of Richmond Law Review*, 54(3): 877–900.

Buist, C.L. & Lenning, E. (2016) *Queer Criminology* (1st ed.), Abingdon: Routledge.

Cole, N.L. (2019) 'How sociologists define human agency: individuals express agency in big and small ways, every day', ThoughtCo, January 22. https://www.thoughtco.com/agency-definition-3026036

Collins, P.H. & Bilge, S. (2020) *Intersectionality* [VitalSource Bookshelf]. https://bookshelf.vitalsource.com/#/books/9781509539697/

Crenshaw, K. (1989) 'Mapping the margins: intersectionality, identity politics, and violence against women of color', *Stanford Law Review*, 43: 1240–1299.

HRW (Human Rights Watch) (2020a) '"Every day I live in fear": violence and discrimination against LGBT people in El Salvador, Guatemala, and Honduras, and obstacles to asylum in the United States', Human Rights Watch, October 7. https://www.hrw.org/report/2020/10/07/every-day-i-live-fear/violence-and-discrimination-against-lgbt-people-el-salvador#

HRW (Human Rights Watch) (2020b) 'Human Rights Watch country profiles: sexual orientation and gender identity', Human Rights Watch, June 22. https://www.hrw.org/video-photos/interactive/2020/06/22/human-rights-watch-country-profiles-sexual-orientation-and

Human Rights Campaign (2020) 'Fatal violence against the transgender and gender non-conforming community in 2020', Human Rights Campaign. https://www.hrc.org/resources/violence-against-the-trans-and-gender-non-conforming-community-in-2020

Potter, H. (2015) *Intersectionality and Criminology* [VitalSource Bookshelf]. https://bookshelf.vitalsource.com/#/books/9781136207464/

Steele, B. (Director). (2014). *Hunted: The War Against Gays in Russia* [Film]. Home Box Office.

Sykes, G.M. (1974) 'The rise of critical criminology', *Journal of Criminal Law and Criminology*, 65(2): 206–213. https://www.jstor.org/stable/1142539?seq=1#metadata_info_tab_contents

Tran, V. (2021) 'Trump administration launches 11th hour attack against LGBTQ people, women, religious minorities with final HHS regulation', Human Rights Campaign. https://www.hrc.org/press-releases/trump-administration-launches-11th-hour-attack-against-lgbtq-people-women-religious-minorities-with-final-hhs-regulation

Wareham, J. (2020) 'Map shows where it's illegal to be gay – 30 years since WHO declassified homosexuality as disease', *Forbes*, May 17. https://www.forbes.com/sites/jamiewareham/2020/05/17/map-shows-where-its-illegal-to-be-gay--30-years-since-who-declassified-homosexuality-as-disease/?sh=728df4c6578a

Woods, J.B. (2015) 'The birth of modern criminology and gendered constructions of the homosexual criminal identity', *Journal of Homosexuality*, 62: 131–166.

1

Gender- and Sexuality-Based Violence among LGBTQ People: An Empirical Test of Norm-Centered Stigma Theory

Meredith G.F. Worthen

LGBTQ people are at higher risk for violence compared with their heterosexual-cisgender counterparts (Katz-Wise & Hyde, 2012; Meyer, 2015), yet few studies consider the unique and overlapping experiences of lesbian women, gay men, bisexual men, bisexual women, trans men, trans women, queer women, and queer men. In particular, the separate but interrelated experiences of LGBTQ people and their intersectional identities of gender and sexuality are critical to examine as they relate to their victimization. Using nationally representative data collected from online LGBTQ panelists ($N = 1,604$), this chapter provides an intersectional investigation of norm-centered stigma theory (NCST) (Worthen, 2020) with hetero-cis-normativity (a system of norms, privilege, and oppression that situates heterosexual cisgender people above all others) as the centralized overarching concept that helps us to understand gender- and sexuality-based violence among LGBTQ people. Specifically, social power axes including gender identity (cisgender woman, cisgender man, transgender woman, and transgender man), sexual identity (lesbian, gay, bisexual), and queer identity (based on self-identification as queer), and interactions among these axes of social power, are investigated as they moderate the relationships between violations of hetero-cis-normativity (LGBTQ identity) and stigmatizing experiences associated with such norm violations (gender- and sexuality-based violence) in order to best understand LGBTQ negativity.

Hetero-cis-normativity and LGBTQ negativity

Because trans people violate the presumption of cisnormativity and LGBQ people violate the 'heterosexual assumption' (Herek, 2007, p. 907), overall, LGBTQ people can be at greater risk for gender- and sexuality-based negativity when compared with cisnormative and heterosexual people (Meyer, 2003; Schilt & Westbrook, 2009; Coulter et al., 2018; Worthen, 2020). Specifically, scholars have argued that violence among LGBTQ people is connected to negativities associated with their violations of hetero-cis-normativity (Schilt & Westbrook, 2009; Ball, 2013; Meyer, 2015; Javaid, 2018; Worthen, 2020). In particular, due to their non-hetero-cis-normative identities, LGBTQ people can be targeted, though in differing ways based on gender and sexuality (to be discussed later). Overall, LGBTQ attacks are often motivated by the desire to reinforce culturally 'appropriate' norms regarding gender and sexual identity through punishing those who violate hetero-cis-normativity (Franklin, 1998; Schilt & Westbrook, 2009; Meyer, 2015; Worthen, 2020).

LGBTQ violence

Queer criminology as a field acknowledges the importance of exploring the ways LGBTQ people endure crime, criminalization, and criminality. In particular, by centering LGBTQ people in queer criminological research, queer criminology allows us to begin to dismantle how hetero-cis-normative biases work to secure the disadvantaged and oppressed social locations of LGBTQ people that can also relate to their experiences with victimization (Ball, 2013; Button & Worthen, 2014, 2017; Panfil, 2017; Worthen, 2020). Though previous work has established that LGBTQ people are at an increased risk of violence (Katz–Wise & Hyde, 2012; Meyer, 2015), there are important differences in the ways that lesbian women, gay men, bisexual men, bisexual women, trans men, trans women, queer women, and queer men can endure such experiences. These groups and their experiences with violence are briefly examined.

Lesbian women

Past work demonstrates that the rate of violence among lesbian women is quite high (Bartle, 2000; Balsam et al., 2005; Katz–Wise & Hyde, 2012; Meyer, 2015; Stacey et al., 2018). For example, nearly one-third (31 percent) of lesbian, bisexual, and gay women (LGB) indicated having been severely beaten or physically abused in childhood, and over one-fifth (21 percent) indicated the same in adulthood in one study ($N = 2,431$) (Morris & Balsam, 2003). Furthermore, there is some evidence that such violence can be normalized among lesbian women. Indeed, in one qualitative study

(n = 13), the majority of lesbian women of color described their experiences with hate-motivated violence as unsurprising because they 'expected' to be 'assaulted for revealing [their] sexuality' (Meyer, 2010, p. 987). However, compared with gay and bisexual men, lesbian women are at lower risk of violence (Herek, 2009; Katz-Wise & Hyde, 2012). Indeed, FBI statistics indicate that only 12.2 percent of sexual orientation bias-motivated crimes are classified as 'anti-lesbian' (FBI, 2018). Thus, lesbian women's violations of heteronormativity may relate to their experiences with gender- and sexuality-based violence in unique ways.

Gay men

Gay men are also at relatively high risk for violence. For example, Katz-Wise and Hyde (2012) found that gay/bisexual men are significantly more likely than lesbian/bisexual women to experience many types of victimization including weapon assault, robbery, physical assault, and sexual harassment. Furthermore, the majority (59.7 percent) of sexual orientation bias-motivated crimes reported to the FBI are classified as 'anti-gay (male)' (FBI, 2018). This may be directly related to hostilities regarding gay men's non-heteronormativity. For example, investigating the motives of heterosexual men who assaulted gay men, Franklin (1998) found that they chose to attack these men because their 'victims violated unwritten codes of appropriate behavior and thus deserved punishment' (Franklin, 1998, p. 8).

Bisexual women

Numerous studies show that bisexual women are at a heightened risk for many different types of victimization (Balsam et al., 2005; Katz-Wise & Hyde, 2012; Meyer, 2015; Coston, 2017). For example, bisexual women (n = 125) were found to experience childhood abuse, domestic violence, physical assault, and sexual assault at significantly higher rates in comparison with heterosexual women (n = 348) in one study (Balsam et al., 2005). In particular, some research demonstrates that bi-negativity may play a significant role in the sexuality-based violence that bisexual women experience in their intimate relationships (Coston, 2017). Bisexual women may also be targeted for violence due to stereotypes associated with hyper-sexualization often found in mainstream media and pornography (Weiss, 2003; Rupp & Taylor, 2010; Worthen, 2020).

Bisexual men

Research indicates that bisexual men report more experiences with childhood trauma, intimate partner violence, sexual assault, and lifetime victimization than heterosexual men (Balsam et al., 2005; Katz–Wise & Hyde, 2012; Meyer, 2015; Stephenson & Finneran, 2017). For example, one study found that close to half (44.7 percent) of bisexual men experienced coercive sexual assault, which was nearly four times the reported coercive sexual assault experiences of heterosexual men (12.6 percent) (Balsam et al., 2005). Bisexual men may also experience negativities associated with cultural perceptions about their masculinities as 'not masculine enough' due to their bisexual identities (Szymanski & Carr, 2008).

Trans women

Trans women are at high risk for both gender- and sexuality-based violence (Schilt & Westbrook, 2009; Greenberg, 2012; Perry & Dyck, 2014; Meyer, 2015; James et al., 2016; Whitfield et al., 2018; Matsuzaka & Koch, 2019). For example, between about 1 in 16 (White) and one in five (American Indian) trans women reported that they had been physically attacked in public by a stranger in the past year in the US Transgender Survey with more than 9,000 trans women respondents. In addition, many experience intimate partner violence (ranging from 28 percent among Asian trans women to 57 percent among American Indian trans women), and more than one in three (37 percent) have been sexually assaulted in their lifetimes (James et al., 2016). In addition, trans women are at extremely high risk for homicide, with nearly four out of five anti-transgender murder victims being trans women of color (Human Rights Campaign, 2018). Thus, trans women's experiences are essential to consider in explorations of LGBTQ violence.

Trans men

Some research demonstrates that trans men have significant experiences with violence (Testa et al., 2012; Buist & Stone, 2014; Meyer, 2015; James et al., 2016; Aparicio-García et al., 2018). Indeed, some research indicates that trans men are at extreme risk of victimization, with half (51 percent) reporting lifetime sexual assault (James et al., 2016) and close to half (45.7 percent) reporting physical attacks due to their trans identity (Testa et al., 2012). Thus, trans men's intersecting experiences are critical to explore as they relate to their victimization.

Queer women

Some studies indicate that self-identified queer women may be at high risk for stigma and discrimination (Alimahomed, 2010; Friedman & Leaper, 2010; Logie & Earnshaw, 2015). For example, compared with LGB women, queer women were found to experience the highest levels of stigma associated with their identity in one online Canadian study ($N = 466$, $n = 206$ queer women) (Logie & Earnshaw, 2015). However, although I examined the cluster of discrimination, harassment, and violence (DHV) among queer women ($n = 135$) in my recent book (Worthen, 2020), no large-scale US research to date has specifically explored the violence among queer-identified women.

Queer men

Some research demonstrates that self-identified queer men endure stigma in various forms (Jones, 2015; Meyer, 2015; Morandini et al., 2017). For example, one small qualitative study ($N = 5$) found that queer men experience 'policing of [their] unconventional performances of gender' from family members especially (Jones, 2015, p. 769). However, other than my exploration of queer men's ($n = 138$) experiences with a composite of DHV (Worthen, 2020), no studies to date have focused on queer men's experiences with violence.

Hetero-cis-normativity and LGBTQ violence

Overall, because LGBTQ people may violate the norms that go along with hetero-cis-normativity, they can be at greater risk for gender- and sexuality-based violence when compared with cisgender people and heterosexuals (Meyer, 2003; Coulter et al., 2018; Worthen, 2020). In addition, due to their differing experiences with social power as related to their gender and sexual identities, LGBTQ people violate hetero-cis-normative assumptions in differing ways that also relate to their likelihood of enduring violence (Meyer, 2010; Katz-Wise & Hyde, 2012; Worthen, 2020). Together, this suggests that both gender and sexuality are important to consider in exploring the relationships between violations of hetero-cis-normativity (LGBTQ identity) and the stigmatizing experiences associated with such norm violations (gender- and sexuality-based violence).

Norm-centered stigma theory

Norm-centered stigma theory (NCST) provides a theoretical framework to better understand these relationships. Put briefly, NCST focuses on the importance of norms/norm violations, social power, and interactions among these (Worthen, 2020). Adding to the established scholarly research about stigma that recognizes the importance of norms and social power in conceptualizing stigma (especially Goffman, 1963; Stafford & Scott, 1986; Link & Phelan, 2001) and other works that recognize how diverse, interacting axes of social power shape varying life circumstances (for example, Crenshaw, 1991; Butler, 1993; Collins, 1999; Davis, 2008), NCST brings these ideas together through its theoretical model and accompanying testable hypotheses. NCST is outlined in three ways: (1) the three tenets of NCST are defined, (2) NCST's theoretical model is described, and (3) hypotheses derived from NCST are provided.

NCST's three tenets

NCST Tenet 1: *There is a culturally dependent and reciprocal relationship between norms and stigma.* Stigma *depends* on norms. Without norms, and in particular norm violations, there is no stigma. In other words, the central element of identifying and understanding stigma *is* norms. Under NCST, this is defined as *norm centrality.* Because both norms and stigma are dependent on culturally bound established standards and expectations about life circumstances, beliefs, behaviors, and identities, they feed off one another. Thus, the relationship between norms and stigma is reciprocal (see also Goffman, 1963; Stafford & Scott, 1986). For the purposes of this project, NCST Tenet 1 is as follows: There is a culturally dependent relationship between *violations of hetero-cis-normativity* and *gender- and sexuality-based violence.*

NCST Tenet 2: *The relationship between norms and stigma is organized by social power dynamics between the stigmatized and the stigmatizers.* NCST defines social power as an organizational element within the links between norms and stigma. In other words, established standards and expectations maintained by a particular group and/or society are embedded within and organized around existing culturally bound infrastructures that privilege some life circumstances, beliefs, behaviors, and identities and oppress others. Norm followers secure privileges that go along with the embodiment/adoption of certain social, familial, cultural, economic, and political norms while norm violators experience oppressive disadvantages and stigma. This creates a hierarchy of non-stigmatized norm followers and stigmatized norm violators that is organized by social power. In other words, NCST recognizes *social power as organizational* in the relationship between norms and stigma (see also Schur, 1983; Jones, 1984; Link & Phelan, 2001). For this project, NCST Tenet 2 is as follows: The relationship between *violations of hetero-cis-normativity* and *gender- and sexuality-based violence* is organized by the social power experiences of *LGBTQ people.*

NCST Tenet 3: *Stigma is inclusive of negativity and social sanctions directed toward norm violations and norm violators justified through social power dynamics.* NCST's third tenet provides a norm-centered, social power justification for negative treatment of the stigmatized. Because societies value upholding norms and rewarding norm followers, the stigma, social sanctions, and negativity norm violators endure become culturally validated. In other words, stigma (and its accompanying negativity) is justified by norms that reflect the privileging of those with social power and the simultaneous oppression of those lacking social power. Here, NCST emphasizes *social power as justification* for the enduring negativity that stigmatized people experience (see also Link & Phelan, 2001). For the purposes of this project, NCST Tenet 3 is as follows: *LGBTQ stigma* is inclusive of negativity and social sanctions directed toward violations and violators of *hetero-cis-normativity* justified through social power dynamics of *gender and sexual identity*.

NCST theoretical model and hypotheses

According to NCST, social power organizes the lens through which the relationship between norm violations and stigma is examined. In particular, there are two lenses: the *stigmatizer lens* and the *stigmatized lens*.[1] The current project utilizes the *stigmatized lens*, which considers how the target of stigma's (that is, the stigmatized) own axes of social power impact their own experiences with negativity, prejudice, and stigma. Specifically, there are two important relationships that NCST outlines (see Figure 1.1). First, there is a direct relationship between norm violations and stigma. For example, as norm violations become more numerous and/or more threatening, stigma increases. Second, the relationship between norm violations and stigma is moderated by social power. Social power impacts the relationship between norm violations and stigma. Together, this leads to the following hypotheses that guide this chapter:

Figure 1.1: Theoretical model of NCST and LGBTQ stigma with model numbers to be examined in Tables 1.2 and 1.3

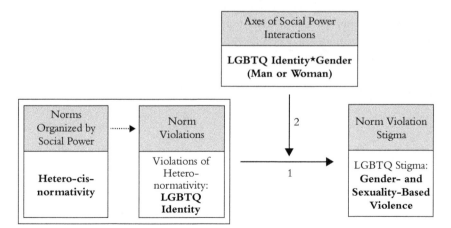

- *Hypothesis 1*: There are significant relationships between being LGBTQ (violating hetero-cis-normativity) and gender- and sexuality-based violence (norm violation stigma).
- *Hypothesis 2:* The relationship between being LGBTQ and gender- and sexuality-based violence is moderated by interactions between being LGBTQ and gender identity (man or woman).

Methods

Data and sample characteristics

The data come from the 2018 LGBTQ and Hetero-cis Population Study (Worthen, 2020) and were collected using panelists recruited from Survey Sampling International (SSI), an international survey research and survey sample provider with over five million US online panel participants. SSI panel members are recruited from online communities, social networks, and the web. SSI profiles, authenticates, and verifies each panel member as a reliable respondent for rigorous research participation. SSI awards incentives to respondents upon survey completion.

A sample of adults aged 18–64 stratified by US census categories of age, gender, ethnicity, and census region was obtained by SSI. For the first sampling frame, a total of 63,466 email invites were sent out by SSI to *only* heterosexual-cisgender potential respondents.[2] A quota of 1,500 respondents (750 hetero-cis men and 750 hetero-cis women) was requested and met ($n = 1,500$). For the second sampling frame, a total of 103,001 email invites were sent out by SSI to *only* LGBT potential respondents. A quota of 1,520 respondents (330 each of lesbian women, gay men, bisexual women, bisexual men; 100 each of trans women and trans men) was requested and met for lesbian women, gay men, and bisexual women; however, quotas were not met for bisexual men ($n = 314$), trans women ($n = 74$), or trans men ($n = 55$). A total of 4,994 individuals accessed the survey by clicking the survey invite link, 4,583 began the survey by answering one or more survey items, and 3,104 respondents completed all items in the survey for a survey start to completion rate of 68 percent. To speak to this study's goals, the current study's sample excludes heterosexual-cisgender people ($n = 1,500$) and only includes LGBTQ people for a total sample size of $N = 1,604$. See Table 1.1 for additional details.

Survey design and implementation

The author created the survey instrument via Qualtrics (an online survey platform). The survey was live on the Internet from November 5, 2018, to November 23, 2018.[3] Through the link provided in the invitation email from SSI, panelists could access the survey via PC, laptop, tablet, or mobile

Table 1.1: Description of LGBTQ sample ($N = 1{,}604$)

	Range	Mean (SD)
Gender Identity		
Cis Man	0–1	0.42 (0.49)
Cis Woman	0–1	0.44 (0.50)
Trans Woman	0–1	0.05 (0.21)
Trans Man	0–1	0.03 (0.18)
Nonbinary	0–1	0.06 (0.24)
Sexual Identity		
Heterosexual	0–1	0.03 (0.17)
Gay or Lesbian	0–1	0.45 (0.50)
Bisexual	0–1	0.45 (0.50)
Pansexual	0–1	0.05 (0.22)
Asexual	0–1	0.03 (0.17)
Queer Identity	0–1	0.20 (0.40)
Sociodemographics		
Caucasian/White★	0–1	0.79 (0.41)
Non-White	0–1	0.21 (0.41)
Latinx Ethnicity	0–1	0.13 (0.34)
Education	1–6	3.79 (1.46)
Town Type (Rural–Large City)	1–4	2.72 (0.98)
Age	18–64	40.69 (14.51)

Note: ★Reference category in regression models.

phone. The survey included 184 closed-ended questions with both multiple- and single-response items. The average time to complete the survey was 25.8 minutes.

Dependent variables: gender- and sexual identity-based DHV

Gender- and sexual identity-based violence were measured using two items. Respondents were asked to respond to the following statement: 'I have experienced violence because of my (select all that apply)'. The respondent could mark 'gender' and/or 'sexual identity/orientation' for this survey item. Those that indicated 'gender' were coded as (1) for gender-based violence and (0) for others. Those that indicated 'sexual identity/orientation' were coded as (1) for sexuality-based violence and (0) for others.

Independent variables: sexual, gender, and queer identities

For sexual identity, respondents were asked 'How would you describe yourself?' with the following response options: heterosexual, gay or lesbian, bisexual, pansexual, and asexual. For gender identity, respondents were asked 'What best describes your gender?' with responses that were coded as cis men (those that indicated 'I identify as a man and my sex assigned at birth was male'), cis women (those that indicated 'I identify as a woman and my sex assigned at birth was female'), trans men (those that indicated 'I identify as a man and my sex assigned at birth was female'), trans women (those that indicated 'I identify as a woman and my sex assigned at birth was male'), and nonbinary (those that indicated 'I am gender-nonbinary, gender fluid, or genderqueer'). Respondents were also asked if they identified as queer (yes/no).

Sociodemographic controls

Previous studies have found significant relationships between sociodemographics and experiences of violence (Herek et al., 1999; Crouch et al., 2000; Grossman et al., 2005; DeKeseredy & Schwartz, 2009; Decker et al., 2015; Stacey et al., 2018); thus, the current study includes racial/ethnic identity, education, town type, and age as sociodemographic controls. For racial identity, the response options were Caucasian/White, African American/Black, Asian American/Pacific Islander, Native American/Alaskan Native, Multi-Racial, and Other Race. Due to the low numbers of non-White respondents, these categories were collapsed into Caucasian/White and non-White. In a separate question for Latinx Ethnicity, respondents were also asked 'Are you Hispanic or Latino/a/x? (A person of Cuban, Mexican, Puerto Rican, South or Central American or other Spanish culture of origin regardless of race)'. *Education* response options were (1) less than high school, (2) high school/GED, (3) some college, (4) Associate's, (5) Bachelor's, or (6) greater than Bachelor's. Town type (where the majority of life was spent) response options were (1) rural, (2) small town, (3) suburb, and (4) large city. *Age* was measured in years (18–64).

Method of analysis

First, it was important to determine the amount of violence that each of the LGBTQ groups experienced. As seen in Figure 1.2, bisexual women reported the highest percentage of gender-based violence (25 percent) and trans women reported the highest percentage of sexuality-based violence (31 percent). Due to their heightened risk of these experiences, these two groups were the focus of the logistic regression models. In the first set of models, NCST was utilized to explore gender-based violence as related to bisexual woman identity. In the second set of models, NCST was utilized to explore sexuality-based violence as related to trans woman identity.

Figure 1.2: Percentage of LGBTQ people reporting gender- and sexuality-based violence ($N = 1,604$)

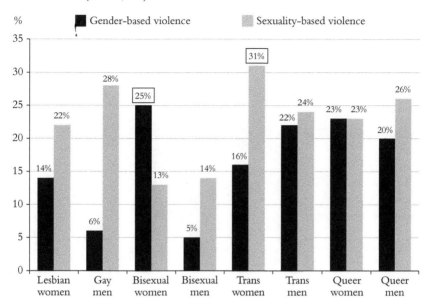

Multi-collinearity was examined using STATA command 'collin' (Ender, 2010), which provides collinearity diagnostics for all variables utilized in each model. The Mean VIF values ranged from 1.09 to 1.10, suggesting no issues with multicollinearity (Allison, 2012).

Results

NCST and gender-based violence

In Table 1.2, the relationships between bisexual identity and gender-based violence are examined using NCST. In Model 1, bisexual identity is not significantly related to gender-based violence. Thus, *Hypothesis 1* is not supported. In Model 2, surprisingly, being a bisexual woman *decreases* the likelihood of experiencing gender-based violence by 0.54 ($p < 0.05$). Thus, *Hypothesis 2* is supported, but in the opposite direction from predicted.

NCST and sexuality-based violence

In Table 1.3, the relationships between trans identity and sexuality-based violence are examined using NCST. In Model 1, trans identity increases the likelihood of sexuality-based violence by 0.72 ($p < 0.05$). Thus, *Hypothesis 1* is fully supported. Similar to the results found in Table 1.2, in Model 2 of Table 1.3, surprisingly, being a trans woman *decreases* the likelihood of

Table 1.2: Logistic regression results with odds ratios and (standard errors) estimating NCST and gender-based violence as related to bisexual woman identity among LGBTQ people (N = 1,604)

	Model 1	Model 2
Norm Violation		
Bisexual identity	1.13 (0.17)	0.67 (0.18)
Social Power Axes Interactions		
Bisexual*Woman identity		0.46* (0.15)
Sociodemographic Controls		
Woman	2.34* (0.38)	3.66* (0.95)
Non-White	1.11 (0.20)	1.11 (0.20)
Latinx Ethnicity	1.02 (0.22)	1.01 (0.22)
Education	1.01 (0.06)	1.01 (0.06)
Town Type (Rural–Large City)	1.00 (0.08)	0.99 (0.08)
Age	0.97* (0.01)	0.97* (0.01)
Mean VIF	1.10	1.10
Pseudo R^2	0.06	0.06

Note: *$p < 0.05$.

experiencing sexuality-based violence by 0.55 (p = 0.07). Thus, *Hypothesis 2* is supported, but again in the opposite direction from predicted.

Controls and goodness of fit

Among the controls, being a woman was significantly related to an increased likelihood of gender-based violence in Table 1.2 (both models). In contrast, being a woman was significantly related to a *decreased* likelihood of sexuality-based violence in Table 1.3 (Model 1 only). In addition, age was negatively related to gender-based violence (both models). No other sociodemographic controls were significant in any models. The pseudo R^2 values were very low and ranged from 0.01 to 0.06.

Discussion

This chapter explored LGBTQ people's experiences with violence with a critical focus on hetero–cis-normativity through the use of norm-centered stigma theory (Worthen, 2020). In particular, NCST's emphasis on the intersectional identities of lesbian women, gay men, bisexual men, bisexual women, trans men, trans women, queer women, and queer men revealed the importance of examining both gender and sexuality when exploring violence among LGBTQ people. Overall, findings demonstrated that some groups report quite high percentages of gender-based violence (bisexual

Table 1.3: Logistic regression results with odds ratios and (standard errors) estimating NCST and sexuality-based violence as related to trans woman identity among LGBTQ people ($N = 1,604$)

	Model 1	Model 2
Norm Violation		
Trans Identity	1.72 (0.37)★	1.10 (0.37)
Social Power Axes Interactions		
Trans★Woman Identity		0.45 (0.20)[†]
Sociodemographic Controls		
Woman	0.76 (0.10)★	1.52 (0.62)
Non-White	1.02 (0.16)	1.01 (0.16)
Latinx Ethnicity	0.99 (0.19)	0.99 (0.19)
Education	0.99 (0.05)	0.99 (0.05)
Town Type (Rural–Large City)	1.08 (0.07)	1.08 (0.07)
Age	0.99 (0.05)	0.99 (0.00)
Mean VIF	1.09	1.09
Pseudo R^2	0.01	0.01

Note: ★$p < 0.05$; [†] $p < 0.10$.

women, 25 percent) and sexuality-based violence (trans women, 31 percent), while other groups are much less likely to report such experiences (gender-based violence among bisexual men, 5 percent; sexuality-based violence among bisexual women, 13 percent) (see Figure 1.2). Such findings both align and contrast with previous research about LGBTQ experiences with violence (Balsam et al., 2005; Katz-Wise & Hyde, 2012; James et al., 2016; Coston, 2017).

In the regression models, results were surprising. Although both bisexual women and trans women reported the highest percentages of gender- and sexuality-based violence in comparison with the other LGBTQ groups, the social power interaction axes representing these intersecting identities of bisexual woman and trans woman *decreased* the likelihood of these experiences with violence. However, it is important to remember that the comparison groups for both sets of models was other LGBTQ people, many of whom reported quite high percentages of these experiences as well. For example, more than 20 percent of queer women and trans men also reported gender-based violence (23 percent and 22 percent, respectively). In addition, more than 20 percent of gay men, queer men, trans men, queer women, and lesbian women reported sexuality-based violence (28 percent, 26 percent, 24 percent, 23 percent, and 22 percent, respectively). Thus, although there are notable differences, there are also some similarities across the LGBTQ groups when it comes to their experiences with gender- and sexuality-based violence. Such findings underscore the significance of continuing to explore LGBTQ violence with careful attention to the cultural responses to the hetero-cis-normativity violations of lesbian women, gay men, bisexual men, bisexual women, trans men, trans women, queer women, and queer men, as some previous work has done (Schilt & Westbrook, 2009; Wodda & Panfil, 2014; Meyer, 2015; Worthen, 2020).

Overall, the use of NCST to explore the relationships between LGBTQ identity and gender- and sexuality-based violence reveals the significance of its three tenets. In particular, results are consistent with NCST's Tenet 1: There is a culturally dependent relationship between *violations of heteronormativity* and *gender- and sexuality-based violence*. Through its focus on the importance of norms (*norm centrality*) as related to stigma, NCST provides a framework with hetero-cis-normativity as central to understanding violence in LGBTQ people's lives. In addition, the social power axes of gender and sexuality interact with one another and are significantly related to violence among LGBTQ people. In these ways, *social power is organizational* in these relationships. This finding supports NCST's Tenet 2: The relationship between *violations of hetero-cis-normativity* and *gender- and sexuality-based violence* is organized by the social power experiences of *LGBTQ people*. Finally, deeply embedded cultural concerns about the ways that LGBTQ people violate hetero-cis-normativity contribute to a cultural *justification* for their victimization (Franklin, 1998; Herek, 2000, 2007; Meyer, 2010). This is in line with NCST's Tenet 3: *Gender- and sexuality-based violence among LGBTQ people* is inclusive of negativity and social sanctions directed toward violations and violators of *hetero-cis-normativity* justified through social power dynamics of *gender and sexual identity*.

Queering criminology in future research

Together, the findings from this chapter illustrate the importance of continuing to 'queer criminology' through centering the complexities of LGBTQ people's lives in discussions of their experiences with victimization. In particular, because cultural responses to violations of hetero-cis-normativity are often at the crux of LGBTQ negativity, norm-centered conversations are essential. NCST (Worthen, 2020) provides a theoretical framework with which to understand these experiences and underscores the need for continued research that can provide more context to these relationships.

Notes

[1] The *stigmatizer lens* examines how the stigmatizer's (that is, the individual who is potentially expressing negativity or passing judgment on another) own axes of social power impact their feelings about the target of stigma. Because the stigmatizer most commonly has more social power than the stigmatized (though not always), both lenses are organized by social power and thus shape the ways NCST is investigated.

2   It is unknown how many of these emails were actually received and read by the potential respondents, so an exact response rate is also unknown. For example, junk mail filters could have prevented potential respondents from seeing the email invitation, some may have opened the email but decided not to click the link to access the survey, and some may have been deemed ineligible due to identity quotas being met as requested by the author set by SSI (five of the eight identity quotas were met).

3   The survey was held open for 19 days in an effort to meet the quotas set for the LGBT groups. Five quotas were met as follows: gay men (five days in), bisexual women (seven days in), lesbian women (eight days in), cis men and cis women (16 days in). The quotas for the remaining three groups (bisexual men, trans men, and trans women) were not met. The survey was closed because SSI believed it was not realistic to expect these quotas to be filled in a reasonable amount of time.

References

Alimahomed, S. (2010) 'Thinking outside the rainbow: women of color redefining queer politics and identity', *Social Identities*, 16(2): 151–168. https://doi.org/10.1080/13504631003688849

Allison, P. (2012) 'When can you safely ignore multicollinearity?', Statistical Horizons. https://statisticalhorizons.com/multicollinearity

Aparicio-García, M.E., Díaz-Ramiro, E.M., Rubio-Valdehita, S., López-Núñez, M.I., & García-Nieto, I. (2018) 'Health and well-being of cisgender, transgender and non-binary young people', *International Journal of Environmental Research and Public Health*, 15(10): 2133. https://doi.org/10.3390/ijerph15102133

Ball, M. (2013) 'Heteronormativity, homonormativity and violence', in K. Carrington, M. Ball, E. O'Brien & J. M. Tauri (eds.), *Crime, Justice and Social Democracy: International Perspectives*, London: Palgrave Macmillan, pp. 186–199. https://doi.org/10.1057/9781137008695_13

Balsam, K.F., Rothblum, E.D., & Beauchaine, T.P. (2005) 'Victimization over the life span: a comparison of lesbian, gay, bisexual, and heterosexual siblings', *Journal of Consulting and Clinical Psychology*, 73(3): 477–487. https://doi.org/10.1037/0022-006X.73.3.477

Bartle, E.E. (2000) 'Lesbians and hate crimes', *Journal of Poverty*, 4(4): 23–43. https://doi.org/10.1300/J134v04n04_02

Buist, C.L. & Stone, C. (2014) 'Transgender victims and offenders: failures of the United States criminal justice system and the necessity of queer criminology', *Critical Criminology*, 22(1): 35–47. https://doi.org/10.1007/s10612-013-9224-1

Butler, J. (1993) 'Critically queer', *GLQ: A Journal of Lesbian and Gay Studies*, 1(1): 17–32.

Button, D. & Worthen, M.G.F. (2014) 'General Strain Theory for LGBQ and SSB youth: the importance of intersectionality in the future of feminist criminology', *Feminist Criminology*, 9(4): 270–297.

Button, D. & Worthen, M.G.F. (2017) 'Applying a General Strain Theory framework to understand school weapon carrying among LGBQ and heterosexual youth', *Criminology*, 55(4): 806–832.

Collins, P.H. (1999) *Black Feminist Thought: Knowledge, Consciousness, and the Politics of Empowerment* (Revised, 10th anniversary, 2nd edn.), Abingdon: Routledge.

Coston, B.M. (2017) 'Power and inequality: intimate partner violence against bisexual and non-monosexual women in the United States', *Journal of Interpersonal Violence*, 36(1–2): 381–405. https://doi.org/10.1177/0886260517726415

Coulter, R.W.S., Bersamin, M., Russell, S.T., & Mair, C. (2018) 'The effects of gender- and sexuality-based harassment on lesbian, gay, bisexual, and transgender substance use disparities', *Journal of Adolescent Health*, 62(6): 688–700. https://doi.org/10.1016/j.jadohealth.2017.10.004

Crenshaw, K. (1991) 'Mapping the margins: intersectionality, identity politics, and violence against women of color', *Stanford Law Review*, 43(6): 1241–1299. https://doi.org/10.2307/1229039

Crouch, J.L., Hanson, R.F., Saunders, B.E., Kilpatrick, D.G., & Resnick, H.S. (2000) 'Income, race/ethnicity, and exposure to violence in youth: results from the national survey of adolescents', *Journal of Community Psychology*, 28(6): 625–641. https://doi.org/10.1002/1520-6629(200011)28:6<625::AID-JCOP6>3.0.CO;2-R

Davis, K. (2008) 'Intersectionality as buzzword: a sociology of science perspective on what makes a feminist theory successful', *Feminist Theory*, 9(1): 67–85. https://doi.org/10.1177/1464700108086364

Decker, M.R., Latimore, A.D., Yasutake, S., Haviland, M., Ahmed, S., Blum, R.W., Sonenstein, F., & Astone, N.M. (2015) 'Gender-based violence against adolescent and young adult women in low- and middle-income countries', *Journal of Adolescent Health*, 56(2): 188–196. https://doi.org/10.1016/j.jadohealth.2014.09.003

DeKeseredy, W. & Schwartz, M. (2009) *Dangerous Exits: Escaping Abusive Relationships in Rural America*, New Brunswick, NJ: Rutgers University Press.

Ender, P. (2010) 'Collinearity issues'. Http://www.philender.com/courses/categorical/notes2/collin.html

FBI (2018) 'FBI hate crimes report'. https://ucr.fbi.gov/hate-crime/2018/topic-pages/victims

Franklin, K. (1998) 'Unassuming motivations: contextualizing the narratives of antigay assailants', in G. M. Herek (ed.), *Stigma and Sexual Orientation: Understanding Prejudice Against Lesbians, Gay Men, and Bisexuals*, Thousand Oaks, CA: SAGE, pp. 1–23.

Friedman, C. & Leaper, C. (2010) 'Sexual-minority college women's experiences with discrimination: relations with identity and collective action', *Psychology of Women Quarterly*, 34(2): 152–164. https://doi.org/10.1111/j.1471-6402.2010.01558.x

Goffman, E. (1963) *Stigma: Notes on the Management of Spoiled Identity*. Englewood Cliffs, NJ: Prentice-Hall.

Greenberg, K. (2012) 'Still hidden in the closet: trans women and domestic violence', *Berkeley Journal of Gender, Law & Justice*, 2: 198–251.

Grossman, S.F., Hinkley, S., Kawalski, A., & Margrave, C. (2005) 'Rural versus urban victims of violence: the interplay of race and region', *Journal of Family Violence*, 20(2): 71–81. https://doi.org/10.1007/s10896-005-3170-y

Herek, G.M. (2000) 'Sexual prejudice and gender: do heterosexuals' attitudes toward lesbians and gay men differ?', *Journal of Social Issues*, 56(2): 251–266. https://doi.org/10.1111/0022-4537.00164

Herek, G.M. (2007) 'Confronting sexual stigma and prejudice: theory and practice', *Journal of Social Issues*, 63(4): 905–925. https://doi.org/10.1111/j.1540-4560.2007.00544.x

Herek, G.M. (2009) 'Hate crimes and stigma-related experiences among sexual minority adults in the United States: prevalence estimates from a national probability sample', *Journal of Interpersonal Violence*, 24(1): 54–74. doi: 10.1177/0886260508316477

Herek, G.M., Gillis, J.R., & Cogan, J.C. (1999) 'Psychological sequelae of hate-crime victimization among lesbian, gay, and bisexual adults', *Journal of Consulting and Clinical Psychology*, 67(6): 945–951. https://doi.org/10.1037/0022-006X.67.6.945

Human Rights Campaign (2018) 'Dismantling a culture of violence: understanding anti-transgender violence and ending the crisis', Human Rights Campaign Foundation. https://assets2.hrc.org/files/assets/resources/2018AntiTransViolenceReportSHORTENED.pdf?_ga=2.47210529.784651472.1561134346-289901230.1554311612

James, S., Herman, J.L., Rankin, S., Keisling, M., Mottet, L., & Ma'ayan, A. (2016) 'The report of the 2015 U.S. Transgender Survey', National Center for Transgender Equality.

Javaid, A. (2018) 'Out of place: sexualities, sexual violence, and heteronormativity', *Aggression and Violent Behavior*, 39: 83–89. https://doi.org/10.1016/j.avb.2018.02.007

Jones, E.E. (1984) *Social Stigma: The Psychology of Marked Relationships*, New York: W.H. Freeman.

Jones, R.G. (2015) 'Queering the body politic: intersectional reflexivity in the body narratives of queer men', *Qualitative Inquiry*, 21(9): 766–775. https://doi.org/10.1177/1077800415569782

Katz-Wise, S.L. & Hyde, J.S. (2012) 'Victimization experiences of lesbian, gay, and bisexual individuals: a meta-analysis', *Journal of Sex Research*, 49(2–3): 142–167. https://doi.org/10.1080/00224499.2011.637247

Link, B.G. & Phelan, J.C. (2001) 'Conceptualizing stigma', *Annual Review of Sociology*, 27(1): 363–385. https://doi.org/10.1146/annurev.soc.27.1.363

Logie, C.H. & Earnshaw, V. (2015) 'Adapting and validating a scale to measure sexual stigma among lesbian, bisexual and queer women', *PLOS ONE*, 10(2): e0116198. https://doi.org/10.1371/journal.pone.0116198

Matsuzaka, S. & Koch, D.E. (2019) 'Trans feminine sexual violence experiences: the intersection of transphobia and misogyny', *Affilia*, 34(1): 28–47. https://doi.org/10.1177/0886109918790929

Meyer, D. (2010) 'Evaluating the severity of hate-motivated violence: intersectional differences among LGBT hate crime victims', *Sociology*, 44(5): 980–995. https://doi.org/10.1177/0038038510375737

Meyer, D. (2015) *Violence Against Queer People: Race, Class, Gender, and the Persistence of Anti-LGBT Discrimination*, New Brunswick, NJ: Rutgers University Press.

Meyer, I.H. (2003) 'Prejudice, social stress, and mental health in lesbian, gay, and bisexual populations: conceptual issues and research evidence', *Psychological Bulletin*, 129(5): 674–697. https://doi.org/10.1037/0033-2909.129.5.674

Morandini, J.S., Blaszczynski, A., & Dar-Nimrod, I. (2017) 'Who adopts queer and pansexual sexual identities?', *The Journal of Sex Research*, 54(7): 911–922. https://doi.org/10.1080/00224499.2016.1249332

Morris, J.F. & Balsam, K.F. (2003) 'Lesbian and bisexual women's experiences of victimization: mental health, revictimization, and sexual identity development', *Journal of Lesbian Studies*, 7(4): 67–85. https://doi.org/10.1300/J155v07n04_05

Panfil, V.R. (2017) *The Gang's All Queer: The Lives of Gay Gang Members*, New York: NYU Press.

Perry, B. & Dyck, D.R. (2014) '"I don't know where it is safe": trans women's experiences of violence', *Critical Criminology*, 22(1): 49–63. https://doi.org/10.1007/s10612-013-9225-0

Rupp, L.J. & Taylor, V. (2010) 'Straight girls kissing', *Contexts*, 9(3): 28–32. https://doi.org/10.1525/ctx.2010.9.3.28

Schilt, K. & Westbrook, L. (2009) 'Doing gender, doing heteronormativity: "gender normals," transgender people, and the social maintenance of heterosexuality', *Gender & Society*, 23(4): 440–464.

Schur, E.M. (1983) *Labeling Women Deviant: Gender, Stigma, and Social Control*, Philadelphia, PA: Temple University Press.

Stacey, M., Averett, P., & Knox, B. (2018) 'An exploration of victimization in the older lesbian population', *Victims & Offenders*, 13(5): 693–710. https://doi.org/10.1080/15564886.2018.1468368

Stafford, M.C. & Scott, R.R. (1986) 'Stigma, deviance, and social control', in S. C. Ainlay, G. Becker, & L. M. Coleman (eds.), *The Dilemma of Difference: A Multidisciplinary View of Stigma*, New York: Springer, pp. 77–91. https://doi.org/10.1007/978-1-4684-7568-5_5

Stephenson, R. & Finneran, C. (2017) 'Minority stress and intimate partner violence among gay and bisexual men in Atlanta', *American Journal of Men's Health*, 11(4): 952–961. https://doi.org/10.1177/1557988316677506

Szymanski, D.M. & Carr, E.R. (2008) 'The roles of gender role conflict and internalized heterosexism in gay and bisexual men's psychological distress: testing two mediation models', *Psychology of Men & Masculinity*, 9(1): 40–54. https://doi.org/10.1037/1524-9220.9.1.40

Testa, R.J., Sciacca, L.M., Wang, F., Hendricks, M.L., Goldblum, P., Bradford, J., & Bongar, B. (2012) 'Effects of violence on transgender people', *Professional Psychology: Research and Practice*, 43(5): 452–459. https://doi.org/10.1037/a0029604

Weiss, J.T. (2003) 'GL vs. BT', *Journal of Bisexuality*, 3(3–4): 25–55. https://doi.org/10.1300/J159v03n03_02

Whitfield, D.L., Coulter, R.W.S., Langenderfer-Magruder, L., & Jacobson, D. (2018) 'Experiences of intimate partner violence among lesbian, gay, bisexual, and transgender college students: the intersection of gender, race, and sexual orientation', *Journal of Interpersonal Violence*, 36(11–12): 088626051881207. https://doi.org/10.1177/0886260518812071

Wodda, A. & Panfil, V.R. (2014) 'Don't talk to me about deception: the necessary erosion of the trans panic defense', *Albany Law Review*, 78: 927–972.

Worthen, M.G.F. (2020) *Queers, Bis, and Straight Lies: An Investigation of LGBTQ Stigma*. New York: Routledge.

2

Queer Pathways

Michael K. Winters

Introduction

Queer criminology aims to shed light on the ways that general criminology has overlooked the specific but interrelated contexts of offending behavior and queerness (Ball, 2014). Although there have been significant attempts to approach the LGBTQ+ populations as both victims and perpetrators of crime, these understandings largely stem from a cisheteronormative understanding of queerness that largely overlooks or misinterprets the individual's sexual minority status and gender expression as a criminological function (Ball et al., 2014). Although queer criminology itself is a new approach, it highlights how cisheteronormative structures create criminal propensity for people of all gender identities and sexual orientations. This chapter examines the pathways to crime approach, which argues that there are specific contextual factors that are related to an individual's position in society and their unique environments. This framework is helpful for fully understanding the role of sexuality and gender expression in offending patterns and in the victimization of the queer community.

Queer/ed criminology

Ostensibly, criminology has developed to favor the experiences of certain subjects and researchers (Ball, 2014); namely, the legacy of criminology paints the views of cisgender heterosexual white men in broad strokes as the de facto perspective. As we will discuss later, feminists highlight the systematic ways in which criminological discourse historically eschewed the unique experiences of women (Daly, 1992; Belknap, 2007), and critical race scholars point out how the nuanced way that race influences criminal propensity, policing, and recourse options was frequently overlooked (Brown, 2006; Burt et al., 2017; Omori, 2019). Similarly, the field of criminology has seen a much-needed influx of scholars who highlight the ways in which sexuality, sexual identity, and gender identity need to be analyzed, as there are some specific avenues in the study of crime, victimization, law, and deviance that benefit from the explicit analysis of the way cisheteronormative policing affects both cisgender heterosexual people and people across the LGBTQ+ spectrum (Ball, 2014).

The legacy of illicit LGBTQ+ existence is still found in the way that queer youth are treated by their schools, families, and the criminal justice system for their LGBTQ+ identities and how this contributes to criminogenic conditions. For instance, public schools are much more likely to punish LGBTQ+ students for public displays of affection compared with their straight peers (Snapp et al., 2015). This disconnect has been shown to negatively impact queer youth's self-esteem and self-efficacy (Meyer, 1995), which – when combined with other stress factors – can increase the likelihood of offending. Similarly, LGBTQ+ youth are the largest relative percentage of homeless youth (Bidell, 2014), as these youth are ejected from their homes or run away due to familial stress stemming from negative responses to their identities (Tierney & Ward, 2017). Finally, queer/ed criminology has roots in the observation that LGBTQ+ youth – namely, transgender and gender-nonconforming youth (Buist & Stone, 2014) – have needs that are not met by the criminal justice system, such as respect for their gender identity in that they are forced to align with a gender assigned at birth or are not allowed to receive hormone treatment.

In addition to LGBTQ+ studies, queer/ed criminology has roots in intersectional feminist criminology (Ball, 2014). Intersectional feminist criminology is accustomed to peeling back the institutional matrices of power that keep people of various identities subjugated in order to maintain a hierarchical society, especially as they relate to masculinity as a dominant structure that subjugates femininity (or, at least, non-masculinity). From criminological and victimological standpoints, intersectional feminism highlights the way both sexual identity and gender expression fail to be considered protected statuses, especially in the realm of hate crime and discrimination protections (Buist & Stone, 2014). Queer/ed criminology expands on this by observing that not only are race and gender factors that contribute to discrimination and oppression, but so too are sexual minority status and gender identity (Ball et al., 2014).

These facets contribute to the way that institutional structures are built in order to maintain a cisheteronormative hierarchy that surveils and polices queer bodies, acts, and spaces differently compared with nonqueer individuals, so much so that legal and financial benefits readily available for nonqueer people to take advantage of are denied to queer people and contested as political discourse (McCandless, 2018). The popular example here would be marriage equality, which was only legalized in the United States in 2015 as a result of the Supreme Court's ruling in *Obergefell v. Hodges*. Marriage is not just a social rite, but a legal and financial decision that disproportionately affected the fair distribution of assets between queer people until gay marriage was made legal.

Stemming from this, a large number of extant studies of LGBTQ+ offenders and victims lean strongly on the role of victimization, trauma, and strain on offending propensity. Trauma and minority stress hypotheses often inform not just the types of offending performed by LGBTQ+ offenders, but also the preceding factors that contribute to these offenses, namely as a result of direct or indirect victimization stemming from institutional, communal, and individual responses to queer identities. As described earlier, many queer youth experience turbulent relationships at home and school as a specific response to their LGBTQ+ identities, which then inform why LGBTQ+ youth are more likely to be homeless (Tierney & Ward, 2017).

The experience of homelessness is a very traumatic event for queer young people, who experience new types of strain – such as shelter, food, or income instability – that compound the unfamiliar issues they now face as openly queer people. Similarly, homelessness is also associated with increased victimization and harassment (Hamilton et al., 2011), which multiplies the hardships a homeless, queer youth could face. This, then, should logically indicate that LGBTQ+ homeless youth are statistically more likely to be drug offenders and sex workers, which current literature supports (McCandless, 2018).

The focus of queer/ed criminology is in the statement that queerness is a *critique position*, rather than a singular focus on queer people as a criminological subject. By understanding how queer individuals are disproportionately policed due to their noncompliance with the cisgender heteronormative structures (Buist & Stone, 2014; Perry & Dyck, 2014), we begin to understand not just how this might affect nonqueer people, but also how these structures interact with those that would disproportionately affect individuals who inhabit non-white, non-male, and cisheteronormative spaces. This chapter argues that a pathways approach to queer criminology will help to expand this notion, and it is to this theoretical tradition that we now turn.

Pathways to crime

The pathways approach, as pioneered by scholars such as Belknap (2007) and Daly (1992), developed out of frustration with the general criminological assumption that men's and women's offending patterns were similar and that results and solutions to issues in men's offending could be translated to women's offending at a one-to-one ratio (Brennan et al., 2012). These early studies noted that women's pathways to offending are markedly different than those of men, and those studies are often dotted with observations on different rates of victimization, different kinds of victimization, and different contexts that call for distinct theoretical and methodological approaches that tease out these differences.

For example, compared with men, women who are arrested are much more likely to be the primary caregiver for their children (Desai et al., 2002; Schubert et al., 2016). These are unique strains that stem from a combination of the socially prescribed role of women as nurturers and caretakers for their children and the grim reality that single-income families are more likely to be in poverty. These contexts should be taken into account, because some solutions may not work for this group of offenders – job training and vocational programs that are often prescribed to male drug offenders, for instance, may mean very little to women who must work both legitimate and criminal jobs in order to meet their needs and those of their families.

The pathways approach to crime and offending can be seen in part as a response to and an adaptation of general strain theories and life-course theories. General strain theories argue that life stressors can influence the likelihood to offend vis-à-vis an individual's responses to everyday stressors (Agnew, 1985, 1992), and life-course theories argue that the everyday social contexts contribute to the overall development of an individual, which in turn impacts their likelihood for offending and victimization (Brennan et al., 2012). Pathways theory argues that this is certainly true for women. For example, most women who commit violence against their partners tend to do so out of retaliation for or in self-defense from violence that they themselves have experienced from their partners and are thus much more likely to experience a victim–offender overlap (Daly, 1992; Brown, 2006; Kobulsky, 2017).

Although intimate partner violence (IPV) can be seen as an indicator of the need for a pathways approach, the most salient example as it relates to this chapter is the tendency for young girls in the juvenile justice system to receive harsher punishments for status offenses – crimes that are the result of the juvenile's status as a legal minor, such as drinking alcohol or truancy – compared with boys (Espinosa et al., 2013; Kruttschnitt, 2013; Agnew & Brezina, 2017), and thus institutional reproach for status offenses may be more indicative of future offending for women than for men. These harsher punishments are suggested to be a response to both the minor's legal infractions *and* the transgression of the gender norms that call for women to be caring, passive, and docile – whereas aggressiveness and offending, in this regard, may seem par for the course for young boys, as social prescriptions of masculinity are in alignment with such patterns of offending (Agnew & Brezina, 2018).

There are three major areas of focus in pathways scholarship that are useful to the construction of queer pathways specifically and queer/ed criminology generally. The first is the role of victimization and trauma in propensity to offend. Daly's (1992) study outlines this in a more typological way specific to women's experiences, but the notion that prior traumatic experiences contribute to offending can be readily applied to queer offenders. Although the experience of physical abuse during adolescence has a general association with future offending (Fagan, 2005; Yoon et al., 2018), women and girls are more likely to experience strain at home as a result of physical, psychological, or sexual abuse, all of which have been shown to be indicators for drug use and physical violence, with the latter usually expressing itself as a form of self-defense from an abusive partner, family member, or legal guardian (Fuentes, 2013; Kruttschnitt, 2013; Simpson et al., 2016).

The second area of focus is developmental pathways to offending, which examines the different ways boys and girls develop as they age, with special emphasis on social influences during the process of maturation. Literature in this field highlights the gendered ways in which strain and stress impact individuals directly and indirectly through their social environments and produce offending behaviors. Boyes et al. (2010) propose a developmental model suggesting that issues (or a lack thereof) with family, school, and community play a considerable role in predicting future offending of all kinds. In gendered pathways studies, this has led to the understanding that men and boys are socialized to *externalize* their response to stressors, such as direct defiance of authority figures and inciting physical violence (McGee & Mazerolle, 2017). Conversely, women and girls are socialized to *internalize* their responses, which manifest as an increased risk for drug abuse, self-harm, and risky sexual behaviors (Kobulsky et al., 2018; Yoon et al., 2018). These pathways influence not only the gendered differences in possible offending tracts, but also the sanctions they are likely to receive.

The third and final area discussed in this chapter is the role that relationships play in pathways to offending. France and Homel (2006) argue that there are both individual and social/societal pathways that influence offending. Where an individual can be socialized to externalize their responses to stressors *without* resulting in offending behavior, there still exists the sociological tendency for families and communities in disadvantaged socioeconomic locations to experience these stressors at a higher level than families and communities in other locations (Vitale et al., 2005). These aspects of the pathways framework have been useful to critical race theorists, who have found that real or perceived discrimination informs offending habits, namely drug use, for Black men (Brody et al., 2012).

Queer pathways

As Daly (1992) notes with regard to women, queer youth offenders typically experience more conflict, strain, and traumatic experiences at home. Like women, queer offenders are more likely to have been sexually and physically victimized than their nonqueer counterparts (Jordan, 2000). Additionally, queer offenders experience trauma stemming from the adversarial positions that their family members and legal guardians take to their queer identities (Tierney & Ward, 2017). Pathways studies have found that such homegrown conflict is especially influential in determining future offending of any kind (Kruttschnitt, 2013), and prior studies have shown that discrimination faced by queer youth offenders is positively associated with future offending (Lehavot & Simoni, 2011). The degree of overlap here remains unknown, but it seems likely that queer women are most likely to have been victimized in multiple ways related to their intersectional identities (Edwards et al., 2015).

The most widely understood way in which discrimination toward queer youth and hostile reactions at home affect future offending is through homelessness as a pathway to offending. Queer youth experience disproportionately high rates of homelessness (Bidell, 2014), so much so that it is understood that LGBTQ+ youth are the highest relative percentage of homeless youth. Despite this, there exist relatively few resources that explicitly target the needs of LGBTQ+ youth, and private foundations are still legally allowed to refuse to help the LGBTQ+ population at their discretion in many states (Dolamore & Naylor, 2018). Homelessness has been accounted for as one of the primary influences on LGBTQ+ youth drug offending (Jordan, 2000), and LGBTQ+ youth are more likely to engage in sex work to support themselves financially compared with their heterosexual and cisgender counterparts (McCandless, 2018).

Even in instances where discrimination toward queer youth does not directly result in homelessness, those who are 'out' must often deal with families, peers, and institutions that are hostile to their identities, while those who are not out must deal with the internalized contradictions of masking their true identities from those around them. Both are sources of strain that influence a variety of queer offending behaviors, including drug offending as mentioned earlier, but also physical violence, theft, and truancy in many instances. Panfil's (2017) study of gay gang members provides a vivid illustration of these outcomes. Openly gay male gang members frequently reported that they lived at home and experienced icy relationships between family members as a result of their sexual identities, whereas others carefully monitored a balance between their 'passing' (posing as heterosexual) behavior and their true identities. While in many cases these factors may not directly influence offending behavior, gang members interviewed in this study expressed their frustration at these conditions.

This echoes the findings of many studies on LGBTQ+ youth offenders and the circumstances surrounding their identity. However, Panfil's study both supports and contradicts the general pathways findings regarding the internalization and externalization of responses to stressors. Peralta and Tuttle (2013) found that straight male perpetrators of violence often rely on gender roles in what they call 'hostile attributions', which are ways that protect challenged masculinity by responding to stress with external responses culminating in violence. Panfil's study found that gay male gang members were protective of their own masculinity, much in the same way that Peralta and Tuttle found with their study of straight men, but the gay gang members were just as likely to *internalize* their stressors and engage in self-destructive offending, such as drug use, as they were to *externalize* their response by engaging in physical violence to display their own masculinity. This suggests that there may be more nuanced ways in which gender pathways and sexual identity can influence offending than existing frameworks might indicate.

Queer pathways to crime can also echo women's pathways to crime in a myriad of ways that reflect the influence of institutions and social structures on offending. Queer youth have often reported that they have faced both official and unofficial sanction at school for expressing their identities (Bidell, 2014). LGBTQ+ victims of bullying, for example, report that their concerns are not seriously addressed by teachers and other administrators, and that those who bully them receive little to no punishment for their actions (Berlan et al., 2010; Snapp et al., 2015). When LGBTQ+ youth are punished for physical violence, most claim that they were acting out of self-defense from homophobic instigation, much in the same way that pathways literature has shown that women arrested for physical violence were acting in response to an incidence of IPV in which they have also been victimized (Fuentes, 2013). Furthermore, Rogers and Rogers (2020) found that trans men's involvement in the criminal justice system stemmed from histories of childhood abuse, victimization, and homelessness, which in turn supports the applicability of a pathways framework as a tool for queer criminology.

Queer pathways: suggestions for theory, research, and practice

A potential approach to help develop this line of thought would be to compare the trends of queer offending and IPV with those of their nonqueer counterparts, especially in terms of victimization as it relates to possible self-defense scenarios (Edwards et al., 2015). Pathways literature has been instrumental in teasing out the role of prior victimization in cisgender women's offending as the result of intimate partner violence in heterosexual relationships (Daly, 1992; Belknap, 2007; Kruttschnitt, 2013). While it is important to understand how this affects queer adults specifically, a comparison with this established pathways framework can help not only to provide a basis for understanding the unique contexts present in queer pathways, but also to untangle queer criminology from a retread of LGBTQ+ studies by offering distinct analyses of gender roles, offending, and cisheteronormativity in offending, victimization, and policing. By exploring these with a pathways framework, queer criminology can shed new light on the way that gendered social structures affect the victimization and offending of people who are *not* queer vis-à-vis their relationships with gender performance. This will help with the establishment of a queer criminology that is rooted in but not dependent on a study of LGBTQ+ people and their experiences (Ball, 2014).

Pathways research has often been conducted with the explicit mindset of creating better measures that expand beyond academic discourse. The pathways approach to women's crime has been developed with an explicit dedication to the creation of better measures that both prevent opportunities for offending and provide better courses of redress that meet the specific needs of women (Reisig et al., 2006). While some available measures could certainly work for queer offenders in a general sense, prior research has found that queer offending can best be curtailed with measures that address the unique circumstances of queer individuals (Dolamore & Naylor, 2018). A pathways approach can help develop options that prevent future offending for queer youth, while also providing clear and precise suggestions for policies to address the needs of queer people.

Boyes et al. (2010) found that addressing contextual and social issues at a familial, community, and school level for young offenders can significantly decrease individual propensity to offend (Albelda et al., 2009). Likewise, studies on queer youth offending have found that many of the issues that spark offending are directly or indirectly tied to the young person's queer identity. Family therapy, with a focus on sensitivity toward the queer youth's identities and teaching acceptance among family members, is an obvious suggestion, as is the development of better school-based approaches that address issues with bullying. For queer youth who have no option but to support themselves without family or community resources, services that are not only available but also open to the specific needs of LGBTQ+ youth, such as the process of coming out or dealing with gender dysphoria, are absolutely vital in preventing drug use as a coping mechanism. These services must also be able to find housing for their youth charges, as homelessness is associated with illicit sex work and drug use in queer offending.

It is often noted in the pathways literature that broad strokes approaches struggle to effectively curtail the likelihood of offending without clearly defined legislation that specifically targets the unique circumstances of an offender (Haw, 2006). For women, policies (especially those with rehabilitative consequences) must be developed with the understanding that they tend to be victims in abusive relationships and that they are the primary caregivers for their children, among other concerns (France & Homel, 2006; Hammersley, 2011; France et al., 2013). A similar approach needs to be taken with the specific circumstances of queerness in mind, namely with regards to discriminatory social welfare programs and the clear lack of well-defined or well-supported protected status measures. For example, 'gay panic' and 'trans panic' defenses are still widely used to excuse violence committed toward queer individuals, with many outcomes leading to the conviction of queer individuals practicing self-defense against their attackers (Michalski & Nunez, 2020). Because some jurisdictions do not clearly define their hate crime statutes in a way that protects vulnerable members of the queer community, these individuals may be just as likely to be convicted of the crimes with which they have been victimized.

It is important to note that many of the findings on LGBTQ+ youth offending have relied strongly on findings that feature gay men and lesbian women as the primary study population. Other sexual minorities such as bisexual and asexual people, as well as transgender and gender-nonconforming individuals, are largely understudied in the field of criminology. However, much like Daly's (1992) findings that women's offenses are born from responses to victimization, Buist and Stone's (2014) study of transgender offenders found that many transgender offenders responded to physical attacks stemming from their gender presentation and transgender identity.

Conclusion

This chapter has provided the structure of a pathways approach to queer criminology. The pathways approach, stemming from the study of women's offending, highlights the differing precedents, contexts, and outcomes of women's crime that are necessary to create a whole picture of crime. Likewise, this chapter argues that a pathways approach to queer crime can do the same, where an understanding of the specific factors that contribute to queer offending behavior can lead to a criminology that better represents the individuals that it studies. Pathways to crime can fill a gap in the understanding of lifelong LGBTQ+ offending, but it is the ability to establish the ways that social structures of cisheteronormativity that can and does affect the propensity to commit crime among both queer and nonqueer individuals (Buist & Lenning, 2015). Future studies should aim to include a pathways framework from the outset, and this should be used to paint a clearer picture of the offending patterns and contextual histories of adult offenders. This can be used to create policies and organizations that are better suited to meet the needs of queer individuals.

References

Agnew, R. (1985) 'A revised strain theory of delinquency', *Social Forces*, 64(1): 151–167.

Agnew, R. (1992) 'Foundation for a general strain theory of crime and delinquency', *Criminology*, 30(1): 47–88.

Agnew, R. and Brezina, T. (2017) *Juvenile Delinquency: Causes and Control*, Oxford: Oxford University Press.

Albelda, R., Schneebaum, A., Badgett, M.V., & Gates, G. (2009) 'Poverty in the lesbian, gay, and bisexual community', UCLA CCPR Population Working Papers.

Ball, M. (2014) 'Queer criminology, critique, and the "art of not being governed"', *Critical Criminology*, 22: 21–34.

Ball, M., Buist, C.L., & Woods, J.B. (2014) 'Introduction to the Special Issue on Queer/ing Criminology: New Directions and Frameworks', *Critical Criminology*, 22: 1–4.

Belknap, J. (2007) *The Invisible Woman: Gender, Crime, and Justice* (3rd edn.), Belmont, CA: Thompson Wadsworth.

Berlan, E.D., Corliss, H.L., Field, A.E., Goodman, E., & Austin, S.B. (2010) 'Sexual orientation and bullying among adolescents in the growing up today study', *Journal of Adolescent Health*, 46(0): 366–371.

Bidell, M.P. (2014) 'Is there an emotional cost of completing high school? Ecological factors and psychological distress among LGBT homeless youth', *Journal of Homosexuality*, 61(3): 366–381.

Boyes, M.C., Hornick, J.P., & Ogden, N. (2010) 'Developmental pathways towards crime prevention: early intervention models', *International Journal of Child, Youth & Family Studies*, 1(2): 97–117.

Brennan, T., Breitenbach, M., Dieterich, W., Salisbury, E.J., & Voorhis, P.V. (2012) 'Women's pathways to serious and habitual crime: a person-centered analysis incorporating gender responsive factors', *Criminal Justice and Behavior*, 39(11): 1481–1508.

Brody, G.H., Kogan, S.M., & Chen, Y. (2012) 'Perceived discrimination and longitudinal increases in adolescent substance use: gender differences and mediational pathways', *American Journal of Public Health*, 102(5): 1006–1011.

Brown, M. (2006) 'Gender, ethnicity, and offending over the life course: women's pathways to prison in the Aloha State', *Critical Criminology*, 14: 137–158.

Buist, C.L. & Lenning, E. (2015) *Queer Criminology: New Directions in Critical Criminology*, New York: Routledge.

Buist, C.L. & Stone, C. (2014) 'Transgender victims and offenders: failures of the United States criminal justice system and the necessity of queer criminology', *Critical Criminology*, 22: 35–47.

Burt, C.H., Lei, M.K., & Simons, R.L. (2017) 'Racial discrimination, racial socialization, and crime over time: a social schematic theory model', *Criminology*, 55(4): 938–979.

Daly, K. (1992) 'Women's pathways to felony court: feminist theories of law-breaking and problems of representation', *Review of Law and Women's Studies*, 2: 11–52.

Desai, S., Arias, I., Thompson, M.P., & Basile, K.C. (2002) 'Childhood victimization and subsequent adult revictimization assessed in a nationally representative sample of women and men', *Violence and Victims*, 17(6): 639–653.

Dolamore, S. & Naylor, L.A. (2018) 'Providing solutions to LGBT homeless youth: lessons from Baltimore's youth empowered society', *Public Integrity: Symposium on the Homeless LGBT Youth Epidemic*, 20(6): 595–610.

Edwards, K.M., Sylaska, K.M., Barry, J.E., Moynihan, M.M., Banyard, V.L., Cohn, E.S., Walsh, W.A., & Ward, S.K. (2015) 'Physical dating violence, sexual violence, and unwanted pursuit victimization: a comparison of incidence rates among sexual-minority and heterosexual college students', *Journal of Interpersonal Violence*, 30(4): 580–600.

Espinosa, E.M., Sorensen, J.R., & Lopez, M.A. (2013) 'Youth pathways to placement: the influence of gender, mental health need and trauma on confinement in the juvenile justice system', *Journal of Youth Adolescence*, 42: 1824–1836.

Fagan, A.A. (2005) 'The relationship between adolescent physical abuse and criminal offending: support for an enduring and generalized cycle of violence', *Journal of Family Violence*, 20: 279–290.

France, A. & Homel, R. (2006) 'Societal access routes and developmental pathways: putting social structure and young people's voice into the analysis of pathways into and out of crime', *The Australian and New Zealand Journal of Criminology*, 39(3): 295–309.

France, A., Bottrell, D., & Haddon, E. (2013) 'The role of habitus and reflexivity in young people managing pathways out of crime', *International Journal of School Disaffection*, 10(1): 11–27.

Fuentes, C.M. (2013) 'Nobody's child: the role of trauma and interpersonal violence in women's pathways to incarceration and resultant service needs', *Medical Anthropology Quarterly*, 28(1): 85–104.

Hamilton, A.B., Poza, I., & Washington, D.L. (2011) '"Homelessness and trauma go hand-in-hand": pathways to homelessness among women veterans', *Women's Health Issues*, 21(4S): S203–S209.

Hammersley, R. (2011) 'Pathways through drugs and crime: desistance, trauma and resilience', *Journal of Criminal Justice*, 39: 268–272.

Haw, K. (2006) 'Risk factors and pathways into and out of crime, misleading, misinterpreted, or mythic? From generative metaphor to professional myth', *The Australian and New Zealand Journal of Criminology*, 39(3): 339–353.

Jordan, K.M. (2000) 'Substance abuse among gay, lesbian, bisexual, transgender, and questioning adolescents', *School Psychology Review*, 29(2): 201–206.

Kobulsky, J.M. (2017) 'Gender differences in pathways from physical and sexual abuse to early substance use', *Children and Youth Services Review*, 83: 25–32.

Kobulsky, J.M., Yoon, S., Bright, C.L., Lee, G., & Nam., B. (2018) 'Gender-moderated pathways from childhood abuse and neglect to late-adolescent substance use', *Journal of Traumatic Stress*, 31: 654–664.

Kruttschnitt, C. (2013) 'Gender and crime', *Annual Review of Sociology*, 39: 291–308.

Lehavot, K. & Simoni, J.M. (2011) 'The impact of minority stress on mental health and substance use among sexual minority women', *Journal of Consulting and Clinical Psychology*, 79(2): 159–170.

McCandless, S. (2018) 'LGBT homeless youth and policing', *Public Integrity: Symposium on the Homeless LGBT Youth Epidemic*, 20(6): 558–570.

McGee, T.R. & Mazerolle, P. (2017) 'Gendered experiences in developmental pathways to crime, extended: editorial introduction', *Journal of Developmental and Life-Course Criminology*, 3: 99–101.

Meyer, I.H. (1995) 'Minority stress and mental health in gay men', *Journal of Health and Social Behavior*, 36(1): 38–56.

Michalski, N.D. & Nunez, N. (2020) 'When is "gay panic" accepted? Exploring juror characteristics and case type as predictors of a successful gay panic defense', *Journal of Interpersonal Violence*, 22:886260520912595, DOI: 10.1177/0886260520912595. Epub ahead of print.

Omori, M. (2019) '"Nickel and dimed" for drug crime: unpacking the process of cumulative racial inequality', *The Sociological Quarterly*, 60(2): 287–313.

Panfil, V.R. (2017) *The Gang's All Queer: The Lives of Gay Gang Members*, New York: New York University Press.

Peralta, R.L. & Tuttle, L.A. (2013) 'Male perpetrators of heterosexual-partner-violence: the role of threats to masculinity', *The Journal of Men's Studies*, 21(3): 255–276.

Perry, B. & Dyck, D.R. (2014) '"I don't know where it is safe": trans women's experiences of violence', *Critical Criminology*, 22(1): 49–63.

Reisig, M.D., Holtfreter, K., & Morash, M. (2006) 'Assessing recidivism risk across female pathways to crime', *Justice Quarterly*, 23(3): 384–405, DOI: 10.1080/07418820600869152

Rogers, S.A. & Rogers, B.A. (2020) 'Tran's men's pathways to incarceration', *Sociological Spectrum*, 41(1): 115–134.

Schubert, E.C., Duinick, M., & Shiafer, R.J. (2016) 'Visiting mom: a pilot evaluation of a prison-based visiting program serving incarcerated mothers and their minor children', *Journal of Offender Rehabilitation*, 55(4): 213–234.

Simpson, S.S., Alper, M., Dugan, L., Horney, J., Kruttschnitt, C., & Gartner, R. (2016) 'Age-graded pathways into crime: evidence from a multi-site retrospective study of incarcerated women', *Journal of Developmental and Life-Course Criminology*, 2: 296–320.

Snapp, S.D., Hoenig, J.M., Fields, A., & Russell, S.T. (2015) 'Messy, butch, and queer: LGBTQ youth and the school-to-prison pipeline', *Journal of Adolescent Research*, 30(1): 57–82.

Tierney, W.G. & Ward, J.D. (2017) 'Coming out and leaving home: a policy and research agenda for LGBT homeless students', *Educational Researcher*, 46(9): 498–507.

Vitale, J.E., Newman, J.P., Serin, R.C., & Bolt, D.M. (2005) 'Hostile attributions in incarcerated adult male offenders: an exploration of diverse pathways', *Aggressive Behavior*, 31: 99–115.

Yoon, S., Voith, L.A., & Kobulsky, J.M. (2018) 'Gender differences in pathways from child physical and sexual abuse to adolescent risky sexual behavior among high risk youth', *Journal of Adolescence*, 64: 89–97.

3

Queer Criminology and the Destabilization of Child Sexual Abuse

Dave McDonald

Throughout the 2010s, queer criminology has firmly established itself as an important orientation within criminology. While its origins date back much further, its emergence was precipitated in particular by the publication of Dana Peterson and Vanessa R. Panfil's (2014) *Handbook of LGBT Communities, Crime and Justice*. This marked a sustained intervention into the field, bringing together a diverse range of voices to challenge an entrenched heteronormativity that has characterized broader criminological scholarship since its inception. In her foreword to the handbook, Jody Miller observes that there is a 'vital need to bring a queer lens to *every* dimension of the field' (2014, p. vii; my emphasis). In the short time following, this has been met with differing perspectives that offer the potential to ameliorate criminology's enduring neglect of sexuality and gender identities, and its momentum is attested by a growing number of collections that have been produced in the time since (Lamble, 2013; Ball et al., 2014; Buist & Lenning, 2015; Dwyer et al., 2016; Lamble et al., 2020). Collectively, this movement has been an important corrective to the tendency to take sex and gender for granted across criminological theorizing.

Across the breadth of this research, one characteristic has been an ongoing self-reflexiveness around the perimeters of what constitutes 'queer criminology'. Put another way, the question of what is *queer* about queer criminology remains open-ended. Much of this work seeks to illuminate issues of crime and justice as they relate to the control of LGBTIQ people

(Ball, 2014; Dwyer, 2014; Peterson & Panfil, 2014; Woods, 2014; Buist & Lenning, 2015). This includes how queer people figure as either offenders or victims, and how they experience institutions and processes of social control. While this work is theoretically informed, it tends to stand in contrast to that which is more explicitly informed by queer theory and which critically eschews an assimilationist stance in preference for a deconstructive approach to identity and/or institutions (see Lamble et al., 2020; Redd & Russell, 2020; Russell, 2020; Ball, 2014). In this way, these latter approaches tend to be less concerned with making a space for LGBTIQ communities within criminology per se, but rather to emphasize the political potentialities that may arise through a destabilization and deconstruction of categories of identity, and the technologies of power upon which they pivot. While these are not necessarily incompatible approaches (Ball, 2016; Woods, 2014), they nevertheless tend to characterize the two broad stances within queer criminology.

In this chapter, I consider how criminological scholarship can make use of the conceptual and analytic tools of queer theory in order to enhance understandings of child sexual abuse. While some critical criminologists have offered valuable critiques of misconceptions and myths associated with the sexual abuse of children (Richards, 2011, 2019; Salter, 2016), it is work that has tended to be located some distance away from queer criminology. What may be gained, I ask, by bringing queer theory to bear upon child sexual abuse? A central feature of queer theory is its attempt to destabilize the homo/hetero binary, and to problematize the ways in which normality and perversion are structured around this distinction. While the homophobic nature of perversion as a concept has been the subject of criticism (Angelides, 2005; Dalton, 2006; Chenier, 2012; McDonald, 2020), the approach I adopt here is somewhat different. My concern is less with perversion and homophobia than it is with examining how *heteronormativity* operates in discussions regarding the sexual abuse of children. Previously I have suggested that the category of the pedophile be considered a subject of queer criminology (McDonald, 2016). Similarly, Walker and Panfil (2017) have thoughtfully argued that queer criminology should extend a place to what they call minor-attracted people. This article in part revisits and refocuses aspects of my earlier argument in order to expand upon perversion as an historical and contemporary concept, and to show how it relies on a heteronormative logic that dominates understandings of child abuse. I argue that by deconstructing the way that normality and perversion are structurally organized as concepts, we can begin to understand how difference is constructed to obscure the institution of the family as the most dominant site in which children are abused.

By employing the tools of queer theory in this way, my objective is twofold: first, in comparison to the narrow rigidity that pervades most contemporary conceptions of child sexual abuse, this enables a more wholistic understanding of offending across a greater plethora of sites. And second, it demonstrates how a theoretical orientation *within* queer criminology can be practically oriented: rather than simply a matter of theory, there are very practical implications at hand in how we think about, and respond to, the abuse of children. I begin by outlining the deconstructive potential of queer theory in unpacking categories and identities, before expanding on how pedophilia may be located in such an approach. I then move to investigate pedophilia as an historical construct and tease out how this past manifests in the contemporary distinction between fixation and regression. In its entirety, by historicizing the contemporary organization of pedophilia as a concept, the chapter seeks to employ the tools of queer theory in order to advance a more just way of thinking about the sexual abuse of children.

Queer theory and identity

While notoriously difficult to define (Sullivan, 2010; Ball, 2016; McCann & Monaghan, 2019), one of the central features of queer theory is its attempt to destabilize the appearance of essentialism that pervades conceptions of sexual orientation and gendered identity. In this respect it is deeply indebted to Michel Foucault (1978, 1980) and his historical approach to subjectivity. In an oft quoted passage from his first volume of *The History of Sexuality*, Foucault remarked that throughout the 19th century, the

> homosexual became a personage,[1] a past, a case history, and a childhood, in addition to being a type of life, a life form, and a morphology ... Homosexuality appeared as one of the forms of sexuality when it was transposed from the practice of sodomy onto a kind of interior androgyny, a hermaphrodism of the soul. The sodomite had been a temporary aberration; the homosexual was now a species. (1978, p. 43)

This statement speaks to Foucault's broader argument about the way that sexuality has come to comprise a key facet of identity, and how the categories on which this relies are taken for granted as objective and ahistorical. These identities did not just appear, of course, but rather are an effect of a broader transformation taking place involving medicine and the human sciences more generally. A key feature of this development throughout the 19th century related to perversion as a concept, which Foucault (1978) linked to his rejection of the repressive hypothesis and to technologies of the confessional. As he did so, he was careful to eschew an essentialized approach to the subject in order to show how it is contingent and constructed. This conception of subjectivity has been taken up by queer theorists to underscore the tenuousness of identity and to resist straightforward categorization – including but not limited to sexed and gendered identities.

With this backdrop to queer theory in mind, how might such a deconstructive approach enhance understandings of pedophilia and child sexual abuse? In the first instance, it helps draw attention to the *constructed* nature of the pedophile. This can be seen in part by the fact that broad social attitudes regarding child sexual abuse change over time (Jenkins, 1998). While it has become commonplace to regard pedophilia with disgust and abhorrence, this has not always been the case. This does not mean that its harms should be minimized. I am drawing an important distinction here between child sexual abuse as a *phenomenon*, and the way that the category of the pedophile has become a shorthand to stand in for those individuals who perpetuate it. This distinction becomes clearer through an interrogation of the origins of pedophilia as a concept, and its more recent usage within psychiatric literature.

The origins of the pedophile

As with the emergence of other categories of 'otherness' that Foucault charted in his *History of Sexuality*, the pedophile was brought into being by psychiatric discourses of perversion that gained precedence in the 19th century. As a concept, it is credited to the noted German psychiatrist Richard von Krafft-Ebing, who first established it in the 1896 edition of his chronicle of sexual perversion, *Psychopathia sexualis: A Medical-Forensic Study* (1998).[2] As I go on to argue, the contemporary organization of normality and perversion dates back to Krafft-Ebing's theorizing, thus revealing the way in which traces of the past continue to structure the present.

For psychiatrists writing at the time of Krafft-Ebing, perversion was regarded in terms either of the 'will' or the 'soul', designating an essentialist conception of the interior condition of the person (Rimke & Hunt, 2002, p. 62). The will was understood to be linked to the mind and reason, whereas the soul denoted psychic identity and was therefore understood as more all-encompassing in nature (Dean, 1996, p. 19). Among a broader array of perversions, it was the latter that were the source of the most concern. Individuals lacking in willpower, or manifesting a perversion associated with a transitory life stage, for example, paled in comparison with those whose perversion was understood as immutable. Importantly, when it came to Krafft-Ebing's conception of pedophilia, this was firmly understood as constitutionally immutable. As he wrote in his introduction to this diagnosis, the offences committed by pedophiles are 'the most horrible perversions and acts, which are possible only to a man who is a slave to lust and morally weak, and, as is usually the case, lacking in sexual power' (1998, p. 369).

One of the chief objectives of Krafft-Ebing's work, as well as that of many comparable psychiatrists writing about sexual abnormality in the late 19th century, was to address relatively explicitly the intersection between psychiatry and law, in particular the question of criminal liability. For Krafft-Ebing, the degree to which these individuals should be held criminally responsible was determined by whether he regarded their perversion to be psychopathological. Where they were understood as psychopathological, their sickness was regarded as more all-encompassing, such that they could not be regarded as liable in a legal sense. At the same time, those whom he regarded as non-psychopathological *could* be considered liable because they were not corrupted by illness to the same extent. Whereas the psychopathological pedophile was ontologically distinct, according to this logic the non-psychopathological offender was regarded as akin to Foucault's abnormal individual in need of correction (Foucault, 2006).

This overarching schema of psychopathology was not intended to minimize the seriousness of the offending that such individuals committed. The point was rather more specific. While many may sexually offend against children, Krafft-Ebing was arguing that it was only in the most exceptional cases that an individual was so sick – in an ontologically complete sense – that they should *not* be held criminally liable. Conversely, while many may be guilty of the *offence*, for few such behavior was understood as the manifestation of an underlying condition. In this way, he sought to distinguish between pedophilia as a diagnosis, which he regarded as an 'erotic' desire for children, and other personality types where individuals engage in sex with minors in the absence of psychopathology. Further, while he did not regard psychopathological pedophiles as criminally liable, he was of course not suggesting that they live free of constraint. 'These unfortunate beings', he wrote, 'should always be looked upon as a common danger to the welfare of the community, and put under strict surveillance and medical treatment' (1998, p. 374). As criminologists have come to know only too well nowadays, positivist ideas of innate sickness were used to instrumentalize an array of harmful interventions which were often extreme in their intrusiveness.

The contemporary organization of pedophilia

While this accounts for the way in which pedophilia was first conceived in the work of Krafft-Ebing, such meanings are of course not static. For the purposes of this chapter, what is particularly significant is how these ideas have influenced more contemporary logics of child sexual abuse. In what follows, I want to draw this out more explicitly. My argument is that the qualification that Krafft-Ebing offered around psychopathology has an important bearing on prevailing ways of thinking about child sexual abuse, with the qualification that notions of responsibility have been paradoxically – even perversely – rewritten in the process. As I will demonstrate, this has had a particular effect in obscuring a key domain in which children are abused.

Whereas Krafft-Ebing organized child sex offenders by reference to psychopathology, in more contemporary psychological theorizing the prevailing orthodoxy distinguishes child sexual abuse according to fixation and regression. This clinical distinction was first introduced by Groth and Birnbaum (1978) and has since been described as having 'become a part of the vernacular used by mental health and legal professionals in classifying and dealing with sexual offenders' (Johnston & Johnston, 1997, p. 361; see also Cossins, 1999; Angelides, 2004a, 2004b, 2005; McDonald, 2020). In their study, Groth and Birnbaum sought to identify sexual attraction and orientation among a random sample of 175 convicted child sex offenders serving periods of imprisonment. They classified offenders into two groups. Fixation was defined by a primary or exclusive sexual attraction towards children, with offending understood as a manifestation of that attraction (Groth & Birnbaum, 1978, p. 176). At the same time, regression was defined by the absence of a primary or exclusive sexual attraction towards children, with offending interpreted as a manifestation of secondary factors such as marital breakdown or unemployment (Groth & Birnbaum, 1978, p. 177). In their study, and in the broader psychological literature that has followed, this distinction has been used to differentiate between pedophiles whose offending is preferential, and those whose offending is circumstantial. In line with the conceptualization of sexual preference, it is held that a fixated pedophile constitutes a greater risk of offending to the greater number of victims.

In many ways this mirrors Krafft-Ebing's distinction between psychopathology and non-psychopathology that I outlined earlier, and it has come to dominate contemporary psychological theorizing. However, the point is not simply that Krafft-Ebing's psychopathological pedophile has become today's fixated pedophile, and that his non-psychopathological pedophile has become today's regressed pedophile. Rather, it is in the way that this basic distinction structures understandings of child sexual abuse according to a schema of normality and perversion. That is, it has been argued that it distinguishes child sexual offending by *type* and *circumstance*: the fixated pedophile represents an 'other', a distinct species or type of person, whereas the regressed offender resembles an otherwise normal individual who in times of stress lacks sufficient willpower or control (Cossins, 1999; Angelides, 2004a, 2004b, 2005; McDonald, 2020). In light of a Foucauldian approach to subjectivity, we can begin to see how these operate not as objective descriptors but as *constructs*. This occurs both in a methodological sense and conceptually. I deal with each in turn.

Methodologically, one problem with the distinction between fixation and regression relates to the basis on which it has been developed. There is a considerable disparity between the actual prevalence of child sexual offences and how this prevalence is – or is not – reflected in official statistics. Despite this, the distinction between fixation and regression takes as a given the assumption that those who are imprisoned for child sexual offences are an accurate representation of offenders more generally. As Cossins has argued persuasively, following Finkelhor:

> The scheme relies on studies which are based on a highly unrepresentative population, that is, convicted offenders who are considered to constitute between one to three per cent of men who sexually abuse children and who are, therefore, likely to be 'the most compulsive, repetitive, blatant, and extreme in their offending'. (1999, p. 47)

Not only does this classification erroneously imply that imprisonment rates are representative of offending populations more generally when in fact they are not, but it also takes for granted the assumption that offenders are truthful about their offending patterns and motivations. This is despite well-established empirical research to suggest that such offenders can frequently be dishonest about their offending (see Cossins, 1999, p. 47).

In comparison with the idea that regressed offenders are less of a threat by virtue of the claim that they lack a primary sexual attraction to minors, Cossins points to research that suggests a significant proportion of incest offenders *also* abuse other children unrelated to them, such that 'it cannot be assumed that incest and extrafamilial offenders comprise distinct and separate categories of child sex offenders' (1999, p. 48). Further problematizing this is more contemporary research that has been conducted with non-offending minor-attracted people that calls into question the assumption that those exhibiting an attraction to minors are necessarily more likely to offend on this basis (Walker & Panfil, 2017). Research on Circles of Support and Accountability (COSAs), for example, has been important in debunking myths about future offending patterns among convicted child sex offenders who report an attraction to minors (Richards, 2011).

In addition to these methodological criticisms – which raise significant questions in their own right about the apparent durability of the distinction – there are further conceptual and political questions. At the center of this critique is the distinction between intrafamilial and extrafamilial offending. Through the alignment the framework constructs between fixation and extrafamilial offending, and between regression with intrafamilial offending or incest, what comes into focus is the way that heteronormative masculinity and the prized institution of the family are evaded or exonerated in this discourse. Throughout the 1970s, when second-wave feminists helped to bring attention to the troubling incidence of child abuse, they were right in pointing to incest and masculinity as central (Angelides, 2004a; Salter, 2016). Since this time, however, the family has receded from view. In its place, the construction of the pedophile as 'other' has filled this void. While it is widely acknowledged that popular conceptions of child sexual abuse rely upon myths or distortions, my queer reading of the emergence of pedophilia as a concept helps to reveal how psychiatry has been complicit in this.

It is not simply that queer theory helps problematize the apparent essentialism of pedophilia as a concept. If one tenet of queer theory is that the homo/hetero definition is a key structuring device of modern Western culture (Sedgwick, 1990), this can be seen in the distinction between fixation and regression. The association the framework draws between homosexuality and fixated pedophilia has been the source of considerable controversy, as has been the way that it normalizes the regressed offender. For example, for Angelides, within the distinction between fixation and regression 'a naturalized deviant sexuality becomes the marker separating "true" pedophiles from so-called normal men' (2004b, n.p.). Similarly, Cossins argues that 'the categories of "fixated" and "regressed" offenders neatly reflect essentialist assumptions about masculine sexuality' (1999, p. 46). At the very time that homosexuality was finally being removed the American Psychiatric Association's *Diagnostic and Statistical Manual* in the 1970s in response to concerted activism (see Chenier, 2012; Walker & Panfil, 2017), it is curious that a homophobic logic regarding the status of perversion found a new route to manifest.

Taken together, these criticisms underpin my broader claim that conceptualizations of child sexual abuse reinforce a narrow emphasis on exceptional forms of abuse at the expense of a holistic understanding of how abuse manifests in practice. While the fixated offender is characterized as innately pedophilic, the regressed offender is normalized. That is, within the scheme of fixation and regression is an implied hierarchy of seriousness in which fixation comes to figure as emblematic of the worst elements of the phenomenon. Thus, considered in the context of the constitutive nature of psychiatric discourses, these are not merely descriptive accounts. Returning to Foucault and his historicization of sexual subjectivity, in the same way that he described a whole apparatus of technology coming to bear upon sodomy in order to produce the homosexual as a kind of unique species or type, so a similar logic is at work in the analytical significance that is placed upon the interior condition of the child sex offender.

Conclusion

Throughout the 1970s and 1980s, feminists were instrumental in shining a spotlight on the sexual abuse of children, with Florence Rush (1980) famously describing it as 'our best kept secret'. Central to this was a recognition of incest as the overwhelming form that this abuse took, and a patriarchal critique that pointed the finger at heterosexual men. Since this time, however, progress has been uneven. Internationally we have seen the rise of public inquiries to respond to the abuse of children in institutions such as schools and churches. However, this has been accompanied by an enduring failure to recognize abuse occurring in the most prized institution of all: the family.

In this chapter I have offered a queer analysis of the history of child sexual abuse in order to reveal how this past continues to structure contemporary understandings and attitudes. By doing so, I have sought to demonstrate how queer criminology can benefit from a theoretically broad approach that seeks not just to speak to LBGTIQ communities about their experiences of crime, victimization, and social control, but that takes seriously what queer deconstruction can offer to understandings of harm and violence. In particular, while criminological accounts of child sexual abuse have critiqued misconceptions and myths relating to the abuse of children, I have shown how psychiatry is complicit within this. Chenier writes that 'public and expert discourses about pedophilia raise important questions about how we in the English-speaking west think, and do not think, about children and childhood, about sexuality, about the family, and about the role of medicine and the criminal and justice systems in regulating them' (2012, p. 173). By expanding the terrain of queer criminology to include pedophilia and child sexual abuse, we can shine an important spotlight on the enduring way in which justice elides this form of harm.

Notes

[1] I am cognizant of the way in which medicalizing discourses have been central to the production of 'the homosexual' as a category, and it is not my intention to reinforce these discourses. Rather, my use of language is intended to reflect the specific contexts to which I am referring.

[2] Note for clarity that the translated edition I refer to throughout was published in 1998.

References

Angelides, S. (2004a) 'Feminism, child sexual abuse, and the erasure of child sexuality', *GLQ: A Journal of Lesbian and Gay Studies*, 10(2): 141–177.

Angelides, S. (2004b) 'Paedophilia and the misrecognition of desire', *Transformations*, 8: n.p. http://www.transformationsjournal.org/wp-content/uploads/2017/01/Angelides_Transformations08.pdf

Angelides, S. (2005) 'The emergence of the paedophile in the late twentieth century', *Australian Historical Studies*, 36(126): 272–295.

Ball, M. (2014) 'What's queer about queer criminology?', in D. Peterson & V. Panfil (eds.) *Handbook of LGBT Communities, Crime, and Justice*, New York: Springer, pp. 531–555.

Ball, M. (2016) *Criminology and Queer Theory: Dangerous Bedfellows?* London: Palgrave Macmillan.

Ball, M., Buist, C.L., & Woods, J.B. (2014) 'Introduction to the special issue on queer/ing criminology: New directions and frameworks', *Critical Criminology*, 22(1): 1–4.

Buist, C. & Lenning, E. (2015) *Queer Criminology*, London: Routledge.

Chenier, E. (2012) 'The natural order of disorder: paedophilia, stranger danger and the normalising family', *Sexuality & Culture*, 16(2): 172–186.

Cossins, A. (1999) 'A reply to the NSW Royal Commission Inquiry into Paedophilia: victim report studies and child sex offender profiles – a bad match?', *Australian and New Zealand Journal of Criminology*, 32(1): 42–60.

Dalton, D. (2006) 'The haunting of gay subjectivity: the cases of Oscar Wilde and John Marsden', *Law, Text, Culture*, 10(1): 72–100.

Dean, C.J. (1996) *Sexuality and Modern Western Culture*, New York: Twayne Publishers.

Dwyer, A. (2014) 'Pleasures, perversities, and partnerships: the historical emergence of LGBT–police relationships', in D. Peterson & V.R. Panfil (eds.), *Handbook of LGBT Communities, Crime, and Justice*, New York: Springer, pp. 149–164.

Dwyer, A., Ball, M., & Crofts, T. (eds.) (2016) *Queering Criminology*, Basingstoke: Palgrave Macmillan.

Foucault, M. (1978) *The History of Sexuality: The Will to Knowledge*, London: Penguin.

Foucault, M. (1980) *Power/Knowledge: Selected Interviews and Other Writings 1972–1977*, New York: Pantheon Books.

Foucault, M. (2006) *Abnormal: Lectures at the Collège de France, 1974–1975*, London: Verso.

Groth, N.A. & Birnbaum, J.H. (1978) 'Adult sexual orientation and attraction to underage persons', *Archives of Sexual Behaviour*, 7(3): 175–181.

Jenkins, P. (1998) *Moral Panic: Changing Concepts of the Child Molester in Modern America*, New Haven, CT: Yale University Press.

Johnston, F.A. & Johnston, S.A. (1997) 'A cognitive approach to validation of the fixated–regressed typology of child molesters', *Journal of Clinical Psychology*, 53(4): 361–368.

Krafft-Ebing, R.V. (1998) *Psychopathia Sexualis* (12th German edn.), New York: Arcade Publishing.

Lamble, S. (2013) 'Queer necropolitics and the expanding carceral state: interrogating sexual investments in punishment', *Law and Critique*, 24(3): 229–253.

Lamble, S., Serisier, T., Dymock, A., Carr, N., Downes, J., & Boukli, A. (2020) 'Guest editorial: queer theory and criminology', *Criminology and Criminal Justice*, 20(5): 504–509.

McCann, H. & Monaghan, W. (2019) *Queer Theory Now: From Foundations to Futures*, London: Red Globe Press.

McDonald, D. (2016) 'Who is the subject of queer criminology? Unravelling the category of the paedophile', in A. Dwyer., M. Ball, & T. Crofts (eds.), *Queering Criminology*, Basingstoke: Palgrave Macmillan, pp. 101–120.

McDonald, D. (2020) 'Classifying the monster: the erasure of familial child sexual abuse in the Wood Royal Commission Paedophile Inquiry', *Griffith Law Review*, 29(1): 91–108.

Miller, J. (2014) 'Foreword', in D. Peterson & V.R. Panfil (eds.), *Handbook of LGBT Communities, Crime and Justice*, New York: Springer, pp. vii–xi.

Peterson, D. & Panfil, V.R. (eds.) (2014) *Handbook of LGBT Communities, Crime and Justice*, New York: Springer.

Redd, C. & Russell, E. (2020) 'It all started here, and it ends here too': homosexual criminalisation and the politics of apology', *Criminology and Criminal Justice*, 20(5): 590–603.

Richards, K. (2011) 'Is it time for Australia to adopt circles of support and accountability (COSA)?', *Current Issues in Criminal Justice*, 22(3): 483–490.

Richards, K. (2019) 'Sympathy for the devil? Child sexual abuse, public opinion and the cycle-of-abuse theory', in C. Lumby & K. Gleeson (eds.), *The Age of Consent: Young People, Sexual Abuse and Agency*, Perth: University of Western Australia Press, pp. 101–115.

Rimke, H. & Hunt, A. (2002) 'From sinners to degenerates: the medicalisation of morality in the nineteenth century', *History of the Human Sciences*, 15(1): 59–88.

Rush, F. (1980) *The Best Kept Secret: Sexual Abuse of Children*, McGraw-Hill.

Russell, E. (2020) *Queer Histories and the Politics of Policing*, Abingdon: Routledge.

Salter, M. (2016) 'The privatisation of incest: the neglect of familial sexual abuse in Australian public inquiries', in Y. Smaal, A. Kaladelfos, & M. Finnane (eds.) *The Sexual Abuse of Children: Recognition and Redress*, Clayton: Monash University Press, pp. 108–120.

Sedgwick, E.K. (1990) *Epistemology of the Closet*, Berkeley: University of California Press.

Sullivan, N. (2010) *A Critical Introduction to Queer Theory*, Edinburgh: Edinburgh University Press.

Walker, A. & Panfil, V.R. (2017) 'Minor attraction: a queer criminological issue', *Critical Criminology*, 25(1): 37–53.

Woods, J.B. (2014) 'Queer contestations and the future of a critical "queer" criminology', *Critical Criminology*, 22(1): 5–19.

4

Queer(y)ing the Experiences of LGBTQ Workers in Criminal Processing Systems

Angela Dwyer and Roddrick A. Colvin

This chapter examines research focused on the work lives of queer criminal processing system professionals. Despite nearly four decades of study, the main focus of research has been on queer officers in policing, specifically lesbian and gay police officers' experiences, with limited research about bisexual and transgender police officers and almost none about nonbinary police officers. Beyond policing, we know very little about queer professionals within other parts of the criminal processing systems, such as the courts or corrections. Furthermore, professionals in prosecution and defense, parole, and other ancillary branches of the system are also seriously understudied. With the limitations on the existing knowledge base, we argue that it would be erroneous to conclude that these employees' full equity and inclusion have been achieved. Instead, the research demonstrates that while there have been some advancements, substantial (and often systemic) discrimination and harassment are still endured by these workers. They remain victims of inequity and exclusion at the hands of both work colleagues and the public. In addition to documenting these queer professionals' experiences, we also discuss their collective efforts to improve internal and external equity for themselves and others.

The context of criminal processing systems

While we have radically reformed aspects of criminal processing systems globally – such as decriminalizing drugs in Portugal and more humanistic approaches adopted in Finnish prisons – other systems continue to compound injustice. Militarized police systems, for instance, continue to serve as the gateway to criminal processing systems worldwide. In much of the world, this translates into disproportionate policing negatively affecting minority populations. The militarized police systems foster a masculine, heterosexist orthodoxy among officers. Within this masculine backdrop, being queer and being a police officer represented dual – often conflicting – identities. Early research focused on how officers reconciled a 'deviant' identity with their law enforcement role as regulators of deviance (Leinen, 1993; Burke, 1993). Although evidence suggests the policing 'cult of masculinity' is buckling (Silvestri, 2017), the adverse effects of hegemonic masculinity have been shown to impact the lives of *all* police officers on the force, not just female officers (Cordner & Cordner, 2011). This is compounded by how criminal processing systems are organized around notions of heteronormativity and cisnormativity. This is not often in the deliberate actions of police officers, probation workers, court officials, lawyers, and community support advocates. It is evident, for instance, that gender equity in policing still refers to female police officers assigned female at birth (Silvestri, 2017) and completely elides transgender women police officers (Panter, 2017b).

People working in these systems also directly discriminate against people because they identify as queer, even though the integration of queer officers has come to be somewhat normalized (Belkin & McNichol, 2002). For example, police officers have been told by supervisors not to touch gay males' hands because they might be diseased (Dwyer, 2012). There are also documented cases where managers of community halfway houses have denied lesbians visits with their same-sex partner yet allow visits for women with opposite-sex partners (Kerrison, 2018). In other cases, transgender people were housed in facilities that do not align with their gender identity when incarcerated (Rodgers et al., 2017). Interactions such as these emerge from an organizational culture of enmeshed masculinity, heteronormativity, and cisnormativity that permeates criminal processing systems and deepens injustice for people identifying as queer. These systems produce challenging outcomes for queer people involved with the systems and perpetuate violence against queer people in broader contexts (Dwyer, 2020). Research suggests that being a queer-identifying criminal processing worker means one may more easily empathize with marginal identities, and doing so can come at significant professional costs (Myers et al., 2004; Charles & Arndt, 2013; Rennstam & Sullivan, 2018).

Gay male criminal processing workers experience widespread discrimination

Scholarly documentation of discrimination and harassment faced by gay criminal processing workers dates back to the earliest works that studied gay police officers. The seminal works by Burke (1993) on officers in the Metropolitan Police in London, and by Leinen (1993) on police officers in the New York Police Department in the United States, document the perceived and actual discrimination and harassment that openly gay male officers faced. During this period, few gay officers served openly in their departments as they would have faced significantly hostile work environments. Contemporary research on employment discrimination suggests that actual or perceived discrimination based on sexuality continues to affect the hiring, firing, and promoting of gay officers (Mennicke et al., 2018; Hodge & Sexton, 2020). Jones and Williams (2015) found that compared with lesbians and bisexual officers, gay male officers were nearly three times as likely to experience discrimination in training in the United Kingdom. In the context of the United States, Colvin (2009) observed that discrimination commonly occurred where supervisory discretion was greatest, namely, promotion, assignments, and evaluations.

Like those that comprise criminal processing systems, male-dominated hegemonic institutions rely on various modes of control and segregation to maintain their status, customs, and traditions as inherently masculine (Swan, 2016). This means gay police officers, for example, who fail to adhere to gender norms can subsequently be assumed to be incompetent and unable to perform job duties (Rumens & Broomfield, 2012). Good police officers are perceived as hypermasculine (Rumens & Broomfield, 2012), with lesbian officers situated as masculine and gay officers seen as feminine (Miller et al., 2003). It is little surprise, then, that gay police officers report the highest level of workplace discrimination (Jones & Williams, 2015), with gay male officers often splitting their 'gay' identity from their 'police' identity in order to survive and closely guarding their gay identities for fear of disclosure in the workplace (Burke, 1993; Leinen, 1993). Disclosing their identity in police workplaces could jeopardize their physical safety and trigger social isolation and exclusion, in addition to negative evaluations, low-level assignments, and being overlooked for promotion (Rumens & Broomfield, 2012). Closeted gay male officers report going above and beyond their job duties and acting hypermasculine so that if their sexuality becomes known, stereotypes about effeminate weakness cannot be applied to them (Collins & Rocco, 2015). However, when gay officers felt they 'blended in' at work and when heterosexual colleagues were supportive, coming out appeared to positively affect workplace interactions, facilitating cohesiveness, team work, and trust (Hamilton et al., 2019).

While our knowledge of police officers has been given recent attention, virtually no queer research exists that exclusively examines other law enforcement sectors, including corrections. Limited research suggests gay and bisexual men struggle with disclosure and safety in prison environments (Yap et al., 2019), and this aligns with the very limited research we have on the experiences of gay and bisexual correctional officers. Mennicke et al. (2018) included four queer corrections officers in their qualitative study of the experiences of queer professionals in criminal processing systems. Their concerns echoed those of their law enforcement colleagues: navigating disclosure of sexuality. Corrections officers feared that other officers would not 'have their backs' in times of need.

Lesbian criminal processing workers' experiences of discrimination are overlooked

Because gay men experience more overt workplace discrimination (Jones & Williams, 2015; Mountz, 2016), and because few legislative frameworks target women's same-sex intimacies, lesbian and bisexual women have mostly avoided explicit criminalization (Dwyer & Rundle, 2019) and their experiences in criminal processing environments have been sidelined. The research focusing specifically on lesbian workers in these systems indicates discrimination (Miller et al., 2003; Couto, 2014; Jones, 2015), although this is often at lower levels than that experienced by gay males in these professions (Colvin, 2015, 2020; Mennicke et al., 2018). For instance, in policing, lesbian officers report significantly negative experiences (Hassell & Brandl, 2009). These include homophobic verbal comments (Charles & Arndt, 2013; Colvin, 2015) and silencing (Rennstam & Sullivan, 2018), being denied promotion (Colvin, 2009; Mennicke et al., 2018) and mentoring (Barratt et al., 2014), having a work colleague disclose their sexuality to others without consent (Colvin, 2015; Jones, 2015), or being labeled a pedophile by other officers (Miller et al., 2003). Discrimination is also evidenced in research with lesbian correctional officers who felt they could not trust their co-workers to back them up and who talked about how they were hypersexualized as insatiable and predatory by colleagues (Mennicke et al., 2018). Lesbian workers were challenged by male supervisors and workers for doing routine shower checks (Mennicke et al., 2018) and were wrongfully accused of sexual misconduct with female inmates in correctional environments.

Research suggests a 'lesbian advantage' (Wright, 2011) for lesbian criminal processing workers in how these roles enable access to male power, but acceptance was also tenuous and tentative. Lesbian officers more easily negotiate police culture because lesbian masculinities align better with police masculinities, making lesbian officers preferred over gay male officers (Burke,

1993; Couto, 2014; Colvin, 2015; Mennicke et al., 2018). Therefore, lesbian officers have more access to leadership positions and feel more comfortable being out (Wright, 2011), but this runs alongside significant disadvantages grounded in sexism (Miller et al., 2003; Myers et al., 2004; Couto, 2014; Moton et al., 2020). For instance, a senior male sergeant with an Australian police organization told a pregnant lesbian officer that 'pregnant women were useless' and that the only reason she was selected for the job was because 'they need a lesbian in the mix' (Victorian Equal Opportunity and Human Rights Commission, 2019, p. 27). Lesbian officers have noted how they are subject to ongoing scrutiny and were unlikely to hear about the good work they did as much as everyone would hear about when they 'mess up' (Mennicke et al., 2018). This is combined with heterosexism that meant lesbian officers often created imaginary heterosexual boyfriends/ husbands to avoid scrutiny (Colvin, 2009, 2012; Galvin-White & O'Neal, 2016), even though this contradicted the truthfulness and trustworthiness considered central to police work (Galvin-White & O'Neal, 2016). Disclosing was important for being seen and protected by other police leaders – heterosexual, cisgender allies, typically of higher rank, would confront heterosexist and cissexist abuse directly in the workplace (Charles & Arndt, 2013).

Transgender criminal processing workers are visible and experience violence

Transgender people experience substantially more victimization than cisgender people (Whittle et al., 2007; Grant et al., 2011; Jauk, 2013); in the workplace especially, they experience more hate incidents than cisgender people (Whittle et al., 2007). Surprisingly, research about transgender workers' experiences in criminal processing systems is almost nonexistent, and this runs alongside endemic violence being perpetrated against transgender people being processed in these systems (Wolff & Cokely, 2007; Hagner, 2010; Miles-Johnson, 2015). They are more likely to be arrested (Stotzer, 2014) and more likely to be harassed by police (Grant et al., 2011; Hodge & Sexton, 2020). If they appear to be a person of color, their chances of harassment are even higher (Nichols, 2010; Grant et al., 2011; Galvan & Barzargan, 2012; Graham et al, 2014). Police profile them as sex workers (Carpenter & Barrett Marshall, 2017), even in training environments (Miles-Johnson, 2015), and they lack knowledge of transgender experiences of family violence, meaning this violence is unreported (Tesch & Bekerian, 2015). These forms of treatment unsurprisingly inform a lack of trust among transgender people towards police (Moran & Sharpe, 2004; Berman & Robinson, 2010). Experiences of incarceration are notably violent for transgender people, where they are often subject to solitary confinement to keep them safe from other inmates, and they are routinely subject to sexual assault (Arkles, 2009).

Research about transgender criminal processing system workers is very limited (Mallory et al., 2013; Panter, 2017a, 2017b). There has been a greater focus on the experiences of transgender police officers than other workers. Transgender officers are subject to serious, protracted, and violent forms of discrimination from law enforcement colleagues. Officers affirming their gender can be rendered redundant because they are deemed unable to search women or men and therefore incapable of fulfilling their basic duties (Little et al., 2002). They are also demoted, misgendered, moved into clerical/administrative positions out of public view, subjected to inappropriate psychological assessment (Mallory et al., 2013), subject to transphobic pejoratives, and excluded from girls' or guys' talk, and their personal belongings are vandalized (Panter, 2017b). They are routinely subjected to verbal harassment, sexual harassment, death threats, indecent exposure, inappropriate touching, being screamed at over the radio, being refused back up at police incidents, and serious violence, including being beaten with a chair (Mallory et al., 2013).

Treatment of transgender correctional workers is equally unsettling, with reports of physical assault by colleagues (including being snapped in the breast and slammed into concrete walls) and threats of being stripped naked and handcuffed to a flagpole (Mallory et al., 2013). Transgender officers in Panter's (2017b) work were physically assaulted by police colleagues outside their own home and dragged off toilets by female colleagues who kicked in the toilet door. The officers involved were not disciplined, sacked, or charged. The culture of criminal processing systems ignores and even perpetuates these types of unconscionable behaviors. This strongly indicates the urgent need for reform in these organizations to safeguard these transgender workers, especially when we are yet to understand how prevalent these behaviors are across different criminal processing system organizations.

Invisible queerness: bisexual and nonbinary criminal processing workers

Bisexual and nonbinary people generally represent invisible groups in research related to criminal processing systems. Evidence suggests they have unsatisfactory experiences with law enforcement generally. Bisexual people, for instance, can be subject to more problematic experiences than gay or lesbian people with these systems (Hodge & Sexton, 2020). In one US-based study, 70 percent of nonbinary respondents reported never, or only sometimes, having been treated with respect by law enforcement (James et al., 2016). These experiences were confirmed in a 2015 community study in the United Kingdom, where 69 percent of nonbinary respondents reported not feeling comfortable being 'out' when seeking support from police (Valentine, 2015). There is little doubt that the experiences of bisexual and nonbinary people are all but invisible in the research on experiences of criminal processing systems as victims and/or offenders, and this invisibility spills over to the experiences of bisexual and nonbinary criminal processing system workers.

Bisexual and nonbinary people are even more invisible in research focused on workers' experiences in criminal processing systems, but they are invisible in different ways. For bisexual workers in criminal processing systems, they are invisible because their experiences are represented in large data sets focused on, for example, gay, lesbian, and bisexual police officers. They represent about 16 percent of the sample of one study of police officers (Jones, 2015). The reports of studies such as these do not elaborate on bisexual police officers' specific experiences, as the results are grouped together with those of other officers (Galvin-White & O'Neal, 2016). Hassell and Brandl (2009) follow suit in their study, in which they found more negative workplace experiences, but again this was for gay, lesbian, and bisexual people combined. The specificity of bisexual experience is completely invisible in studies of the experiences of criminal processing workers, and their specific issues and voices are yet to be documented. There is a significant need for studies that elaborate the experiences of bisexual criminal processing workers so that organizations can support them more appropriately.

Equally invisible in the research on the experiences of criminal processing workers are nonbinary people, but they occupy a level of invisibility above bisexual people: nonbinary criminal processing system workers literally do not exist in the extant research. Research collapses data about nonbinary people into the umbrella group of transgender people (James et al., 2016). Where we might typically find some examples of experience in research focused on police, unlike that focused on gay, lesbian, and transgender identifying police officers, we have no research focused on nonbinary law enforcement officers. The very little evidence we might glean emerges from the experiences nonbinary people have with law enforcement. Given that younger people are more often identifying as nonbinary or gender-fluid than previous generations (The Trevor Project, 2021), it is essential to start to disaggregate these data and better understand the lived experiences of nonbinary and gender-fluid criminal processing workers. This is especially important given the highly sex-segregated nature of the restrooms, locker rooms, and uniforms used in criminal processing systems and how some nonbinary people report fluidity in their gender identity or report no strong preference either way (James et al., 2016). This fluidity of experience for nonbinary people may not necessarily be accommodated in systems so strictly organized around a binary notion of sex. One nonbinary officer noted in a newspaper interview, 'I've had some interesting comments of "oh did you lose a bet?" Usually my response back to that is more of a form of a question: "Do you ask your mom if she lost a bet when she wears a dress?"' (Reyna-Rodriguez, 2019). These comments seem suggestive of some significant concerns that require further documentation in isolation from the experiences of other queer criminal processing system workers.

Conclusion

In this chapter we have overviewed the current state of policing for queer criminal processing workers, dominated somewhat by the research knowledge that we have about queer police officers, meaning the issues we raise are often speculative for transgender, bisexual, and nonbinary officers. Research collapses the experiences of people within queer communities, but this chapter has made a concerted effort to examine the unique experiences of gay men, lesbians, transgender, bisexual, and nonbinary criminal processing workers. Several consistent themes emerged from the literature for queer criminal processing system workers.

First, although gay and lesbian criminal processing system workers, such as police, have made positive advancements, research suggests that harassment and discrimination still persist. In policing, gay men report higher levels of harassment and discrimination than lesbian women, and lesbian officers face sexism and other challenges because of stereotyping in masculinist police culture. Transgender officers face very serious forms of harassment and violence, and we surmise nonbinary officers will face similar challenges as their presence increases in policing. It is clear that police organizational culture is changing in a way that accommodates more sexuality diversity, but there is some way to go until this change makes the working environments of criminal processing system workers safer for transgender workers, and we are yet to even know what the experiences are for nonbinary and bisexual workers.

Second, while the literature suggests that workers in criminal processing systems who disclosed their sexuality and/or gender identity report higher levels of satisfaction and support within policing and corrections, deciding when to disclose, and whom to disclose to, continues to be a challenge. Queer criminal processing system workers often weigh up the costs and benefits of disclosure and hide their sexuality or gender diversity when disclosure is impossible. Bisexual criminal processing system workers are again completely elided in these conversations, where they may pass as heterosexual because they have an opposite sex partner, but they could be hiding their bisexual identity because they do not want to be pushed by people they work with to 'choose a side'. We suspect nonbinary officers will likely face even more intense scrutiny given how police organizations, in their current design, continue to be sex-segregated, male-dominated spaces, and frequently do not enable any form of fluidity in choice of uniforms, for instance.

Third, queer criminal processing system workers will continue to face both internal and external challenges with visibility. For example, again in policing, while efforts have been made to improve community relations with visible gay and lesbian police officers in many communities, few efforts have been made to increase transgender and nonbinary police officers' public visibility. We surmise that transgender and nonbinary criminal processing workers might sooner hide their identities to 'fit in' with the binary system that is so entrenched because it may be too challenging to try to negotiate new spaces (such as unisex toilets) and new resources (such as nonbinary uniform options) to enable them to affirm their identities in these masculinist workplaces. This is highlighted well in research demonstrating that, even if queer police officers are favorably received within their police departments, they may encounter challenges from other criminal processing system workers, victims, offenders, their families and friends, and the general public that interact with police.

The research overviewed in this chapter highlights the importance of additional research on queer criminal processing workers – workers that queer sexuality, sex, and gender. We need targeted research on the specific experiences of different identities based around sexuality, gender, and sex diversity. The invisibility of bisexual and nonbinary criminal processing system workers will perpetuate spaces where these workers feel unsafe – their voices will remain unheard. The violence experienced by transgender criminal processing system workers clearly needs to be addressed as a matter of some urgency, and policy decisions need to involve these workers. These issues leave little doubt about the need for specifically targeted empirical research documenting the experiences of transgender, nonbinary, and bisexual workers in criminal processing systems, in addition to the need for robust, challenging conversations about how to make spaces safer for these workers in every possible way. More frequent and deeper research would provide better information about the opportunities and challenges for these criminal processing system workers to improve their workplace experiences and conditions worldwide.

References

Arkles, G. (2009) 'Safety and solidarity across gender lines: rethinking segregation of transgender people in detention', *Temple Political & Civil Rights Law Review*, 18(2): 515–560.

Barratt, C.L., Bergman, M.E., & Thompson, R.J. (2014) 'Women in federal law enforcement: the role of gender role orientations and sexual orientation in mentoring', *Sex Roles*, 71: 21–32.

Belkin, A. & McNichol, J. (2002) 'Pink and blue: outcomes associated with the integration of open gay and lesbian personnel in the San Diego Police Department', *Police Quarterly*, 5(1): 63–95.

Berman, A. & Robinson, S. (2010) *Speaking Out: Stopping Homophobic and Transphobic Abuse in Queensland*, Brisbane, Queensland: Australian Academic Press.

Burke, M.E. (1993) *Coming Out of the Blue: British Police Officers Talk About Their Lives in "the Job" as Lesbians, Gays and Bisexuals*, London: Burns & Oates.

Carpenter, L.F. & Barrett Marshall, R. (2017) 'Walking while trans: profiling of transgender women by law enforcement, and the problem of proof', *William & Mary Journal of Race, Gender, and Social Justice*, 24(1): 5–38.

Charles, M.W. & Arndt, L.M.R. (2013) 'Gay- and lesbian-identified law enforcement officers: intersection of career and sexual identity', *The Counseling Psychologist*, 41(8): 1153–1185.

Collins, J.C. & Rocco, T.S. (2015) 'Rules of engagement as survival consciousness: gay male law enforcement officers' experiential learning in a masculinised industry', *Adult Education Quarterly*, 65(4): 295–312.

Colvin, R.A. (2009) 'Shared perceptions among lesbian and gay police officers: barriers and opportunities in the law enforcement work environment', *Police Quarterly*, 12(1): 86–101.

Colvin, R.A. (2012) *Gay and Lesbian Cops: Diversity and Effective Policing*, Boulder, CO: Lynne Rienner Publishers.

Colvin, R.A. (2015) 'Shared workplace experiences of lesbian and gay police officers in the United Kingdom', *Policing: An International Journal of Police Strategies & Management*, 38(2): 333–349.

Colvin, R. (2020) 'The emergence and evolution of lesbian and gay police associations in Europe', *European Law Enforcement Research Bulletin*, 20(1). https://bulletin.cepol.europa.eu/index.php/bulletin/article/view/406

Cordner, G. & Cordner, A. (2011) 'Stuck on a plateau? Obstacles to recruitment, selection, and retention of women police', *Police Quarterly*, 14(3): 207–226.

Couto, J.L. (2014) *Covered in Blue: Police Culture and LGBT Police Officers in the Province of Ontario*, Victoria, British Columbia: Royal Roads University.

Dwyer, A. (2012) 'Policing visible sexual/gender diversity as a program of governance', *International Journal of Crime and Justice*, 1(1): 14–26.

Dwyer, A. (2020) 'Queering police administration: how policing administration complicates LGBTIQ-police relations', special issue on 'Gender identity and expression and sexual orientation (LGBTQ+) in the public and nonprofit contexts', *Administrative Theory and Praxis*, 42(2): 172–190.

Dwyer, A. & Rundle, O. (2019) 'Made wrong, excluded, and ignored: 'Lesbians and the law', *The Journal of Lesbian Studies*, 23(3): 295–305.

Galvan, F. & Bazargan, M. (2012) *Interactions of Latina Transgender Women with Law Enforcement*, Los Angeles, CA: Bienestar Human Services Incorporated.

Galvin-White, C.M. & O'Neal, E.N. (2016) 'Lesbian police officers' interpersonal working relationships and sexuality disclosure: a qualitative study', *Feminist Criminology*, 11(3): 253–284.

Graham, L.F., Crissman, H.P., Tocco, J., Lopez, W.D., Snow, R.C., & Padilla, M.B. (2014) 'Navigating community institutions: Black transgender women's experiences in schools, the criminal justice system, and churches', *Sexuality Research and Social Policy*, 11(4): 274–287.

Grant, J., Mottet, L., Tanis, J., Harrison, J., Herman, J., & Keisling, M. (2011) 'Injustice at every turn: a report of the National Transgender Discrimination Survey', National Center for Transgender Equality and National Gay and Lesbian Task Force. Accessed August 18, 2020, from https://www. transequality.org/sites/default/files/docs/resources/NTDS_Report.pdf

Hagner, D. (2010) 'Fighting for our lives: the D.C. Trans Coalition's campaign for humane treatment of transgender inmates in District of Columbia correctional facilities', *The Georgetown Journal of Gender and the Law*, 11(3): 837–868.

Hamilton, K.M., Park, L.S., Carsey, T.A., & Martinez, L.R. (2019) '"Lez be honest": gender expression impacts workplace disclosure decisions', *Journal of Lesbian Studies*, 23(2): 144–168.

Hassell, K.D. & Brandl, S.G. (2009) 'An examination of the workplace experiences of police patrol officers: the role of race, sex, and sexual orientation', *Police Quarterly*, 12(4): 408–430.

Hodge, J.P. & Sexton, L. (2020) 'Examining the blue line in the rainbow: the interactions and perceptions of law enforcement among lesbian, gay, bisexual, transgender and queer communities', *Police Practice and Research*, 21(3): 246–263E.

James, S., Herman, J., Rankin, S., Keisling, M., Mottet, L., & Anafi, M.A. (2016) 'The report of the 2015 U.S. Transgender Survey', National Center for Transgender Equity. https://transequality.org/sites/default/files/docs/usts/USTS-Full-Report-Dec17.pdf

Jauk, D. (2013) 'Gender violence revisited: lessons from violent victimisation of transgender identified individuals', *Sexualities*, 16(7): 807–825.

Jones, M. (2015) 'Who forgot lesbian, gay, and bisexual police officers? Findings from a national survey', *Policing*, 9(1): 65–76.

Jones, M. & Williams, M.L. (2015) 'Twenty years on: lesbian, gay and bisexual police officers' experiences of workplace discrimination in England and Wales', *Policing and Society*, 25(2): 188–211.

Kerrison, E.M. (2018) 'Risky business, risk assessment, and other heteronormative misnomers in women's community corrections and reentry planning', *Punishment and Society*, 20(1): 134–151.

Leinen, S.H. (1993) *Gay Cops*, New Brunswick, NJ: Rutgers University Press.

Little, C., Stephens, P., & Whittle, S. (2002) 'The praxis and politics of policing: problems facing transgender people', *Queensland University of Technology Law and Justice Journal*, 2(2): 226–243.

Mallory, C., Hasenbush, A., & Sears, B. (2013) 'Discrimination against law enforcement officers on the basis of sexual orientation and gender identity: 2000 to 2013', The Williams Institute, UCLA School of Law.

Mennicke, A., Gromer, J., Oehme, K., & MacConnie, L. (2018) 'Workplace experiences of gay and lesbian criminal justice officers in the United States: a qualitative investigation of officers attending a LGBT law enforcement conference', *Policing and Society*, 28(6): 712–729.

Miles-Johnson, T. (2015) '"They don't identify with us": perceptions of police by Australian transgender people', *International Journal of Transgenderism*, 16(3): 169–189.

Miller, S.L., Forest, K.B., & Jurik, N.C. (2003) 'Diversity in blue: lesbian and gay police officers in a masculine occupation', *Men and Masculinities*, 5(4): 355–385.

Moran, L.J. & Sharpe, A.N. (2004) 'Violence, identity and policing the case of violence against transgender people', *Criminology and Criminal Justice*, 4(4): 395–417.

Moton, L., Blount-Hill, K., & Colvin, R. (2020) 'Squaring the circle: exploring lesbian experience in a heteromale police profession', in C.D.M. Coates & M. Walker-Pickett (eds.), *Women and Minorities in Criminal Justice: An Intersectionality Approach*, Dubuque, IA: Kendall Hunt Publishing Company.

Mountz, S. (2016) 'That's the sound of the police: state-sanctioned violence and resistance among LGBT young people previously incarcerated in girls' juvenile justice facilities', *Affilia: Journal of Women and Social Work*, 31(3): 287–302.

Myers, K.A., Forest, K.B., & Miller, S.L. (2004) 'Officer friendly and the tough cop: gays and lesbians navigate homophobia and policing', *Journal of Homosexuality*, 47(1): 17–37.

Nichols, A. (2010) 'Dance Ponnaya, dance! Police abuses against transgender sex workers in Sri Lanka', *Feminist Criminology*, 5(2): 195–222.

Panter, H. (2017a) 'Pre-operative transgender motivations for entering policing occupations', *International Journal of Transgenderism*, 18(3): 305–317.

Panter, H. (2017b) *Transgender Cops: The Intersection of Gender and Sexuality Expectations in Police Cultures*, Abingdon: Routledge.

Rennstam, J. & Sullivan, K.R. (2018) 'Peripheral inclusion through informal silencing and voice: a study of LGB officers in the Swedish police', *Gender, Work and Organization*, 25(2): 177–194.

Reyna-Rodriguez, V. (2019) 'Non-binary police officer finds inclusivity at ISUPD', *Iowa State Daily*, November 19. https://www.iowastatedaily.com/diversity/iowa-state-university-police-department-non-binary-police-officer-lgbtqia-and-diversity/article_87ed6c84-0b16-11ea-a394-a301e5cfd246.html

Rodgers, J., Asquith, N.L., & Dwyer, A. (2017) 'Cisnormativity, criminalisation, vulnerability: transgender people in prisons', Tiles Briefing Paper, 12. https://www.utas.edu.au/__data/assets/pdf_file/0004/944716/Briefing_Paper_No_12_J_Rodgers_N_Asquith_A_Dwyer.pdf

Rumens, N. & Broomfield, J. (2012) 'Gay men in the police: identity disclosure and management issues', *Human Resource Management Journal*, 22(3): 283–298.

Silvestri, M. (2017) 'Police culture and gender: revisiting the "cult of masculinity"', *Policing*, 11(3): 289–300.

Stotzer, R.L. (2014) 'Law enforcement and criminal justice personnel interactions with transgender people in the United States: a literature review', *Aggression and Violent Behavior*, 19: 263–277.

Swan, A.A. (2016) 'Masculine, feminine, or androgynous: the influence of gender identity on job satisfaction among female police officers', *Women & Criminal Justice*, 26(1): 1–19.

Tesch, B.P. & Bekerian, D.A. (2015) 'Hidden in the margins: a qualitative examination of what professionals in the domestic violence field know about transgender domestic violence', *Journal of Gay & Lesbian Social Services*, 27(4): 391–411.

The Trevor Project (2021) 'The Trevor Project research brief: diversity of nonbinary youth', West Hollywood, CA: The Trevor Project. https://www.thetrevorproject.org/wp-content/uploads/2021/07/Diversity-of-Nonbinary-Youth_-July-Research-Brief.pdf

Valentine, V. (2015) 'Non-binary people's experiences in the U.K.', Scottish Trans Alliance. https://www.scottishtrans.org/wp-content/uploads/2016/11/Non-binary-report.pdf

Victorian Equal Opportunity and Human Rights Commission (2019) 'Proud, visible, safe: responding to workplace harm experienced by LGBTI employees in Victoria Police, Melbourne, Victoria'. Accessed August 14, 2020, from https://www.police.vic.gov.au/veohrc-review

Whittle, S., Turner, L., & Al-Alami, M. (2007) 'Engendered penalties: transgender and transsexual people's experiences of inequality and discrimination', The Equalities Review, United Kingdom.

Wolff, K.B. & Cokely, C.L. (2007) '"To protect and to serve?": An exploration of police conduct in relation to the gay, lesbian, bisexual, and transgender community', *Sexuality & Culture: An Interdisciplinary Quarterly*, 11(2): 1–23.

Wright, T. (2011) 'A "lesbian advantage"? Analysing the intersections of gender, sexuality and class in male-dominated work', *Equality, Diversity and Inclusion: An International Journal*, 30(8): 686–701.

Yap, L., Simpson, S., Richters, J., Donovan, B., Grant, L., & Butler, T. (2019) 'Disclosing sexuality: gay and bisexual men's experiences of coming out, forced out, going back in and staying out of the "closet" in prison', *Culture, Health & Sexuality*, 22(11): 1222–1234. DOI: 10.1080/13691058.2019.1668963

'PREA Is a Joke': A Case Study of How Trans PREA Standards Are(n't) Enforced

April Carrillo

'PREA is a joke' is a direct quote from a study by the LGBTQ+ prison abolition society Black & Pink,[1] who interviewed 1,100 currently incarcerated LGBTQ+ people about their experiences. The full quote reads, 'I have been raped at nearly every level 5 camp in MO. PREA is a joke' (Black & Pink, 2015, p. 43). PREA, the Prison Rape Elimination Act of 2003, was meant to protect incarcerated people from sexual assault by utilizing a systemic method of preventative procedures and reporting (United States, 2003). In 2012, the Department of Justice expanded PREA standards to include how correctional institutions should accommodate trans and intersex people currently incarcerated (PCI)[2] regarding body searches, placement, access to gender-affirming items, and unique care needs (National Standards to Prevent, Detect, and Respond to Prison Rape, 2012). These new standards included a stipulation that if state Departments of Corrections (DOCs) are not compliant, they could lose 5 percent of funding from the Department of Justice (National Standards to Prevent, Detect, and Respond to Prison Rape, 2012). Thus, when utilizing these guidelines, trans people should be able to choose who searches them inside a facility, have access to hormones, bras, binders, and so forth, and be placed in facilities where they feel safe (National Standards to Prevent, Detect, and Respond to Prison Rape, 2012).

However, in practice, it has been found that many states do not follow these PREA guidelines and in fact repeatedly violate the rights supposedly guaranteed to trans PCIs. In Black & Pink's (2015) report, other PREA guidelines were found to have been specifically violated, as 44 percent of trans inmates were denied access to hormones, 31 percent were denied the chance to receive a medical diagnosis for gender dysphoria, and only 21 percent of trans folx were able to access gender-affirming underwear and/or cosmetic items. Further, in a 2020 report to track where trans PCIs are housed, 'out of 4,890 transgender state prisoners in 45 states and Washington, D.C., only 15 cases in which a prisoner was housed according to their lived gender were confirmed' (Sosin, 2020, para. 9). But this number is not entirely accurate, as seven states refused to disclose where trans PCIs were housed, and five states did not respond to requests for information (Sosin, 2020). Additionally, when reviewing PREA compliance pertaining to trans issues by analyzing official state DOC policies, only Pennsylvania's were in line with PREA standards, while Delaware held the current best practices at the time (albeit after a lawsuit from the American Civil Liberties Union (ACLU) in 2016) (Oberholtzer, 2017). This is unacceptable, as trans folx should not have to wonder if they will be incarcerated in facilities that will provide them with competent care. Yet even if a state refuses to abide by these standards, as previously mentioned, there will only be a 5 percent loss of total federal grants, a penalty that is minimal at best. For instance, in 2014, Governor Rick Perry of Texas wrote an open letter to Attorney General Eric Holder, which publicly stated that the Texas DOC would not abide by PREA and would forfeit the 5 percent (Qiao Chen, 2014). Perry called PREA standards 'impossible' and encouraged other governors to reject what Perry claimed were unrealistic goals to achieve in Texas prisons and jails (Qiao Chen, 2014). However, the only penalty Texas faced was the loss of $810,796 out of their overall $3 billion DOC budget, only a loss of roughly 0.03 percent (Texas Department of Criminal Justice, 2013; Sontag, 2015). Thus, the federal standard that is supposed to protect incarcerated folx from sexual assault and hold institutions accountable has no teeth. Meanwhile, while other 'renegade states' (that is, those that openly disregarded PREA) joined Texas in 2015, including Arizona, Florida, Idaho, Indiana, and Utah (Sontag, 2015), issues with PREA compliance still linger even five years later.

As a specific example, Illinois, a state that has seemingly good policies on the books in terms of PREA and trans folx, is actually failing in practice. In December 2019, the Illinois DOC was put under a federal injunction from the United States District Court, pending a lawsuit from the ACLU on behalf of six trans PCIs in Illinois DOC custody who accuse multiple facilities of not providing adequate treatment and who claim they have faced harassment from correctional staff (Associated Press, 2018). While the lawsuit is being litigated, the current federal injunction has seven standards the Illinois DOC must uphold to be in compliance, which include providing necessary care and items to alleviate gender dysphoria, to protect trans PCIs from cross-gender strip searches, and to inform the court on training of correctional staff concerning trans cultural competency (*Monroe v. Baldwin*, 2019). This injunction also specifies that the Illinois DOC 'must cease the policy and practice of allowing the Transgender Committee to make the medical decisions regarding gender dysphoria and develop a policy to ensure that decisions about treatment for gender dysphoria are made by medical professionals' (*Monroe v. Baldwin*, 2019, p. 1). The use of transgender committees describes a practice of using an appointed committee or council to assess trans PCIs on a case-by-case basis on whether they qualify for trans-specific services, and then which services they will be given access to (Routh et al., 2015). However, while those on the committee are supposed to be knowledgeable about trans issues, concerns about how these panels reach their conclusions is justified (Faithful, 2009). In a review of DOC policies throughout all 50 states concerning trans PCIs (primarily trans women in male facilities), Routh et al. (2015) found that while six states actively had these types of committees on the books, nine other states did not have any written policy towards trans folx, 11 states required a medical diagnosis of gender dysphoria to provide services, and 28 states denied trans folx necessary medical treatment, even if they were diagnosed while in state custody.

Furthering these complications, under the Trump administration, the US Department of Justice announced changes to its policy concerning trans PCIs in 2018. Under the guise of 'maintaining security and good order in Federal Prisons' (US Department of Justice, 2018, p. 1), the letter explicitly noted that the use of biological sex, not gender identity, would be used to determine housing, to limit the cell and/or unit assignments, and to assess if the person poses a threat to others with histories of trauma (US Department of Justice, 2018). The new policy includes the phrase '[i]n order for an inmate to be considered for transfer to another institution of the same sex as the inmate's current facility …' (US Department of Justice, 2018, p. 2), whereas the original standards included gender identity. Moreover, another change reads as follows: 'The TEC (Transgender Executive Council) may also consider facility-specific factors, including inmate populations, staffing patterns, and physical layouts (for example, types of showers available)' (US Department of Justice, 2018, p. 2). But this is markedly different from the previous phrasing, which stated that PCIs would be housed by 'gender identity when appropriate' (US Department of Justice, 2018, p. 6). This reveals that before the policy change, the TEC did see gender identity as a valid reason for moving someone to a facility that matched their gender identity rather than their biological sex.

Thus, this case study will be an analysis of the inconsistent use of PREA towards trans PCIs, specifically centering around the experience of Naomi, a 53-year-old Black trans woman who served a prison sentence in two separate facilities during her incarceration. These facilities represent the duality of action and inaction taken concerning her trans identity. It is notable that Naomi was not transferred to another state (both facilities were in Virginia), but that the two facilities used different procedures concerning PREA. Naomi is a participant in a broader qualitative research study of 44 trans folx that focused on their experiences with the criminal legal system (law enforcement, courts, and corrections).

Naomi

Naomi was arrested as a result of a bench warrant after she missed her court date. However, even before her incarceration, the details around her arrest are disturbing and worth mentioning: it is not just the carceral system that has an issue with trans people, but the criminal legal system as a whole. Naomi was arrested for possession of an illegal substance and paraphernalia, but she was also charged with distribution, since no one believed that the amount she had was only for personal use. She felt that when officers came to her residence after the bench warrant was issued, their response was excessive.

> Uh, it was actually embarrassing because it was ... I knew everyone that was in the neighborhood I was in and they pulled up like three deep. They had people in the back of the apartment complex. It was just a big thing [laughs]. Yeah, they had like three cars, which probably had like two people each. And then, they had a guy that was in the back. I guess they didn't want me to run out the back door.

After her arrest, Naomi was placed in the general population in the local jail before her transfer to a regional facility.

> That was kinda scary because I was put in the regular population. I couldn't have a wig, couldn't have makeup, so I didn't. I had to be placed with men and, and it was the regular cell with a bunch of guys. And I just always had that fear of what would ... what is my experience gonna be like, you know because everyone is not, acknowledged about transgenders.[3]

At the regional jail, Naomi noted a difference between it and the local jail, describing the regional jail as more accommodating, with stricter supervision, and noting that she was housed with only one cellmate. This was a marked difference from the previous facility, where Naomi noted the supervising officer would not leave his office unless he absolutely had to, despite complaints from her and other PCIs.

Unable to afford her own representation, Naomi was assigned a public defender whom she met twice, once as an introduction, and the second time right before a plea deal was finalized.

> I remember not seeing him again until my court date, like five minutes before I was going in. Then he came to me to tell me that um, he has worked out a deal with the Commonwealth for ten years, and my whole facial expression changed and everything. And I was like, I can't do double digits. I'm going to be 50 years old and I can't do, I don't want to do 10 years.

Her lawyer informed her that the deal was made because of her past history, which mostly consisted of petty larceny, due to the fact that Naomi left home at 16 because her parents rejected her coming out as gay. Thus, like many LGBQ+ and trans folx, Naomi engaged in various forms of underground economies to commit petty larceny and engage in sex work for survival. The public defender warned she could face 30 years for the amount of substances in her possession at the time of her arrest, but when she told the judge in open court she did not feel this lawyer was representing her best interests, the judge informed her that if she rejected her representation, they would have to start the process over. Naomi reluctantly agreed to five years of probation and five years of incarceration for a non-violent drug offense, for substances that she used recreationally and did not sell to anyone.

After sentencing, Naomi was transferred to Tulip Correctional Center (TCC),[4] a level 3, mid-tier security facility in Virginia. The placing counselor informed her that because she had asked to be in a single cell instead of a dormitory, he would have to override the system to get her into a level 3 security facility, even though her conviction was appropriate for a level 2 security facility. The justification was that TCC would give Naomi access to cells with a single roommate instead of being in a pod with the general population. Ironically, Naomi did not have many issues with other PCIs at TCC; most of her issues were with correctional staff and other personnel. For instance, while she had been taking hormones for a number of years before being incarcerated, Naomi did not have a medical diagnosis for gender dysphoria or documented paperwork for taking hormones. Like the majority of Black & Pink's (2015) trans PCI participants who took hormones before incarceration, Naomi had been taking street-based hormones for years. Thus, TCC would not allow her to continue to take hormones until she obtained such paperwork, even though Naomi had visible breasts, and TCC also refused to provide her bras. Not allowing a trans person to continue their hormone use, regardless of where they previously obtained the hormones, can have devastating effects. Accounts from trans people who were denied hormones while incarcerated describe transition reversal, which includes the diminishment of primary and secondary characteristics such as loss of breast tissue, redistribution of fat, muscle definition, and hair loss or growth (Kellaway, 2015; Leland, 2019). Moreover, in addition to the physical changes, the psychological impact creates further damage, since trans folx who need hormones for their transition can experience heightened anxiety, depression, suicide ideation, and suicide attempts without them (APA, 2020). Thus, when they are denied hormones and do not consent to the process of de-transitioning, it can cause a whirlwind of mental health issues that are reinforced by physical changes.

When Naomi inquired about how to start the paperwork process in order to gain access to hormones, she was informed that she needed to meet with a psychiatrist. Naomi made numerous requests to see the psychiatrist and was told each time that it would be arranged soon, but days and months passed. Naomi was not allowed access to her hormones, and while she never explicitly mentioned that she experienced any negative side effects, these physical and mental changes would have likely affected her. So Naomi took action and began to file grievances and complaints to draw attention to her situation.

> So finally, I wrote it up and told them they had this form called the 1983 form, which you can file, so that DOC would take a look at it or the courts will start looking into what's going on and I kind of based it on discrimination. And, within a month, I was being shipped.[5]

The 1983 Prisoner Complaint Form under the Civil Rights Act allows PCIs to file grievances that will be reviewed by the United States District Court, Western District in Virginia. Even though Naomi was transferred to another facility shortly after filing the form, the process took three years, with Naomi filing grievances and requesting hormones, bras, and other necessary items that are supposed to be provided to all incarcerated trans folx. Disturbingly, TCC already had a large population of trans women, as observed by Naomi, and she knew that some of them were receiving hormones, bras, and other accommodations, but only because they had a medical diagnosis in their records. Thus, not only did TCC ignore Naomi's requests for assistance, the facility in fact knew how to care for trans people, as they were already providing that support for others.

Naomi was shipped to Orchid Correctional Center (OCC), where her treatment was markedly different from her experience at TCC and aligned with PREA guidelines. At OCC, she immediately met with a team, which included medical staff, a psychiatrist, an assistant warden, and a building manager, who was Naomi's biggest advocate. At the start of her two-year stay at OCC, Naomi was immediately given proper clothing (including bras) and her own cell, which she sometimes shared with a cellmate; she started meeting with the psychiatrist to get paperwork for her hormones; and she was given one of the higher-paying jobs in the prison. While this was noticeably different from her treatment at TCC, especially concerning resources, OCC did come with its challenges. For instance, when Naomi started to meet with the psychiatrist, the psychiatrist admitted that she did not know how to treat Naomi, so the psychiatrist bought a book about another trans person's journey to use for the treatment plan.

> So she's [psychiatrist] in that, no education with that. So what does that tell me? This is a woman that is a professional, you know, she should have had just … that's what they need they need in there. They need training, they need to have classes with that, they need to have seminars or workshops.

So, even though OCC had the right idea, there were still hiccups, and the facility often turned to Naomi to consult her about next steps, which placed the responsibility of providing care in her hands. Thus, there is a high likelihood that if Naomi had not known what she needed or had not asked, OCC would have been unable to provide her essential items and/ or resources.

However, the starkest difference between TCC and OCC was the fact that Naomi had a proactive advocate who helped her with the necessary paperwork and dealt with any harassment Naomi faced. In this case it was the building manager, Ms. Forthright.[6] Ms. Forthright was solely responsible for getting Naomi a job taking care of the older PCIs, arranging access to the psychiatrist, and taking care of interpersonal issues between her and other PCIs or staff. Naomi described how she felt like a queen in OCC because other PCIs knew they would immediately face consequences from Ms. Forthright if they harassed her. Further, in terms of correctional staff, Naomi stated that when an incident occurred, she would tell Ms. Forthright and action would be taken the next day. She described one such incident:

> There was one [correctional officer] that I had to constantly let know, Look, you kind of disrespect me when you come in a pod and you refer to me as a gentleman or you refer to me as a male. And like I said, [Ms. Forthright] already done briefed these officers before they come in the building that she has two transgenders in here. And they will come in at count time and they'd be like, 'Okay, gentlemen, it's time to get up for count,' you know? And then, when we would approach him, and I would be like, Do you have to use the word gentlemen?
> [Officer] Oh, oh, I forgot. I forgot.

Which um, a couple of them I will say, yeah it was a thing that they do or was doing. It's hard to go ahead and change right away. But some of them, I just thought that they was being ridiculous with it. But I got to a point where I just brushed it off. And it's nothing that I could really do to change it because I am under them more or less. So it's no need to really get on them about it. I did approach Ms. Forthright about a few of them and she took them out of her building. She wouldn't allow them to work in our building.

Naomi recalled that three or four times Ms. Forthright at the very least moved the officers out of the building to another part of the prison, or they would not be seen again.

Cleopatra, a criminal legal practitioner and cisgender friend of Naomi's, met her through the Virginia DOC. Cleopatra, who was there during the interview, informed me that 'I have never in all the years that I have been at DOC seen anyone treated so well like she was, and they, uh, made sure that she had everything that she needed'. Working together, Naomi and Cleopatra have been advocating for trans PCIs after Naomi's incarceration, even though correctional facilities have denied having trans PCIs. They work with individual trans PCIs on specific issues they are having with their facilities concerning their gender identity. They also try to track as many trans PCIs as possible in the Virginia DOC as they do not think DOC numbers are accurate based on Naomi's experience. As Naomi stated, '[t]hat's what me and her [Cleopatra] are trying to get to the bottom of because me from being in there ... know there's transgenders. I mean, at one camp that I was at, TCC, there were like 50 or so of us [trans folx] in one unit.'

Policy implications

Thus, using Naomi's case as a framework, I have two specific policy recommendations to address these issues with trans folx to better align them with established PREA guidelines and meet the ultimate goal of ensuring humane and just treatment of trans folx in the corrections system (in tandem with working towards substantial, long-term reform). These suggestions are to increase cultural competency and to better enforce PREA guidelines. As evidenced by Naomi's experience, there are vast disconnects between the guidelines outlined in PREA and the actual enforcement of the standards. Notably, while Naomi knew her rights and what she needed, TCC, her first facility, was unwilling to be cooperative, while OCC provided her necessary items and services without hesitation. However, trans folx should not have to wonder whether the facility they have been sent to will be affirming of their existence or even follow the law.

Cultural competency

Despite her own experiences, after having been incarcerated, Naomi has been advocating and speaking together with Cleopatra at Virginia DOC events to try to educate correctional staff. Naomi believes the biggest problem is correctional staff's lack of knowledge of the unique challenges and issues of trans folx, and that this needs to be addressed.

> It's really not in a bad way. It's just a thing of them not understanding. There's not enough education or training for these officers. Just like in DOC, there's not enough training with the officers that are in there to get them the knowledge of dealing with transgenders when they come into that building.

Increasing cultural competency by way of better training is a fairly obvious solution. Drawing from Naomi's quote, one of her greatest concerns about DOC staff is that they are unsure of how to handle trans PCIs. Thus, hoping that correctional officers' base of knowledge about trans folx will be founded on affirming sources is wishful thinking. Further, while the TCC correctional staff addressed Naomi incorrectly and the administration did not provide the necessary resources or take responsibility for her protection, the affirming staff at OCC still had eerily parallel issues. For instance, despite the existence of Naomi's team at OCC, Naomi still had to struggle with staff misgendering her and her psychiatrist not knowing how to treat her. Hence, these issues are also systemic, so better cultural competency training is important, as even a willing and open staff face similar issues to those of non-affirming staff.

Naomi's account fortunately does not include instances of her being repeatedly victimized by correctional staff or other PCIs in more physically damaging ways. However, I believe what makes her account more compelling is that she did not experience the typical myriad of sexual and/ or physical assaults or unfair stints in solitary confinement often reported by incarcerated trans women. The presentation of consistent microaggressions against her identity, the denial of appropriate care, and the disregard for her needs shows that these actions, while seemingly 'harmless', are common, and therefore persistent. If Naomi had been assaulted at the hands of correctional staff or another PCI, the institution would have been forced to acknowledge that it had happened and that they had (mis)handled it. This would have been a pivotal moment that Naomi could use to advocate for herself to outside attorneys, sympathetic staff, and even during a PREA investigation. But by putting off an appointment to a psychiatrist, ignoring requests for a medical diagnosis, and not providing bras, facilities such as TCC can use these administrative ills as a way to shrug off responsibility and blame a flawed system. Thus, the need for cultural competency is even greater in a case such as Naomi's, since if a correctional facility adequately trained their staff, it would be likely to prevent these occurrences in the future. Further, even if an officer failed to be supportive of trans rights, as long as their place of employment had a strong stance on trans rights, they would be less likely to discriminate against trans inmates.

Enforcing PREA guidelines

The fact that trans PCIs have had rights to services since 2012 under the federal guidelines of PREA, yet Naomi was unable to take advantage of them until she was shipped from one facility to another after 2012, is unacceptable. Naomi struggled for three years, despite her history of living as a woman, having visible breasts, and previous hormone use, to receive affirming care from TCC. Naomi exhausted methods of reporting, consistently filing grievances and figuring out how she could advocate for things that should have been provided to her through PREA. The intentional gatekeeping by TCC staff hindered Naomi's care and prevented her from receiving services she needed. Further, the 5 percent grant penalty that exists for state DOCs that do not follow PREA is not enough. Direct impacts such as a higher percentage penalty, consistent inspections from PREA officers (not employed by DOCs) to ensure compliance, and direct access of inmates to outside advocates are just some of the many steps all DOCs can take to improve the safety and care of all incarcerated folx.

Further, even when individual staff violated PREA guidelines or simply ignored them, it was up to the facility to determine whether they were to face any consequences. From Naomi's account, none of the staff at TCC who prevented her care were properly disciplined or even reprimanded for their actions. And alarmingly, there is a strong possibility that the only reason guards received any punishment at OCC was because of Naomi's team and Ms. Forthright. Thus, while a level of access and care is supposed to be provided to all trans PCIs under PREA, there is no guarantee of it, as evidenced by Naomi's experience. Moreover, it is fair to assume that Ms. Forthright's influence only went so far, since some guards were never seen again at OCC, while others were only moved to other buildings. This could be for a number of reasons, but simply moving a bad actor without any sort of discipline, training, or further interaction with the PCI will not prevent future discriminatory behavior.

Conclusion

While Naomi's account is only one of many, her unique experience of being in two separate facilities in the same state, observing how PREA is and is not enforced, is valuable. After being transferred, Naomi was able to serve the rest of her sentence in a facility that allowed her to have affirming and life-saving care until she was released. And this treatment should be the standard, not the exception, especially considering there are guidelines in place for correctional facilities to follow concerning trans folx. The reality is that PREA enforcement is not standardized, and this leaves vulnerable not only trans PCIs, but all incarcerated people who may experience sexual assault or mistreatment due to their sexual orientation, gender expression, or any other behavior outside cisgender, heteronormative standards. Naomi should not be considered lucky to have been transferred to OCC, and other trans PCIs should not have to file endless amounts of paperwork for an institution to take their identity seriously. It's frightening that trans folx who are incarcerated can end up without affirming treatment because they are denied it by a group of people who are appointed to determine the validity of their identity, they do not have an advocate either inside or outside the facility, or they get the runaround as Naomi did. If DOCs actually take PREA seriously and acknowledge the rights of trans folx under federal standards as well as increase cultural competency, it will improve the treatment of all incarcerated folx as institutions take standards more seriously. But if 'trans rights are human rights' is not a compelling argument, maybe putting state DOCs at higher financial and legal risk will.

Notes

[1]   Black & Pink is an abolition organization that supports LGBTQ+ and HIV-positive folx who are incarcerated. Their efforts include letter writing, court support, and spreading information about prisoner rights.

[2]   The use of people currently incarcerated/person currently incarcerated (PCI) rather than inmate or prisoner (except in direct quotes) seeks to humanize these folx in the abolitionist tradition (Ellis, 2020).

[3]   This is the exact language of the participant, but it is important for cisgender folx to only use transgender as in transgender people, a transgender person, or transgender folx.

[4]   The names of both facilities have been changed to protect Naomi's identity, but all other information is unchanged.

[5]   Shipped: sent to another prison.

[6]   Not her real name.

References

APA (American Psychological Association) (2020) 'What is gender dysphoria?', Psychiatry.org. https://www.psychiatry.org/patients-families/gender-dysphoria/what-is-gender-dysphoria

Associated Press (2018) 'Six transgender inmates sue Illinois Corrections Department', NBC News, January 31. https://www.nbcnews.com/feature/nbc-out/six-transgender-inmates-sue-illinois-corrections-department-n843476

Black & Pink (2015) 'Coming out of concrete closets: a report on Black & Pink's National LGBTQ Prisoner Survey'. https://www.issuelab.org/resources/23129/23129.pdf

Ellis, E. (2020) 'An open letter to our friends on the question of language', Unpublished manuscript.

Faithful, R. (2009) Transitioning our prisons toward affirmative law: examining the impact of gender classification policies on US transgender prisoners', *The Modern American*, 5(1): 3–9. https://digitalcommons.wcl.american.edu/cgi/viewcontent.cgi?article=1012&context=tma

Kellaway, M. (2015) 'DOJ tells state prisons: denying trans inmates hormone therapy is unconstitutional', *The Advocate*, April 8. https://www.advocate.com/politics/transgender/2015/04/08/doj-tells-state-prisons-denying-trans-inmates-hormone-therapy-uncons

Leland, J. (2019) 'How a trans solider took on the jail that denied her medication and won', *The New York Times*, February 15._https://www.nytimes.com/2019/02/15/nyregion/transgender-jail-hormone-therapy.html

Monroe, Melendez, Stamps, Vision, Kuykendall, and Reed v. Baldwin, Meeks, & Hinton, Case No. 18-CV-00156-NJR-MAB (IL 2019). https://www.aclu-il.org/sites/default/files/field_documents/preliminary_injunction.pdf

National Standards to Prevent, Detect, and Respond to Prison Rape; DOJ Final Rule, 77. Fed. Reg. 119 (June 20, 2012) (to be codified at 28 CFR pt. 115).

Oberholtzer, E. (2017) 'The dismal state of transgender incarceration policies', Prison Policy Initiative, November 8. https://www.prisonpolicy.org/blog/2017/11/08/transgender

Qiao Chen, K. (2014) 'Perry: federal anti-prison rape standards "impossible" to achieve', *The Texas Tribune*, March 21. https://www.texastribune.org/2014/03/31/perry-anti-prison-rape-standards-impossible

Routh, D., Abess, G., Makin, D., Stohr., Hemmens, C., & Yoo, J. (2015) 'Transgender inmates in prisons: review of applicable statutes and policies', *International Journal of Offender Therapy and Comparative Criminology*, 61(6): 645–666. DOI: 10.1177/0306624X1560374

Sontag, D. (2015) 'Push to end prison rapes loses earlier momentum', *The New York Times*, May 12. https://www.nytimes.com/2015/05/13/us/push-to-end-prison-rapes-loses-earlier-momentum.html

Sosin, K. (2020) 'Trans, imprisoned – and trapped', *NBC News*, February 26. https://www.nbcnews.com/feature/nbc-out/transgender-women-are-nearly-always-incarcerated-men-s-putting-many-n1142436

Texas Department of Criminal Justice (2013) *Agency Operating Budget 2014*, The State of Texas. https://www.tdcj.texas.gov/documents/bfd/Agency_Operating_Budget_FY2014.pdf

United States (2003) *Prison Rape Elimination Act of 2003*, Washington, DC: US GP.

US Department of Justice (2018) *Transgender Offender Manual, Change Notice*, US Department of Justice. https://www.bop.gov/policy/progstat/5200-04-cn-1.pdf

6

Queerly Navigating the System: Trans★ Experiences Under State Surveillance

Rayna E. Momen

Introduction

The criminalization of trans★ lives in the United States is largely the result of stigmatization in the cis- and heteronormative society and being subjected to trans-antagonism.[1] Societies' adherence to rigid gender and sexuality dichotomies influences the laws and rules that regulate behavior and fails to recognize and legitimate trans people as valid human beings deserving of human rights (Spade, 2015). Gender shapes how we are perceived and valued; challenging normative gender identities can bring far-reaching consequences (Worthen, 2016).

The pervasive challenges trans people face because of their gender identity impacts their trajectories, compromises mental and physical health, impedes achievement of economic stability, pushes them into the survival economy, heightens the risk of victimization, and increases their propensity to encounter the criminal legal system (CLS)[2] and come under correctional control (MAP & CAP, 2016a).[3] In effect, trans people are under constant surveillance, whether or not they are behind bars or on probation or parole.[4] Whereas probation is imposed pre-trial or in place of incarceration, parole is for eligible people granted early release from prison after serving a period of time.

This chapter uses a queer criminological and intersectional lens to explore barriers to full participation in society for trans people throughout social institutions (that is, entry) and the pathways these barriers create that lead to CLS involvement, which are compounded by intersecting identities (for example, race, class). It illustrates what we know about the overrepresentation of trans people in the CLS, emphasizing both those under community supervision and those released from incarceration (that is, re-entry), barriers to re-entry and compliance with probation and parole, and aspects of these systems that raise concerns about cultural competence in service provision. The limited literature informs a discussion of interventions that could reduce CLS encounters and the related harms and describes a model trans-inclusive pathway to entry and re-entry as a means of reimagining justice for trans people.

Queer criminology and intersectionality

Mainstream criminology has historically pathologized and criminalized queer people in social scientific inquiry (Woods, 2014), hence the importance of a critical, queer lens. Buist and Stone (2014) contend that '[t]ransgender identities, lives, and experiences are not well known in our society' (p. 44). Queer criminology 'investigates, criticizes, and challenges heteronormative systems of oppression in the context of the criminal legal system' (Buist & Lenning, 2016, p. 120). This chapter disrupts the oppressive frameworks that shape the scope of trans encounters with the CLS and suggests avenues for mitigating the extent to which trans people find themselves entangled in the system.

Trans people are not a homogeneous group. Oparah (2012) contends that the category transgender 'is internally differentiated and marked by both marginalization and privilege' (p. 245). Trans people with stacked oppressions are not disproportionately victimized and criminalized solely because of transphobia. Rather, intersecting identities (that is, race, ethnicity, class) come into play, shaping their interactions with people and systems in their everyday lives. Trans people of color have unique experiences from their white trans counterparts, just as trans women have different experiences than trans men and gender nonconforming people. Thus, an intersectional approach is warranted (Crenshaw, 1989) to interrogate these oppressive systems and examine how they catapult trans people into arenas of work and social life that increase their propensity for contact with the CLS.

Overrepresentation in the criminal legal system

An estimated 1.4 million US adults identify as trans (Flores et al., 2016). Hawaii has the largest estimated percentage of trans adults per capita in the nation aged 18 and older, with West Virginia having the largest percentage of trans youth aged 13–17 (Herman et al., 2017). The US locks up more people per capita than any other country in the world (Sawyer & Wagner, 2020), holding roughly 2.3 million people behind bars and 4.4 million under community supervision, including probation, parole, and pre-trial (Bradner et al., 2020). We do not know how many of these 4.4 million are trans, warranting trans-specific data collection.

The Bureau of Justice Statistics estimated that more than 3,200 trans adults were incarcerated in US prisons and jails (Beck, 2014). With roughly 95 percent of the incarcerated population eventually returning to society, more trans people in prisons means more re-entering society. They are disproportionately represented among those reporting ever having spent time in a prison or jail (16 percent of all trans adults), compared with all other US adults (5 percent). By gender, 21 percent of trans women reported prior incarceration, compared with 10 percent of trans men (MAP & CAP, 2016a). Disparities also hold for race, with Grant et al. (2011) reporting close to 17 percent of trans Americans and 50 percent of Black trans people having been imprisoned.[5] In addition, CLS involvement was two times higher for trans veterans than for their non-trans counterparts (Brown & Jones, 2015).

General population rates show 1,726 people per 100,000 under community supervision, with higher rates for Black people compared with their white counterparts (Bradner et al., 2020). Trans people likely comprise a disproportionate share, highlighting the importance of re-entry and supervision practitioners understanding concerns specific to such individuals (Poole et al., 2002). Trans people likely commit similar crimes to their cisgender counterparts; however, data on the most frequent encounters, which are interactions with police that lead to arrest (Buist & Lenning, 2016), and the primary offenses for which trans people are convicted are lacking. Buist and Lenning (2016) suggest that CLS actors take into account the role that non-normative gender and sexualities play in shaping criminality in relation to how individuals experience the world. For example, trans people engaged in the survival economy are prone to 'a broad range of criminal acts, from minor vagrancy offenses all the way up to felonious behavior such as prostitution or theft' (Buist & Lenning, 2016, pp. 91–92).

Trans youth are also overrepresented in the juvenile legal system (Marksamer, 2008; Kahle & Rosenbaum, 2020), and these disparities have gendered and racial components. Early encounters with the CLS lead to heightened risk as adults (Lydon et al., 2015). Trans youth are also differentially targeted for non-normative gender identities, expressions, and behaviors (Marksamer, 2008; MAP & CAP, 2016a), have similar pathways to the CLS (for example, survival crimes), and experience confinement in juvenile detention in ways that mirror trans adults' experiences in prisons in several respects (Marksamer, 2008).

Barriers to entry and re-entry

Due to their gender identity, trans people face significant barriers to safely maneuver through society and achieve economic stability, which impacts their lived experiences and may be independent of CLS involvement. Barriers include family rejection, unwelcome school environments, employment and housing discrimination (MAP & CAP, 2016a), limited access to healthcare and gender-affirming care (Jauk, 2013), obstacles to obtaining identification documents with accurate gender markers (Spade, 2015), and legal discrimination (Buist & Lenning, 2016).

These barriers contribute to the lack of safe, stable housing; transportation issues; lower incomes and employment rates; and health disparities. These trends are exacerbated for trans people of color, who experience higher rates of poverty, homelessness, and unemployment compared with their white trans peers (Grant et al., 2011), the highest rates of HIV infection, higher rates of sex work, and more harassment by police (MAP & CAP, 2016a). Trans immigrants face the added threat of deportation and other unique concerns.[6] Many trans people are thus pushed into the survival economy to meet their basic needs, where they are over-policed and subject to discriminatory enforcement of laws relating to HIV and the sex and drug trades. Unfair targeting by law enforcement contributes to higher rates of arrests and convictions. LGBT people also experience discrimination in legal proceedings, leading to higher rates of imprisonment and harsher punishments than their heterosexual counterparts (MAP & CAP, 2016a). Early encounters with the CLS make it harder to stay out of the system over time (Buist & Lenning, 2016).

Trans people with criminal convictions face added barriers, whether they serve time behind bars or under community supervision (MAP & CAP, 2016a). These include discrimination for having a criminal background; trans-exclusive re-entry programs; restrictive parole and probation conditions; lack of cultural competence among probation, parole, and re-entry practitioners; and, for those deemed 'sex offenders',[7] a host of unique barriers. Trans women with a history of incarceration are disproportionately people of color and have lower socioeconomic status, less education, and public or no health insurance (Reisner et al., 2014). They also have more reported health indicators, such as HIV-positive status and history of sex work, compared with trans people who have never been incarcerated. In addition, Creasy (2017) found that trans women re-entrants 'have unique challenges that are not addressed in standard re-entry programs due to similar stigma and discrimination that led to their incarceration' (p. 9). With such high rates of trans incarceration, and nearly two-thirds of all re-entrants recidivating in the first three years post-release (Alper et al., 2018), knowing the rate of trans recidivism would inform how often trans people under community supervision violate conditions, but such data are lacking (Creasy, 2017). At the same time, recidivism rates provide an incomplete picture with respect to who returns to prison and why.

Community supervision and re-entry

Trans individuals on probation or parole typically face a set of standardized conditions that must be met to remain in the community, while supervised by a probation or parole officer (PO). The most technical of violations, such as a missed appointment, can land them in prison or send them back to prison. Standard conditions may relate to mobility (for example, geographical residential constraints, permission to change residence); reporting (for example, as early as 24 hours after release from prison and scheduled times thereafter); employment (for example, maintain a job, permission to change jobs); behavior (for example, maintain appropriate behavior, abidance of laws); weapons (for example, unable to possess or have access to such); substances (for example, abstain from drugs and alcohol; avoid places that sell such); monetary (for example, pay a monthly fee); contact (for example, no unapproved contact with someone who has a felony conviction); and privacy (for example, allow POs to come to their home or place of employment without intervening; subject to searches of residence or vehicle at any time). Additional rules may apply to people with certain sex offense and other cases (US Probation and Pretrial Services, 2016).

For trans individuals, such conditions may pose significant obstacles to compliance. For example, a trans person who lacks identification with the appropriate gender marker may face barriers to obtaining a job (MAP & CAP, 2016a). If lacking transportation and support systems, they may be unable to afford bus fare (if public transportation is available) and thus struggle to attend PO appointments or arrive for a scheduled job interview. Addressing trans-specific barriers to compliance can greatly aid in breaking cycles of justice-involvement.

Probation and parole

For juveniles adjudicated delinquent, probation is the most prevalent outcome (Livsey, 2012). Much like adult probation, compliance conditions for juveniles are often standardized, in place to surveil youth at the expense of having 'positive value in youth development' (National Juvenile Defender Center, 2016, p. 2), and written in a way that is challenging for youth to understand, making it harder to comply.

Despite their role in assisting trans people with compliance and successful re-entry, the Movement Advancement Project and the Center for American Progress (MAP & CAP, 2016b) find that 'many parole, probation, and re-entry programs are understaffed, underfunded, and focus heavily on employment or treatment for substance use' (p. 33). Thus, the difficulties trans people face in meeting their basic needs outside these foci are absent consideration in such programs. Buist and Lenning (2016) further assert that 'probation officers who are already tirelessly overworked would require the appropriate training in order to understand, at the very least, the unique experiences of Queer people under their correctional supervision' (p. 92).

There is a dearth of literature on trans people's experiences with POs, and on the extent to which they are knowledgeable about issues trans people under supervision are likely to face. Probation practitioners are apt to encounter trans people 'at some point during their career, possibly as an offender,[8] maybe as a colleague or as a friend' (Poole et al., 2002, p. 227). However, to equip practitioners with the tools to properly assist trans people under supervision is not without its concerns, including lack of protocol for learning the trans status of the person under supervision to better identify trans-inclusive needs, challenges with reintegration for trans people who are used to social isolation, lack of awareness of trans-inclusive support systems for referral, trans-exclusive housing assignments for those with custodial sentences (that is, eventually going to prison), and personal biases impacting effective engagement with trans people (Poole et al., 2002).

Poole et al.'s (2002) research helped shape high-level suggestions for trans-inclusive training among probation practitioners. These entail understanding that trans-specific concerns will arise at various stages in the CLS; always showing respect (for example, using preferred pronouns); including trans people in relevant decision-making processes; establishing boundaries to ensure privacy and bodily integrity; and understanding that trans people may be more likely to present with comorbidities, such as chemical dependency or mental health issues, because of how they have come to cope with the stress of existing as trans. They also recognize that experiencing transphobia for expressing one's gender identity can elicit harmful and criminalized behavior. Limited trans-specific information in the CLS leaves probation practitioners lacking the competence needed to adequately serve this population (Poole et al., 2002).

Re-entry

More than 650,000 people are released from prisons in the US each year (US Department of Health and Human Services, n.d.), and another 100,000 juveniles leave confinement in detention centers and other placements, such as residential facilities or foster care (Lee, 2018). When trans youth and adults are released, they often return to the same environments they encountered before becoming justice-involved. If these environments are unhealthy, their chances of future justice-involvement rise. As adults, incarcerated trans people may leave prison for a halfway house or treatment facility, on parole, or without any form of supervision. Some are released to the streets with little money or support.

Imprisoned trans people should be assisted in preparing for the re-entry process while incarcerated (Zettler, 2019). Many re-entry programs are not well suited for trans people (MAP & CAP, 2016a) and fail to account for intersectional differences. Staff often lack the training to assist in re-entry and efforts to gain compliance with supervision for diverse populations. This lack of cultural competence on the part of practitioners must be addressed so that trans people are not forced to compensate for deficiencies beyond their control, which impacts their ability to stay out of the system.

Research shows that support systems are critical for trans people, independent of being under correctional control (Graham, 2014). The MAP and CAP (2016b) assert that prisons are charged with assisting incarcerated people with educational attainment and the skills needed to search for employment, which are critical for re-entry. To what extent this support is provided to imprisoned trans people is unclear. Large-scale research on re-entry programs points to the failure to address women re-entrants' needs (Scroggins & Malley, 2010). Zettler (2019) highlights gender differences in re-entry challenges, risks, and needs for women and men. Though research on women's re-entry has been explored, less is known about 'the gendered process' of re-entry (Middlemass & Smiley, 2019). If such programs fall short of meeting women's needs, it follows that they also fail to meet trans people's needs. With women being the fastest growing population of incarcerated people (Dernberger, 2017), and with trans people being overrepresented in the CLS, the need for gender- and trauma-responsive services as part of community supervision and re-entry cannot be overstated.

Placing trans people in halfway houses without attending to their unique needs can be particularly harmful, exposing them to harassment and violence at the hands of peers and staff. Too often, trans people are sent to sex-segregated halfway houses that do not align with their gender identity and can face consequences such as the threat of reincarceration for expressing the gender with which they identify (MAP & CAP, 2016a). These barriers must be addressed in order to prevent trans people from being placed into dangerous and hostile environments that further inhibit their chances of successful re-entry.

Trans-inclusive pathways to entry and re-entry

Since trans people often face family rejection, high dropout rates, disproportionate homelessness and underemployment, and lack equitable access to healthcare and gender-affirming care, they often end up in the survival economy and have more health disparities (including rates of suicide), as well as CLS involvement. These indicators are more pronounced for trans people of color and likely differ for trans women, trans men, nonbinary genderqueer people, and those with other non-normative gender identities. Trans people who have come under correctional control face the added stigma of a criminal conviction, further diminishing their life chances.

Reversing these trends requires everything from changes in laws and culture, including a belief that trans people deserve equal rights, to a commitment to change at the individual and structural levels. It necessitates attending to intersectionality in order to meet the needs of all trans people, rather than a select few. While education can be key to broadening our understanding of trans lives and why we ought to care about them, education alone will not reverse the course. The Trump administration implemented a number of harmful anti-LGBTQ policies that hindered the ability of interventions to have large-scale impacts. In the current climate, the most impactful changes are those made outside the legal system and largely rest on the concept of mutual aid. As seen with hate crime legislation, changes in laws alone do little to curb violence; trans people, especially those of color, face an epidemic. Legal changes mean little if they are not fully implemented and lack oversight and evaluative components. Change, then, must go beyond statutes and codes.

Panfil (2017) asserts that '[w]ithin criminology and criminal justice, there is also the issue of how to extrapolate information for prevention and intervention purposes, but we must first try to unearth the mechanisms at play' (p. 228). In the case of trans CLS involvement, the mechanisms are often negative familial responses to having trans children and structural barriers that severely limit full entry to society, coupled with navigating a world that is hostile toward anyone who is not straight, white, male, masculine, and higher-income. There is a need for meaningful statistics along with rich qualitative data to unearth the scope of trans community supervision and re-entry experiences.

Best practices exist concerning appropriate treatment of trans people in various arenas and should be utilized by such professionals. High-level recommendations should be considered based on ages (youth versus adult) and stages (before CLS involvement, during, and after) and take into account whether one has a criminal history and what that looks like (for example, felony conviction, drug conviction, sex offense). For example, the following recommendations draw on the literature and speak to changes that would lead to more successful outcomes for trans youth who come into contact with the CLS: ensure due process by informing youth and their caregivers of their right to legal counsel, as research shows many youth waive this right without consulting a lawyer (Marksamer, 2008); for youth adjudicated delinquent and placed on probation, we must change the language on conditions for compliance (a sixth- to eighth-grade level is recommended) to ensure they understand how to comply; use preferred pronouns, allow trans youth to express their gender identity, and provide gender-inclusive spaces while under supervision; provide POs with ongoing trans-inclusive training; and use alternatives to juvenile confinement in all cases.

Changing the narrative about trans people can help reframe the conversation. More people are taking notice of the unique challenges trans people face when they encounter the CLS. For example, the webinar 'Transgender Experiences and Resistance in the Criminal Legal System', co-hosted by Black & Pink (Boston) and MassEquality,[9] was held in June 2020. This all-trans panel included formerly incarcerated people and focused on lived experiences, covering such topics as what it is like to exist in this world as trans, intersectionality, white supremacy, the harms of the carceral state, self-care, abolition, and other reforms. Panels such as this not only center trans voices but also offer first-hand accounts that shed light on what the literature fails to capture. In an era of COVID-19, the ability to distribute information digitally on a mass scale can help raise the level of cultural competency surrounding trans exclusion.

Trans-aid model

A national, comprehensive trans-aid model exists in theory to address the barriers to entry and re-entry that trans people face, so that trans people in all states, of all ages and backgrounds, have access to services that afford them better life chances and opportunities. An interactive map would illustrate the scope of available services including where they are located and how they can be accessed. This model would demonstrate that the right interventions can serve as protective factors that reduce the chances of encountering the CLS and mitigate the harms associated with such contact. It would be informed by research and best practices and include metrics for measuring progress and formative evaluation. With a network of likeminded individuals who are tired of seeing so many trans people get caught in a web of harm and who are unwilling to wait around for more inclusive leadership, the passage of anti-discrimination and anti-racism laws, the end to the wars on drugs and poverty, and a society that is ready to move beyond the gender binary, such a model is possible. That said, it requires impassioned volunteers willing to share their expertise, educate and advocate, and sometimes, just listen.

Grassroots organizations have been working to elevate trans people, with and without criminal legal histories, for years. Often led by trans people, they understand the needs of this population. Whether they rely on mutual aid or have nonprofit status, they exist to disrupt pathways to the survival economy and provide a range of services, yet little attention is given in scholarly circles. A select few include G.L.I.T.S., INCITE!, Jen Love Project, Queer Detainee Empowerment Project, Trans Employment

Program, Transgender Emergency Fund, Transgender Gender-Variant & Intersex Justice Project, and Transgender Women of Color Collective.[10] Coordinating with these organizations, which are doing what they can with the resources they have to positively impact trans lives, can go a long way in closing gaps that exist in certain areas.

The model requires significant financial support and staff to operate, which means writing and winning grants and figuring out how to help trans people without funding along the way. It also requires space to offer a range of services and, amid the COVID-19 pandemic, safety measures and heavily virtual services. The model entails taking meaningful actions that improve trans people's trajectories. These include providing trans youth rejected by their families with safe housing, and housing for trans people living on the streets;[11] offering alternatives to completing high school for trans youth who are unsafe at school, and educational support for trans adults; employment assistance, including hiring trans people and paying them a living wage; providing affordable trans-inclusive healthcare through partnerships with qualified professionals; offering support for those with trauma, mental health issues, and those living with HIV; as well as other services, such as assistance obtaining identification documents with accurate gender markers and retaining culturally competent legal counsel when applicable.

An example of a service this model would provide to trans youth across the US follows. Trans youth face high rates of harassment and bullying in schools, leading to disproportionate dropout rates with few protections in place. Policies requiring the use of preferred pronouns, access to restrooms that align with one's gender identity, and anti-discrimination clauses are scarce and do little to stop transphobic treatment when institutional cultures remain unchanged. Trans youth deserve a safe learning environment, and if schools fail to provide this, another path must be made. Thus, the model would ensure trans youth have alternative options for completing high school, through homeschooling, online, or in-person instruction with inclusive educators. Youth who experience harassment and bullying and who drop out of school face higher rates of CLS involvement. Thus, affording them a means for completing high school and intervening when they are being harmed can help disrupt the trans school-to-prison pipeline.

Eventually, perhaps, we will catch up to the fact that a society that operates by oppressing trans people in ways that set them up to be less stable and more vulnerable to victimization and criminalization expends significant resources doing so (that is, time, money, and energy), while missing out on the valuable contributions a diverse citizenry brings and, in more extreme cases, at the expense of trans' lives. This same society would stand to gain from expanding its definition of gender beyond the binary, welcoming trans individuals in all life arenas, and affording them full protections, allowing for a citizenry that can focus on supporting one another in meeting their basic needs, living authentically, doing their best work, and moving toward a world where everyone has enough.

Conclusion

What little is known of how trans people experience state surveillance is primarily from select reports collected by LGBTQ+ advocacy organizations dedicated to improving the lives of people with non-normative gender and sexual identities (Buist & Lenning, 2016). Due to insufficient data collected by CLS actors, we are unsure how many trans people are under correctional control, the types of offenses for which they are arrested and convicted, their rates of parole, community supervision violations, and recidivism. The limited evidence suggests that the biggest pathway to the CLS for trans people is engagement in the survival economy, which begs the question: what would the scope and prevalence of trans offending look like without structural barriers that create the conditions for encountering the system? Our system of punishment does little to repair harm and too often causes harm. Despite a growing abolition movement, advocates recognize the need to minimize the harmful impacts while working toward systemic change. Lydon et al. (2015) assert that '[w]hile we remain committed to the abolition of prisons, we recognize that meeting the needs and ending the daily suffering of LGBTQ prisoners is also an urgent necessity' (p. 6).

We must do more to change exclusionary systems and the cultural norms around which they operate. Following Dernberger (2017), '[e]xploring how institutions and systems of power amplify or moderate the stigmatization of LGBT individuals can lead to increased understanding of gaps in public policy and the need for more targeted interventions' (pp. 120–121). Queer criminology focuses on 'disrupting, challenging, and asking uncomfortable questions that produce new ways of thinking about the lives of LGBTQ people and criminal justice processes' (Dwyer et al., 2016, p. 3). This chapter disrupts the narrative that people with criminal histories are straight, white males and that trans people are victims without agency (Panfil, 2017). The focus on trans people's experiences under correctional control responds to the call to 'queer' criminology (Woods, 2014), challenging us to reorient the conversation toward who makes the rules that trans people often appear unable to follow (Buist & Lenning, 2016).

Notes

[1] There has been a move 'to denote trans* with an asterisk to signify the fluidity and openness of the category' (Jauk, 2013, p. 822). However, the asterisk will not be repeated in the remainder of the chapter.

[2] 'The conscious choice to avoid the more common phrase "criminal justice system" reflects an acknowledgement of the reality that this system has not produced anything remotely

approximating justice for the vast majority of people in the United States—particularly for people of color, poor people, immigrants, and queers—since its inception, but rather bears major responsibility for the continuing institutionalization of severe, persistent, and seemingly intractable forms of violence and inequality' (Mogul et al., 2011, p. xx).

[3] Not all people under correctional control are guilty of the crimes for which they are convicted.

[4] 'The Sentencing Reform Act of 1984 eliminated federal parole for new court commitments and required federal courts to impose a term of supervised release after imprisonment as part of the original sentence to prison' (Carson, 2020, p. 15).

[5] For more on people-first language for those with CLS involvement, see Ellis (2005).

[6] 'Even an arrest for a minor offense can result in detention and ultimately deportation for immigrants, in some cases regardless of immigrant status' (MAP & CAP, 2016a, p. 10).

[7] People labeled 'sex offenders' face unique barriers; some states require they be added to a sex offender registry, including people as young as 14. Trans people face heightened risk of being charged with a sex crime due to being over-policed if engaged in sex work, assumed to be sex workers, and wrongfully punished for consensual sex with no economic ties (Booth, 2019).

[8] The term 'offender' is a misnomer; it criminalizes individuals based on behaviors, or alleged behaviors, which often leads to stigma.

[9] For more on Black & Pink (Boston), see www.blackandpinkma.org; for MassEquality, see https://www.massequality.org; for the webinar, see https://youtu.be/JPwyRCZ73DI

[10] For more on these trans-inclusive resources, see G.L.I.T.S. https://www.glitsinc.org; INCITE! https://incite-national.org; Jailhouse Lawyer's Handbook http://jailhouselaw. org; Jen Love Project https://jenloveproject.org; Queer Detainee Empowerment Project http://www.qdep.org; Trans Employment Program https://transemploymentprogram. org; Transgender Emergency Fund https://transemergencyfund.org; Transgender Gender-Variant & Intersex Justice Project http://www.tgijp.org; Transgender Women of Color Collective https://www.twocc.us

[11] On November 13, 2020, G.L.I.T.S. opened the first housing complex purchased by and for trans people; see https://www.pix11.com/news/local-news/queens/first-housing-complex-purchased-by-trans-community-for-trans-community-opens-in-queens

References

Alper, M., Durose, M.R., & Markman, J. (2018) *2018 Update on Prisoner Recidivism: A 9-Year Follow-up Period (2005–2014)*, Washington, DC: US Department of Justice, Office of Justice Programs, Bureau of Justice Statistics.

Beck, A.J. (2014) 'Sexual victimization in prisons and jails reported by inmates, 2011–12', Bureau of Justice Statistics. https://www.bjs.gov/content/pub/pdf/svpjri1112_st.pdf

Booth, D. (2019) '"… Except sex offenders": registering sexual harm in the age of #MeToo', in K.M. Middlemass & C. Smiley (eds.), *Prisoner Reentry in the 21st Century: Critical Perspectives of Returning Home*, New York: Routledge, pp. 219–231.

Bradner, K., Schiraldi, V., Mejia, N., & Lopoo, E. (2020) More work to do: Analysis of probation and parole in the United States, 2017–2018. Columbia Justice Lab. https://doi.org/10.7916/d8-hjyq-fg65

Brown, G.R. & Jones, K.T. (2015) 'Health correlates of criminal justice involvement in 4,793 transgender veterans', *LGBT Health*, 2(4): 297–305.

Buist, C.L. & Lenning, E. (2016) *Queer criminology*, New York: Routledge.

Buist, C.L. & Stone, C. (2014) 'Transgender victims and offenders: failures of the United States criminal justice system and the necessity of queer criminology', *Critical Criminology*, 22(1): 35–47.

Carson, E.A. (2020) *Prisoners in 2018*, Washington, DC: US Department of Justice, Bureau of Justice Statistics. https://www.bjs.gov/content/pub/pdf/p18.pdf

Creasy, S. (2017) 'Previously incarcerated transgender women: experiences, needs, and resiliencies', Master's thesis, University of Pittsburgh.

Crenshaw, K.W. (1989) 'Demarginalizing the intersection of race and sex: a Black feminist critique of antidiscrimination doctrine, feminist theory and antiracist politics', *The University of Chicago Legal Forum*, 140: 139–167.

Dernberger, B.N. (2017) 'Limited intersectional approaches to veteran and former prisoner reintegration: examining gender identity and sexual orientation', *Sociological Imagination*, 531(1): 100–131.

Dwyer, A., Ball, M., & Crofts, T. (2016) 'Queering criminologies', in A. Dwyer, M. Ball, & T. Crofts (eds.), *Queering Criminology*, London: Palgrave Macmillan, pp. 1–11.

Ellis, E. (2005) 'An open letter to our friends on the question of language', The Center for NuLeadership. https://static1.squarespace.com/static/58eb0522e6f2e1dfce591dee/t/596e3ef9bf629a2270909252/1500397309561/Open+Letter+On+The+Question+of+Language.pdf

Flores, A.R., Herman, J.L., Gates, G.J., & Brown, T.N.T. (2016) 'How many adults identify as transgender in the United States?', The Williams Institute, UCLA School of Law. https://williamsinstitute.law.ucla.edu/wp-content/uploads/How-Many-Adults-Identify-as-Transgender-in-the-United-States.pdf

Graham, L.F. (2014) 'Navigating community institutions: Black transgender women's experiences in schools, the criminal justice system, and churches', *Sexuality Research and Social Policy*, 11(4): 274–287.

Grant, J.M., Mottet, L.A., Tanis, J., Harrison, J., Herman, J.L., & Keisling, M. (2011) 'Injustice at every turn: a report of the national transgender discrimination survey', Washington, DC: National Center for Transgender Equality and National Gay and Lesbian Task Force.

Herman, J.L., Flores, A.R., Brown, T.N., Wilson, B.D., & Conron, K.J. (2017) 'Age of individuals who identify as transgender in the United States', The Williams Institute, UCLA School of Law. http://williamsinstitute.law.ucla.edu/wp-content/uploads/Age-Trans-Individuals-Jan-2017.pdf

Jauk, D. (2013) 'Gender violence revisited: lessons from violent victimization of transgender identified individuals', *Sexualities*, 16(7): 807–825.

Kahle, L.L. & Rosenbaum, J. (2020) 'What staff need to know: using elements of gender-responsive programming to create safer environments for system-involved LGBTQ girls and women', *Criminal Justice Studies*, 34(1): 1–15. https://doi.org/10.1080/1478601X.2020.1786281

Lee, C.H. (2018) *Juvenile Justice Guidebook for Legislators*. Denver, CO: National Conference of State Legislatures.

Livsey, S. (2012) 'Juvenile delinquency probation caseload, 2009', United States. National Juvenile Court Data Archive. https://ojjdp.ojp.gov/sites/g/files/xyckuh176/files/pubs/239082.pdf

Lydon, J., Carrington, K., Low, H., Miller, R., & Yazdy, M. (2015) 'Coming out of concrete closets: a report on Black & Pink's National LGBTQ Prisoner Survey'. https://www.blackandpink.org/wp-content/upLoads/Coming-Out-of-Concrete-Closets.-Black-and-Pink.-October-21-2015..pdf

MAP & CAP (Movement Advancement Project and Center for American Progress) (2016a) 'Unjust: How the broken criminal justice system fails transgender people'. https://www.lgbtmap.org/policy-and-issue-analysis/criminal-justice-trans

MAP & CAP (Movement Advancement Project and Center for American Progress) (2016b) 'Unjust: How the broken criminal justice system fails LGBT people of color'. https://www.lgbtmap.org/file/lgbt-criminal-justice-poc.pdf

Marksamer, J. (2008) 'And by the way, do you know he thinks he's a girl? The failures of law, policy and legal representation for transgender youth in juvenile delinquency courts', *Sexuality Research & Social Policy*, 5(1): 72–92.

Middlemass, K.M. & Smiley, C. (2019) 'Section III: Gender, criminality, and reentry', in K.M. Middlemass & C. Smiley (eds.), *Prisoner Reentry in the 21st Century: Critical Perspectives of Returning Home*, New York: Routledge, pp. 141–145.

Mogul, J.L., Ritchie, A.J., & Whitlock, K. (2011) *Queer (In)justice: The Criminalization of LGBT People in the United States*, Boston, MA: Beacon Press.

National Juvenile Defender Center (2016) 'Issue brief: promoting positive development: the critical need to reform youth probation orders'. https://www.njjn.org/uploads/digital-library/Promoting_Positive_Development.pdf

Oparah, J.C. (2012) 'Feminism and the (trans)gender entrapment of gender nonconforming prisoners', *UCLA Women's Law Journal*, 18(2): 239–271.

Panfil, V.R. (2017) *The Gang's All Queer: The Lives of Gay Gang Members*, New York: NYU Press.

Poole, L., Whittle, S., & Stephens, P. (2002) 'Working with transgendered and transsexual people as offenders in the probation service', *Probation Journal*, 49(3): 227–232.

Reisner, S.L., Bailey, Z., & Sevelius, J. (2014) 'Racial/ethnic disparities in history of incarceration, experiences of victimization, and associated health indicators among transgender women in the US', *Women & Health*, 54(8): 750–767.

Sawyer, W. & Wagner, P. (2020) 'Mass incarceration: the whole pie 2020', Prison Policy Initiative. https://www.prisonpolicy.org/reports/pie2020.html

Scroggins, J.R. & Malley, S. (2010) 'Reentry and the (unmet) needs of women', *Journal of Offender Rehabilitation*, 49(2): 146–163.

Spade, D. (2015) *Normal Life: Administrative Violence, Critical Trans Politics, and the Limits of Law*, Durham, NC: Duke University Press.

US Department of Health and Human Services (n.d.) 'Incarceration and Reentry'. https://aspe.hhs.gov/incarceration-reentry

US Probation and Pretrial Services, Northern District of West Virginia (2016) 'Standard conditions of probation and supervised release'. https://www.wvnp.uscourts.gov/conditions-supervision

Woods, J.B. (2014) '"Queering criminology": Overview of the state of the field', in D. Peterson & V. Panfil (eds.), *Handbook of LGBT Communities, Crime, and Justice*, New York: Springer, pp. 15–41.

Worthen, M.G. (2016) *Sexual Deviance and Society: A Sociological Examination*, New York: Routledge.

Zettler, H. (2019) 'The gendered challenges of prisoner reentry', in K.M. Middlemass & C. Smiley (eds.), *Prisoner Reentry in the 21st Century: Critical Perspectives of Returning Home*, New York: Routledge, pp. 157–171.

7

Sex–Gender Defining Laws, Birth Certificates, and Identity

Jon Rosenstadt

As the subject of multiple laws, court rulings, and vested public interest, sex and gender nonbinary people are increasingly subjected to scrutiny and enforced politicization, medicalization, and criminalization. By legally defining sex and gender as permanently interconnected and bodies as either male or female from birth based on the perceived ability of sexual reproduction, proponents of sex-gender-confirming proposed legislation seek to establish that one's sex-gender is determined through scientific, thus inarguable, fact. In January 2019, the Utah Vital Statistics Act Amendments bill (H.B. 153, 2019), was proposed, which would legally define sex and gender – assumed congruent – as inherently and permanently either male or female. However, the strict language used in the proposed bill provides definitions for what is considered legally male and female that are so explicit that nonbinary bodies, even those bodies that doctors would typically assign as male or female, would 'literally fall outside of the only categories the court recognizes as human' (Lloyd, 2005, p. 170). A failure of the proposed legislation to account for the myriad of natural bodily formations beyond the binary male/female indicates a failure to include personhood or humanity for people whose bodies do not match the required function in the text of the law. This potentially marks transgender, intersex, and nonbinary people as existing outside the category of legally human by denying their identity in relation to the available legal male/female markers, such as accurate birth certificates and legal identification documents, which, in turn, impact access to employment, housing, healthcare, finances, education, and interactions within the criminal justice system.

By examining the purposefully specific language used in H.B. 153 and comparing it with previous incarnations of similar legislation, I show how exclusionary legislation fails to represent the vast differences in sex-gender present within the human body, potentially defining multitudes of people out of societal and legal existence. Through an examination of the structure and language of the proposed bill and an examination of how the sciences noted in proposed legislation fail to account for the variances in bodily formations, I position sex and gender nonbinary people as not only not included in, but intentionally prevented from, being considered legally human.

Proposed legislation

Sex-gender-confirming proposed legislation is designed to enact control on bodies deemed non-normative by refocusing debates regarding personal identity into politically aligned negations of choice in the name of protecting compulsory heterosexuality as a function of expected and accepted family formation and child rearing.[1] Given the rigid definitions of either male or female, transgender, intersex, and nonbinary bodies no longer legally exist (Buist & Stone, 2014). The existing literature identifies key issues and risks that have developed through this practice, including how sex-gender is categorized to perpetuate stigma surrounding nonbinary bodies and how proposed legislation is based on incorrect, outdated, and often misleading science to further enact legal violence against people who fail to conform to legal standards of sex-gender. In this section, I examine how legal sex is determined and categorized, reviews potential sex-presentation changes and the impact of these choices, and evaluates the potential legal concerns for individuals both in changing their legal sex and when their legal sex does not match their presented identity.

This type of proposed legislation situates bodies that do not conform to binary gender politics as deviant and potentially fraudulent utilizing homophobic and transphobic rhetoric (Lee & Kwan, 2014). Determinations of one's legal sex (Hutton, 2017, p. 65) are typically based on the physical appearance of genitalia that is observed at the time of birth (Pemberton, 2013) and enforced when entered into the legal records via birth certificate. Laws surrounding sex-gender emphasize the legitimacy of a birth certificate as the foremost signifier of a person's legally approved identity (Hutton, 2017). By defining what a person's legal sex is, human bodies are conditioned into social and legal boundaries that affect potential outcomes for the remainder of their lives.

Medicalization

Medicalization, society, and the law, as spheres of influence on bodily purpose and autonomy, operate individually and in tandem to perpetuate overly simplistic determinations of sex and gender that rely on heterosexist scripts of normativity. Society and social constructs of gender become increasingly important when infants are born with ambiguous genitals. In the case of intersex infants, doctors make surgical choices that 'provide the right genitals to go along with the socialization' (Kessler, 1990, p. 17). At birth, or at the time a birth certificate is initially created, if the infant's physical genitalia are underdeveloped or otherwise fails to meet visual expectations, other factors may be utilized to determine the infant's sex, including 'chromosomes, gonads, external morphology, internal morphology, hormonal patterns, [and] phenotype' (Lugones, 2007, p. 195). The use and deployment of these 'determining' factors vary widely and are influenced directly by societal values, which 'presumes an unambiguous binary sex paradigm in which all individuals can be classified neatly as male or female' (Greenberg, 2002, p. 112). Unambiguous categories of sex, including partially male and/or partially female, are characteristic of intersex (Lugones, 2007), a category of sex that is a medical value but not a legal or social value for the purposes of records. Intersex classifications typically rely on visual examinations of ambiguous genitalia but include a range of formations from the visible morphology to the chromosomal (Holmes, 2008), which may not appear until later in life (Fausto-Sterling, 2000). Statistics indicate that 1 to 4 percent of the population is born intersex (Lugones, 2007).

Intersex individuals, much like transgender individuals, do not have their sex-gender legally recognized and thus exist outside the sex binary (Buist & Stone, 2014, p. 40). Rather than provide or expand the definitions of sex-gender to include those that cannot identify as male or female, intersex individuals are routinely 'surgically and hormonally turned into males or females' (Lugones, 2007, p. 195). These medical interventions further reify how 'normal' genitals should appear in a medical context in order to be accepted within the wider social sphere. Intersex surgical interventions are frequently performed to align visible genitalia with socially accepted perceptions of how a male or a female should appear, act, and function, rather than for specific medical necessity. Secondary views on sex-gender-confirming surgeries among intersex bodies fail to consider informed choices and patient-centered medical care via informed consent from either the person being altered or their caregivers (Rubin, 2015). Bodily autonomy would allow for an elected personal sex, implying 'a right to recognition without being limited by preselected category' (Hutton, 2017).

Legal and scientific remedies to defining sex-gender beyond the binary have failed to consistently provide a single definition (Buist & Stone, 2014), and existing definitions are based on incorrect sex-gender binary sciences that rely on 'sexual dimorphism and heteronormative gender development' (Rubin, 2015). Chromosomal tests remain inaccurate because they focus on defining sex as either XX or XY and fail to include potentials for other chromosomal formations (Fausto-Sterling, 2000). Testosterone and estrogen testing similarly assumes that binary bodies have one or the other (that is, males have testosterone, females have estrogen) and fail to recognize the existence of varying levels of multiple types of hormones across all bodies (Sapolsky, 1998). Finally, testing assumes that sex-gender legitimacy is only achieved when the various tests (chromosomal, visual, gonadal, and genital) are congruent (Hutton, 2017). When congruence fails, infants are unnecessarily medicalized (Rubin, 2015) and surgically altered (Lugones, 2007, p. 195; ISNA, n.d.) until congruence is reached in order to match bodies to acceptable cultural and legal definitions of male or female (Holmes, 2008; Hutton, 2017). Surgical interventions focus on social expectations of anatomical purpose and preferential appearance, rather than healthy gonadal function; infants born with inadequate penises can be surgically given vulvas/vaginas (Greenberg, 2002), while infants born with enlarged clitorises may have their otherwise healthy genitals 'shaved down' (Baskin & Rink, 2004).

Legitimate bodies and legal barriers

The medicalization of the anatomy of nonbinary bodies, specifically in visible formation, creates lifelong legal concerns. A lack of recognition relegates those same bodies to legal invisibility and social inauthenticity (Hutton, 2017). Beginning at birth, people's lives are invariably controlled by the sex-gender designation on their birth certificates, which is maintained through social expectations (Kessler, 1990). When people can change their sex-gender identity socially but not legally, they face additional barriers (Pemberton, 2013). These barriers disproportionately impact transgender and gender nonconforming people, who are frequently misgendered and misnamed across arenas that only provide space for legal names and genders to be accepted (Tilleman, 2010). Similarly, legally changing one's name due to sex-gender confirmation is met with resistance due to assumptions of deviance and deception (Williams, 2015). Notions of deviance and deception are critical sites of transphobic engagements within legal systems (Lloyd, 2005; Lee & Kwan, 2014). To legitimize their identities, transgender and gender nonconforming individuals are often required to prove that they have undergone some form of costly gender confirmation procedure, up to and including surgery, to be legally recognized by courts in states that allow these changes (Lloyd, 2005; Buist & Stone, 2014).

Additional restraints applied to the bodies of transgender and nonbinary people are directly related to the ability to change their birth certificate to match their preferred or actualized identities. Birth certificates are used to obtain driver's licenses, marriage documents, proof of identity forms, housing, employment, and education, and they influence interactions with/in criminal justice systems. Nonbinary individuals are at risk because their identity defies legal categorization of gender assignment. When a person's visible and legal identities fail to match, they can be denied medical care (Pemberton, 2013) or the ability to use bathrooms and other gendered spaces (Barnett et al., 2018); they risk being outed to housing authorities and employers (Pemberton, 2013); and they face negative interactions with/in criminal justice systems (Buist & Stone, 2014; Forbes, 2014). Until the passing of marriage equality, they were legally denied marriage, divorce, management of estates, and custody of children (In re estate of Gardiner, 2002; *Kantaras v. Kantaras*, 2004; *Beatie v. Beatie*, 2014).

Method

I examine how sex-gender-confirming proposed legislation frames bodies as either inherently male or female to delimit the ability for people to make personal choices relating to their own identities, and how rigid definitions prevent those that would not identify with their birth sex-gender from being legally classified as human. H.B. 153 was specifically designed to determine if, when, and how a birth certificate could be amended, including which sections. To frame the potential risks that the proposed bill could have enforced on nonbinary bodies, I reviewed other instances in which states legally enforced regulations on modifying birth certificates in relation to sex-gender determinations utilizing Lambda Legal's (2018) 'Changing Birth Certificate Sex Designations' database. A review of this database identified three states that currently do not allow birth certificate changes relating to sex-gender identity: Kansas, Ohio, and Tennessee. Following a review of each of the state laws, Ohio's Chapter 3705.15 Registration of Unrecorded Birth – Correction of Birth Record (2006) was selected for inclusion in my research due to the known long-term effects of the state's sex-gender restrictions, notably through the controlling case law In re Ladrach (1987). The resulting data were evaluated utilizing a summative content analysis to examine how legal and medical language is used and to identify greater legal potentialities when sex-gender is explicit and rigidly defined.

Analysis

The implications of identity formation and the legal control over bodies form realities for queer, transgender, and gender nonbinary people that have lasting effects beyond their ability to have legal documents that match their identities. What is considered a person's *legal* sex-gender has historically impacted all facets of their lives. When H.B. 153 was proposed in 2019, the bill was clearly intended to strike a blow to transgender people's rights, even though the actual text was written to appear neutral so that it could apply to all citizens. Legislation often intentionally appears non-biased while lawmakers ignore racialized, sexualized, gendered, and privileged themes (Alexander, 2011). Additionally, the way laws are enforced by authorities allows the personal values and biases of those with the power to enforce laws to be expressed without legal resistance (Alexander, 2011; Buist & Stone, 2014; Williams, 2015). In evaluating the text of these types of bills, I identify the explicit and underlying language of sex-gender determining legislation including purpose, functions, and legal implications. I also evaluate how bodies that cannot be framed within the law as male or female become marked as *neither* and, potentially, not legally human.

Sex-gender laws: purposes, functions, and legal implications

H.B. 153 was proposed to define and clarify how sex-gender indicators on birth certificates were initially completed and potentially amended while also providing strict definitions for what would be legally considered either male or female, without potential inclusion for nonbinary and intersex people. The bill indicates that "'sex' means male or female, *the innate and immutable characteristics established at conception and that can be confirmed before or at birth'* (emphasis added, 2019). Additional definitions for male and female were modified to state that 'Female' means an individual with ovaries who is confirmed before or at birth to have external anatomical characteristics that appear to have the purpose of performing the natural reproductive function of providing eggs and receiving sperm from a male donor; and that 'Male' means an individual with testes who is confirmed before or at birth to have external anatomical characteristics that appear to have the purpose of performing the natural reproductive function of providing and delivering sperm to a female recipient. Additionally, the bill also removed previous wording that would allow a person's birth certificate to be changed when that person had a name or sex change that was approved by a court (my critique of this bill, including the potential for the erasure of gender nonconforming and nonbinary bodies, utilizes previous legislation and court rulings of significance).

In 1996, Ohio passed Chapter 3705.15 Registration of Unrecorded Birth – Correction of Birth Record, which outlined how a birth certificate may be adjusted or corrected, specifically in reference to incorrectly identified personal statistics such as birth date, name, birth location, or incorrectly marked sex-gender. While the bill did not specifically note personal sex-gender changes, it may be used to impede a person's choice to transition; similar to H.B. 153, there are clear discrepancies between the stated purpose of the bill and its use in preventing people from transitioning.

Critically, Ohio's Chapter 3705.15 cited In re Ladrach (1987) as controlling case law – an appellant case set to determine whether Elaine Ladrach, a trans woman, could legally marry her male partner. This case referenced previous instances in which Elaine had attempted to have her identity legally recognized; in April 1986, the court granted her the right to change her name because the court recognized that she had undergone gender-confirmation surgery. In September 1986, Elaine requested a marriage license to marry her male partner, but the court denied the request, claiming that marriage was between a male and female, and because Elaine's birth certificate still identified her as male, she could not legally marry her male partner. Finally, she filed a Complaint for Declaratory Judgment in January 1987 with the purpose of demanding that her previous gender-confirmation surgeries, medical records, and history be evaluated by the court to have her birth certificate amended to reflect her identity. The court required that Elaine be examined by a doctor, who reported that she had 'normal female external genitalia [and] he would classify Elaine as a female [but] when questioned by applicant's counsel as to whether a chromosomal test would show Elaine to be a female he replied "highly unlikely"' (In re Ladrach, 1987). The court ruled against the request to correct her birth certificate, which prevented her from marrying her partner, indicating that

> it is generally accepted that a person's sex is determined at birth by an anatomical examination by the birth attendant. This results in a declaration [of] either 'boy' or 'girl' [which] then becomes the person's *true sex* and the respondent's operation, therefore, *cannot affect her true sex*. (emphasis added, 1987)

The use of medical experts in courts to provide definitions of either male or female, especially in relation to transgender court cases, is common, but a uniform definition has not been consistently utilized (Buist & Stone, 2014). Additionally, a ruling in favor of Elaine based on the doctor's inspection of her visible genitalia would reify the expectation of surgical intervention and the formation of 'normative' genitalia. In re Ladrach has been cited in numerous court cases across the country, including to deny a marriage license in Massachusetts (In re Application for Marriage License for Nash, 2003) and to deny an amended birth certificate following gender-confirmation surgery in Maryland (In the matter of R. W. Heilig, 2002). It has been used to prevent a widow from retaining her deceased husbands' estate due to her sex change in Ohio (In re estate of Gardiner, 2002), to prevent a legal name change in Ohio (In re Change of Name of DeWeese, 2002), and to prevent a couple that was legally married in Hawaii from divorcing in Arizona, where their marriage was not recognized by the state (*Beatie v. Beatie*, 2014). It was also used to void a marriage and parental rights because of one partner's sex assigned at birth in Florida (*Kantaras v. Kantaras*, 2004).

The legal implications for the proposed Utah bill, and bills like it, have profound effects on transgender, intersex, and gender nonconforming people. While the bill itself attempts to remain neutral by avoiding directly alienating transgender, intersex, and nonbinary people through omission and using broad language, the true purpose is clear when evaluating the historical implications of previous legislation.

Framing a body as male or female (or neither)

Laws such as H.B. 153 frame bodies with sex-gender markers as either male or female at birth using a classification that excludes the existence of nonbinary or transitioning bodies (Buist & Stone, 2014, p. 39) while treating the binary male/female model as normal. A key factor of H.B. 153 is the authors' definitions of what constitutes male or female, utilizing rigid structures of genital appearance and supposed purpose that indicates sex-gender is formed at or before birth. Representative Nelson, who introduced H.B. 153, stated that the bill 'is based on the scientific and medical fact that an individual's sex is determined at conception by chromosomal make-up and is not subject to change or self-determination later in life … What is a physical fact at birth, gender, is put on the birth certificate' (Tanner, 2019). At no point in the wording of H.B. 153 does chromosomal testing for sex appear to be utilized to determine sex-gender, and the decision to indicate permanent sex-gender identity is based solely on a medical professional's visual evaluation of external genital structures.

According to the Mayo Clinic's (2017) publication 'Pregnancy Week by Week', external genitalia begin to form around the 11th week of pregnancy. By focusing on physical appearance and assumed purpose of external genitals at conception, and by excluding other testing including chromosomal or a review of internal organs, H.B. 153 fails to account for the potentiality of various bodies and identities beyond what would be considered an ideal male or female (Hutton, 2017; ISNA, n.d.). Furthermore, this bill assumes that sex should be immediately determined from the moment of conception by visual inspection while simultaneously refusing chromosomal testing, the only way to determine sex early in pregnancies.

Bodies with genitals that do not specifically match the explicit descriptions afforded by H.B. 153 may not be considered legally human if those genitals, which could normally be considered as belonging to a male or female, are unformed, under-formed, or otherwise atypical. Because the law identifies the existence of ovaries and testes, for female and male respectively, the absence or non-normative development of either implies that the infant cannot be sexed under the law. Furthermore, because the law only allows for the visual inspection of genitalia, it fails to rectify how specific genitalia and organs that are internal are to be observed; ovaries within the body and testes that have not dropped prior to or at birth are not visible without additional technologies that are not afforded by the law. Because the law does not indicate how infants should be sexed beyond an external visual review, it is unclear how doctors would determine the existence of ovaries, and one could argue that all females remain un-sexed until they receive sperm *and* become pregnant. Similarly, it is unclear how the law defines an intersex infant that has visible testes and functioning ovaries, or an infant that has a visible labia and undescended testicles. The existence of multiple genital, genetic, or bodily formations that would be considered intersex, including chromosomal and mixed gonadal formation (Fausto-Sterling, 2000; ISNA, n.d.), which may not be found until later in life, could be impacted as to define those bodies as legally nonexistent. Furthermore, if the law allowed for additional tests beyond visual evaluations, the law does not indicate how potentially non-normative bodies should be identified or reconciled; sex-gender markers on legal forms are required to indicate either male or female, emphasizing the potential for unnecessary and damaging surgeries. Bodies that would be considered intersex at any stage in life, but which are identified and recorded as male or female at birth, would be required to maintain that identity for the remainder of their life regardless of their personal identification or surgical choices.

Additionally, sexual purpose is a key factor in the revisions proposed for determining sex-gender; females have ovaries for the *purpose of receiving sperm*, whereas males have testes for *the purpose of delivering sperm* (H.B. 153, 2019). This maintains that genitals only exist for procreation and defines personhood from the moment of conception as the ability to perform sexual reproduction. However, because H.B. 153 includes the expected purpose of either delivering or receiving sperm, it fails to accord personhood to those that fail to or are unable to have penis–vaginal intercourse, or whose production of sperm or eggs is not directly related to, or in contact with, the other. A similar implication can be made that one's sex-gender is not legally definable until both a visual inspection of genital formation and an act of heterosexual sex has been completed. This argument would additionally find that the act of heterosexual sex would occur only following the socially enforced marriage of consenting adults, thus indicating that only heterosexual, married, monogamous, fully developed, binary adults could constitute as legally being either male or female. Similarly, bodies that are unable to produce sperm or eggs – due to age, performance, inability, lack of necessary organs, or medical conditions – would be unable to continue identifying themselves as either male or female. For those whose sexual reproductive abilities change with time – through menopause, infertility, and/or inability – their positions of maleness or femaleness also become a site of potential concern. Menopause socially situates bodies as falling out of essential womanhood (Dillaway, 2005), while erectile dysfunction endorses the social view that sexual ability defines masculinity and acceptance as a male (Thompson & Barnes, 2013). Similarly, surgical intervention at any stage in life, including the removal of organs due to injury or medical need (hysterectomy, testicle removal, and so on), cancer, tubal ligation, or vasectomy, could eliminate one's legally defined sexual purpose and, thus, sex-gender categorization. The authors' emphasis on genital purpose is situated within the religious context of sexual purpose and child rearing (Dore, 2015) and fails to account for the myriad of potential sex and gender identities.

Conclusion

As the Utah Vital Statistics Act Amendments bill so narrowly defined sex-gender and failed to account for a wide range of bodily formations and other sex-gender determining factors, sexualities, and so forth, it is unclear how these proposed changes would be enforced as infants age into adulthood and their bodies continue to develop. Proposed legislation such as H.B. 153 seeks to legally classify the body as a fixed, immutable, monolithic object that is unable to change, with intent to legally define who has the right to exist and be recognized as existing, while reifying potential personhood and citizenship for fetuses. The either purposeful or negligent failure of the law to account for the myriad of natural bodily formations beyond the binary male/female indicates a failure to include personhood or humanity for people with unacceptable or nonvisible genital formations, the existence of intersex and queer people, or the likelihood that a person's body may change naturally or function differently over time. The proposed bill fails both to consider how bodies function and to account for societal expectations of bodily autonomy and purpose, instead emphasizing preferential normative genital configurations. Preventing the change of birth certificates further destabilizes transgender, intersex, and nonbinary people's access to legal categories associated with birth certificates. And, as the sex-gender listed on birth certificates is critical in gaining access to legal documents such as driver's licenses and identification cards, this in turn becomes critical for employment, housing, healthcare, finances, and education, and it impacts interactions with/in the criminal justice system. People whose sex-gender fails to match their legally defined sex-gender thus are placed at a disadvantage to be recognized as legally human.

It would be disingenuous to claim that any/all of the groups identified here as potentially at risk would actually be targeted by H.B. 153. However, the far-reaching impact of previous case laws and bills identify a roadmap for how laws can be manipulated to serve alternative purposes and goals.

By deconstructing the language of this kind of legislation, it is possible to identify who is impacted and, more importantly, how few people would be able to maintain access to the only legally recognized categories of humans. Proposals of legislation such as this are not new or isolated incidents and, because bills/laws have far-reaching legal, social, and political implications as detailed in my research, scholars and professionals in the legal and medical fields have a duty to both identify and upend these actions. By carefully examining the language of these bills and laws and contrasting them with historical actions that operate in similar veins, it is possible to identify what can cause the most harm to marginalized groups. Additionally, the language of identity in legal and medical arenas must be interrogated and enhanced to provide more possibilities for human understanding and acceptance in order to prevent the delimiting of personhood, humanity, and potential for legal recognition for those who face disproportionate risks.

Note

1 As the proposed legislation conflates sex and gender as being one in the same, this chapter utilizes *sex-gender* as interconnected.

References

Alexander, M. (2011) *The New Jim Crow*, New York: The New Press.

Barnett, B.S., Nesbit, A.E., & Sorrentino, R.M. (2018) 'The transgender bathroom debate at the intersection of politics, law, ethics, and science', *The Journal of the American Academy of Psychiatry and the Law*, 46: 232–241.

Baskin, L. & Rink, R. (2004). 'Implications of female genital innervation', Paper presented at the American Academy of Pediatrics Section on Urology, San Francisco, CA.

Beatie v. Beatie, Arizona Court of Appeals. No. 1 CA-CV 13-0209 (2014).

Buist, C.L. & Stone, C. (2014) 'Transgender victims and offenders: failures of the United States criminal justice system and the necessity of queer criminology', *Critical Criminology*, 22(1): 35–47.

Dillaway, H.E. (2005) '(Un)natural menopausal bodies: how women think and act in the face of a reproductive transition and gendered beauty ideals', *Sex Roles*, 50(1–2): 1–17.

Dore, C. (2015) 'Republicans on abortion rights', *Think*, Spring: 9–18.

Fausto-Sterling, A. (2000) *Sexing the Body: Gender Politics and the Construction of Sexuality*, New York: Basic Books.

Forbes, A. (2014) 'Define "sex": legal outcomes for transgender individual in the United States', in D. Peterson & V.R. Panfil (eds.), *Handbook of LGBT Communities, Crime, and Justice*, New York: Springer, pp. 387–403.

Greenberg, J.A. (2002) 'Definitional dilemmas: male or female? Black or white? The law's failure to recognize intersexuals and multiracials', in T. Lester (ed.), *Gender Nonconformity, Race, and Sexuality: Charting the Connections*, Madison: University of Wisconsin Press, pp. 102–126.

H.B. 153, 2019 General Session. (Utah) (2019).

Holmes, M. (2008) *Intersex: A Perilous Difference*, Selinsgrove, PA: Susquehanna University Press.

Hutton, C. (2017) 'Legal sex, self-classification and gender self-determination', *Law and Humanities*, 11(1): 64–81.

In re Application for Marriage License for Nash, 2003-Ohio-7221 (2003).

In re Change of Name of DeWeese, 148 Ohio App.3d 201, 2002-Ohio2867 (2002).

In re estate of Gardiner, Kansas Supreme Court. No. 85,030 (2002).

In re Ladrach, 32 Ohio Misc. 2d 6, 513 N.E.2d 828 (1987).

In the matter of R. W. Heilig, No. 38, September Term (2002).

ISNA (Intersex Society of North America) (n.d.) 'How common is intersex?'. https://isna.org/faq/frequency

Kantaras v. Kantaras, Florida Second District Court of Appeal. No. 2D03-1377 (2004).

Kessler, S. J. (1990) 'The medical construction of gender: case management of intersexed infants', *Signs: Journal of Women in Culture and Society*, 16(11): 3–26.

Lambda Legal (2018) 'Changing birth certificate sex designations: State-by-state guidelines'. https://www.lambdalegal.org/know-your-rights/article/trans-changing-birth-certificate- sex-designations

Lee, C. & Kwan, P. (2014) 'The trans panic defense: masculinity, heteronormativity, and the murder of transgender women', *Hastings Law Journal*, 66(10): 77–132.

Lloyd, A.W. (2005) 'Defining the human: are transgender people strangers to the law?', *Berkeley Journal of Gender, Law, & Justice*, 20: 150–195.

Lugones, M. (2007) 'Heterosexualism and the Colonial/Modern Gender System', *Hypatia*, 22(1): 186–209.

Mayo Clinic (2017) 'Pregnancy week by week'. https://www.mayoclinic.org/healthy-lifestyle/pregnancy-week-by-week/in-depth/prenatal-care/art-20045302

Pemberton, S. (2013) 'Enforcing gender: the construction of sex and gender in prison regimes', *Signs: Journal of Women in Culture and Society*, 39(11): 151–171.

Registration of Unrecorded Birth – Correction of Birth Record, Ohio Rev. Code § 3705.15 (2006).

Rubin, D. (2015) 'Provincializing intersex', *Frontiers*, 36(3): 51–83.

Sapolsky, R. (1998) *The Trouble With Testosterone*, New York: Scribner.

Tanner, C. (2019) '"A person's sex is no more subject to change than a person's age": Utah lawmaker defends bill to block changes to birth certificates', *The Salt Lake Tribune*, January 23. https://www.sltrib.com/news/politics/2019/01/23/utah-lawmaker-wants/

Thompson, E.H. & Barnes, K. (2013) 'Meaning of sexual performance among men with and without erectile dysfunction', *Psychology of Men & Masculinity*, 14(3): 271–280.

Tilleman, M. (2010) '(Trans)forming the provocation defense', *The Journal of Criminal Law and Criminology*, 100(4): 1659–1688.

Williams, J.R. (2015). '"I don't like gays, okay?" Use of the "gay panic" murder defense in modern American courtrooms: the ultimate miscarriage of justice', *Albany Law Review*, 78(3): 1129–1169.

8

Effects of Intimate Partner Violence in the LGBTQ Community: A Systematic Review

Rosalind Evans and Illandra Denysschen

Introduction

Intimate partner violence (IPV) is a much broader term than domestic abuse and it describes a devastating social and global issue. Domestic abuse, originally classified as an act between a man and a woman where the male figure was the perpetrator in most reported cases, reduces the likelihood of inclusion for the LGBTQ community. According to the Centers for Disease Control and Prevention (2019), using the National Intimate Partner and Sexual Violence Survey, in their 2015 report, one in four women and one in ten men have experienced contact sexual violence, physical violence, and/ or stalking by an intimate partner during their lifetime and have reported some form of IPV-related impact (CDC, 2019). By broadening the term to be more inclusive of LGBTQ and underserved individuals, IPV was established. The boundaries of research conducted to discuss IPV within the LGBTQ community have been severely shortsighted. There is a vast amount of research done quantitatively and qualitatively looking into IPV within couples of opposite sex, but there is a dearth of research about the LGBTQ+ community as a whole. The majority of IPV research within the LGBTQ+ community involves lesbian women and gay men, and less research has been done to highlight the issues faced by both men and women who are bisexual. Transgender and queer individuals tend to be overshadowed in research unless there is a specific focus on this community, with gender elements such as non-gender-conforming or nonbinary individuals being excluded from much needed research.

> In the U.S., non-binary refers to transgender people who have a gender identity not aligned with their assigned sex at birth, and who identify outside of the traditional male-female binary, such as genderqueer, genderfluid, or gender nonconforming. (Reisner & Hughto, 2019, p. 1)

Most of the research into IPV within the LGBTQ+ community can be attributed to the passing of the Violence Against Women Reauthorization Act (VAWA) (2013), which has provided further opportunities to gain awareness of the impact of IPV. The Act incorporated more funding for research and preventative programs for IPV throughout the United States. The Act also incorporated protections for individuals encompassing sexual orientation and gender identity. This created an opportunity for scholars to provide literature focusing on various aspects of IPV pertaining to causes, reports, and prevention resources. Although this topic has been researched over the past few decades there have been limited studies focusing on IPV and the LGBTQ community (Rothman et al., 2011; Finneran & Stephenson, 2013a; Buller et al., 2014; Badenes-Ribera et al., 2016; Longobardi & Badenes-Ribera, 2017). This is a troubling concern for a community that often experiences discrimination and marginalization in society (Rothman et al., 2011; Longobardi & Badenes-Ribera, 2017; Semprevivo, 2021). It is critical to capture data on this population and to be aware of their experiences to inform future policy, research methodologies, theoretical frameworks, and best practices when working to provide services to the community.

The National Intimate Partner and Sexual Violence Survey findings in the 2010 report of Victimization by Sexual Orientation revealed that 'individuals who self-identify as lesbian, gay, and bisexual have an equal or higher prevalence of experiencing IPV, SV, and stalking as compared to self-identified heterosexuals' (Walters et al., 2013, p. 8). It was also noted that bisexual women had an even higher disproportionate rate of experiencing components of IPV. Walters et al.'s (2013) findings indicated that 44 percent of lesbian women and 61 percent of bisexual women experienced stalking, rape, or physical violence by their intimate partner. In addition to reports of bisexual women, 40 percent of gay men and 47 percent of bisexual men reported these experiences with their intimate partners (Walters et al., 2013). These numbers provided awareness of the striking concerns of IPV within LGBTQ relationships. A study by Semprevivo (2021) also provided awareness of the impacts of gender and sexual orientation in dating and sexual violence victimization of youth. From her research, she discovered that

LGBQ students reported higher rates of dating violence victimization (16% LGBQ vs. 6% Heterosexual) and sexual violence victimization (16% LGBQ vs. 7% Heterosexual), and were 2.4 times more likely to experience dating violence victimization and 2 times more likely to experience sexual violence victimization than heterosexual students. (p. 11)

The researcher's findings reveal the significant impacts of IPV even among LGBQ youth. One might wonder if these results are impacted by the approach of sex education within the school system and the lack of policies put in place to create safe and affirming spaces for LGBTQ students. Nevertheless, this recent research provides awareness of the vital need of resources, trainings, and services to address LGBTQ IPV focusing on adolescents and adults.

Data from the 2015 Transgender Survey shows 47 percent of respondents had experienced sexual assault at some point in their lifetime. It is important to note that these findings are only an indication from individuals who disclose or report these experiences. It is common for individuals within the LGBTQ community to refrain from reporting their intimate partners. One main factor is discrimination and fear of the police, hospitals, or even shelters (Finneran & Stephenson, 2013b; Strickler & Drew, 2015; Longobardi & Badenes-Ribera, 2017). The 2015 U.S. Transgender Survey report contained data on experiences and treatment of individuals who were transgender. The researchers' findings revealed that one in five (20 percent) respondents who were incarcerated in jail, prison, or juvenile detention in the past year were sexually assaulted by facility staff during that time (James et al., 2016, p. 191). Additionally, 52 percent of respondents who stayed at one or more homeless shelters in the past year reported being physically harassed, physically attacked, and/or sexually assaulted for being transgender (James et al., 2016, p. 176).

Although the 2013 VAWA was passed to provide more resources and to prevent these experiences, and the 2019 Reauthorization Act provides additional resources, it is evident that there are striking concerns of experiences of IPV in the LGBTQ community. The proposal by representatives Ayanna Pressley and Maire Newman for the Reauthorization Act brings awareness to the lack of resources and support to the LGBTQ community and survivors of IPV, particularly among the transgender community. Pressley informed NBC Out that 'Congress's efforts have overlooked the hurt and harm felt by LGBTQ+ survivors, especially trans women of color' (Yurcaba, 2021, p. 1). The new amendment presented by the representatives would offer the first grant program to further expand resources and services specifically to LGBTQ survivors of IPV. This amendment is presented at a time where there is a continued rise in violence toward the LGBTQ community, especially the transgender community, considering the continued increase in violent deaths. The Human Rights Campaign (HRC) has reported an alarming rate of violent deaths toward transgender or gender non-confirming people, with a disproportion rate in violence towards Black transgender women (HRC, 2021).

The status of the reauthorization of the VAWA, the presented evidence of the continued violence toward the LGBTQ community, and the lack of literature on these topics encouraged the authors to further explore this gap. There is a need to identify current literature that addresses the criminal justice system's responses to the LGBTQ community's experiences with IPV. Therefore, the scholars seek to conduct a systematic review capturing studies published after the passing of the 2013 VAWA to provide content on LGBTQ individuals' experiences of IPV, the criminal justice system, and resources for prevention. The scholars aim to contribute to the limited literature on this topic to provide awareness of research, best practices, and implications for policy.

Methods

The current study conducted an electronic search utilizing the following seven databases: Soci Index, Criminal Justice Abstracts, Academic Search Complete, APA psych articles, APA psych info, Legal Connections, and JSTOR. A Google Scholar search was also conducted to identify supportive literature for the study. Initial database inquiries presented a staggering number of articles with IPV as the main search term, with over 20,000 results. Narrowing the criteria to limit the article inclusion for this study was done by incorporating inclusion and exclusion criteria, as well as utilizing keywords to identify relevant articles. The authors utilized the following search terms: intimate partner violence (IPV), LGBTQ, transgender, nonbinary, gender nonconforming, and criminal justice. The authors then administered a search with inclusion criteria to further narrow down the articles.

Inclusion criteria

Studies had to include the following *inclusion criteria*: (1) Articles needed to be published after 2013. (2) Articles needed to be published in a peer review scholarly journal. (3) Articles needed to include or focus on participants that identified within the LGBTQ community. (4) Articles needed to include a focus on intimate partner violence and the criminal justice/legal system. (5) Articles also needed to be full-text and in English.

The results of the search using keywords across databases resulted in 521 articles that had potential relevance to the topic of interest for this literature review. The authors conducted a search of articles published from 2013–2020 to maintain the inclusion criteria. Article titles and abstracts were then reviewed for relevance to the current literature review. The authors reviewed the articles that were in full-text and English and obtained 47 articles. Implementing the keyword search, reviewing the title, abstract, and date of publication in relevance to the focus of the current literature review, 37 articles were excluded. Ten articles that met all inclusion criteria were selected for the literature review. Once the authors reviewed the references of the ten articles, five additional articles were eligible and met the inclusions criteria to be added to the literature review. This process concluded with a total of 15 articles incorporated in the literature review. Figure 8.1 provides a visual representation of the strategy process.

Figure 8.1: Flow chart indicating article search strategy

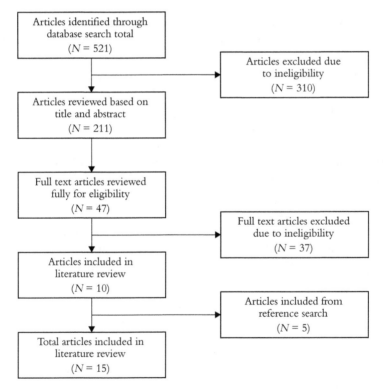

Analysis

The authors reviewed each article and affirmed that experiences of IPV and engagement with the criminal justice system were present. The articles in the current literature review encompassed various research methodologies including quantitative, qualitative, mixed methods, theoretical, as well as literature/systematic reviews. The research designs incorporated secondary analysis, semi-structured interviews, and surveys providing empirical evidence of experiences. The findings across articles highlighted an awareness of experiences with barriers to services, minority stressors, engagement with the police and legal systems, and important policy implications.

Results

Table 8.1 summarizes the information procured from the literature reviewed in relation to the effects of IPV in the LGBTQ community and experiences with the criminal justice system. The table includes the authors/year of publication, article title, sample/population, method, and themes. In reviewing the articles, the authors noted five key themes that stood out across the literature: (1) Legal system: various steps of the legal system that a victim of IPV has the potential to encounter. The articles reviewed involved interactions with police as well as reporting to authoritative figures (police, shelters, mental health professionals, and so on). (2) Intervention: elements such as enhancing community awareness, deduction of minority stress, and how to effectively respond to LGBTQ IPV victims were noted in the articles. (3) Policy: articles focusing on policy looking at the federal level, state level, as well as organizational-level policies that determine resources and services needed for LGBTQ IPV victims. (4) Social services: articles emphasizing services in terms of shelters, housing resources, hospitals, and therapeutic needs for LGBTQ survivors of IPV. (5) Training: articles noting how a *lack* of training for individuals within the legal system as well as service systems have caused many IPV survivors to not disclose their victimization or seek assistance when they need it the most. The researchers offered recommendations to address the necessity of continuing to advocate for training as well as affirming practices for LGBTQ survivors of IPV.

Themes

Legal system

In reviewing literature focused on IPV in the LGBTQ community and the criminal justice system, the authors noted several studies highlighting the impacts of the legal system on the LGBTQ community. The theme 'legal system' was determined by the consistent reference to treatment by law enforcement toward the LGBTQ community as well as laws that impact the LGBTQ community due to lack of inclusivity. Scholars illuminated the dire need to address inadequate policies and unacceptable treatment by the legal system that impacts the LGBTQ IPV community

Table 8.1: Literary summary of IPV in the LGBT community articles

Authors/year	Article title	Sample/population	Method	Area of focus
Decker, Littleton, & Edwards (2018)	An updated review of the literature on LGBTQ+ intimate partner violence	LGBTQ+ Community	Literature Review	Intervention Legal System (Reporting)
Langenderfer-Magruder, Whitfield, Walls, Kattari, & Ramos (2016)	Experiences of intimate partner violence and subsequent police reporting among lesbian, gay, bisexual, transgender, and queer adults in Colorado: comparing rates of cisgender and transgender victimization	(N = 1,139) LGBTQ Identified Participants	Quantitative: Survey design	Legal System (Reporting & Police)
Tesch & Bekerian (2015)	Hidden in the margins: a qualitative examination of what professionals in the domestic violence field know about transgender domestic violence	(N = 10) Participants (4) Domestic Violence Advocates (6) Active Researchers	Qualitative: Phenomenological Structured Interviews	Policy Social Services Training Legal System (Police)
Lantz (2020)	Victim, police, and prosecutorial responses to same-sex intimate partner violence: a comparative approach	Same-sex Identified Participants	Quantitative Secondary Data Analysis	Legal System (Police) Social Services
Baker, Buick, Kim, Moniz, & Nava (2013)	Lessons from examining same-sex intimate partner violence	Same-Sex Identified participants	Literature Review	Legal System

(continued)

Table 8.1: Literary summary of IPV in the LGBT community articles (continued)

Authors/year	Article title	Sample/population	Method	Area of focus
Morin (2014)	Re-traumatized: how gendered laws exacerbate the harm for same-sex victims of intimate partner violence	LGBTQ Community	Theoretical Paper	Legal System (Police) Social Services
Jordan, Mehrotra, & Fujikawa (2020)	Mandating inclusion: critical trans perspectives on domestic and sexual violence advocacy	(N = 10) Trans Identified Participants	Qualitative Study: Semi Structured Interviews	Social Services Policy Training Legal System
Lippy, Jumarali, Nnawulezi, Williams, & Burk (2020)	The impact of mandatory reporting laws on survivors of intimate partner violence: intersectionality, help-seeking and the need for change	(N = 2,462) Survivors 8% Identified Bisexual 4% Identified Gay or Lesbian 2% Identified Transgender or Gender Nonconforming 4% Identified Sexually Fluid	Convergent Mixed Method Qualitative: Survey Analysis Quantitative: Inductive Content Analysis	Legal System (Police) Social Services Policy
Guadalupe-Diaz & Jasinski (2017)	"I wasn't a priority, I wasn't a victim": challenges in help seeking for transgender survivors of intimate partner violence	(N = 18) Trans-Identified Participants	Qualitative: Grounded Theory Semi Structured Interviews	Social Services Legal System (Police)
Finneran & Stephenson (2013a)	Gay and bisexual men's perceptions of police helpfulness in response to male–male intimate partner violence	(N = 989) Gay and Bisexual Identified Men	Quantitative: Survey Design	Legal System (Police)

(continued)

Table 8.1: Literary summary of IPV in the LGBT community articles (continued)

Authors/year	Article title	Sample/population	Method	Area of focus
Goodmark (2013)	Transgender people, intimate partner abuse, and the legal system	Transgender Community	Theoretical Paper	Legal System (Police) Social Services Policy Intervention
Calton, Cattaneo, & Gebhard (2016)	Barriers to help seeking for lesbian, gay, bisexual, transgender, and queer survivors of intimate partner violence	LGBTQ Community	Literature Review	Legal System Policy Social Services Training
Langenderfer-Magruder, Walls, Whitfield, Kattari, & Ramos (2020)	Stalking victimization in LGBTQ adults: a brief report	(N = 1,116) LGBTQ Identified Participants	Quantitative: Secondary Data Analysis	Legal System (Reporting & Police)
Scheer, Martin-Storey, & Baams (2020)	Help-seeking barriers among sexual and gender minority individuals who experience intimate partner violence victimization	LGBTQ Community	Literature Review	Legal System (Police) Social Services Intervention
Strickler & Drew (2015)	Starting and maintaining LGTBQ antiviolence programs in a southern state	LGBTQ Community	Descriptive Field Research	Social Services

(Baker et al., 2013; Finneran & Stephenson, 2013a; Goodmark, 2013; Lippy et al., 2020; Langenderfer-Magruder et al., 2020; Lantz, 2020).

Research conducted by Finneran and Stephenson (2013a) focused on gay and bisexual men's perceptions of police helpfulness in response to IPV in which both the perpetrator and the victim are male. Their findings revealed that the majority of the sample (59.1 percent) reported perceiving that contacting the police would be less helpful for a gay or bisexual male IPV victim than for a heterosexual female IPV victim. From these findings the researchers informed readers 'that efforts must be made to improve both the supply of police assistance (that is, its quality and effectiveness) and gay/bisexual men's demand for this assistance (that is, their perceptions of its quality and effectiveness, in order words, police legitimacy' (Finneran & Stephenson, 2013a, p. 360).

The researchers also discussed the importance of police improving their communication with the LGBTQ community and increasing legitimacy in their efforts to report and assist with IPV encounters. Another study focusing on stalking victimization of the LGBTQ community and reporting revealed that transgender, bisexual, and queer participants had the lowest prevalence of reporting their victimization (Langenderfer-Magruder et al., 2020). The researchers also mentioned the impact of stigma toward the community and the additional marginalization they face, which impacts their reporting to the police. Research by Baker et al. (2013) reviewed how historically social stigma and marginalization has significantly influenced laws, policies, and treatment toward LGBTQ people and their experiences with IPV. The researchers offer the perspective to incorporate an ecological lens to view IPV among the LGBTQ community including influences of culture and gender. 'By focusing on the ways that ideological or superstructure frames influence laws and those who enforce them, we may learn about the social changes still needed to eliminate IPV' (Baker et al., 2013, p. 9). Learning about these social changes can further assist in identifying supportive interventions and services for the community.

Interventions

The theme 'intervention' was identified within the literature through discussions on ways interventions could be incorporated at various levels to prevent IPV and legal system abuses in the LGBTQ community. Interventions were suggested within the criminal justice system to address oppression, discrimination, and stigma toward LGBTQ IPV survivors. Recommendations were also presented in the literature to provide interventions and trainings for service providers and communities in efforts to bring awareness to violence prevention. Goodmark (2013) suggested providing interventions within the community to educate people on violence prevention to decrease and potentially eliminate the involvement of the criminal justice system, which has often oppressed the LGBTQ community. This was especially noted when working to provide inclusive and supportive interventions for those identifying within the transgender community. Langenderfer-Magruder et al. (2016) presented similar implications for agencies to provide affirming interventions and programs to address IPV for the transgender community. Implications for affirming theoretical frameworks were also expressed, for example, 'IPV-related service providers (for example victim advocates) should ensure that their theoretical approaches to intervention are comprehensive enough to meet the needs of LGBTQ clients and trans-identified clients in particular' (Langenderfer-Magruder et al., 2016, p. 866).

Research by Decker et al. (2018) highlights the importance of providing interventions through clinical implications to offer prevention techniques of inclusive education on IPV to educators, clinicians, and counselors. Their review of literature on LGBTQ IPV post-2015 brought attention to the lack of literature on prevention and thus revealed a need for future research to focus on interventions and preventative techniques to decrease IPV. Therefore, the researchers emphasized the urgent need for universal primary prevention programs for IPV. 'Universal primary prevention programs would likely prove effective for reducing IPV among LGBTQ+ youth because they address shared risk and protective factors' (Decker et al., 2018, p. 270). In addition to providing recommendations for interventions to address LGBTQ IPV, researchers recommended agencies to review their policies, their inclusivity in language, and their approaches to provide affirming and supportive resources and services.

Policy

Policy was acknowledged as a theme from the articles due to collective literature demanding policy changes to incorporate more inclusion, protection, and resources for the LGBTQ community experiencing IPV. Scholars shed light on the negligence and lack of policies set in place to protect this community from further violence and discrimination (Goodmark, 2013; Tesch & Bekerian, 2015; Calton et al., 2016; Jordan, et al., 2020). The findings from the articles presented in our study provide awareness of the significance of incorporating policies that will allow prevention of violence as well as funding for inclusive resources and services to the LGBTQ community.

Creating inclusivity within policy can not only address the treatment of the LGBTQ community by the legal system but can also incorporate supportive changes in treatment from social services within organizations, agencies, and the broader community. As stated, the proposed reauthorization of the

VAWA is intended to offer funding for grant programs to enhance resources and services for LGBTQ IPV survivors. The articles discussed in this section document the significance of affirming and inclusive policies.

Research conducted by Jordan et al. (2020) included ten in-depth interviews with transgender people who worked in domestic violence and sexual violence advocacy organizations. Their study highlighted five themes related to ongoing inequalities for transgender survivors. One theme brought awareness to the continued exclusion of policies to provide inclusive services to the transgender community. Their study brought further awareness to the lack of implementation of inclusive policy changes within organizations and agencies after the passing of the VAWA.

Calton et al.'s (2016) study evaluated the interactions between survivors and sources of help to try to maximize the utility of each encounter. Within their research efforts, the authors identified barriers such as limited understanding of the problem of LGBTQ IPV, stigma, and systemic inequities. Within the justice system (that is, civil courts, law enforcement, prosecution, and emergency shelters), many survivors of IPV who do not receive adequate assistance or who are discriminated against by an individual who represents a larger system are more reluctant to reach out for assistance when they need it the most. The researchers offered several recommendations to address the barriers faced by the LGBTQ community, which included recommendations for practice, theory, and policy. The researchers expressed the need to continue advocating for implementation of laws and affirming policies that will offer legal protections for the LGBTQ community (Calton et al., 2016). In addition, it was recommended to advocate for the regulation of VAWA. This regulation would essentially hold organizations and agencies accountable for following mandates of VAWA to ensure supportive and inclusive services for the LGBTQ community.

Lantz (2020) advised that inclusive policies should be enacted and examined within the criminal justice system to address LGBTQ IPV survivors' needs for accessibility and access to resources, stating that 'important policy implication of these results concerns the need to further evaluate safe housing options, and related policies, which may be both accessible and protective for such nontraditional victims of IPV' (p. 219). The scholars' research illuminates the connectivity of policy and social services in our society.

Social services

The theme 'social services' was derived from findings and future implications among several articles in the current study. The researchers of these articles addressed the insufficiency of affirming and supportive services offered for LGBTQ IPV survivors. In addition, the articles presented findings on the need to offer inclusive safe spaces for the community, particularly shelters, to create spaces that take into consideration the gender of survivors (Goodmark, 2013; Morin, 2014; Calton et al., 2016; Guadalupe-Diaz & Jasinski, 2017; Lantz, 2020; Scheer et al., 2020). Furthermore, researchers also focused on the scarcity of funding for social services to provide adequate resources to the community and trainings to agency workers (Morin, 2014; Guadalupe-Diaz & Jasinski, 2017; Scheer et al., 2020).

Guadalupe-Diaz and Jasinski (2017) conducted a qualitative study with 18 trans-identified survivors of IPV. Their findings provided awareness that many of their participants avoided formal forms of support and sought out support from friends and family due to barriers they faced from social service providers based on gender. It was indicated that the participants could not find services or spaces that were accepting and affirming of their identities. The researchers expressed the urgency for more trans-inclusive services as well as more educational programs that offer safe and approachable spaces for IPV survivors (Guadalupe-Diaz & Jasinski, 2017).

While Morin (2014) expressed a similar call to action for more educational trainings and inclusive services for LGBTQ survivors of IPV, the scholar also stressed the vital necessity of funding. Morin expressed the importance of policymakers supporting local, federal, and national efforts to fund programs to address violence toward the LGBTQ community and survivors of IPV. It is noted that this funding can be allocated to support culturally competent trainings for service providers and law enforcement. In addition, the funding could support prevention programing for adults and adolescents (Morin, 2014).

Lippy et al. (2020) expressed similar recommendations supporting Morin's research to focus on changes from policymakers to address supportive services for LGBTQ IPV survivors. Their research reviewed IPV survivors seeking services and the impact of mandated reporting laws. Through their findings the researchers brought awareness to the challenges LGBTQ IPV survivors face when seeking formal services. The challenges revolved around barriers faced due to their identities including sexual orientation, gender identity, and race. The researchers recommended for policymakers and advocates to review these laws to identify ways to promote more opportunities for survivors to seek help. In addition, they suggested for social service providers at agencies to also examine their policies in efforts to create a more inclusive and welcoming space for survivors to seek affirming services (Lippy et al., 2020).

Strickler and Drew (2015) expressed the significance of offering services to LGBTQ IPV survivors due to the unfortunate common reports of negative experiences in seeking services from traditional service providers, such as 'experiences of social marginalization, social stigmatization, and actual or perceived discrimination, punishment, and/or re-victimization when seeking services' (p. 86). Having awareness of the continued marginalization and service disparities toward the community, Strickler and Drew assisted in the development of the antiviolence project with a mission to focus on LGBTQ health and safety. The project involved a community-based approach that highlighted social constructs and involvement from community members when providing services and resources to address LGBTQ IPV. The framework behind the project included the following values: co-advocacy, community centered, intersectionality, racial justice, praxis, confidentiality, self-determination, support, accountability, transparency, and principled struggle (Strickler & Drew, 2015). These elements would work to address the social stigma and marginalization that commonly takes place toward LGBTQ IPV survivors. It also incorporates an empowerment perspective by involving LGBTQ IPV survivors as leaders and advocates to address the changes needed for adequate and inclusive services and policies.

Training

While there was significant evidence of the importance of supportive social services and funding for programs to support LGBTQ IPV survivors, the authors noted multiple articles addressing the critical value of training. The trainings recommended encompassed macro and micro aspects, which included law enforcement, court systems, service providers at shelters, clinics, and community organizations (Morin, 2014; Tesch & Bekerian, 2015; Calton et al., 2016; Jordan et al., 2020; Lantz, 2020).

Lantz's (2020) study examining police responses to same-sex IPV incidents illustrates the importance of offering training for law enforcement to address preconceived notions of IPV in LGBTQ relationships. The researcher suggested trainings should include an overview on specific concepts that impact the community, such as the potential harm in disclosing their sexual orientation or gender identity. Findings from Tesch and Bekerian (2015) supported the recommendations of training for law enforcement. It was revealed that during the time of their study, police officers often did not receive training to properly assist with LGBTQ IPV incidents, especially incidents that include the transgender community.

The researchers highlighted a history of mistreatment and conflict the transgender community experienced from law enforcement. They offered the following recommendation to address the historical context of this treatment along with barriers the LGBTQ community experiences: 'law enforcement officers should consider offering trainings in how to best respond to the needs of victims of domestic abuse; something that could be empirically evaluated for efficacy in future research' (Tesch & Bekerian, 2015, p. 408). Another recommendation was for law enforcement to be more affirming and accessible to the transgender community. If this approach was still in need of further development due to lack of training, a liaison was suggested to be present to assist with LGBTQ IPV incidents.

Although the necessity of training for law enforcement was evident within the articles, there was also evidence of a need for training service providers. Scheer et al. (2020) specifically discussed sexual gender minority (SGM) affirmative training for healthcare settings, agencies, and even the legal system. The researchers also incorporated techniques such as SGM inclusive language, awareness of oppression toward the LGBTQ community, along with minority stresses experienced by the community to be included in these trainings. In addition, they suggested highlighting the strengths and resilience of the community in trainings to bring further awareness of the perseverance of the community, which often faces adversities.

Discussion

The findings of the current review revealed various factors involving the LGBTQ community and the experiences of IPV in the criminal justice system. Minority stress factors such as stigma; fear of being 'outed' to family, friends, and work colleagues; and internalized homophobia are but a few factors on the individual level that contribute to victims of IPV not reporting their abuse. Findings from the individual level suggest that on a systematic level there are major barriers for victims to seek assistance. The fear of seeking help on the victim's side makes it difficult for those who want to help to actually assist individuals to get away from a volatile situation. In addition to these discussed factors, the authors identified gaps concerning gender variables of individuals seeking assistance for IPV, even though protections were put in place with VAWA (2013) to specifically provide protections and support for this underserved and marginalized population. Based on these findings, it provides the opportunity to address future implications focusing on policy, future research, training, and interventions.

Conclusion: implications

The current study sheds light on the continued need for research to address policy implications for treatment of LGBTQ IPV survivors and the legal system. Policies revolving around protection orders, access to safe housing, shelters, and the legal system are still identified to be discriminatory to the LGBTQ population and especially to the transgender community. Accountability for safety and prevention is imperative within the legal system and social services at a federal and state level to address this marginalized and oppressed community. This accountability starts with providing vital inclusive and affirming services, protective policies, ongoing trainings, and supportive funding to deconstruct barriers toward the LGBTQ community.

In considering future research, the authors noted it is imperative to capture experiences from the LGBTQ community through empirical and longitudinal studies to understand these experiences over time in accessing services and interactions with the legal system instead of a snapshot of experiences. Furthermore, research should include larger sample sizes and diverse experiences of intersecting identities to provide further awareness of experiences and needs among the community.

Lastly, an absence of adequate diversity infrastructure for officers and service providers can create barriers and manifest additional risk to the wellbeing and safety of the LGBTQ community. By administering trainings that shed light on inclusive approaches and evidence-based interventions these public servants can become more aware and better equipped to meet the community's needs. This can strengthen a sense of safety, acceptance, and trustworthiness for IPV survivors. Therefore, persistent advocacy for changes while supporting and empowering survivors is imperative.

References

Badenes-Ribera, L., Bonilla-Campos, A., Frias-Navarro, D., Pons-Salvador, G., & Monterde-i-Bort, H. (2016) 'Intimate partner violence in self-identified lesbians: a systematic review of its prevalence and correlates', *Trauma, Violence, & Abuse*, 17(3): 284–297.

Baker, N., Buick, J., Kim, S., Moniz, S., & Nava, K. (2013) 'Lessons from examining same-sex intimate partner violence', *Sex Roles*, 69(3–4): 182–192. https://doi-org.ezproxy.ollusa.edu/10.1007/s11199-012-0218-3

Buller, A.M., Devries, K.M., Howard, L.M., & Bacchus, L.J. (2014) 'Associations between intimate partner violence and health among men who have sex with men: a systematic review and meta-analysis', *PLoS Medicine*, 11(3): 1–12.

Calton, J.M., Cattaneo, L.B., & Gebhard, K.T. (2016) 'Barriers to help seeking for lesbian, gay, bisexual, transgender, and queer survivors of intimate partner violence', *Trauma, Violence, & Abuse*, 17(5): 585–600.

CDC (Centers for Disease Control and Prevention) (2019) 'Preventing intimate partner violence'. https://www.cdc.gov/violenceprevention/intimatepartnerviolence/fastfact.html

Decker, M., Littleton, H.L., & Edwards, K.M. (2018) 'An updated review of the literature on LGBTQ intimate partner violence', *Current Sexual Health Reports*, 10(4): 265–272. https://doi.org/10.1007/s11930-018-0173-2

Finneran, C. & Stephenson, R. (2013a) 'Gay and bisexual men's perceptions of police helpfulness in response to male–male intimate partner violence', *Western Journal of Emergency Medicine*, 14(4): 354–362.

Finneran, C. & Stephenson, R. (2013b) 'Intimate partner violence among men who have sex with men: a systematic review', *Trauma, Violence, & Abuse*, 14(2): 168–185.

Goodmark, L. (2013) 'Transgender people, intimate partner abuse, and the legal system', *Harvard Civil Rights-Civil Liberties Law Review*, 48(51): 51–104.

Guadalupe-Diaz, X.L. & Jasinski, J. (2017) '"I wasn't a priority, I wasn't a victim": challenges in help seeking for transgender survivors of intimate partner violence', *Violence Against Women*, 23(6): 772–792. https://doi.org/10.1177/1077801216650288.

HRC (Human Rights Campaign) (2021) 'Fatal violence against the transgender and gender non-conforming community in 2021'. https://www.hrc.org/resources/fatal-violence-against-the-transgender-and-gender-non-conforming-community-in-2021

James, S.E., Herman, J.L., Rankin, S., Keisling, M., Mottet, L., & Anafi, M. (2016) 'The report of the 2015 U.S. Transgender Survey', Washington, DC: National Center for Transgender Equality. https://transequality.org/sites/default/files/docs/usts/USTS-Full-Report-Dec17.pdf

Jordan, S.P., Mehrotra, G.R., & Fujikawa, K.A. (2020) 'Mandating inclusion: critical trans perspectives on domestic and sexual violence advocacy', *Violence Against Women*, 26(6–7): 531–554.

Langenderfer-Magruder, L., Walls, N.E., Whitfield, D.L., Kattari, S.K., & Ramos, D. (2020) 'Stalking victimization in LGBTQ adults: a brief report', *Journal of Interpersonal Violence*, 35(5–6): 1442–1453.

Langenderfer-Magruder, L., Whitfield, D.L., Walls, N.E., Kattari, S.K., & Ramos, D. (2016) 'Experiences of intimate partner violence and subsequent police reporting among lesbian, gay, bisexual, transgender, and queer adults in Colorado: comparing rates of cisgender and transgender victimization', *Journal of Interpersonal Violence*, 31(5): 855–871.

Lantz, B. (2020) 'Victim, police, and prosecutorial responses to same-sex intimate partner violence: a comparative approach', *Journal of Contemporary Criminal Justice*, 36(2): 206–227.

Lippy, C., Jumarali, S.N., Nnawulezi, N.A., Williams, E.P., & Burk, C. (2020) 'The impact of mandatory reporting laws on survivors of intimate partner violence: intersectionality, help-seeking and the need for change', *Journal of Family Violence*, 35(3): 255–267.

Longobardi, C. & Badenes-Ribera, L. (2017) 'Intimate partner violence in same-sex relationships and the role of sexual minority stressors: a systematic review of the past 10 years', *Journal of Child and Family Studies*, 26(8): 2039–2049.

Morin, C. (2014) 'Re-traumatized: how gendered laws exacerbate the harm for same-sex victims of intimate partner violence', *New England Journal on Criminal & Civil Confinement*, 40(2): 477–497.

Reisner, S. L. & Hughto, J. M. (2019) 'Comparing the health of non-binary and binary transgender adults in a statewide non-probability sample', *PLoS One*, 14(8): e0221583.

Rothman, E.F., Exner, D., & Baughman, A.L. (2011) 'The prevalence of sexual assault against people who identify as gay, lesbian, or bisexual in the United States: a systematic review', Trauma, *Violence, & Abuse*, 12(2): 55–66.

Scheer, J.R., Martin-Storey, A., & Baams, L. (2020) 'Help-seeking barriers among sexual and gender minority individuals who experience intimate partner violence victimization', in B. Russell (ed.), *Intimate Partner Violence and the LGBT+ Community*, Cham: Springer, pp. 139–158.

Semprevivo, L.K. (2021) 'Dating and sexual violence victimization among lesbian, gay, bisexual, and questioning youth: considering the importance of gender and sexual orientation', *Journal of Aggression, Maltreatment & Trauma*, 30(5): 662–678.

Strickler, E., Jr. & Drew, Q. (2015) 'Starting and sustaining LGBTQ antiviolence programs in a southern state', *Partner Abuse*, 6(1): 78–106.

Tesch, B.P. & Bekerian, D.A. (2015) 'Hidden in the margins: a qualitative examination of what professionals in the domestic violence field know about transgender domestic violence', *Journal of Gay & Lesbian Social Services*, 27(4): 391–411. https://doi-org.ezproxy.ollusa.edu/10.1080/10538720.2015.1087267

Violence Against Women Reauthorization Act Pub. L. No. 113-4, 127 STAT. 54 (2013) https://www.congress.gov/bill/113th-congress/senate-bill/47/text

Violence Against Women Reauthorization Act, H.R. 1585, 116th Cong. (2019) https://www.congress.gov/bill/116th-congress/house-bill/1585?q=%7B%22search%22%3A%5B%22H.R.+1585%22%5D%7D&r=1&s=1

Walters, M.L., Chen J., & Breiding, M.J. (2013) 'The National Intimate Partner and Sexual Violence Survey (NISVS): 2010 Findings on victimization by sexual orientation', Atlanta, GA: National Center for Injury Prevention and Control, Centers for Disease Control and Prevention.

Yurcaba, J. (2021) 'Exclusive: Violence Against Women Act to offer support to LGBTQ survivors', NBC News Out Politics and Policy, March 17. https://www.nbcnews.com/feature/nbc-out/exclusive-violence-against-women-act-offer-support-lgbtq-survivors-n1261331

9

Health Covariates of Intimate Partner Violence in a National Transgender Sample

Victoria Kurdyla, Adam M. Messinger,
and Xavier L. Guadalupe-Diaz

Upwards of half of transgender individuals in the United States will experience abuse by a romantic or sexual partner in their lifetimes (James et al., 2016). This intimate partner violence (IPV) can include psychological (that is, verbal or controlling), physical, or sexual abuse, as well as anti-transgender identity abuse (hereafter termed 'identity abuse') whereby the abuser leverages the survivor's transgender status as a means of control. Research on smaller transgender samples indicates that IPV victimization is associated with an increased risk of several adverse health conditions (AHCs), including but not limited to negative mental health effects, substance use, and poor physical health (for example, Messinger & Guadalupe-Diaz, 2020; Peitzmeier et al., 2020). However, research with more representative transgender samples is needed to verify these associations. Additionally, the transgender IPV literature has not examined the possible associations between the full range of IPV forms and AHC types, nor between IPV forms and the number of different AHC types experienced. Clarifying the connections between distinct IPV forms and AHC types will have important implications for transgender-specific screening protocols and service provision.

Through a secondary analysis of the 2015 U.S. Transgender Survey (USTS) – the largest national sample of transgender individuals to date ($N = 27{,}715$; James et al., 2016) – the current paper elucidates the connection between

IPV form and AHC type. Controlling for demographics, regressions assessed whether type of IPV (identity, controlling, physical, and sexual) each predict several AHCs – psychological distress, suicidal ideation, illicit drug use, prescription drug misuse, binge alcohol use, poor general health, and HIV positive status – as well as the number of different AHC types experienced.

Adverse health conditions (AHCs) and IPV victimization

Research on predominantly cisgender survivors has found IPV victimization to be associated with poor mental and physical health as well as alcohol and substance use, with scholars positing that these associations are a direct outcome of or coping mechanisms for IPV victimization (Carbone-Lopez et al., 2006; Devries et al., 2014; Cafferky et al., 2016). Although one may speculate that similar patterns exist for transgender survivors, IPV–AHC links may actually be weaker among transgender populations, where baseline rates of depression, suicidal ideation, and substance use are reported to be higher than for cisgender populations (Benotsch et al., 2013; Tebbe & Moradi, 2016).

While studies on transgender IPV have found connections between IPV and certain AHCs, this picture is incomplete. Research on transgender samples has consistently shown that IPV is associated with psychological distress (White-Hughto et al., 2017; Goldenberg et al., 2018; Parsons et al., 2018; Bukowski et al., 2019; Peitzmeier et al., 2019) and illicit drug use (Brennan et al., 2012; Keuroghlian et al., 2015; Parsons et al., 2018). However, findings have been less clear regarding the association between IPV and two other AHCs: binge alcohol use and HIV status. For example, Peitzmeier et al. (2019) found no association between binge alcohol use and identity IPV among transgender people, but this study did not include other forms of IPV. Meanwhile, two studies with transgender samples used a composite substance abuse variable (with binge alcohol use being one of several possible qualifying conditions) but drew conflicting conclusions regarding the association between substance abuse and IPV (Keuroghlian et al., 2015; Goldenberg et al., 2018). Similarly, Brennan et al. (2012) found a positive association between IPV and HIV positive status among transgender people, but other studies on transgender samples found no association between IPV and HIV status (Goldenberg et al., 2018), nor with any sexually transmitted infection (Peitzmeier et al., 2019). Additionally, researchers have not explored the associations between IPV and suicidal ideation, prescription drug use, and physical health for transgender survivors.

Another underexamined question is whether IPV victimization among transgender people is associated with experiencing a greater number of AHC types. In a sample of transgender people, Parsons et al. (2018) found a positive association between IPV and experiencing a greater number of 'syndemics', including polydrug use and depression, as well as child sexual abuse and IPV. Because their syndemic count variable included non-AHC violence items and excluded a variety of AHC types, their study only hints at – but cannot confirm – that transgender IPV survivors are more likely to experience a greater variety of AHC types than non-survivors.

Importantly, even when publications in this literature identified a significant relationship between IPV and an AHC type, only certain forms of IPV were separately assessed. For example, some of the aforementioned studies measured only one form of IPV, such as physical IPV (Bukowski et al., 2019) or identity IPV (Peitzmeier et al., 2019). Other studies operationalized IPV as a composite measure, integrating participants who experienced any combination of different IPV types (Brennan et al., 2012; Keuroghlian et al., 2015; White–Hughto et al., 2017; Goldenberg et al., 2018; Parsons et al., 2018). Such operationalizing obscures potential differences in the relationships between AHCs and distinct forms of IPV. Additionally, prior transgender research on IPV and AHC associations has often relied upon smaller samples (n = 131–493). The resulting issue of decreased generalizability – in combination with the previously discussed lack of specificity in IPV measures, and a narrow range of AHC types assessed – highlights the need for research with larger and more geographically diverse transgender samples, which, in turn, can accommodate analyses comparing distinct IPV forms and AHC types.

The present study

While researchers have found a link between some IPV forms and some AHC types, no research to our knowledge has fully explored the possible associations between each form of IPV victimization and a broad range of AHCs, or IPV's impact on the number of AHC types experienced in transgender populations. Informed by the literature, we first hypothesize that each AHC type is positively associated with at least one form of IPV victimization. For our second hypothesis, we predict that each IPV form is positively associated with experiencing a greater number of AHC types.

Methods

The present research tests the hypotheses through a secondary data analysis of the U.S. Transgender Survey. In 2015, the National Center for Transgender Equality collected online surveys from a purposive and snowball sample of 27,715 transgender adults from all 50 states, Washington, DC, and several US territories and military bases. This represents the largest known study to date of the US transgender population, defined inclusively as those whose gender identity differs from their sex assigned at birth, irrespective of whether they self-identify as 'transgender'. Due to low proportions of missing data, listwise deletion of missing data was utilized. All analyses in this chapter apply age and racial–ethnic sampling based upon the 2014 US Census Bureau's American Community Survey. (For a complete methodology report, see James et al., 2016.)

Measures

Demographics

Several respondent characteristics were controlled for in the analysis. *Gender* categories included crossdresser, trans woman, trans man, assigned female at birth genderqueer/nonbinary (AFAB GQ/NB), and assigned male at birth genderqueer/nonbinary (AMAB GQ/NB). *Sexual orientation* categories included identifying as asexual, bisexual, gay/lesbian/same-gender-loving, heterosexual, pansexual, queer, or an unlisted sexual orientation. Mirroring the US Census Bureau's American Community Survey, participants' *race-ethnicity* was categorized as Alaska Native/American Indian only (ANAI), Asian American or Native Hawaiian/Pacific Islander (NHPI) only, African American only, Latinx only, White or Middle Eastern/North African (MENA) only, or Multiracial/Unlisted race. *Citizenship status* categories included citizen, documented resident, or undocumented resident.

Homelessness status was coded 0 if never and 1 if ever experiencing homelessness. *Disability status* was coded as 0 if they did not identify and 1 if they identified as a person with a disability. *Transgender outness* measures the mean degree of outness about one's transgender identity, coded as being out to (1) none, (2) some, (3) most, or (4) all people in their life. This measure averaged a series of survey items assessing outness to a range of acquaintance types. *Gender visual conformity* measured the self-reported frequency with which a participant is perceived by others to be transgender, coded as (1) visual nonconformers (responses 'always' and 'most of the time'), (2) somewhat visual conforming (response 'sometimes'), and (3) visual conformers (responses 'rarely' and 'never'). *Household annual income* was coded as follows: (0) no income; (1) $1–9,999; (2) $10,000–24,999; (3) $25,000–49,999; (4) $50,000–100,000; (5) $100,00 or more. A continuous age item was recoded as (1) 18–24, (2) 25–44, (3) 45–64, and (4) 65 or older. For complete details of how each of the variables was measured in the questionnaire and coded, please see Messinger et al. (2021).

Lifetime intimate partner violence (IPV) victimization

Adapted from the National Intimate Partner and Sexual Violence Survey (Breiding et al., 2014), participants were asked: "Have any of your romantic or sexual partners ever …?" followed by a series of yes/no items measuring various tactics of identity, controlling, physical, and sexual IPV lifetime victimization. Participants who endorsed at least one tactic of a particular IPV form were coded as having experienced that IPV form, resulting in four any/none composite measures: *identity IPV* (if a partner ever would not let them have their hormones, threatened to 'out' them, told them that they were not a 'real' woman or man, or pressured them to detransition to their sex assigned at birth), *controlling IPV* (if a partner ever tried to keep them from seeing or talking to family or friends, kept them from having money for their own use, kept them from leaving the house when they wanted to, hurt someone they love, threatened to hurt a pet or threatened to take a pet away from them, would not let them have other medications, stalked them, threatened to use their immigration status against them, or made threats to physically harm them), *physical IPV* (if a partner ever slapped them, pushed or shoved them, hit them with a fist or something hard, kicked them, hurt them by pulling their hair, slammed them against something, tried to hurt them by choking or suffocating them, beaten them, burned them on purpose, or used a knife or gun on them), and *sexual IPV* (if a partner ever forced them to engage in 'sexual activity', or had ever perpetrated against them 'unwanted sexual contact' such as 'oral, genital, or anal contact or penetration, forced fondling, rape'). (An additional controlling IPV item – 'threatened to call the police on you' – was omitted from analysis because of a strong possibility that this measures perpetration rather than victimization.) Participants were coded a 0 if they did not answer yes to any of the answered IPV tactics for that measure or if they were not asked any of the IPV questions due to never having been in a romantic or sexual relationship. Participants were coded as missing if they skipped more than one-third of the measure's items.

AHCs

Seven AHCs were measured. Regarding the first three AHCs – illicit drug use, prescription drug misuse, and binge alcohol use – participants were asked a choose-all-that-apply substance use screener: "Have you ever had a drink of any type of alcoholic beverage, smoked part or all of a cigarette, or used any of the other following substances?" Participants were coded as having engaged in *past-30-day illicit drug use* if they endorsed 'Illegal or illicit drugs (such as cocaine, crack, heroin, LSD, meth, inhalants like poppers or whippits)' for the substance abuse screener, and if they also indicated on a follow-up question that they 'last used any illegal/illicit drug' within the past 30 days. Participants were coded as having engaged in *past-30-day prescription drug misuse* if they endorsed 'Prescription drugs (such as Oxycontin, Xanax, Adderall, Ambien) that weren't prescribed to you, or that you didn't take as prescribed' for the aforementioned substance abuse screener, and if they also answered on a follow-up question that they 'last used any prescription drugs not prescribed or not prescribed to you' within the past 30 days. Participants were coded as having engaged in *past-30-day binge alcohol use* if they endorsed 'Alcohol (such as beer, wine, or hard liquor)' for the substance abuse screener, if they also indicated on a follow-up question that they 'last drank an alcoholic beverage' within the past 30 days, and if they provided any non-zero numeric answer to the subsequent contingency question: 'During the past 30 days, on how many days did you have 5 or more drinks on the same occasion? By "occasion," we mean at the same time or within a couple of hours of each other.'

In addition, *most-recently-tested HIV positive status* was coded as 1 (a positive most-recent HIV test) if participants indicated on a screening question that they had 'ever been tested for HIV' and, on a follow-up question, answered that 'result of your most recent HIV test' was 'HIV positive or reactive, meaning I have HIV'. The variable was coded as 0 (not having a positive most-recent HIV test) if participants had never been tested for HIV, or if they had been tested and were HIV negative, received unclear test results, or never received their test results. *Self-reported current general health* was coded as 1 (high general health) if participants answered excellent, very good, or good – and it was coded as 0 (low general health) if participants answered either fair or poor – to the question: 'Would you say that in general your health is …' As operationalized by the USTS research team (James et al., 2016), participants were dichotomously coded as experiencing 'serious' *past-30-day psychological distress* if they received a total score of at least 13 out of 24 on the Kessler Psychological Distress Scale K6, which assesses the frequency (on a four-point scale of none, a little, some, or all the time) with which participants in the past 30 days felt six indicators of psychological distress: so sad that nothing could cheer them up, nervous, restless or fidgety, hopeless, that everything was an effort, or worthless (Kessler et al., 2003). Lastly, participants were coded as experiencing *past-year suicidal ideation* if they answered 'yes' (rather than 'no') to the question: 'The next few questions are about thoughts of suicide. At any time in the past 12 months did you seriously think about trying to kill yourself?'

Number of AHC types experienced

Finally, a count variable was constructed to assess the *number of AHC types experienced*, from zero (did not experience any AHCs) to seven (experienced all seven assessed AHC types). Being coded as 1 on any of the aforementioned AHCs increased this count variable by one. Due to a small number of participants experiencing six or seven AHC types (weighted *n* = 67), for regression analyses, participants were coded as five on this variable if they experienced five, six, or seven AHC types.

Analytic method

In addition to weighted univariate analyses, seven weighted logistic regressions each included as a dependent variable one of the seven different adverse outcomes (past 30 days psychological distress, past year suicidal ideation, past 30 days illicit drug use, past 30 days prescription drug misuse, past 30 days binge alcohol use, most recently tested HIV status, self-reported current general health), with all four of the IPV types included as predictors in every model. Lastly, a weighted linear regression analysis was conducted that utilized the adverse outcome count as the dependent variable, again with all four IPV type variables included as predictors. All models also adjusted for gender, sexual orientation, race-ethnicity, citizenship status, ever being homeless, disability status, transgender outness, visual conformity, household income, and age.

Results

Turning to Table 9.1, the sample was comprised predominantly of trans women (33.4 percent), trans men (29.4 percent), and AFAB GQ/NB individuals (27.7 percent), with less than 10 percent identifying as either AMAB GQ/NB or crossdressers. Most identified as LGBQ+ (85.2 percent), White/MENA only (62.8 percent), US citizens (97 percent), never homeless (69.7 percent), and without a disability (72.4 percent). Participants were on average out about their transgender status to some-to-most people in their lives ($M = 2.61$, SD = 0.65). They tended to report medium to high gender visual conformity ($M = 2.46$, SD = 0.69), a mean annual household income of \$25,000–49,999 ($M = 2.94$, SD = 1.41), and a mean age of 31 (SD = 12.95).

Turning to Table 9.2, over *half* (55.2 percent) experienced some form of IPV victimization within their lifetimes, with participants most likely to experience controlling (38.2 percent) and physical IPV (35.2 percent), followed closely by anti-transgender identity IPV (27.7 percent) and sexual IPV (22.6 percent). Regarding adverse health conditions, on average participants reported their current general health to be between 'good' and 'very good' ($M = 2.69$, SD = 1.04). Within the past 30 days, the most prevalent AHCs were psychological distress (39.2 percent) and binge alcohol use (26.6 percent), followed more distantly by prescription drug misuse (7 percent) and illicit drug use (3.7 percent). An alarming 48.3 percent experienced suicidal ideation within the past year. Of the full non-missing sample – including both those who have (weighted $n = 14,692$) and have not ever been tested for HIV (weighted $n = 12,096$) – 1.4 percent reported their most recent test to be positive; however, when limiting the denominator to those who have ever been tested, the positive rate nearly doubles to

Table 9.1: Sample demographics ($N = 27{,}715$)

Variable	Weighted n	Weighted % or M (SD)
Gender		
Crossdresser	674	2.5
Trans Woman	8,971	33.4
Trans Man	7,892	29.4
AFAB GQ/NB	7,449	27.7
AMAB GQ/NB	1,848	6.9
Sexual Orientation		
Asexual	2,670	10.0
Bisexual	3,829	14.3
Gay or Lesbian	4,236	15.8
Heterosexual	3,965	14.8
Pansexual	4,790	17.9
Queer	5,659	21.1
Unlisted Sexual Orientation	1,683	6.3
Race-Ethnicity		
ANAI only	178	0.7
Asian American/NHPI only	1,368	5.1
African American only	3,377	12.6
Latinx only	4,456	16.6
White/MENA only	16,844	62.8
Multiracial/Unlisted Race	609	2.3
Citizenship Status		
US Citizen	26,126	97.4
Documented Resident	608	2.3
Undocumented Resident	99	0.4
Has Ever Been Homeless	8,104	30.3
Has a Disability	7,389	27.6
Transgender Outness (M, SD)	25,928	2.61 (0.65)
Gender Visual Conformity (M, SD)	25,928	2.46 (0.69)
Household Annual Income Bracket (M, SD)	24,585	2.94 (1.41)
Age (M, SD)	26,833	30.99 (12.95)

Notes: Results weighted for racial-ethnic composition of US population. AFAB GQ/NB = assigned female at birth *and* either nonbinary or genderqueer identified; AMAB GQ/NB = assigned male at birth *and* either nonbinary or genderqueer identified; ANAI = Alaska Native or American Indian; NHPI = Native Hawaiian or Pacific Islander; MENA = Middle Eastern or North African. Household annual income bracket = 0 (no income), 1 ($1–9,999), 2 ($10,000–24,999), 3 ($25,000–49,999), 4 ($50,000–100,000), 5 ($100,000 or more).

Table 9.2: Prevalence of lifetime IPV victimization and recent adverse health conditions ($N = 27,715$)

Variable	Weighted n	Weighted % or M (SD)
Lifetime Intimate Partner Violence (IPV)		
Anti-Transgender Identity IPV	7,427	27.7
Controlling IPV	10,243	38.2
Physical IPV	9,411	35.2
Sexual IPV	6,042	22.6
Any IPV	14,773	55.2
Past-30-Day Illicit Drug Use	976	3.7
Past-30-Day Prescription Drug Misuse	1,850	7.0
Past-30-Day Binge Alcohol Use	7,102	26.6
Most-Recently-Tested HIV Positive Status	376	1.4
Self-Reported Current General Health (M, SD)	27,691	2.69 (1.04)
Past-30-Day Psychological Distress	10,308	39.2
Past-Year Suicidal Ideation	12,948	48.3
# of Adverse Health Conditions Experienced		
0	824	3.2
1	8,198	31.8
2	8,603	33.4
3	5,741	22.3
4	1,962	7.6
5	371	1.4
6	66	0.3
7	1	0.0
M (SD)	26,630	2.05 (1.07)

Notes: Results weighted for racial-ethnic composition of US population. IPV = intimate partner violence. Any IPV = experiencing anti-transgender identity, controlling, physical, and/or sexual IPV during lifetime. # of adverse health conditions experienced = coded as +1 for each of the following experienced: any lifetime IPV, past-30-day illicit drug use, past-30-day prescription drug misuse, past-30-day binge alcohol use, most-recently-tested HIV positive status, low or poor self-reported current general health, past-30-day psychological distress, and past-year suicidal ideation.

2.6 percent, with an additional 1.3 percent reporting either unclear results or never receiving the results. Lastly, on average, participants experienced two AHCs (SD = 1.07). Nearly all participants (96.8 percent) experienced at least one AHC, with the majority experiencing one (31.8 percent), two (33.4 percent), or three AHCs (22.3), and far fewer experiencing four (7.6 percent) or five to seven AHCs (1.7 percent).

Bivariate logistic regressions (tables available upon request from second author) indicated that most assessed AHCs were significantly positively associated with each other (OR = 1.38–9.60, $p < 0.05$). Exceptions involved HIV positive status (which was significantly *negatively* associated with psychological distress and suicidal ideation – OR = 0.50–0.58 – and *not* associated with low general health, prescription drug misuse, or binge alcohol use) or low general health (which, beyond not being associated with HIV status, was also not associated with illicit drug use). However, with the exception of sexual IPV not being associated with HIV status, bivariate logistic regressions found that each form of IPV (identity, controlling, physical, and sexual IPV) significantly positively predicted each assessed AHC (OR = 1.17–2.07, $p < 0.05$). Likewise, using the recoded AHC count variable (with five to seven AHCs coded as five), bivariate ordinal logistic regressions found each IPV form to significantly positively predict the number of AHCs experienced (OR = 1.40–1.87, $p < 0.05$).

Multiple regression results are reported in Table 9.3. Seven logistic regression models respectively tested whether each IPV form (identity, controlling, physical, and sexual IPV) predicted the different assessed AHCs, controlling for the remaining three IPV forms, as well as gender, sexual orientation, race-ethnicity, citizenship status, ever being homelessness, disability status, transgender outness, visual conformity, household income, and age. Although not all IPV forms were associated with all AHCs, every association that was significant ($p < 0.05$) indicated that IPV was associated with *greater* odds of experiencing AHCs (OR = 1.12–1.66). Moreover, experiencing physical IPV was found to significantly associate with *greater* odds of experiencing the greatest variety of AHC types, for a total of five different AHCs: suicidal ideation, binge alcohol use, prescription drug misuse, HIV positive status, and illicit drug use (OR = 1.12–1.66). Next, sexual IPV was significantly associated with *greater* odds of experiencing four different AHCs: prescription drug misuse, low general health, suicidal ideation, and psychological distress (OR = 1.24–1.36). Anti-transgender identity IPV and controlling IPV each respectively was significantly associated with *greater* odds of two different AHCs – with identity IPV predicting suicidal ideation and psychological distress (OR = 1.32–1.42) and controlling IPV predicting suicidal ideation and prescription drug misuse (OR = 1.15–1.24). Re-examining these same findings through the lens of the dependent variables reveals that suicidal ideation was the AHC type significantly predicted by the greatest number of IPV forms (all four IPV forms), followed by prescription drug misuse (predicted by three IPV forms) and psychological distress (predicted by two IPV forms), followed by illicit drug use, binge alcohol use, HIV positive status, and low general health (each predicted by one IPV form).

Finally, multiple ordinal logistic regressions (again using the recoded AHC count as the dependent variable, with five to seven AHCs coded as five) also found all four IPV forms to be significantly associated with *greater* odds of participants experiencing a greater number of AHC types (OR = 1.13–1.31; see Table 9.3). This is perhaps not surprising, given that, as noted earlier, every IPV form was significantly linked with at least two different AHC types.

Table 9.3: Adjusted odds ratios predicting adverse health conditions

	Illicit Drug Use (weighted n = 20,934)	Prescription Drug Misuse (weighted n = 20,956)	Binge Alcohol Use (weighted n = 21,050)	HIV Positive Status (weighted n = 21,104)
	aOR (95% CI)	aOR (95% CI)	aOR (95% CI)	aOR (95% CI)
Identity IPV	1.00 (0.81–1.26)	1.02 (0.87–1.19)	1.07 (0.97–1.18)	0.62 (0.38–1.02)
Controlling IPV	1.12 (0.88–1.43)	1.24 (1.03–1.49)★	1.03 (0.93–1.15)	1.65 (0.94–2.88)
Physical IPV	1.66 (1.33–2.08)★	1.45 (1.21–1.73)★	1.44 (1.30–1.59)★	1.64 (1.02–2.65)★
Sexual IPV	1.28 (0.99–1.67)	1.24 (1.05–1.47)★	1.08 (0.97–1.20)	0.96 (0.55–1.67)

	Low General Health (weighted n = 21,120)	Psychological Distress (weighted n = 20,754)	Suicidal Ideation (weighted n = 21,115)	ACH # (weighted n = 20,393)
	aOR (95% CI)	aOR (95% CI)	aOR (95% CI)	aOR (95% CI)
Identity IPV	1.06 (0.94–1.19)	1.42 (1.28–1.57)★	1.32 (1.20–1.46)★	1.27 (1.17–1.37)★
Controlling IPV	1.10 (0.97–1.25)	1.09 (0.97–1.22)	1.15 (1.04–1.27)★	1.13 (1.04–1.23)★
Physical IPV	0.90 (0.80–1.02)	1.05 (0.94–1.17)	1.12 (1.02–1.24)★	1.31 (1.20–1.42)★
Sexual IPV	1.26 (1.11–1.42)★	1.36 (1.22–1.51)★	1.30 (1.17–1.44)★	1.27 (1.16–1.39)★

Notes: ★ = $p < 0.05$.
aOR = adjusted odds ratios. IPV = intimate partner violence lifetime victimization. ACH # = number of adverse health conditions experienced, coded as 0 (0 AHC), 1 (1 AHC), 2 (2 AHCs), 3 (3 AHCs), 4 (4 AHCs), and 5 (5–7 AHCs). Ordinal logistic regression used to predict ACH #, and logistic regression for all other models. All models adjusted for IPV (identity, controlling, physical, and sexual IPV victimization), gender, sexual orientation, race-ethnicity, citizenship status, ever homelessness, disability status, transgender outness, visual conformity, household income, and age. Results weighted for racial–ethnic composition of US population.

Conclusion

Through secondary analysis of the USTS, the present study expanded the existing transgender IPV literature by assessing possible associations between all forms of IPV (not just one form or a composite form) and a broad range of AHC types. This was also the first study to examine whether IPV among transgender people predicts experiencing a greater number of IPV types, and it was also the first in this particular literature to utilize a nationally representative transgender sample.

Despite the fact that transgender people face disproportionately high baseline rates of AHCs such as depression, suicidal ideation, and substance abuse (see Benotsch et al., 2013; Tebbe & Moradi, 2016), each AHC was positively associated with at least one form of IPV. Of particular note was suicidal ideation, which was the singular AHC type associated with every form of IPV. This finding is reminiscent of Testa et al. (2012), which found that transgender survivors (albeit of any physical or sexual violence, not necessarily IPV) are at higher risk for suicidal ideation and attempts, as well as substance abuse. Lastly, while previous studies (Brennan et al., 2012; Keuroghlian et al., 2015; Goldenberg et al., 2018) had found conflicting results between IPV, substance abuse, and HIV status, the current findings illustrated that illicit drug use, prescription drug misuse, binge alcohol use, and HIV positive status were each indeed associated with at least one form of IPV. Finally, the results show that all IPV types are associated with experiencing a greater number of AHC types. This is particularly important as it shows that no matter the type of IPV experienced, transgender survivors of intimate partner violence (T-IPV survivors) are likely to suffer from multiple negative health covariates.

There are several implications for service providers working with T-IPV survivors. First, service providers should note that all forms of IPV were significantly associated with suicidal ideation. Suicidality already disproportionately affects transgender populations, and IPV may further exacerbate this risk (Wolford-Clevenger et al., 2018). Because transgender people may already experience familial rejection and isolation from community, friends, and workplaces, IPV may exacerbate suicidality arising from existing stressors. A holistic service approach would address existing, transgender-specific AHC risk factors that are further compounded by IPV survival. Second, service providers should be acutely prepared to address a broad range of AHCs and underlying trauma linked to all forms of IPV. T-IPV survivors may require more intensive, multilayered safety planning that addresses gaps in areas such as housing, employment, and healthcare. In this regard, transgender IPV survivors should be screened for AHCs, and vice versa. Lastly, because all forms of IPV were associated with experiencing a greater number of AHC types, service providers should tailor intervention efforts that assess and address multiple forms of violence as they relate to a wide range of deleterious health covariates, including substance abuse, HIV risk, poor general health, and forms of psychological distress. T-IPV service providers should be prepared to tap into a wide network of transgender-affirming resources that address the unique overlap of needs facing transgender survivors.

There are some limitations to the study, as well as future directions for research. The utilized data measured IPV across the lifespan of participants, while most AHC measures were assessed for the last 30 days or past year. Given that IPV could have occurred at any point in a respondent's lifetime, time order is unclear. Future research should employ qualitative methods or longitudinal designs to parse out time order, so as to investigate whether these AHCs are in fact causal variables, outcomes, or perhaps are exacerbated by other underlying factors.

References

Benotsch, E.G., Zimmerman, R., Cathers, L., McNulty, S., Pierce, J., Heck, T., Perrin, P.B., & Snipes, D. (2013) 'Non-medical use of prescription drugs, polysubstance use, and mental health in transgender adults', *Drug and Alcohol Dependence*, 132(1–2): 391–394. https://doi.org/10.1016/j.drugalcdep.2013.02.027

Breiding, M.J., Smith, S.G., Basile, K.C., Walters, M.L., Chen, J., & Merrick, M.T. (2014) 'Prevalence and characteristics of sexual violence, stalking, and intimate partner violence victimization—National Intimate Partner and Sexual Violence Survey, United States, 2011', *Morbidity and Mortality Weekly Report*, 63(8): 1–18. [Retrieved September 2020 from http://www.cdc.gov/mmwr/pdf/ss/ss6308.pdf].

Brennan, J., Kuhns, L.M., Johnson, A.K., Belzer, M., Wilson, E.C., & Garofalo, R. (2012) 'Syndemic theory and HIV-related risk among young transgender women: the role of multiple, co-occuring health problems and social marginalization', *American Journal of Public Health*, 102(9): 1751–1757.

Bukowski, L.A., Hampton, M.C., Escobar-Viera, C.G., Sang, J.M., Chandler, C.J., Henderson, E., Creasy, S.L., & Stall, R.D. (2019) 'Intimate partner violence and depression among Black transgender women in the USA: the potential suppressive effect of perceived social support', *Journal of Urban Health*, 96(5): 760–771.

Cafferky, B.M., Mendez, M., Anderson, J.R., & Stith, S.M. (2016) 'Substance use and intimate partner violence: a meta-analytic review', *Psychology of Violence*, 8(1): 110–131.

Carbone-Lopez, K., Kruttschnitt, C., & Macmillan, R. (2006) 'Patterns of intimate partner violence and their associations with physical health, psychological distress, and substance use', *Public Health Reports*, 121(4): 382–392.

Devries, K.M., Child, J.C., Bacchus, L.J., Mak, J., Falder, G., Graham, K., Watts, C., & Heise, L. (2014) 'Intimate partner violence victimization and alcohol consumption in women: a systematic review and meta-analysis', *Addiction*, 109: 379–391.

Goldenberg, T., Jadwin-Cakmak, L., & Harper, G.Q. (2018) 'Intimate partner violence among transgender youth: associations with intrapersonal and structural factors', *Violence and Gender*, 5(1): 19–24.

James, S.E., Herman, J.L., Rankin, S., Keisling, M., Mottet, L., & Anafi, M. (2016) 'The report of the 2015 U.S. transgender survey', National Center for Transgender Equality, https://www.ustranssurvey.org

Kessler, R.C., Barker, P.R., Colpe, L.J., Epstein, J.F., Gfroerer, J.C., Hiripi, E., Howes, M.J., Normand, S.-L.T., Manderscheid, R.W., Walters, E.E., & Zaslavsky, A.M. (2003) 'Screening for serious mental illness in the general population', *Archives of General Psychiatry*, 60(2): 184–189.

Keuroghlian, A.S., Reisner, S.L., White, J.M., & Weiss, R.D. (2015) 'Substance use and treatment of substance use disorders in a community sample of transgender adults', *Drug and Alcohol Dependence*, 152: 139–146.

Messinger, A.M. & Guadalupe-Diaz, X.L. (2020) *Transgender Intimate Partner Violence: A Comprehensive Introduction*, New York: New York University Press.

Messinger, A.M., Kurdyla, V., & Guadalupe-Diaz, X.L. (2021) 'Intimate partner violence help-seeking in the U.S. transgender survey', *Journal of Homosexuality*, 1–25, advance online publication. https://doi.org/10.1080/00918369.2021.1901506

Parsons, J.T., Antebi-Gruszka, N., Millar, B.M., Cain, D., & Gurung, S. (2018) 'Syndemic conditions, HIV transmission risk behavior, and transactional sex among transgender women', *AIDS and Behavior*, 22(7): 2056–2067, https://doi.org/10.1007/s10461-018-2100-y

Peitzmeier, S.M., Hughto, J.M.W., Potter, J., Deutsch, M.B., & Reisner, S.L. (2019) 'Development of a novel tool to assess intimate partner violence against transgender individuals', *Journal of Interpersonal Violence*, 34(11): 2376–2397.

Peitzmeier, S.M., Malik, M., Kattari S.K., Marrow, E., Stephenson, R., Agenor, M., & Reisner, S.L. (2020) 'Intimate partner violence in transgender populations: systematic review and meta-analysis of prevalence and correlates', *American Journal of Public Health*, 110(9): e1–e14, https://doi.org/10.2105/AJPH.2020.305774

Tebbe, E.A. & Moradi, B. (2016) 'Suicide risk in trans populations: an application of minority stress theory', *Journal of Counseling Psychology*, 63(5): 520–533. https://doi.org/10.1037/cou0000152

Testa, R.J., Sciacca, L.M., Wang, F., Hendricks, M.L., Goldblum, P., Bradford, J., & Bongar, B. (2012) 'Effects of violence on transgender people', *Professional Psychology: Research and Practice*, 43(5): 452–459.

White-Hughto, J.M., Pachankis, J.E., Willie, T.C., & Reisner, S.L. (2017) 'Victimization and depressive symptomology in transgender adults: the mediating role of avoidant coping', *Journal of Counseling Psychology*, 64(1): 41–51.

Wolford-Clevenger, C., Frantell, K., Smith, P.N., Flores, L.Y., & Stuart, G.L. (2018) 'Correlates of suicide ideation and behaviors among transgender people: a systematic review guided by ideation-to-action theory', *Clinical Psychology Review*, 63: 93–105.

10

Serving Transgender, Gender Nonconforming, and Intersex Youth in Alameda County's Juvenile Hall

Alexandria Garcia, Naseem Badiey,
Laura Agnich Chavez, and Wendy Still

Transgender, gender nonconforming, and intersex (TGNCI) youth are acutely vulnerable to poor mental health outcomes.[1] Justice-involved TGNCI youth are at even greater risk of trauma, victimization, suicide, and self-harm (Markshamer & Tobin, 2014; Lydon et al., 2015; James et al., 2016; Hughto et al., 2018; Malkin & DeJong, 2019). TGNCI youth in juvenile detention facilities face additional challenges related to housing and medical care. Providing quality care for this vulnerable subpopulation is an important challenge for juvenile justice professionals.

Since 2000 California has passed successive legislation to protect TGNCI youth in public schools, state programs, and juvenile detention facilities. Among these was SB 518 (2007), the California Juvenile Justice Safety and Protection Act, which made California the first state to adopt a comprehensive bill of rights for young people confined in juvenile justice facilities. The law protected lesbian, bisexual, gay, and transgender (LBGT) youth from discrimination in the state's juvenile justice facilities and served as the foundation for subsequent legislation that provided specific protections for TGNCI youth. In 2019, Title 15 of the California Code of Regulations (CCR) was expanded to include definitions around gender and to provide specific protections for LGBQ and TGNCI youth in detention facilities. Title 15 section 1352.5, 'Transgender and intersex youth', requires the development of written policies and procedures ensuring respectful and equitable treatment of transgender and intersex youth. These requirements built on national legislation such as the 2003 Prison Rape Elimination Act (PREA), which intended to prevent sexual violence in all custodial correctional settings operated by federal, state, and local governments (juvenile, adult, community corrections, and immigration). According to Smith (2008), data collection resulting from PREA created visibility for the issue of sexual violence in custody. For example, in the first baseline survey in 2005, juvenile agencies reported rates of sexual violence three to seven times higher than adult facilities – both staff sexual misconduct and youth-on-youth sexual abuse (see Beck & Harrison, 2006).

In California, probation departments are responsible for running youth detention facilities. As such, they are tasked with ensuring the physical safety and psychological well-being of incarcerated TGNCI youth. While legal protections from discrimination and sexual abuse are a critical step in safeguarding the physical and psychological well-being of TGNCI youth, legislation is not sufficient. Juvenile justice agencies must also develop internal policies and protocols and provide training that prepares staff to administer safe and professional care for this vulnerable group. This necessitates understanding the unique characteristics and needs of TGNCI youth, considering research regarding sex, gender, gender identity, trauma and triggers, and youth health, as well as training staff on legislation, policies, and procedural changes (see Table 10.1 for applicable definitions).

This chapter examines the Alameda County Probation Department's (ACPD) experience in developing policies and protocols for transgender youth in Juvenile Hall from 2012 to 2019. Drawing on interviews with line staff, supervisors, and executive management, we offer a practitioner's perspective in discussions on how juvenile detention facilities can improve care of TGNCI youth, while offering a number of insights that can inform processes of policy development in jurisdictions across the country. First, informal practices intended to protect TGNCI youth may render them invisible from a data collection perspective, impeding the development of policies and services to address youth needs. Second, staff training is a continuous process that requires repeated reinforcement of the objective of policies and procedures, as well as support for staff whose social and cultural norms don't align with policy changes. Third, if done thoughtfully, creating a safe space in juvenile detention for TGNCI youth to express their gender identity in the way they choose does not pose safety risks for youth or staff, and the potential benefits outweigh challenges. Finally, the process benefits from clear objectives communicated by department leadership and holding staff accountable to enact required changes. Staff accountability is particularly important, as some staff may think that these policy changes conflict with their personal beliefs. Regardless of staff beliefs, however, staff behavior

Table 10.1: Definition of terms from the ACPD Juvenile Facilities Manual

Term	Definition
Cisgender	A person whose gender identity corresponds to the gender they were assigned at birth.
Gender Nonconforming	A person whose appearance or manner does not conform to traditional masculine and feminine gender norms of their assigned sex at birth.
Intersex	A person whose sexual or reproductive anatomy or chromosomal pattern does not seem to fit the typical definitions of male or female. Intersex medical conditions are sometimes referred to as Disorders of Sex Development (DSD) (US 28 CFR § 115.5).
Nonbinary	An umbrella term for people with gender identities that fall somewhere outside the traditional conceptions of strictly either female or male. People with nonbinary gender identities may or may not identify as transgender, may or may not have been born with intersex traits, may or may not use gender-neutral pronouns, and may or may not use more specific terms to describe their genders, such as: agender, genderqueer, gender fluid, Two Spirit, bigender, pangender, gender nonconforming, non-cisgender, or gender variant.
Transgender	A person whose gender identity is different from their assigned sex at birth and who lives, or desires to live, in accord with their gender identity.
Trans Man	A person who was assigned female at birth, but identifies as, and desires to live as, a man.
Trans Woman	A person who was assigned male at birth, but identifies as, and desires to live as, a woman.

Note: Terms and definitions taken from ACPD Juvenile Facilities Manual policy 1352.5, Chapter: Classification and Separation, Section: Transgender and Intersex Youth.

must align with the written policies and expectations communicated by leadership. Moreover, the case of Alameda County Juvenile Hall may help dispel assumptions that may negatively impact TGNCI youth in custody, identify potential challenges, and offer strategies for approaching similar processes of organizational change.

TGNCI youth and the juvenile justice system

Lesbian, gay, bisexual, transgender, and queer or questioning people, particularly those who are people of color and low income, have disproportionate contact with the criminal justice system (Center for American Progress, 2016). As a result of overpolicing, bias, sexual violence, trauma, workplace discrimination, high rates of poverty, and homelessness, this population experiences higher levels of incarceration (Amnesty International, 2005; Lydon et al., 2015; Mallory et al., 2015; Thomas, 2020). TGNCI youth face all these issues, as well as family alienation, bullying and harassment in schools, exploitation, and abuse. As a result of the numerous challenges they face, TGNCI youth suffer worse outcomes than both their LGB and non-LGB cisgendered peers, with TGNCI youth of color suffering the worst outcomes (The Trevor Project, 2019). TGNCI youth in juvenile justice facilities face additional challenges such as misgendering, inappropriate searches, and lack of adequate medical care.

Historically, the absence of policies to protect against prejudice and abuse, and to ensure equitable and non-discriminatory treatment for TGNCI youth in detention, has contributed to the trauma of incarceration. Without the implementation of departmental policies in juvenile detention institutions, the care of TGNCI youth in juvenile detention facilities has proceeded in an ad hoc fashion, with frontline staff having a large measure of discretion over how to serve these youth on a day-to-day basis. The risk of such approaches is that staff may be influenced by a set of erroneous assumptions about TGNCI youth that position them as either targets or perpetrators of sexual violence, and that place these risks as inherent to their identities rather than stemming from trauma caused by prejudice and mistreatment. This may include the belief that merely having a TGNCI youth in a housing unit will cause conflict with other youth. It is true that TGNCI individuals experience high levels of sexual abuse and assault in their lives, with even higher rates for individuals of color and those living with disabilities (Kenagy, 2005). However, subjecting TGNCI youth to punitive measures under the guise of safety concerns, such as placing them in solitary confinement, can be traumatizing and dangerous for youth, especially those with preexisting mental health conditions.

Policy and procedural change implementation in the Alameda County Probation Department

Located within the Juvenile Justice Center in San Leandro, California, the Alameda County Juvenile Hall has 12 housing units, of which five are currently in use.[2] Prior to being admitted into Juvenile Hall, youth are assessed using the Juvenile Detention Risk Assessment Instrument (JDRAI). The JDRAI is a decision-making tool used by Juvenile Hall intake staff to determine whether a youth should be booked into Juvenile Hall or released with a Notice to Appear pending the district attorney's decision to file charges for their alleged offense. Using a JDRAI to determine whether a youth is admitted into the Juvenile Hall helps to ensure that only youth with serious offenses, a high likelihood of reoffending, and/or who are likely to fail to appear for a hearing date are detained (NCCD, 2015). Juvenile Hall staff are extensively trained in all aspects of how to interact with youth during and after the intake process. Youth who are admitted into the Juvenile Hall go through a process of evaluation that, per the ACPD's policies, includes asking the youth about their gender identity and gender expression.

Prior to the ACPD's development of policies on TGNCI youth, however, Juvenile Hall administration made significant and progressive advancements in the approach to TGNCI youth. For example, intake staff began consulting youth regarding their preferences in housing unit placement, allowed them to choose clothing and undergarments in line with their gender identity, called them by their pronouns and names, and provided them with medical help for non-surgical gender affirming body alterations such as penis tucking. Juvenile Hall staff even made available appointments with a beautician and permitted youth to wear hairstyles reflective of their gender identity.

Despite these achievements, however, absent policies to govern the treatment or classification of TGNCI youth admitted to Juvenile Hall, staff did not have a standardized approach to serving this vulnerable subpopulation. Rather, staff used ad hoc approaches to address youths' needs based on their gender identity. Without standardized processes, everything was done on a 'case-by-case' basis, which granted staff a large amount of discretion in the care of TGNCI youth. For example, staff typically tried to divert TGNCI youth brought to Juvenile Hall intake, believing they would not be able to accommodate their unique needs. While in line with the ACPD's goal of diverting all youth when possible so as to minimize the impact of contact with the juvenile justice system, whether diversion is always the best option for TGNCI youth entering the hall remains unknown. Given the struggles TGNCI youth face with homelessness, abuse, and discrimination in their families and communities, diversion without adequate social supports may not always be the best option. As such, there was a clear need for policies and procedures to guide staff in making decisions about booking TGNCI youth into the hall. Accordingly, the treatment of TGNCI youth without guidance or understanding of the complex struggles both inside and outside the hall via an ad hoc approach was problematic. Absent clear policies, staff at times relied on the experience of other local probation departments to inform their approaches to TGNCI youth, further emphasizing the need for internal mechanisms of standardization.

Since 2012, the ACPD has worked to improve equity and outcomes for LGBT youth in Juvenile Hall, beginning with the department's participation in Alameda County's multi-agency LGBT task force, which aimed to adopt LGBT-inclusive non-discrimination policies and provide enhanced supportive services. While this process did not immediately result in substantive plans and policies for ACPD, in the years following the inception of the task force a process was initiated within the department to develop a policy framework for TGNCI youth based on non-discrimination and legislative guidelines. In 2016, with the hiring of new Chief Probation Officer Wendy Still, the department embarked on a process of organizational change that included the creation of a new Policy and Standards Compliance Unit in 2017. The Policy and Standards Compliance Unit was tasked with updating a backlog of approximately 500 policies. As part of the effort and in line with revisions to Title 15, which mandated the addition of policies to protect TGNCI and LGBQ youth, more than 60 policies related to this subpopulation were found to be in need of update. After a long period of development, in 2019 a series of policies were published creating a much needed sense of direction and standardization in the treatment of TGNCI youth.

Policy Number 1349, the Federal Prison Rape Elimination Act of 2003, of the Juvenile Facilities Manual, was published on August 8, 2019, and was the first ACPD policy that impacted TGNCI youth. Policy 1349 governs the classification and separation of youth, aligned with the Federal Prison Rape Elimination Act (PREA) Juvenile Facilities Standards and Title 15 of the California Code of Minimum Standards for Juvenile Facilities. Policy 1349 establishes the department's guidelines for PREA compliance and specifies that staff, volunteers, interns, and contractors who contact youth in custody must receive training on how to communicate professionally with LGBTQI and gender nonconforming youth. In addition, 'staff must not consider LGBTQI identification or status as an indicator of likelihood of being sexually abusive' (ACPD, 2020, p. 16). In the event of a sexual abuse incident, the policy further specifies that the Sexual Abuse Incident Review Board must 'consider whether the incident or allegation was motivated by race, ethnicity, gender identity, LGBTQI identification, status or perceived status, gang affiliation, or was motivated or otherwise caused by other group dynamics within the facility' (ACPD, 2020, p. 29).

On December 18, 2019, three additional policies were published, one in a new section of the Juvenile Facilities policy manual titled 'Transgender and intersex youth'. This new policy specified that ACPD staff must respect each youth's gender identity, refer to each youth by their chosen names (with the exception of gang or street names), use a youth's gender pronouns regardless of their legal name, and permit youth to dress and groom themselves in a manner consistent with their gender identity. Further, staff are prohibited from conducting physical searches of TGNCI youth for the purpose of determining their anatomical sex. In addition, youth must not be automatically housed according to their external anatomy, but rather according to their gender identity and recommendations from the youth's medical or behavioral health providers. Finally, the policy mandates that facilities superintendents or designees must ensure that TGNCI youth have access to medical and behavioral health providers who are sufficiently knowledgeable and able to provide care and treatment to them.

Key insights from the case of Alameda County Juvenile Hall

In examining the case of Alameda County Probation's efforts since 2012 to update policies and processes to enact a non-discrimination and gender-affirming approach to serving TGNCI youth in Juvenile Hall, our team identified several key insights regarding data collection, staff training and professional development, youth safety and well-being, and communication strategies that may be instructive to other jurisdictions embarking on similar processes of development.

TGNCI data collection

The first key insight from the case of Alameda County Juvenile Hall is that informal or ad hoc practices intended to protect TGNCI youth may render them invisible from a data collection perspective, impeding the development of policies and services to address youth needs. Historically, the ACPD has not collected data on youth's transgender status or sexuality. This is in part because the juvenile case management system, PRSIM, did not have fields for that information. It also reflects staff efforts to safeguard youth privacy, believing that keeping their gender identity out of the system may protect them from harm. Yet the failure to record information on gender identity in the case management system effectively rendered TGNCI youth invisible and as a result inhibited the ability of the department to improve services and track outcomes for this subpopulation (Irvine, 2010; Canfield et al., 2020). As a result, the exact number of TGNCI youths coming in and out of the Alameda County Juvenile Hall remains unknown, and their outcomes have not been tracked. Anecdotally, staff have reported working with roughly one or two TGNCI youth a year. In October 2020, ACPD launched a new juvenile case management system, Tyler Supervision, which is designed to track gender identity and sexuality. This new system, along with the department's new policies, enables ACPD to accurately capture data regarding TGNCI youth, so the department can better understand and meet their needs by tracking their outcomes, and analyze data to improve program and service delivery.

The invisibility of TGNCI youth in probation data systems reflects a broader phenomenon within the juvenile justice system. While it is difficult to estimate the exact number of LGBT youth impacted by the juvenile justice system, studies conducted over the years have attempted to do so and have found varying results (Thomas, 2020). Discrepancies such as these are attributable to factors such as poor data collection and an individual's unwillingness to identify as LGBT, all of which contribute to the inability of researchers to fully understand the scope of impact of the juvenile justice system on LGBTQ+ youth (Thomas, 2020). For TGNCI youth specifically, representative figures are even more elusive, with few studies collecting data disaggregating TGNCI youth from the broader LGBT population (Jonnson et al., 2019; Thomas, 2020).

Issues of data collection and disaggregation are complicated by the challenges faced by youth in coming out as TGNCI. Many young people keep their transgender status private out of fear of retaliation or violence (Brumbaugh-Johnson & Hull, 2019), or of family rejection. In Alameda County Juvenile Hall, staff have honored youth's request to conceal their transgender status. For example, Juvenile Hall staff recounted an instance where a transgender youth wished to dress according to their gender identity while in the hall, but not when in court. In this situation, staff sensitivity to the complexities and challenges of the coming out process for transgender youth was an important factor in ensuring the youth's physical and mental well-being. In order to respect a youth's individual coming-out process while not rendering the population invisible, a process of data collection should be established that respects individual privacy and takes into consideration the fluid nature of gender identity.

Staff training and professional development

The second key insight from the case of Alameda County Juvenile Hall is that staff training is a continuous process that requires repeated reinforcement of the objective of policies and procedures, as well as support for staff whose social and cultural norms don't align with policy changes. While supervisors provide staff a lot of support, they observed that more training was needed to walk staff through each policy change. Immediately after the updated Title 15 department policies were approved, Juvenile Facilities leadership embarked on training staff on the policies. Phase One trainings began prior to the COVID-19 pandemic with suicide prevention, program and recreation, positive reinforcement, positive separation, and room confinement. Phase Two trainings began in October 2020. These include searches, classification, emergency codes, use of force, active shooter, and fire. Issues that impact TGNCI youth are weaved through all these policies. One such example is the classification of youth in Juvenile Hall and ensuring safety. Furthermore, while staff have received additional training specific to working with LGBT youth, a common issue vocalized was the need for training that specifically centered around the department's new policies impacting LGBT youth.

Interviews with staff and training evaluation documents reveal that PREA and LGBT training received to date was, overall, effective. A supervisor in Juvenile Hall claimed that while staff had a lot of questions about it during the training, by the time the training ended, 'most of them were like, you know what, I get it. The kids do have that choice because you know, they do have a choice to identify how they identify. And we just have to respect that' (Institutional Supervisor interview, August 2020). According to the superintendent of Juvenile Hall, the training process has not been difficult. 'Staff didn't even have any questions. Years ago, it was a hot topic and staff had a lot of questions. It wasn't an issue. The practice is already established. There is no confusion. It's clear' (Juvenile Hall Superintendent interview, October 2020).

Despite these reported training successes, staff emphasized the need for training specific to the department's new policies regarding TGNCI youth, providing staff a safe space to discuss and better understand issues relevant to a marginalized population. A supervisor explained that the department could do a better job of laying out expectations with regard to new policies:

> There's some of us who do read the policies, and stay on top of everything, and we don't necessarily need to go to a training class. But line staff need it. They need to sit down so that they can ask their questions. So that it can be very clear what the expectations are from the department ... with new policies with processes that need to take place. (Unit Supervisor interview, August 2020)

As a result of the feedback obtained through this study, the ACPD has undertaken the process of identifying trainings to better meet staff needs in recognition of their concerns.

In addition, some staff have worked in Juvenile Hall for 25 years. This older cohort has a very different approach and perspective to the job than newer staff. One challenge was around the issue of physical searches. As one supervisor noted:

> There is a specific training that is given to all staff with regards to a youth's choice [as to] who they want to pat search them, especially when they identify as transgender or non-conforming, because they do have that choice. They have the ability to tell us ... I know biologically I'm male [but identify as female and] I want a female staff to do my pat search. All we do is note in the use folder that this is what they would like. ... A lot of staff at the beginning of that training ... really had a problem with it, because they were like, 'You mean to tell me that if a biological female [trans man] tells me I'm going to search them as a male I have to search them?' And unfortunately, yes, because that's the choice that they have made based on how they identify themselves. (Institutional Supervisor interview, September 2020)

Careful attention should be paid to the amount of training and education youth receive on the topic of TGNCI youth. For example, staff observed that the librarian and teachers in Juvenile Hall overwhelmed youth with content on LGBTQ issues. While well intentioned, some youth felt that discussions of gender and sexuality overshadowed discussions about race, reconciliation, and broader tolerance issues. Staff were concerned that, if not handled in a balanced way, educational content and discussions on gender and sexuality could potentially result in resentment toward TGNCI youth in the housing units. In general, staff indicated that training should be inclusive of intersectional identities (see Crenshaw, 1989). While the number of TGNCI youth served by the Alameda County Juvenile Hall is generally low, because the majority of youth the Hall serves are youth of color, it is important for staff to understand how race may intersect with a youth's various identities, gender and sexual identity included (see also Irvine & Canfield, 2017).

Youth safety and well-being

The third key insight from the case of Alameda County Juvenile Hall is that while it may be challenging initially to create a safe space in juvenile detention for TGNCI youth to express their gender identity in the way they choose, if done thoughtfully, it does not pose safety risks, and the potential benefits outweigh the challenges. In the Alameda County Probation experience, it was safe to house transgender youth in the boys' or girls' units per their choice, and to allow them to express their gender identity how they choose in Juvenile Hall. In fact, it was important for their well-being.

Various processes were already in place to ensure youth safety while in detention. Many of these stemmed from PREA guidelines. Despite the absence of any major incidents or assaults related to youths' gender identity, staff did recognize that bullying and intolerance could still pose a risk to TGNCI youths' psychological well-being while housed in Juvenile Hall. A staff member who served as the PREA compliance manager stated:

> I just wanted to make sure that they felt safe, because I know how kids can be. They can be cruel. I would check in like once a week and just make sure that they were okay, let them know that there's someone who is looking out for them, and if they needed anything to let us know. And they would tell us, you know, they would let us know if kids were making them feel uncomfortable, or if things were being said, and then we will deal with it. We've done a few ... tolerance sessions with groups of kids where we just talk about being tolerant of people's choices, and being tolerant of the fact that we all have a right to think and act differently and we just have to be respectful and mindful of that. (Institutional Supervisor interview, September 2020)

Some staff still believed that housing transgender youth in units based on their gender classification posed safety risks to the TGNCI youth.

Specifically, the concern was over placing a trans male in the boys' unit, because 'the girls tend to be a little bit more accepting … they were just a little bit more open and accepting to having a transgender in their unit' (Institutional Supervisor interview, September 2020). However, staff also indicated that youth were for the most part tolerant of their TGNCI peers.

> For the most part, the kids, they understood. I think the younger kids still couldn't quite understand, the maturity level wasn't quite there. And we may have had one or two older kids who would make comments during the training sessions with the kids. I would normally pull them to the side and let them know that we all have something about us that is unique and different, and how would you like it if someone teased you about your haircut or about the way you wear your clothes or the choices that you make? Normally, in the course of a one-on-one conversation, you find out that there's other underlying issues. Maybe there's someone in the household that identifies as LBGTQ and they haven't been very accepted into the family. So a lot of it has been learned behavior of how to react to them. (Institutional Supervisor interview, September 2020S)

While staff perceptions of potential threats to TGNCI youth safety have not been substantiated, they do demonstrate how the process of developing policies and protocols for the housing of TGNCI youth is essential to bringing staff with varying cultural and social norms, and differing preconceived notions about the behavior and security of youth, together into a common, department-sanctioned approach.

In examining the experience of Alameda County Juvenile Hall staff in implementing new policies impacting TGNCI youth, it became apparent that the process of policy development benefits from clear objectives communicated by department leadership. ACPD began a process of strategic planning in 2017 and clearly communicated that respect for clients' diverse backgrounds would be diffused into each strategic goal by committing to the success of every client and their family. Executive leadership frequently communicate with staff regarding ACPD values, particularly with respect to tolerance and diversity.

Communication strategies

A final key insight that can be gleaned from the case of Alameda County Juvenile Hall is that policy development and implementation, as well as the overall care of TGNCI youth, benefit from clear objectives communicated by leadership across the department. Communication issues were first evident in the lack of knowledge staff had about the county's LGBT task force. Despite being a large, multi-agency effort, the extent of the ACPD's participation in the task force was not widely known across the department. Information about the ACPD's participation had seemingly been lost over time as staff who participated in the task force retired, taking their knowledge with them. Loss of knowledge associated with turnover is a problem that many probation departments face, however the lack of communication about the task force left a level of ambiguity surrounding the care of LGBQ and TGNCI youth for more than a decade.

Outside of communication issues associated with staff turnover, another common issue was the need for clear communication about TGNCI youth policy and procedures from department leadership. Across interviews, staff expressed the need for clear direction from management with respect to the expectations of staff care of LGBQ and TGNCI youth in the absence of a formal set of procedures. Post-policy implementation, this desire for increased communication from leadership was echoed in staff's desire for group discussions between line staff and leadership where questions and concerns could be heard. Both before and after TGNCI policies were published, a clear need for the development of the department's communication infrastructure was highlighted and further echoed the needs presented in the case of staff turnover.

While a series of improvements have been made in the areas of intra-department communication in the years since Chief Still took over the leadership of the ACPD in 2016 (implementation of policy briefs, new training memos, monthly departmental update videos to staff, and so on), staff still felt that better communication would improve knowledge of and familiarity with policies. If staff are to perform their duties up to ACPD standards with the best interest of TGNCI and all youth in mind, they must be well versed in departmental protocols and procedures. Then they can be held accountable for ensuring adherence to guidance from leadership, training, and departmental policies regarding proper and equitable treatment of youth. In response to this, Chief Still explained, 'staff accountability is so important, because it sends a message: what are the values of the organization, what behaviors will be tolerated, that changes culture more than anything else we do'.

Conclusion

Alameda County's experience in implementing policies and procedures for TGNCI youth offers several insights for other jurisdictions. First, it highlights the importance of building a data-driven basis for improving services and tracking outcomes. Prioritizing data collection is the responsibility of department leadership and requires careful policies that protect youth privacy and safety but do not retraumatize vulnerable youth.

Second, it exemplifies the need for departments to have clear objectives about what they want to achieve for this population in terms of services and outcomes. Finally, it illustrates the importance of having clear policies and procedures, open communication, and ongoing training available to staff to guide them in supporting TGNCI youth. This type of change management – one that aims to institutionalize non-discrimination – would benefit from a strategic planning process whereby an overarching objective is identified and communicated clearly from the top down to line staff. This would help staff understand that each policy and procedural change is working toward a common departmental goal. Concerted communication of strategic values regarding the provision of high-quality care and services to youth with intersectional marginalized identities would improve the policy implementation process for TGNCI youth.

The department's strategic vision and commitment to communicating ACPD goals from the top down likely contributed to the overall successful implementation of policy change for TGNCI youth. At the same time, the department's strategic vision will guide improvements identified as necessary in this chapter. With a goal to be a data-driven organization, the new case management system that went live in October 2020 was designed to capture data on youth gender identity and expression, and training will continue to improve based on valuable staff feedback.

ACPD's experience is transferrable to other jurisdictions across the country, and it also informs debates about how to protect the most vulnerable TGNCI youth in our society. Both the youth population in Juvenile Hall and Juvenile Hall staff reflect the demographically diverse communities of Alameda County. Furthermore, the drivers of legislative change in California will prompt similar changes in other states, requiring probation departments and juvenile facilities to embark on processes of policy development for TGNCI youth. Moreover, the work done by the ACPD serves as an example to other jurisdictions as to how thoughtful and intentional change via training, policy development, and technological advancement can improve the quality of care for justice-involved LGBQ+ and TGNCI youth. It is imperative that public institutions work to create safe environments for these youth, drawing on theoretical advancements in the field of criminology (see Kahle, 2018). The work that Alameda County has done is by no means sufficient, but it is the beginning of a movement in a positive direction for juvenile justice institutions and may serve as a model for change elsewhere in the country.

Notes

[1] In a study by Veale et al. (2017), for example, two-thirds of transgender youth reported recent self-harm.

2   According to the 2019 'Reductions in juvenile detention in Alameda County' report, over
     the previous ten years the Alameda County Juvenile Hall had seen a population decrease
     of over 65 percent, contributing to the use of less space within the hall.

References

ACPD (Alameda County Probation Department) (2020) 'Title 15, California Code of Regulations: Minimum Standards for Juvenile Facilities Penal Code Sections 835a, 3407, and 22820'. https://probation.acgov.org/probation-assets/files/1357-Use-of-Force.pdf

Amnesty International (2005) 'Stonewalled: police abuse and misconduct against LGBT people in the United States'.

Beck, A.J. & Harrison, P.M. (2006) 'Sexual violence reported by correctional authorities, *2005*', US Department of Justice, Office of Justice Programs.

Brumbaugh-Johnson, S.M. & Hull, K.E. (2019) 'Coming out as transgender: Navigating the social implications of a transgender identity', *Journal of Homosexuality*, 66(8): 1148–1177.

California Code of Regulations. Title 15. *1352.5. Transgender and Intersex Youth.* https://govt.westlaw.com/calregs/Document/IED0C9A7B314743 0A89DF6AFBEFD64A75?viewType=FullText&originationContext=doc umenttoc&transitionType=CategoryPageItem&contextData=(sc.Default)

Canfield, A., Irvine, A., Wilber, S., & Larrabee-Garza, M. (2020) 'The whole youth model: how collecting data about sexual orientation, gender identity, and gender expression (SOGIE) helps probation and youth courts build more authentic relationships focused on improved well-being', *LGBTQ Policy Journal*, June, https://lgbtq.hkspublications.org/2020/06/22/ the-whole-youth-model-how-collecting-data-about-sexual-orientation-gender-identity-and-gender-expression-sogie-helps-probation-and-youth-courts-build-more-authentic-relationships-focused-on-impro/

Center for American Progress (2016) 'Unjust: how the broken criminal justice system fails LGBT people of color'.

Crenshaw, K. (1989) 'Demarginalizing the intersection of race and sex: a black feminist critique of antidiscrimination doctrine, feminist theory and antiracist politics', *University of Chicago Legal Forum*, 1(8): 139–167. http:// chicagounbound.uchicago.edu/uclf/vol1989/iss1/8

Hughto, J.M.W., Clark, K.A., Altice, F.L., Reisner, S.L., Kershaw, T.S., & Pachankis, J.E. (2018) 'Creating, reinforcing, and resisting the gender binary: a qualitative study of transgender women's healthcare experiences in sex-segregated jails and prisons', *International Journal of Prisoner Health*, 14(2): 69–88.

Irvine, A. (2010) 'We've had three of them: addressing the invisibility of lesbian, gay, bisexual, and gender nonconforming youths in the juvenile justice system', *Columbia Journal of Gender and Law*, 19: 675–701.

Irvine, A. & Canfield, A. (2017) 'Reflections on new national data on LGBQ/GNCT youth in the justice system', *LGBTQ Policy Journal*, 7: 27–36.

James, S., Herman, J., Rankin, S., Keisling, M., Mottet, L., & Anafi, M. A. (2016) 'The report of the 2015 US Transgender Survey', National Center for Transgender Equality. https://transequality.org/sites/default/files/docs/usts/USTS-Full-Report-Dec17.pdf

Jonnson, M.R., Bird, B.M., Li, S.M., & Viljoen, J.L. (2019) 'The prevalence of sexual and gender minority youth in the justice system: a systematic review and meta-analysis', *Criminal Justice and Behavior*, 46(7): 999–1019.

Kahle, L. (2018) 'Feminist and queer criminology: a vital place for theorizing LGBTQ youth', *Sociology Compass*, 12(3): e12564.

Kenagy, G.P. (2005) 'The health and social service needs of transgender people in Philadelphia', *International Journal of Transgenderism*, 8(2–3): 49–56.

Lydon, J., Carrington, K., Low, H., Miller, H., & Yazdy, M. (2015) 'Coming out of concrete closets: a report on Black & Pink's national LGBTQ prisoner survey', Black and Pink.

Malkin, M.L. & DeJong, C. (2019) 'Protections for transgender inmates under PREA: a comparison of state correctional policies in the United States', *Sexuality Research and Social Policy*, 16(4): 393–407.

Mallory, C., Hasenbush, A., & Sears, B. (2015) 'Discrimination and harassment by law enforcement officers in the LGBT community', The Williams Institute. https://escholarship.org/content/qt5663q0w1/qt5663q0w1.pdf

Markshamer, J. & Tobin, H.J. (2014) 'Standing with LGBT prisoners: an advocate's guide to ending abuse and combating imprisonment'. https://transequality.org/sites/default/files/docs/resources/JailPrisons_Resource_FINAL.pdf

NCCD (National Council on Crime and Delinquency) (2015) 'Traditional risk assessments vs. detention screening instruments'. https://www.nccdglobal.org/sites/default/files/publication_pdf/detention_screening_instruments_-_prediction_and_validity.pdf

Smith, B.V. (2008) 'The Prison Rape Elimination Act: implementation and unresolved issues torture', *Criminal Law Brief*, 3(2): 10–18.

The Trevor Project (2019) 'Research brief: data on transgender youth'. https://www.thetrevorproject.org/2019/02/22/research-brief-data-on-transgender-youth/

Thomas, C.R. (2020) 'Ethical and legal issues in the care of transgender youth in the juvenile justice system', *Ethics, Medicine and Public Health*, 13: 100464.

Veale, J.F., Watson, R.J., Peter, T., & Saewyc, E.M. (2017) 'Mental health disparities among Canadian transgender youth', *Journal of Adolescent Health*, 60(1): 44–49.

11

Liberating Black Youth across the Gender Spectrum Through the Deconstruction of the White Femininity/ Black Masculinity Duality

Angela Irvine-Baker, Aisha Canfield, and Carolyn Reyes

The National Memorial for Peace and Justice was conceived and developed by Bryan Stevenson and the Equal Justice Institute in Birmingham, Alabama, to remember the history of lynching Black people as well as how the practice of lynching morphed into the contemporary incarceration and capital punishment of Black people. When one visits this memorial, there are plaques that tell a brief story for each lynched Black person for whom the Equal Justice Institute was able to find a record. Five examples of these plaques follow:

'Oliver Moore was lynched in Edgecombe County, North Carolina, in 1930 for frightening a white girl.'

'David Walker, his wife, and their four children were lynched in Hickman, Kentucky, in 1908 after Mr. Walker was accused of using inappropriate language with a white woman.'

'Frank Dodd was lynched in DeWitt, Arkansas, in 1916 for annoying a white woman.'

'Mary Turner, eight months pregnant, was lynched in Georgia in 1918 for publicly speaking out against her husband's lynching the day before.'

'Laura Nelson was raped and lynched in Okema, Oklahoma, in 1911 for allegedly shooting a sheriff while trying to protect her son.'

While the information provided is minimal, these plaques capture a pattern of Black men, women, and children being killed for the trivial actions of breaking social norms with white women.

Historians' writings explain this extreme pattern of punishment. Authors such as Brett (2020) and Hamad (2018, 2019) show how white women were socially constructed in a way that justified both their protection from and the punishment of Black people. This protection of white women and the punishment of Black people became inextricably linked. In addition to the lynching and incarceration of Black people, white women as 'damsels in distress' were used to justify federal decisions that impacted many Indigenous and other people of color. Examples include the expansion of the United States, resulting in the mass killing and rapes of Indigenous people from North and Central America, limiting the immigration of Chinese men, and the internment of Japanese families (Brett, 2020). However, for the purpose of this chapter, we will focus on the duality between white femininity and Black masculinity.

Contemporarily, we see white women apply their power to monitor Black behavior (Brett, 2020). Using their whiteness to orchestrate illegitimate threats to their safety, women such as Amy Cooper leverage public resources to complain about an 'African American man' who disagrees with her behavior, a practice that has been reinforced by a social history that certifies that their identity is a public safety priority. We see countless examples of this behavior, such as that of Jennifer Schulte, who called police to report a Black family barbecuing at Lake Merritt in Oakland, California. After harassing the family and repeatedly calling police until they arrived, she reported that she was 'really scared' and insinuated that her physical safety was threatened (Zhao, 2018, para. 10). In another incident, Teresa Klein accused nine-year-old Jeremiah Harvey, a Black boy, of groping her in a corner store and called the police to report the incident. Jeremiah's mother, who was with her son at the time of the alleged incident, was also accused by Klein of acting aggressively toward the woman. The accusations were later disproved by footage reviewed on the store's security camera. This reinforces Brett's (2020) argument that 'this narrative encourage[s] white women to jump to accusations of sexual violence to protect themselves against social embarrassment' (Francis & Hutchinson, 2018, para. 10). Similarly, within interpersonal conflicts with women of color, white women cry strategically to escape accountability when confronted by their own wrongdoing. As described by Ajayi (2019, para. 3), '[w]hite women tears are especially potent and extra salty because they are attached to the symbol of femininity. These tears are pouring out from the eyes of the one chosen to be the prototype of womanhood. Moreover, the potential consequences of these actions by white women can be severe, leading to poor job reviews, layoffs, and criminalization for Black people.'

At the exact time that white women have been represented as helpless, Black men have been represented as aggressive, violent predators (Brett, 2020). This leads to perceptions of Black men as bigger and more capable of causing physical harm than white men, even when they are not (Wilson, Hugenberg et al., 2017). It also leads to perceptions that Black boys are older and less innocent than their white peers (Goff et al., 2014).

Within this duality of white femininity and Black masculinity, Black women have been portrayed as more masculine than white women. In 1851, Sojourner Truth gave a speech in Akron, Ohio, entitled 'Ain't I a woman' in which she highlights how Black women were never treated the same as white women and, through her central question, suggests that Black women aren't seen as women:

> That man over there says that women need to be helped into carriages and lifted over ditches and to have the best place everywhere. Nobody ever helps me into carriages or over mud puddles or gives me any best place! And ain't I a woman? (National Park Service, 2017, para. 4)

Goff et al. (2008b) explore how white people continue to misgender Black women and fail to see them as feminine. In their study, they asked 292 white undergraduate students in the Northeast to categorize pictures and videos of Black and white men and women. Overall, the study found that participants made the highest number of gender categorization errors for Black women, and that 'maleness' was highly associated with Black women.

The methods employed by society to uphold white femininity have been twofold. As already illustrated, one method has been the offensive tactic of vilifying men and masculine people of color, particularly Black men, and rendering them imminent threats to the physical safety of white femininity. Yet there are strategies employed by white women against Black women and feminine-of-center Black people that are equally deleterious. Researchers have outlined how white feminism oppresses Black women within the gender justice movement (Hill Collins, 1990; Ortega, 2006; Williams, 2019). White women are so focused on being oppressed as women that they 'don't see their heelprint' on Black women's faces (Audre Lorde quoted by Ortega, 2006, p. 56). A defensive tactic aimed at preserving white femininity is also in place and driving the punishment of feminine-of-center Black boys and Black transgender women within the justice system. The degree of protection afforded to white femininity rests upon its exclusivity and narrowly defined parameters – from physical features to mannerisms and etiquette to social/familial expectations (Hill Collins, 1990, p. 67). Those whose race, sex assigned at birth, gender identity, physical features, and socioeconomic status are not in close proximity to white femininity but are perceived to be encroaching on or appropriating it are disproportionately swept into the justice system, a fate met similarly by Black men but with insidious implications. As evidenced by the statistics on Black youth in the justice system in the subsequent sections, the existential threat to white femininity posed by Black and feminine individuals assigned male at birth is played out in youth court and probation systems.

The dehumanization and association of masculinity with Blackness by white people have consequences within the court system. Goff et al. (2008a, 2014) proved that white police who dehumanize Black people by associating them with apes are more likely to support violence against Black children perceived to be suspects. These findings may also lead other actors such as judges and other justice stakeholders to justify unnecessary punishment and treatment of Black youth (Tonnesen, 2013).

Certainly, empirical research on race and ethnic disparities shows that Black children are more likely to experience exclusionary school discipline, arrest, and incarceration (Morris, 2012; Davis et al., 2014; Irvine & Canfield, 2016; John Ridolfi, 2016; Morris, 2016; Irvine & Canfield, 2017; Irvine et al., 2017). Moreover, these forms of punishment are linked. Even though Black and white students behave in the exact same ways, Black students are suspended and expelled at higher rates when compared with white students (Fabelo et al., 2011; National Center for Education Statistics, 2011; US Department of Education Office for Civil Rights, 2014; Hirschfield, 2018), are more likely to be engaged with school-based law enforcement efforts (Shollenberger, 2013; US Department of Education Office for Civil Rights, 2014; Hirschfield, 2018), and are more likely to become incarcerated because of these histories of school suspensions and expulsions (Sedlak & Bruce, 2010; Irvine & Yusuf, 2016; Hirschfield, 2018). In the end, Black youth are the most overrepresented of all youth in the court system, comprising 42 percent of the 2015 juvenile detention population compared with an estimated 16.5 percent of youth ages 10–17 in the general population (Sickmund et al., 2017).

The gender spectrum

Yet not all research discusses Black youth who fall outside the gender binary of girls and boys. Let us explain what we mean. All youth are assigned a sex when they are born. While most youth have been assigned male or female, some hospitals in the United States and other places in the world have started to offer other options that do not adhere to just these two options – two options that create a gender binary. Some hospitals recognize that there are babies born with sex characteristics that are both male and female and should therefore be identified as intersex.

Separate from sex assigned at birth, all people have a gender identity and a gender expression. Gender identity is each person's internal sense of their gender. Gender expression is how each person externally performs their gender identity through chosen pronouns, names, clothing, and hairstyles, and, different from sex assigned at birth, these two categories are constructed and informed by social and cultural norms, not biology.

The variety of gender identities and gender expressions that exist among individuals creates what we call the gender spectrum. When people identify with a gender that corresponds with their assigned sex at birth, they are cisgender. When people express their gender in a way that corresponds with their gender identity, they are gender conforming. When people identify or express a gender that is something different than what they were assigned at birth, they might be transgender, genderqueer, gender nonbinary, gender expansive, two-spirit, or gender nonconforming (GNC).[1] This variety creates gender identities and expressions on a broad spectrum rather than a simple binary of male/female, boy/girl, man/woman, masculine/feminine.

This chapter explores how the overcriminalization of Black youth across the entire gender spectrum sits within the white femininity/Black masculinity duality and, conversely, how we must deconstruct this duality in order to liberate all Black youth. Much work has been done within the justice field to identify programs aimed at changing what is perceived to be the criminal behavior of Black youth. This approach entirely ignores the greater driver of incarceration: the social construction of Blackness as masculine, aggressive, and violent. This view of Blackness shapes justice stakeholders' views of culpability and risk level, raising the severity of charges and lengthening the time that Black youth are held in secure facilities.

Gender nonconforming and transgender youth in the court system

An emerging body of research shows that lesbian, gay, bisexual, pansexual, questioning, transgender, genderqueer, gender nonbinary, and gender nonconforming youth are also overrepresented in the court system (Irvine & Canfield, 2017; Wilson, B.D.M. et al., 2017; Irvine et al., 2019a). While 6–7 percent of the general population is estimated to be LGBQT+, 20 percent of all youth in the justice system report being LGBQ/GNCT (Irvine & Canfield, 2017; Irvine et al., 2019a). This number jumps to 40–50 percent of youth assigned female at birth (Irvine & Canfield, 2017; Irvine et al., 2019a). Notably, understanding the exact degree to which gender nonconforming, gender nonbinary, and transgender youth of color are overrepresented is more difficult.

Since this is a relatively new field of study, there are not always statistics that break out numbers specifically for Black youth. Research across multiple race and ethnic identities shows that very small numbers of adults and youth in the general population identify as transgender. Studies show that 0.3–0.8 percent of adults and 0.67 percent of youth identify as transgender (Flores et al., 2016; Williams Institute, 2020). However, a growing number of youth identify as genderqueer, gender nonbinary, or gender nonconforming (Olson-Kennedy et al., 2016). Unfortunately, it is more difficult to measure this latter group. One study asked parents about their children's gender identity and expression. Between 1.3 and 5 percent said that their children 'wish to be the opposite sex' and between 1 and 12.9 percent said that their children 'behave like the opposite sex'. The authors have access to several databases that might provide more accurate comparisons between cisgender and gender conforming and GNCT youth.

Analysis of a survey that we conducted in 2016 with 700 seniors attending school in one public school district in California finds that 7.8 percent of the respondents identified as transgender, gender nonbinary, or gender nonconforming. Broken down by current gender identity, 7.6 percent of youth who were assigned male at birth said they were GNCT, 6.1 percent of youth who were assigned female at birth said they were GNCT, and another 0.4 percent of youth reported another sex assigned at birth and said they were GNCT (Irvine, 2020a).[2]

Analysis of another survey that we conducted in 2014 with 4,044 youth in secure out-of-home placements in California could compare the responses to the exact same questions: 12.7 percent of respondents to this court system survey indicated that they are transgender, gender nonbinary, genderqueer, or gender nonconforming. Broken down by current gender identity, 10.5 percent of youth who were assigned male at birth said they were GNCT, 21.2 percent of youth who were assigned female at birth said they were GNCT, and another 0.5 percent of youth reported another sex assigned at birth and said they were GNCT (Irvine, 2020b).

Comparing these two analyses, we see that GNCT youth are overrepresented within the court system, though there is heightened risk for youth who were assigned female at birth. If you look specifically at the proportion of youth assigned male at birth compared with the youth assigned female at birth, there is a noticeable difference. A national sample of 1,400 youth found that 10.1 percent of youth assigned male at birth within the justice system reported being gender nonconforming or transgender compared with 17.0 percent of youth assigned female at birth (Irvine & Canfield, 2017). Similarly, a sample of 4,044 youth held within county-run secure facilities in California found that 9.9 percent of youth assigned male at birth reported being gender nonconforming or transgender compared with 22.4 percent of youth assigned female at birth (Irvine et al., 2017). In both samples, over 85 percent of the youth were of color. As such, we see masculine-of-center youth assigned female at birth arrested and charged within the justice system at alarming rates.

Analysis of court system data to describe the criminalization of Black youth

In order to understand the criminalization specifically of Black youth across the gender spectrum, we analyzed system data from more than 3,614 youth from three youth courts in Ohio, three probation departments in New York, and the youth court in Connecticut (see Appendix A for a more detailed description of our methods). Fifty-four percent of these youth were Black: 2.7 percent were Black and Latinx, while 51.3 percent were Black and not Latinx.

In order to illustrate the full impact of the white femininity/Black masculinity duality on Black youth across the gender spectrum, we calculated relative rate indices that compare the incarceration rates of cisgender, gender conforming white girls for violent felonies and weapons charges to the incarceration rates of cisgender, gender conforming Black girls, GNCT Black youth who were assigned female at birth, GNCT Black youth who were assigned male at birth, and cisgender, gender conforming Black boys (Irvine, 2020c).

We found that for every cisgender, gender conforming white girl:

• who is arrested for a violent felony: there are six cisgender, gender conforming Black girls, 16 GNCT Black youth who were assigned female at birth, 19 GNCT Black youth who were assigned male at birth, and 34 cisgender, gender conforming Black boys;
• who receives a sustained charge for a violent felony: there are six cisgender, gender conforming Black girls, 34 GNCT Black youth who were assigned female at birth, 24 GNCT Black youth who were assigned male at birth, and 52 cisgender, gender conforming Black boys;
• who is arrested for a weapons charge: there are six cisgender, gender conforming Black girls, 18 GNCT Black youth who were assigned female at birth, 16 GNCT Black youth who were assigned male at birth, and 34 cisgender, gender conforming Black boys;
• who receives a sustained charge for a weapons charge: there are six cisgender, gender conforming Black girls, 51 GNCT Black youth who were assigned female at birth, 13 GNCT Black youth who were assigned male at birth, and 61 cisgender, gender conforming Black boys.

These findings show that the lowest arrest and sustained charging rates for violent felonies and weapons charges are experienced by cisgender, gender conforming white girls and the highest rates are experienced by cisgender, gender conforming Black boys. In general, cisgender, gender conforming Black girls are arrested and adjudicated six times more frequently than their white counterparts. Transgender, genderqueer, gender nonbinary, and gender nonconforming Black youth are also experiencing high rates of arrest and adjudication, with masculine-of-center Black girls or transgender Black boys experiencing higher rates than their feminine-of-center counterparts in three of the four categories. They are virtually the same in the fourth category of arrests for violent crimes.

These findings reinforce the authors' argument that the criminalization of Black youth – whether cisgender and gender conforming, gender nonconforming, or transgender – is driven by the social constructions within the Black masculinity/white femininity duality. We do see a pattern where Black boys and masculine-of-center Black youth have the highest rates of criminalization. Nonetheless, we see arrest and charging patterns reflect the construction of Black youth across the gender spectrum as masculine, aggressive, violent, and inhuman.

Recommendations for liberating Black youth from the juvenile justice system

Given how the Black masculinity/white femininity duality drives the staggering overcriminalization of Black youth, the authors provide four recommendations to the field of youth justice transformation so that we may ultimately humanize and treasure Black youth across the gender spectrum:

1. develop a deeper understanding and practice of intersectionality;
2. develop intersectional youth programs that allow for gender fluidity and affirm race and gender;
3. organize youth to fight the white femininity/Black masculinity duality;
4. train staff to build authentic relationships and conduct data-driven reforms.

We discuss these recommendations in more detail here.

1. Develop a deeper understanding and practice of intersectionality

The youth justice field, including the philanthropic institutions funding reform work, must begin to recognize that all youth have a race/ethnicity, gender identity, and gender expression that are inextricably bound to one another. Gender cannot be seen as a binary nor can it be seen as separate from race. In so doing, we can see that while individual cisgender, gender conforming white girls have had to navigate terrible circumstances before entering the justice system, there are many forces in place to protect them from excessively punitive system responses. At the same time, social and systemic responses to particular forms of Black femininity and masculinity are driving Black youth across the gender spectrum into being arrested and adjudicated at alarming rates. In order to liberate Black youth, we must intentionally deconstruct both the protections of white femininity and the dehumanization and punishment of Black bodies. This does not mean arresting or incarcerating white girls at the same rate as Black youth. Rather, we must think of ways to protect Black youth across the gender spectrum from the dangers of the court system.

2. Develop intersectional youth programs that allow for gender fluidity and affirm Blackness

Emanating from this philosophical framework, the field must amplify gender and race affirming services that create off-ramps from the justice system. Emerging research points to the failure of traditionally white-facilitated gender-specific programs and other 'evidence-based practices' to effectively transition youth of color from the justice system (Irvine-Baker et al., 2019). In fact, the segregation of youth into programs for either boys or girls underpins a gender binary that reinforces negative social constructions of femininity and masculinity (Irvine-Baker et al., 2019). At the same time, many existing programs for justice-involved adults and youth fail to effectively serve Black people because they do not recognize and address the strengths of the Black community (Jones, 2020). Instead, programs such as those created by members of the EBP+ Collaborative should be lifted as alternatives to incarceration (EBP+ Collaborative, 2018). These programs are all led by Black, Latinx, and Indigenous leaders serving youth from their communities with serious and violent charges. They work to magnify the individual strengths and leadership of youth of color across the gender spectrum, provide opportunities for spiritual growth, and create forward movement in youths' lives (EBP+ Collaborative, 2018).

3. Organize youth and their communities to fight the white femininity/ Black masculinity duality

Aside from programs that serve individual youth, organizers and advocates should weave efforts to deconstruct the white femininity/Black masculinity duality into the larger movement to end youth incarceration. Advocates working to transform the youth justice field should develop curricula and plan events that educate people about how social and systemic responses to both race and gender combine to drive Black youth across the gender spectrum into the justice system.

This work does not have to be limited to Black organizers. All people within the movement can work to deconstruct the duality. White women in particular must take responsibility to acknowledge and deconstruct the ways in which white femininity benefits them and harms others, particularly those in Black communities. All movement leaders can educate the public about how Black youth are burdened with violent and weapons charges even when they haven't hurt anybody – and how this overcharging is a function of the views of Black youth being masculine, aggressive, violent, and inhuman.

4. Train staff to build authentic relationships and conduct data-driven reforms

Advocates, community-based programs, and state and county agencies should train staff how to talk to youth about their race, gender identity, and gender expression in a way that affirms youth as whole people. The Whole Youth Project (Canfield et al., 2020) provides an example of such training. This approach begins with authentic conversations between staff and youth. Data collection is achieved through a series of questions aimed at gaining a deeper understanding of young people, the circumstances of their lives that contribute to disparate suffering and punishment, and how justice professionals might best meet their needs and promote their well-being. Once data is collected, it can be analyzed to identify opportunities for new practices that counter the ongoing dehumanization and overcriminalization of Black youth.

Conclusion

This chapter lays out how a duality between white femininity and Black masculinity was socially constructed over time to justify the punishment of Black people. The impact of this duality has been a staggering overcriminalization of Black youth across the gender spectrum, with Black girls being arrested and adjudicated for violent and weapons charges six times more often than white girls; GNCT Black youth being arrested and adjudicated for violent and weapons charges 16 to 51 times more often than white girls; and Black boys being arrested and adjudicated for violent and weapons charges 34 to 61 times more often than white girls.

Through 2019 and 2020, much organizing and movement building has focused on defunding the police and passing policies to eliminate police violence within Black communities. Yet the police and court practices of overarresting and overcharging Black youth are anchored in the protection of white femininity.

Ironically, as Brett (2020) points out, this protection actually infantilizes white women. It is also ephemeral – a construct that protects white men far more than it protects white women. This is seen in the failure to prosecute white men for even the most heinous crimes against white women (Brett, 2020).

Since this duality only serves white men, a multiracial coalition of people across the gender spectrum should work to dismantle both social constructions – the damsel in distress and the violent Black man. Both must be dismantled to liberate Black youth.

The police and courts will not stop harming Black children in the name of protecting white women until we destroy the anchor – the idea of white femininity. And if white women can themselves insist that the oppression of Blackness no longer happens in their name, we will more easily achieve a moment where the police and the courts will see Black youth for who they are. Black youth will regain their innocence, an ability to move safely through the world, and the space to be brilliant.

Appendix A: Methods
The court system data used in this chapter were collected as part of the authors' Whole Youth Project. With the intention of collecting sexual orientation, gender identity, and gender expression data across the country, Ceres Policy Research broadly disseminated a request for applications. We chose Equality Ohio, which was working with three counties in Ohio (Lucas, Montgomery, and Cuyahoga); the New York State Division of Criminal Justice Services, which had chosen three pilot counties in New York (Suffolk, Onondaga, and Schenectady); and the Court Support Services Division of the Connecticut Judicial Branch, which serves all counties in the state.

Ceres trained trainers in each county that, in turn, trained their pilot departments and collected sexual orientation, gender identity, and gender expression (SOGIE) data for between 6 and 12 months. At the end of the first grant period, we had SOGIE data from close to 3,500 unique youth across all sites. These were matched to other justice data to create a database that included arrest charges, sustained court charges, risk assessment data, placement information, and detention information.

Respondents varied across sex at birth, race/ethnicity, gender, and sexual orientation:

- The majority of youth (67 percent) were assigned male at birth and 33 percent of youth were assigned female at birth. There were no youth who indicated that they had been identified as intersex through the course of their lifetime.
- Youth of color are overrepresented within the incarcerated LGBQ/ GNCT population: 68 percent of respondents are youth of color. Broken

down, 50 percent of respondents are African American or Black (not Latinx), 0.6 percent of respondents are Asian, 14 percent of respondents are Latinx, 0.3 percent of respondents are Native American, 32 percent of respondents are white (not Latinx), and 3 percent of respondents have a mixed race or ethnic identity.

- Youth of color disclosed being LGBQ/GNCT at the same rate as white youth.
- 15.3 percent of respondents identify as either lesbian, gay, bisexual, questioning, gender nonconforming, or transgender:
  - 3 percent of respondents are straight and gender nonconforming or transgender;
  - 8 percent of respondents are lesbian, gay, or bisexual and gender nonconforming or transgender;
  - 4.3 percent of respondents are lesbian, gay, or bisexual and gender conforming.

Notes

[1] The Human Rights Campaign provides an online glossary of terms here: https://www. hrc.org/resources/glossary-of-terms. The Trevor Project reports that 25 percent of LGBTQ youth identify as nonbinary and provides a longer list of gender identities: https://www.thetrevorproject.org/2019/10/29/research-brief-diversity-of-youth-gender-identity/

[2] This sample only contained five Black youth, so we cannot complete an intersectional analysis of Blackness and the gender spectrum in this section.

References

Ajayi, L. (2019) 'About the weary weaponizing of white woman tears', Awesomely Luvvie Blog, April 17. https://www.awesomelyluvvie. com/2018/04/weaponizing-white-women-tears.html

Brett, M. (2020) 'Amy Cooper played the damsel in distress. That trope has a troubling history', *The Washington Post*, May 28. https://www. washingtonpost.com/outlook/2020/05/28/amy-cooper-played-damsel-distress-troubling-history-this-trope/

Canfield, A., Irvine-Baker, A., Wilber, S., & Garza, M. (2020) 'The whole youth model: how collecting data about sexual orientation, gender identity, and gender expression (SOGIE) helps probation and youth courts build more authentic relationships focused on improved well-being', *LGBTQ Policy Journal*, June 22, Harvard Kennedy School, Cambridge, MA.

Davis, A., Irvine, A., & Ziedenberg, J. (2014) 'Stakeholders' views on the movement to reduce youth incarceration', National Council on Crime and Delinquency. http://nccdglobal.org/sites/default/files/publication_pdf/deincarceration-summary-report.pdf

EBP+ Collaborative (2018) 'The EBP-PLUS model: liberating youth, families, and community from the justice system, Policy Brief #1. http://bit.ly/ebp-policy-brief

Fabelo, T., Thompson, M.D., Plotkin, M., Carmichael, D., Marchbanks, M.P., & Booth, E.A. (2011) 'Breaking schools' rules: a state-wide study of how school discipline relates to students' success and juvenile justice involvement', Council of State Governments Justice Center and Public Policy Research Institute. https://knowledgecenter.csg.org/kc/system/files/Breaking_School_Rules.pdf

Flores, A.R., Herman, J.L., Gates, G.J. & Brown, T.N.T. (2016) 'How many adults identify as transgender in the U.S.?', The Williams Institute, University of California, Los Angeles. https://williamsinstitute.law.ucla.edu/publications/trans-adults-united-states/

Francis, E. & Hutchinson, B. (2018) '"I don't forgive this woman, and she needs help": Black child wrongly accused of grabbing "Cornerstone Caroline"', ABC News, December 16. https://abcnews.go.com/US/white-woman-apologizes-alleging-black-child-assaulted-york/story?id=58505763

Goff, P.A., Eberhardt, J.L., Williams, M.J., & Jackson, M.C. (2008a) 'Not yet human: implicit knowledge, historical dehumanization, and contemporary consequences', *Journal of Personality and Social Psychology*, 94(2): 292–306. https://doi.org/10.1037/0022-3514.94.2.292

Goff, P.A., Thomas, M.A., & Jackson, M.C. (2008b) '"Ain't I a woman?": Towards an. intersectional approach to person perception and group-based harms', *Sex Roles*, 59: 392–403. https://doi.org/10.1007/s11199-008-9505-4

Goff, P.A., Jackson, M.C., DiLione, B.A.L., Culotta, C.M., & DiTomasso, N.A. (2014) 'The essence of innocence: consequences of dehumanizing Black children', *Journal of Personality and Social Psychology*, 106(4): 526–545.

Hamad, R. (2018) 'How white women use strategic tears to silence women of colour', *The Guardian*, May 8. https://www.theguardian.com/commentisfree/2018/may/08/how-white-women-use-strategic-tears-to-avoid-accountability

Hamad, R. (2019) *White Tears/Brown Scars*, New York: Catapult Books.

Hill Collins, P. (1990) *Black Feminist Thought: Knowledge, Consciousness, and the Politics of Empowerment*, Abingdon: Routledge.

Hirschfield, P.J. (2018) 'Trends in school social control in the United States: explaining patterns of decriminalization', In J. Deakin, E. Taylor, & A. Kupchik (eds.), *The Palgrave International Handbook of School Discipline, Surveillance, and Social Control*, Cham: Palgrave Macmillan, pp. 43–64. https://doi.org/10.1007/978-3-319-71559-9_3

Irvine, A. (2020a) '2016 survey of Eastside Union School District seniors' [SPSS File], Oakland, CA: Ceres Policy Research.

Irvine, A. (2020b) '2014 survey of youth held in secure out-of-home placements in California [SPSS File], Oakland, CA: Ceres Policy Research.

Irvine, A. (2020c) '2020 compilation of court system data from three counties in OH, three counties in NY and Connecticut' [SPSS File], Oakland, CA: Ceres Policy Research.

Irvine, A. & Canfield A. (2016) 'The overrepresentation of lesbian, gay, bisexual, questioning, gender nonconforming, and transgender youth within the child welfare to juvenile justice crossover population', *Journal of Gender, Social Policy & the Law*, 24(2): 243–261.

Irvine, A. & Canfield, A. (2017) 'Reflections on new national data on LGBQ/GNCT youth in the justice system', *LGBTQ Policy Journal, Harvard Kennedy School*, VII (Spring): 27–36.

Irvine, A. & Yusuf, A. (2016) 'New information about the school-to-prison pipeline: up to nine in ten juvenile justice-involved youth have been disciplined in school', Impact Justice. https://static1.squarespace.com/static/58ba8c479f7456dff8fb4e29/t/58de63a62994caabca662c5f/1490969510805/school-to-prison-pipeline-final.pdf

Irvine, A., Jordan, S., & Soto, D. (2019a) 'Youth of color in systems: juvenile justice', in K.J. Conron & B.D.M. Wilson (eds.), *LGBTQ Youth of Color Impacted by the Child Welfare and Juvenile Justice Systems: A Research Agenda*, Los Angeles: Williams Institute, University of California, Los Angeles, pp. 52–57. https://williamsinstitute.law.ucla.edu/wp-content/uploads/LGBTQ-YOC-Social-Services-Jul-2019.pdf

Irvine, A., Wilber, S., & Canfield A. (2017) 'Lesbian, gay, bisexual, questioning, and gender nonconforming girls and boys in the California juvenile justice system: a practice guide', Impact Justice and the National Center for Lesbian Rights.

Irvine-Baker, A., Jones, N., & Canfield, A. (2019) 'Taking the "girl" out of gender-specific programming in the juvenile justice system', *American Review of Criminology*, 2: 321–336.

John Ridolfi, L. (2016) 'Stemming the rising tide: racial and ethnic disparities in youth incarceration and strategies for change', W. Hayward Burns Institute. https://burnsinstitute.org/wp-content/uploads/2020/09/Stemming-the-Rising-Tide-_compressed.pdf

Jones, M.D. (2020) The Araminta approach: a social-emotional, culturally affirming model for criminal justice involved Black women', Because Black is Still Beautiful. https://static1.squarespace.com/static/58ba8c479f7456dff8fb4e29/t/5f554aadfab9b365a24630df/1599425199338/ARAMINTA+APPROACH+PDF.pdf

Morris, M. (2012) 'Race, gender, and the school-to-prison pipeline: expanding our discussion to include Black girls', African American Policy Forum. http://schottfoundation.org/sites/default/files/resources/Morris-Race-Gender-and-the-School-to-Prison-Pipeline.pdf

Morris, M. (2016) *Pushout: The Criminalization of Black Girls in Schools*, New York: New Press.

National Center for Education Statistics (2011) 'Table 14. Percentage of public school students in 9th through 12th grade who had ever been suspended or expelled, by sex and race/ethnicity: 1999, 2003, and 2007', in *Youth Indicators 2011. America's Youth: Transitions to Adulthood*. https://nces.ed.gov/pubs2012/2012026/tables/table_14.asp

National Park Service (2017) 'Sojourner Truth: Ain't I a woman?' https://www.nps.gov/articles/sojourner-truth.htm

Olson-Kennedy, J., Cohen-Kettenis, P.T., Kreukels, B.P.C., Meyer-Bahlburg, H.F.L., Garofalo, R., Meyer, W., & Rosenthal, S.M. (2016) 'Research priorities for gender nonconforming/transgender youth: gender identity development and biopsychosocial outcomes', *Current Opionion in Endocrinology, Diabetes, and Obesity*, 23(2): 172–179.

Ortega, M. (2006) 'Being lovingly, knowingly ignorant: white feminism and women of color', *Hypatia*, 21(3): 56–74. https://muse.jhu.edu/article/199102

Sedlak, A. & Bruce, C. (2010) 'Youth characteristics and backgrounds: findings from the Survey of Youth in Residential Placement', Office of Juvenile Justice and Delinquency Prevention, Office of Justice Programs, US Department of Justice. https://www.ncjrs.gov/pdffiles1/ojjdp/227730.pdf

Shollenberger, T.L. (2013) 'Racial disparities in school suspension and subsequent outcomes: evidence from the National Longitudinal Survey of Youth 1997', Paper, Closing the School Discipline Gap: Research to Practice Conference, Washington, DC. https://www.civilrightsproject.ucla.edu/resources/projects/center-for-civil-rights-remedies/school-to-prison-folder/state-reports/racial-disparities-in-school-suspension-and-subsequent-outcomes-evidence-from-the-national-longitudinal-survey-of-youth-1997

Sickmund, M., Sladky, T.J., Kang, W., & Puzzanchera, C. (2017) 'Easy access to the census of juveniles in residential placement', National Center for Juvenile Justice. https://www.ojjdp.gov/ojstatbb/ezacjrp/

Tonnesen, S.C. (2013) '"Hit it and quit it": responses to Black girls' victimization in school', *Berkeley Journal of Gender, Law & Justice*, 28(1): 1–29.

US Department of Education Office for Civil Rights (2014) 'Civil rights data collection. Data snapshot: school discipline', Issue brief no. 1. http://www2.ed.gov/about/offices/list/ocr/docs/crdc-discipline-snapshot.pdf

Williams Institute (2020) 'LGBT population in the United States: fact sheet'. https://williamsinstitute.law.ucla.edu/publications/lgbt-youth-pop-us/

Williams, M.T. (2019) 'How white feminists oppress Black women: when feminism functions as white supremacy', *Chacruna*, January 16. https://chacruna.net/how-white-feminists-oppress-black-women-when-feminism-functions-as-white-supremacy/

Wilson, B.D.M., Jordan, S.P., Meyer, I.H., Flores, A., Stemple, L. & Herman, J. (2017) 'Disproportionality and disparities among sexual minority youth in custody', *Journal of Youth and Adolescence*, 46(7): 1547–1561. https://link.springer.com/article/10.1007%2Fs10964-017-0632-5

Wilson, J.P., Hugenberg, K., & Rule, N.O. (2017) 'Racial bias in judgments of physical size and formidability: from size to threat', *Journal of Personality and Social Psychology*, 113(1): 59–80. https://psycnet.apa.org/doiLanding?doi=10.1037%2Fpspi0000092

Zhao, C. (2018) '"BBQ Becky," white woman who called cops on Black BBQ, 911 audio released: "I'm really scared! Come quick!"', *Newsweek*, September 4. https://www.newsweek.com/bbq-becky-white-woman-who-called-cops-black-bbq-911-audio-released-im-really-1103057

12

'I Thought They Were Supposed to Be on My Side': What Jane Doe's Experience Teaches Us about Institutional Harm against Trans Youth

Vanessa R. Panfil and Aimee Wodda

A pressing issue for the child welfare and juvenile justice systems is the treatment of LGBTQ youth in facilities and under the care of the state, particularly transgender youth. Unfortunately, these youth often do not receive affirming, effective care, nor responsible and suitable placements. Thus, while young trans people may experience interpersonal harm, they also face *institutional harm* perpetuated by police, courts, juvenile correctional facilities, child welfare agencies, and other institutional entities, which repeatedly occurs in what seems to be a coordinated effort to allow violence and stigma to flourish as they fail to protect these youth.

We explore the facets of this issue by focusing on the case study of Jane Doe, a transgender teen whose plight caught the eye of activists and the media. She had been under the custody of the Department of Children and Family (DCF) Services from early childhood and had repeatedly experienced sexual assault while under the care of the state. She also spent time in an adult carceral facility – including in solitary confinement – despite not having been charged with a crime and was briefly psychiatrically hospitalized. Nowhere was she given meaningful support for her gender transition. For years prior to being institutionalized, Jane Doe experienced pervasive, severe physical and sexual abuse from family members on the basis of her transgender identity, had engaged in survival sex, and was coping with the pain of her trauma through illicit drug use. Despite a lawsuit filed on her behalf, it seemed that the only respite Jane had from harmful placements was aging out of DCF care.

Jane Doe's story is tragic and, although extreme in some instances, crystallizes many relevant issues for transgender youth in the juvenile justice and child welfare systems. We complement our analysis of this case study with relevant empirical data about LGBTQ youths' experiences in families, schools, communities, the child welfare system, and the juvenile justice system. Doing so allows us to paint a portrait of the structural issues at play in instances of serious system failure, as with Jane Doe. Consistent with the practical goals of this volume, we discuss ten policy recommendations we see as stemming from this case. Our recommendations are targeted at various levels of intervention, including institutional, interpersonal, and even society-wide. We aim to address transphobic and trans-exclusionary practices enacted by families and the state, as well as draw from empirical evidence regarding youth under state custody more generally.

Jane Doe's story

To facilitate our discussion of the mistreatment of LGBTQ youth while in state custody, we explore the case of 'Jane Doe', a 16-year-old Latina trans teen whose story was detailed extensively by the media and championed by trans activists. While the state failed Jane in many ways, including mandating her to various inappropriate placements and failing to address the hideous trauma she suffered from an early age, it also inadequately supported her gender transition.

Jane had been in DCF custody in Connecticut from the age of five and had experienced sexual assault and abuse while under the 'care' of the state, both in state-run juvenile facilities and at the hands of family members while in foster care. She shared her life history with the court in an attempt to force the adults in control of her case to understand where she was coming from and what she was going through in isolation. Between the ages of eight and 12, Jane Doe experienced violent, transphobic punishments for behaviors such as playing with dolls and wearing lipstick. For example, at age 11, Jane was experimenting with lipstick while wearing a dress. Her aunt came into the room, slapped her, and said 'you're a boy, what the fuck is wrong with you!' (*Jane Doe v. Connecticut Department of Corrections et al.*, 2014). Other punishments included beatings and being locked in a room for two days without food and water in retaliation for notifying someone about the abuse. She experienced extreme, repeated sexual violence from older male relatives, including her cousin and her sister's father, across the ages of 8–15. These were coupled with graphic death threats and physical harm, which included long-lasting bodily damage to her bowels.

At Connecticut Children's Place (CCP), a DCF residential facility for abused and neglected children, Jane was also forced to perform oral sex on multiple staff members, sometimes in the facility itself. Other times, the sexual abuse happened offsite. At age 15, Jane went to live with a friend she had met at CCP. She began experimenting with a variety of drugs to numb her physical and emotional pain. She sold sex in order to survive. She and her friend found themselves in a number of precarious positions; at one point they were injected with drugs, held in a house for three weeks, and forced to sell sex. They appealed to a customer who ultimately helped them. Doe thinks back on that time – not so long ago – with resignation: 'I feel so numb to it all and ever since this has happened, I feel numb to everything because I could go missing and no one would care' (*Jane Doe v. Connecticut Department of Corrections et al.*, 2014, p. 7). After she escaped captivity, she lived for some time with her aunt, with whom Jane said she smoked crack and sold sex. Later, she was housed in another residential facility for foster youth, this time in Massachusetts.

Local and then national media outlets took up Jane's story in April 2014 after she was transferred from a residential facility in Massachusetts to a high-security adult women's prison in Connecticut, where she was placed in solitary confinement 'for her own protection' but had not been charged with a crime. An obscure statute (Connecticut Statute 17a-12) allowed for the transfer of Doe into 'any facility administrators find appropriate'. 'Protection' is perhaps a kind reading into the State of Connecticut's decision, as her placement in solitary confinement occurred because adults reportedly did not know what to do with her (Katz, 2014). Part of the issue, some suspect, was state mishandling of her transgender identity (Kovner, 2015). Attorney Chase Strangio met with Doe and argued for her release, saying that '[i]solation puts people in closer contact with staff and leads to more abuse in a private setting' (Deniflee, 2014). Indeed, even a casual glance at Jane Doe's file would reveal layers of trauma that could only deepen by placement in solitary confinement – a practice widely considered torture, particularly for those under 18 (Clark, 2017). Solitary confinement requires individuals to be 'locked down' for 22 or 23 hours per day. DCF officials argued that the placement was necessary, as Doe was violent with staff and other youth at the facilities where she had earlier been placed (Katz, 2014). In court documents and letters to the governor and the head of DCF, Jane acknowledged that she has a tendency to act out when upset; it is not surprising that a young person with her extensive and continuing traumatic history would experience behavioral issues. Specifically, she said, 'I have a lot of stuff built up inside me and don't know how to deal with it at times. They tell me that trauma changes people and makes them act out. Believe me, it does' (Doe, 2014). When DCF was unsympathetic to the trauma that caused her to get into conflicts and instead placed her in solitary confinement, she lost faith that DCF had her best interests in mind, lamenting, 'I thought they were supposed to be on my side' (Doe, 2014).

Doe was released from the adult prison after 78 days and sent to a children's psychiatric center, where she was accused of assaulting a fellow youth and a staff member. She was then transferred to the Connecticut Juvenile Training School – a male facility. There, she was referred to only by her assigned birth name, staff used male pronouns for her, and she was not allowed to wear any feminine garb or accessories despite the fact that DCF had previously supported her hormonal transition (Deniflee, 2014). Further, she was placed in solitary confinement once again.

While in the care of the state, Jane Doe experienced abuse, discrimination, isolation, and misgendering. A court document shows her thorough desire to be whole, to be treated as human:

> I wanted to be a little kid again in my mother's arms and all I wanted was someone to tell me they loved me, that everything would be alright, and that I will never have to live the way I was again. But that never happened and will not happen and I've become okay accepting that this is my life as a transgender 16 year old sex worker who ... does any drugs anyone gives her, from pills, shrooms, k2, angel dust, pcp, acid, and anything to become numb, and will probably not make it to age 25. (*Jane Doe v. Connecticut Department of Corrections et al.*, 2014, p. 7)

In a later statement to the press, Doe reflected on her resilience: 'What I have survived would have destroyed most people. I'm not going to let it destroy me. I can't change what has happened, but I can build a future just like every other 16 year old' (Doe, 2014).

Despite the efforts of transgender activists such as Laverne Cox, Tourmaline, Janet Mock, and Chase Strangio, Jane Doe's legal team was not able to facilitate her release from custody. News about her case tapered off around 2015 and a Facebook post dated May 5, 2017, on the 'J4J: Justice for Jane' page shared this good news: 'She has aged out of DCF and is now happily living her life as an independent adult. She has a nice support network and a job.' While we cannot know what the future will hold for Jane Doe, we hope that examples like hers will become fewer and farther between as institutional supports move toward nurturing and enriching LGBTQ youth rather than actively harming them by stigmatizing, pathologizing, and criminalizing their same-sex desires and gender identities. And, regarding direct interpersonal harm perpetrated by those who are supposed to 'guard' or 'serve' these young people, we hope shifts toward affirmation and acceptance will also shift narratives that have historically allowed these young people's trauma to be ignored, downplayed, or thought to be brought about by their own behavior or identity.

A mirror of trans experiences

While we acknowledge that Jane Doe's experience is in some ways extreme, we want to reiterate that many of her experiences in the criminal and juvenile justice systems mirror larger patterns. Transgender individuals who are incarcerated are often housed according to their assigned birth sex instead of their gender identity, prevented from grooming or dressing themselves in ways that are consistent with their gender identity, addressed by inaccurate pronouns, placed in solitary confinement, denied medical treatment such as hormone therapy, and blamed for their own sexual victimization (Mogul et al., 2011). Youth in juvenile facilities face many of these same challenges. As young people, they face the added challenge of their transgender identity being pathologized as being the cause of their delinquency or 'dysfunction' and thus encounter staff efforts to change, control, or punish their gender identity, all of which are profoundly harmful (Majd et al., 2009). These experiences will be addressed in additional depth as we discuss the policy recommendations stemming from the lessons Jane Doe's experience teaches us.

Practical lessons learned and policy recommendations

Lesson 1: support early intervention programs for families at risk of violence

Effective violence prevention takes many forms and can start prenatally. One model program identified by the Blueprints for Violence Prevention Program was the Nurse–Family Partnership, which 'sends nurses to the homes of low-income, first-time mothers, beginning during pregnancy and continuing for 2 years after the birth of the child' (Mihalic et al., 2004, pp. 18–19). The portion of the program delivered while the children are infants and toddlers is meant 'to provide support and to teach skills designed to alter the parent–child interaction, improve the developmental life course of the child, and promote a positive maternal life course' (p. 18). In addition to improving maternal health, the program substantially reduced rates of child abuse and neglect (including emergency room visits for injuries and ingestions) by teaching effective parenting skills and coping mechanisms. For the youth whose families had received home visits, the long-term positive impacts were decreased rates of running away, substance use, being arrested, and being convicted of a crime. The program was also highly cost effective. Had Jane Doe's family received this kind of intervention – focused on improving parent and child well-being and educating about healthy child development – she may have had a very different start to life, and a completely different life trajectory.

Lesson 2: engage in society-wide efforts to reduce transphobia

Admittedly, this lesson is a particularly slippery one to pin down in terms of actionable policy suggestions, but one thing is clear: visibility of LGBTQ people in society, especially if known personally, helps lead to their acceptance. In a large-scale survey of LGBT people, over two-thirds said that greater social acceptance has resulted from more Americans personally knowing someone who is LGBT, and two-thirds similarly said that well-known public figures (both LGBT and not) have helped change societal perspectives (Pew Research Center, 2013b). Shifts in public opinion about LGBT people have indeed arisen from visibility of LGBT people; for example, in a survey of individuals who shifted their perspective from being opposed to same-sex marriage to supporting it, one-third said the shift happened because they know someone who is gay or lesbian, while about one-fifth said that the world has changed and the shift is inevitable (Pew Research Center, 2013a). Although a majority of Americans may not know a transgender person in their daily lives (or think they know one, at least), the fact that there are a handful of highly visible transgender actors, authors, and athletes – such as Laverne Cox, Janet Mock, Chaz Bono, and Caitlyn Jenner, to name a few – bodes well for an increased recognition, if not understanding, of trans identity. We posit that greater visibility of transgender people, including discussion of the challenges they face, can also cultivate empathy for this population and thus lead to greater acceptance.

Although individual-level prejudices against transgender people may take some time to subside, we emphasize that institutions and localities must end cissexist policies now. Legal protections are of the utmost importance: they affect equitable access to employment, housing, healthcare, and more. Transgender people in the United States and globally have been subject to punitive laws that criminalize them, fail to ensure equity in access to basic human needs, and fail to protect them from discrimination, harassment, and violence (Walker et al., 2018). A US Supreme Court decision (*Bostock v. Clayton County, Georgia*, 2020) affirmed that Title VII protections from workplace discrimination on the basis of sex also apply to gay/lesbian and transgender employees. While we hope this will set a positive precedent for future decisions in related arenas, there is still much movement that can happen on the ground right now.

Lesson 3: implement comprehensive sex education

Comprehensive sex education – in contrast to abstinence-only education, which is the modal form of education in the US – includes affirming messages about LGBTQ identity and teaches about bodily autonomy, consent, safer sex practices, and many other medically accurate and developmentally appropriate topics (Wodda & Panfil, 2021). Not only would such education affirm transgender identity and improve youths' understandings of their bodies and sexual rights, it could also empower youth to speak up if they have experienced coercive or abusive sexual contact. For instance, the transformative justice organization generationFIVE argues that the lack of sex-positive, developmentally appropriate, LGBTQ-inclusive sex education – and thus no nuanced discussion of consent and sexual rights – 'can also leave lesbian, gay, bisexual, transgender, and queer children and youth particularly vulnerable to sexual abuse and targeting' (generationFIVE, 2017, p. 15). Author and activist Janet Mock (2014) discusses this issue in her autobiography *Redefining Realness*, where she explains how denial and repression of her identity as an 11-year-old transgender girl left her vulnerable to sexual abuse by her father's girlfriend's 15-year-old son without feeling empowered to tell anyone. Although we in no way suggest that children should be tasked with preventing their own sexual abuse (and should instead lay that blame solely on sexual predators), comprehensive sex education helps instill confidence and understanding of sexual autonomy and consent, and ideally it will not only facilitate healthy consensual relationships but also provide a strong statement that sexual abuse is not acceptable or deserved, and that it should be told to a trusted adult. We also hope that adults so entrusted will take the appropriate steps to protect children and prevent their future victimization.

Lesson 4: do not treat youth forced into survival sex as offenders

Youth who sell or trade sex to acquire basic necessities such as food, clothing, and shelter are engaging in what has been aptly deemed 'survival sex'. Unfortunately, youth are often criminalized for survival sex, even if under different circumstances they would be considered a victim instead of a perpetrator. For example, a 40-year-old having sex with a 15-year-old would typically be deemed statutory rape or child molestation, even if the child 'consented', since most age-of-consent laws state that a 15-year-old is too young to legally consent. However, when that sex becomes transactional, youth are often criminalized. This fact is even more appalling considering that homelessness is a key issue leading to survival sex for LGBTQ youth – particularly youth of color – and the whole reason they were homeless in the first place is because they were rejected by homophobic or transphobic families of origin and foster care placements (see, for example, Dank et al., 2015). Although LGBTQ youth are estimated to make up only 5–7 percent of the total youth population, they make up 20–40 percent of the homeless youth population (Quintana et al., 2010), and a recent study of LGBTQ young people involved in survival sex found that 58 percent of them were living in a shelter or on the street (Dank et al., 2015). Regarding transgender youth specifically, they are eight times more likely than non-transgender youth to trade sex for a safe place to stay (Freeman & Hamilton, 2008). Criminalizing youth for doing what they can to survive in perilous environments into which they have been forced is completely unacceptable and counterproductive to trans youth's well-being and success.

Lesson 5: provide access to drug treatment

It is clear from Jane Doe's story that transgender youth who have experienced unimaginable trauma and adversity may use drugs to cope. Further, experiences of anti-transgender discrimination may themselves be a form of trauma that trans youth are coping with through drug use. The National Transgender Discrimination Survey found that '[e]ight percent (8%) of study participants reported currently using alcohol or drugs specifically to cope with the mistreatment that they received as a result of being transgender or gender non-conforming, while 18% said they had done so in the past but do not currently' (Grant et al., 2011, p. 81). Instead of criminalizing youth for drug offenses, drug treatment should be made available to them, as should other forms of healthcare to improve their physical and mental health. As with many issues we discuss in this chapter, the relative unavailability and high cost of (private) drug treatment is a more systemic issue for various reasons, including the perception that drug use constitutes an individual's moral failing instead of a complex medical problem that may exist alongside other mental health concerns (for example, Paltrow, 2001). When Jane Doe says she 'uses any drugs anyone gives her … to become numb', we should take that very seriously and respond accordingly with care and treatment, especially since our societal and institutional failings led her to use drugs to cope.

Lesson 6: improve trauma-informed care in the juvenile justice and child welfare systems

Society and its institutions are increasingly realizing the importance of trauma-informed care. In their brief on why trauma-informed care is important for LGBTQ youth, the National Resource Center for Mental Health Promotion and Youth Violence Prevention (n.d.) notes that a trauma-informed approach would include acknowledging and addressing the impact of trauma and supporting resilience and healing. They argue that 'LGBTQ youth ... often move through educational and service environments that, at best, do not understand what they need and at worst, cause harm. ... Adopting a trauma-informed approach means changing the practices, policies, and culture of a school or agency to ensure an environment that is conducive to health and wellness for all, particularly those exposed to trauma' (p. 1). Similarly, we advocate for juvenile justice systems, child welfare systems, and schools to adopt a trauma-informed approach for all youth that is also responsive to traumas experienced by LGBTQ youth specifically.

Regarding children specifically, acting-out behaviors are beginning to be recognized as related to maltreatment, instead of a reflection on that youth's inherent 'badness'. However, LGBTQ youth are still often blamed for their trauma, especially sexual trauma, suggesting they somehow invited it or brought it on themselves. A consistent finding in the literature on LGBTQ youths' experiences in the juvenile justice system is the attempt to make gay or trans identity a treatment issue, suggesting that it originated from childhood trauma and can be 'addressed' (that is, 'cured') by addressing other treatment issues (for example, Majd et al., 2009). This is the opposite of the sort of trauma-informed care we are advocating for. Instead, we support treatment modalities that acknowledge the trauma of stigma, shame, and rejection that are fueled by societal homophobia and transphobia; in other words, they are not inherent to that youth's transness but rather to harmful reactions by families, schools, and the crimino-legal system.

LGBTQ youth are overrepresented in both the juvenile justice system and the child welfare system at a rate of more than double their representation in the general youth population, and they are similarly overrepresented in the crossover child welfare/juvenile justice population (Hunt & Moodie-Mills, 2012; Irvine & Canfield, 2016). The policies and practices that actively funnel youth from the child welfare system to the juvenile justice or adult criminal justice systems have collectively been described as the 'foster care-to-prison pipeline'. Processes by which this occurs include foster parents or staff in state-run facilities calling police for minor or technical infractions, an increased risk of homelessness leading to survival crimes, increased rates of arrest in school because a parent is not present to advocate for them, and criminalization of mental illness resulting in arrest for a mental health crisis. Furthermore, 'Black youth, LGBTQ youth and those with mental illnesses are more likely to be in foster care, and discrimination in the system exacerbates these populations' already disproportionate vulnerabilities to criminalization' (Anspach, 2018). As with Jane Doe, detention has been used as a 'default' to deal with trans youth (Hunt & Moodie-Mills, 2012). Trauma-informed care and emphases on treatment and support, instead of criminalization, are needed for youth in foster care.

Lesson 7: believe youth who claim abuse in residential placements

Jane Doe experienced sexual assault while in the 'care' of the state, both in residential foster placements and by staff in a juvenile facility. There has been a historical tendency to disbelieve youth who accuse facility staff of abuse. For example, juvenile justice system actors have claimed that girls are allegedly needy, manipulative, whiny, difficult, harder to work with (having 'too many issues'), and prone to acting promiscuously and fabricating stories of abuse, which prevents their claims of abuse in facilities from being taken seriously – all while there have been confirmed cases of shocking and pervasive abuse of girls in facilities leading to arrests and convictions (Chesney-Lind & Irwin, 2006). Because of Jane Doe's history and treatment needs, she may very well have been seen as needy, difficult, and having 'too many issues', which prevented her claims of abuse from being taken seriously. While the #MeToo movement has helped sensitize society to the widespread sexual harassment and assault faced by women and girls (including transgender women and girls), youth who are sent to juvenile facilities are frequently seen as untrustworthy by virtue of actions that led to them ending up in a facility – even if those actions were the result of prior mistreatment. This belief system can provide cover for those who wish to harm youth in facilities and should not be allowed to continue.

Lesson 8: ban solitary confinement

As mentioned previously, solitary confinement can be considered a form of torture, especially for children (Clark, 2017). Although transgender people may be placed into solitary confinement as a form of 'protective custody' from fellow inmates, it can actually exacerbate the conditions under which staff can abuse them, as it physically and socially isolates trans inmates from others to whom they could report abuse, or who could witness it (Deniflee, 2014). Solitary confinement typically entails being in a private cell for 23 or more hours a day, preventing access to programming, services, treatment, visits, and certain items. Adult transgender women who have spent time in solitary confinement reported severe psychological symptoms such as depression and hallucinations, and some have engaged in serious self-harm while in isolation (Baus et al., 2006). Sometimes thought of as a 'punishment within a punishment', LGBT inmates who have been placed in solitary confinement may find isolation so psychologically damaging that being in general population – even if they have experienced numerous instances of physical and sexual assault while there – is preferable to isolation (see, for example, the experience of Roderick Johnson described in Mogul et al., 2011, pp. 92–94). In Jane Doe's case, her isolation was because of a perceived lack of other options and happened before she had ever been adjudicated for an offense, which constitutes an egregiously poor use of this already poor housing option. Further, the fact that she had been isolated and starved as a child as punishment for reporting abuse is eerily similar to the ways transgender people often experience solitary confinement: being punished for others' failure to protect them.

Lesson 9: house youth according to their gender identity

Advocates have long suggested housing transgender youth according to their gender identity instead of their assigned birth sex — barring some sort of safety objection or discomfort from the transgender youths themselves (Majd et al., 2009). In Jane Doe's case, housing her among male peers and staff may have been not only disaffirming to her identity as a young woman, but also a direct threat to her feelings of safety and security, as all of her sexual abusers had been men or boys, some even in juvenile facilities. Housing placements based on gender identity are now specifically recommended by the updated Prison Rape Elimination Act guidelines, though these were not in place at the time of Jane Doe's juvenile placements.

Lesson 10: support youths' gender identities in facilities, including expression and medical care

As should be clear, juvenile justice settings can hardly be called affirming — juvenile justice staff have forcibly removed transgender girls' hair extensions, fingernails, and clothing (Majd et al., 2009). Transgender identity has also been demonized and pathologized by staff as a treatment issue in itself, with coercive attempts made to 'convert', control, and punish transgender youth. For example, one young trans woman's 'treatment plan' included her receiving 'help with gender confusion and appropriate gender identity' while housing her in a boys' facility, 'which included staff prohibiting her from growing her hair out or having any feminine accessories' (Majd et al., 2009, p. 65). We could recount many examples of trans youth being forced to conform; we argue that if youth were appropriately housed according to their gender identity, this point would effectively be moot. It is transphobia and a fundamental misunderstanding of transgender identity that drive this 'intervention'. Instead, youth should be supported in exploring these identities, even while in restrictive environments.

Appropriate medical care, including trans-affirming therapy and hormone treatments, are rare among juvenile justice settings, as they are also relatively uncommon for incarcerated adults (Mogul et al., 2011). However, these are vitally important for well-being, both physical and mental; they are also important for the overall 'therapeutic' experience of juvenile residential treatment. Without such care, youth suffer. For example, one formerly incarcerated transgender youth said of the facility staff who denied them access to medical treatment, 'I said I'm going to get sick if I do not get my hormones, but no one listened, and it seemed like no one cared. The justice system doesn't care' (Mallon & Perez, 2020, p. 222). Even when transgender people can secure appropriate diagnoses and prescriptions from medical personnel, facilities can fail (or outright decline) to provide that care, as they did with Jane Doe, representing a serious institutional failure (see also Baus et al., 2006). Although some states such as New York have model policies for trans youth that seek to affirm them, provide appropriate care, and keep them safe (see, for example, Mallon & Perez, 2020), many states – including those that housed Jane Doe – have a long way to go to support trans youth. Luckily, affirming treatment is fully realizable.

Conclusion

Our list of suggested policy changes is by no means exhaustive but is intended to be illustrative and thought-provoking regarding a reconceptualization of what youth in the child welfare and juvenile justice systems need to succeed. Jane Doe's case, along with the experiences of so many other transgender youth – and LGBTQ youth more broadly – illustrate a number of serious failures in the protection, treatment, and affirmation of transgender youth by institutions ostensibly meant to get them back on track. Some of our recommendations, such as early intervention, comprehensive sex education, drug treatment, and trauma-informed care, will benefit all youth, not just those who are LGBTQ. Other recommendations are meant to benefit youth who find themselves in the system, such as decriminalizing our response to survival strategies, believing youth who claim abuse, and banning solitary confinement. While our recommendations for youth in facilities – such as housing according to gender identity and affirming youth's sexual and gender identities – apply most strongly to LGBTQ youth, other youth may benefit as well. Finally, some recommendations, such as reducing transphobia, require a concerted effort among multiple institutions. We encourage all practitioners, advocates, and stakeholders to pursue avenues outside the juvenile justice system for trans youth and to seriously reconsider our legacy of homophobic and transphobic actions within these institutions.

References

Anspach, R. (2018) 'The foster care to prison pipeline: what it is and how it works', *Teen Vogue*, May 25. https://www.teenvogue.com/story/the-foster-care-to-prison-pipeline-what-it-is-and-how-it-works

Baus, J., Hunt, D., & Williams, R. (2006) *Cruel and Unusual* [Documentary], Reid Productions.

Bostock v. Clayton County, Georgia (2020) https://www.supremecourt.gov/opinions/19pdf/17-1618_hfci.pdf

Chesney-Lind, M. & Irwin, K. (2006) 'Still "the best place to conquer girls": girls and the juvenile justice system', in A.V. Merlo & J.M. Pollock (eds.), *Women, Law, and Social Control* (2nd ed.), London: Pearson, pp. 271–291.

Clark, A.B. (2017) 'Juvenile solitary confinement as a form of child abuse', *The Journal of the American Academy of Psychiatry and the Law*, 45(3): 350–357.

Dank, M., Yahner, J., Madden, K., Bañuelos, I., Yu, L., Ritchie, A., Mora, M., & Conner, B. (2015) 'Surviving the streets of New York: experiences of LGBTQ youth, YMSM, and YWSW engaged in survival sex', Urban Institute.

Deniflee, N. (2014) 'Connecticut trans teen ignites prison reform push', *WeNews*, July 22. https://womensenews.org/2014/07/connecticut-trans-teen-ignites-prison-reform-push/

Doe, J. (2014) 'Jane Doe: imprisoned DCF 16-year-old speaks', *The Hartford Courant*, April 24. https://www.courant.com/opinion/op-ed/hc-op-doe-imprisoned-dcf-girl-tells-her-story-0425-20140424-story.html

Freeman, L. & Hamilton, D. (2008) 'A count of homeless youth in New York City: 2007', Empire State Coalition of Youth and Family Services.

generationFIVE (2017) *Ending Child Sexual Abuse: A Transformative Justice Handbook*. http://www.generationfive.org/wp-content/uploads/2017/06/Transformative-Justice-Handbook.pdf

Grant, J.M., Mottet, L.A., Tanis, J., Harrison, J., Herman, J.L., & Keisling, M. (2011) 'Injustice at every turn: a report of the National Transgender Discrimination Survey', National Center for Transgender Equality and National Gay and Lesbian Task Force.

Hunt, J. & Moodie-Mills, A. (2012) 'The unfair criminalization of gay and transgender youth: an overview of the experiences of LGBT youth in the juvenile justice system', Center for American Progress.

Irvine, A. & Canfield, M.P.P. (2016) 'The overrepresentation of lesbian, gay, bisexual, questioning, gender nonconforming and transgender youth within the child welfare to juvenile justice crossover population', *American University Journal of Gender, Social Policy & the Law*, 24(2): 243–261.

Jane Doe v. Connecticut Department of Corrections et al. (2014) https://www.documentcloud.org/documents/1113035-4-14-14affidavit-redacted-reduced.html

Katz, J. (2014) 'Teen's violent history left state no option', *The Hartford Courant*, April 21. https://www.courant.com/opinion/op-ed/hc-op-katz-transgender-girl-york-prision-0422-20140421-story.html

Kovner, J. (2015) 'CT court reverses transfer of transgender teen to prison', *The Hartford Courant*, June 8. https://www.courant.com/news/connecticut/hc-transgender-girl-rights-violated-0609-20150608-story.html

Majd, K., Marksamer, J., & Reyes, C. (2009) 'Hidden injustice: lesbian, gay, bisexual, and transgender youth in juvenile courts', Legal Services for Children, National Juvenile Defender Center, and National Center for Lesbian Rights.

Mallon, G.P. & Perez, J. (2020) 'The experiences of transgender and gender expansive youth in juvenile justice systems', *Journal of Criminological Research, Policy and Practice*, 6(3): 217–229.

Mihalic, S., Fagan, A., Irwin, K., Ballard, D., & Elliott, D. (2004) 'Blueprints for violence prevention', Center for the Study and Prevention of Violence.

Mock, J. (2014) *Redefining Realness: My Path to Womanhood, Identity, Love & So Much More*, New York: Simon & Schuster.

Mogul, J.L., Ritchie, A.J., & Whitlock, K. (2011) *Queer (In)justice: The Criminalization of LGBT People in the United States*, Boston, MA: Beacon Press.

National Resource Center for Mental Health Promotion and Youth Violence Prevention (n.d.) 'Adopting a trauma-informed approach for LGBTQ youth: a two-part resource for schools and agencies. Part 1: Why use a trauma-informed approach with LGBTQ youth?' https://healthysafechildren.org/sites/default/files/Trauma_Informed_Approach_LGBTQ_Youth_1.pdf

Paltrow, L.M. (2001) 'The war on drugs and the war on abortion: some initial thoughts on the connections, intersections and the effects', *Southern University Law Review*, 28(3): 201–254.

Pew Research Center (2013a) 'Growing support for gay marriage: changed minds and changing demographics', March 20. https://www.pewresearch.org/politics/2013/03/20/growing-support-for-gay-marriage-changed-minds-and-changing-demographics/

Pew Research Center (2013b) 'Social acceptance: a survey of LGBT Americans: attitudes, experiences and values in changing times', June 13. https://www.pewsocialtrends.org/2013/06/13/a-survey-of-lgbt-americans/

Quintana, N.S., Rosenthal, J., & Krehely, J. (2010) 'On the streets: the federal response to gay and transgender homeless youth', Center for American Progress.

Walker, A., Sexton, L., Valcore, J., Sumner, J., & Wodda, A. (2018) 'Transitioning to social justice: transgender and non-binary individuals', in C. Roberson (ed.), *Routledge Handbook of Social, Economic, and Criminal Justice*, Abingdon: Routledge, pp. 220–233.

Wodda, A. & Panfil, V. R. (2021) *Sex-Positive Criminology*, Abingdon: Routledge.

13

The Role of Adolescent Friendship Networks in Queer Youth's Delinquency

Nayan G. Ramirez

Introduction

Involvement in crime or delinquency spikes during the adolescent years (Gottfredson & Hirschi, 1990), yet relatively few studies have explored the role that sexual orientation plays in involvement in delinquency (Himmelstein & Brückner, 2011; Conover-Williams, 2014; Koeppel, 2015; Beaver et al., 2016). Prior work that has addressed this research question has had various limitations due to the difficulty of collecting data on sexual orientation, low sample sizes, lack of longitudinal data, and also the increased likelihood of misreporting by adolescent respondents (Savin-Williams & Joyner, 2014). These issues have led to inconsistencies in our understanding of queer youth's offending patterns. In this chapter, queer youth are defined as individuals who self-identified as gay, lesbian, bisexual, or who were uncertain about their sexual orientation during young adulthood.

Only recently have studies begun to assess how sexual orientation relates to involvement in delinquency. Focusing on criminal justice and school sanctions, Himmelstein and Brückner (2011) found that queer youth who reported same-sex attraction or who self-identified as lesbian, gay, or bisexual were more likely to receive some type of official sanction (for example, school expulsion, juvenile arrest, be stopped by the police). Similarly, Conover-Williams (2014) found that queer youth had a higher prevalence and frequency of delinquent involvement and were more likely to commit property and sex-related crime compared with their straight peers. Other recent studies (Koeppel, 2015; Beaver et al., 2016) find similar patterns in queer youth's involvement in delinquency. Additionally, these studies suggest that gender and sexual orientation interact to create different patterns of delinquent involvement, with queer girls more likely to engage in delinquent behaviors compared with queer boys. In this chapter, I explore whether characteristics related to peer friendship networks during adolescence help explain differences in delinquent involvement on the part of queer youth. I also discuss how we can apply findings from this research to help queer youth become better integrated socially within schools during adolescence.

Queering theoretical peer explanations

Criminological theories have largely ignored the role of queer criminology in their explanations of why individuals become involved with crime, yet socializing with others is key to both being exposed to and learning different types of attitudes and behaviors, including delinquency. Two competing criminological theoretical frameworks that help explain differences in delinquency are learning (Sutherland, 1939; Burgess & Akers, 1966) and strain (Agnew, 1992) theories. These two theories allow us to explore the relationship between queer criminology and mainstream criminological theories by exploring the role of friendship network characteristics in queer youth's delinquency.

Differential association (Sutherland, 1939) and social learning (Burgess & Akers, 1966) theories propose that we learn behaviors as we interact socially with other people. During childhood, parents are the primary influence in teaching their children how to behave. However, during adolescence, with the increased prominence of peers, friends become much more central to new behaviors learned by teenagers. Behaviors that increase status or popularity are likely to be learned by teenagers seeking to fit in; for example, teenagers may be more likely to start drinking if they think it will improve their social standing (Dijkstra et al., 2010). Alternatively, new peer relationships can expose teenagers to different social networks that may be engaged in certain behaviors previously unknown to the youth, such as substance use (Kreager & Haynie, 2011). Thus, understanding where queer youth are positioned in their school's social hierarchy is important for understanding their level of social integration and potential peer influences.

In contrast to learning theories, strain theories propose that poor social integration may account for differences in delinquency. One of Agnew's (1992) main propositions is that delinquency arises from negative relationships with others, particularly when there is a mismatch between how an individual wants to be treated and how they are treated by their peers. For example, if a queer boy attempts to join a peer group from which he is rejected, the introduction of the negative stimulus (that is, peer rejection) is likely to increase his feelings of strain. Theoretically, this strain then leads him to be pressured into delinquency due to the resulting negative emotions that are associated with peer rejection, such as disappointment, anger, sadness, and fear. Altogether, mainstream criminological theories provide us possible avenues to explore how sexual orientation may influence the lives of queer youth during adolescence; however, few studies have examined this underexplored area.

Gendered opportunities for delinquency

Femininity and masculinity affect the criminal opportunities available to different individuals. More 'masculine' individuals may provide a greater number of delinquent opportunities, while more 'feminine' individuals may result in fewer opportunities. Criminological research has consistently shown that men are more likely to engage in delinquency compared with women (Steffensmeier & Allan, 1996; Kruttschnitt, 2013). It is unclear whether the composition of teenagers' friendship networks matter more or whether peer rejection prevents certain teenagers from having the opportunity for greater delinquency. Regardless, criminological theories explain that peer rejection and/or social isolation may lead to fewer opportunities to learn delinquent behaviors and attitudes (Sutherland, 1939; Burgess & Akers, 1966; Warr, 1993). In contrast, strain theories (Agnew, 1992; Broidy & Agnew, 1997) suggest that the frustration that arises from experiencing strains can lead individuals to externalize their feelings, resulting in greater delinquent involvement.

The current study

Examining the friendship networks of queer youth can help us disentangle what aspects of friendship networks lead to delinquent involvement. In this chapter, I assess whether differences exist in queer youths' delinquent involvement and whether any differences in the network characteristics of queer youth affect their involvement in delinquency. Although prior research largely suggests that queer youth may be more likely to engage in delinquency, I anticipate that because of differential treatment of youth based on their adherence to typical gendered ideals, queer boys will be less likely to engage in the behaviors compared with heterosexual boys. However, because queer girls may not perform typically feminine behaviors, I predict that their level of delinquent involvement will be greater than that of their heterosexual female peers.

Methods

Data

This chapter uses data collected from the evaluation of the PROSPER Peers longitudinal study, which followed approximately 10,000 students annually across eight waves of data collection beginning at 6th grade through 12th grade. During these waves, students were asked to nominate, or name, their best and five closest friends in their grade, providing full social network data for their school. Students also self-reported their involvement in various behaviors, including delinquency. To examine differences between queer youth and their heterosexual peers during adolescence, my analyses focus on a random subsample of 1,852 young adults who responded to a sexual identity question in two follow-up surveys immediately following adolescence.

Sample

A key issue when assessing issues related to queer individuals is how best to identify the subpopulation. In the past, adolescence researchers have cautioned that adolescents may be more likely to misreport certain types of responses in self-report surveys (Fan et al., 2006; Robinson & Espelage, 2011; Durso & Gates, 2013). At ages 19 and 21, a random subsample of respondents from both cohorts that participated in the in-school survey were asked to complete follow-up surveys. As part of the follow-up surveys, respondents were asked to self-identify their sexual orientation as either heterosexual (attracted to people of the opposite sex), homosexual (attracted to people of the same sex), or bisexual (attracted to people of both sexes). I use responses to the sexual identity question from the age 19 and 21 follow-up surveys as a retrospective indicator of respondents' sexual orientation during adolescence. The retrospective approach used in this chapter is consistent with suggestions from researchers on how to best use sexual identity data (Savin-Williams & Joyner, 2014) due to misreporting of same-sex romantic attraction in the Add Health survey.

Measures

Delinquency

The dependent variable, delinquency, is a variety score of 12 delinquency items asking about involvement across various behaviors in the past 12 months. Examples of the delinquent items included in the measure include theft, vandalism, and fighting. Prior research supports the use of variety scores (that is, a sum total of the items) when scaling delinquent behavior (Sweeten, 2012). To create the delinquency outcome, all items were first dichotomized (0 = 'never' versus 1 = 'once or more in the past 12 months') and then summed to reflect the total number of delinquent items a respondent was involved in during the prior year.

Sexual orientation and gender

Sexual orientation was constructed using respondents' answers to the sexual identity question asked during the study's follow-up waves at ages 19 and 21. The survey question asked: 'Do you feel that you are ...' with 'heterosexual', 'homosexual', 'bisexual', 'not sure', 'don't know', and refused as possible response options. Queer youth was operationalized as any individuals who identified consistently queer at both follow-up waves ('homosexual' or 'bisexual'), as 'not sure' or 'don't know' during both of the follow-up waves, or individuals who identified as queer ('homosexual' or 'bisexual') at one wave and 'not sure', 'don't know', or 'refused' at the other wave. Gender is coded as 0 for girls and 1 for boys in the study.

Social network characteristics

The potential network mediators include centrality measures such as indegree (number of friendship nominations received, or how many individuals named the respondent as a friend) and outdegree (number of friendship nominations sent, or how many individuals the responded named as a friend). I also include social isolation, which is measured as receiving zero incoming friendship nominations and sending zero outgoing friendship nominations. Finally, I also include a measure related to friendship composition, which is the proportion of same-sex friends a respondent named.

Control variables

All regression models include additional control variables for demographic characteristics and other factors that may influence youth's delinquency. The first covariate is school grades ('What grades do you generally get in school?'), measured from 'Mostly lower than D's' to 'Mostly A's'. Family relations ($\alpha = 0.81$) was the average of several standardized subscales assessing the quality of relationships between parents and children. This measure reflects affective quality, joint activities of family members, parenting practices as they relate to supervision and discipline, and family cohesion. School adjustment and bonding ($\alpha = 0.81$) was the mean of eight items reflecting students' attitudes toward their teachers and schools, with higher scores reflecting greater positive attitudes. Risk and sensation seeking ($\alpha =$

0.75) was a mean of three items measuring how often respondents do things for fun and excitement with little regard for consequences (Zuckerman, 1994). In addition to the aforementioned control variables, I also included three covariates assessing whether the respondent identified as white, lived in a two-parent household, and whether the respondent received free or reduced lunch. Finally, I also included the average of every respondent's friends' delinquency in the final model of each analyses.

Plan of analyses

The analyses proceed in three stages. First, I establish the patterns of delinquent involvement by sexual orientation and gender. Second, I assess whether differences exist in adolescents' friendship networks by comparing the network characteristics of queer youth with those of their straight peers using a series of t tests to make comparisons within-gender. Third, I test whether any of the patterns between the network variables and sexual orientation mediate the relationship between sexual orientation, gender, and delinquency using negative binomial regression models. I employ a cluster option with the regression models using the respondent as the cluster variable to reduce bias in the standard errors of the coefficients given the multiple observations per respondent across time in the study.

Results

Descriptive statistics

Table 13.1 presents descriptive statistics for all variables used in this chapter's analyses. On average, there were 11,049 observations across the eight waves of the study for the 1,852 participants. There were 119 individuals who identified as queer (6.4 percent) and 1,733 individuals who identified as heterosexual (93.6 percent). The analytic sample reflects a percentage of the queer population that is comparable to national prevalence estimates (Kann et al., 2016).

Patterns of delinquent involvement

Figure 13.1 demonstrates the patterns of delinquent involvement by sexual orientation and gender. Queer boys appear to follow very similar patterns of delinquent involvement to straight girls. Conversely, patterns of delinquent involvement for queer girls are very similar to the patterns for straight boys. Next, I conducted a series of t tests examining whether there were statistically significant differences by sexual orientation within gender. Queer boys had statistically significant fewer ($p < 0.05$) delinquent acts at 8th

Table 13.1: Descriptive statistics for analytic sample variables

	Mean	RSE	Min	Max
Behavioral Outcome				
Delinquency	1.35	0.04	0.00	12.00
Sexual Orientation and Gender Variables				
Sexual orientation (ref. heterosexual)	0.06	0.01	0.00	1.00
Gender (ref. girls)	0.46	0.01	0.00	1.00
Network Characteristics				
Indegree	3.93	0.05	0.00	20.00
Outdegree	3.84	0.03	0.00	7.00
Social isolation	0.03	0.00	0.00	1.00
Proportion of same-gender friends	0.46	0.01	0.00	1.00
Control Variables				
School grades	4.30	0.02	1.00	5.00
Family relations	−0.09	0.01	−2.31	0.85
School adjustment and bonding	3.78	0.01	1.00	5.00
Risk and sensation seeking	2.18	0.02	1.00	5.00
White	0.91	0.01	0.00	1.00
Two-parent household	0.80	0.01	0.00	1.00
Free and reduced lunch	−0.54	0.04	−1.70	3.43
Average of friends' delinquency	1.32	0.02	0.00	12.00

Notes: N = 11,049 observations across waves; RSE = robust standard errors.

Source: PROSPER Peers Longitudinal Study

Figure 13.1: Delinquent involvement by sexual orientation and gender

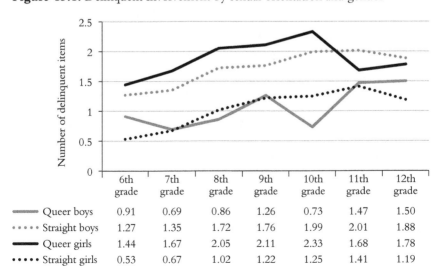

	6th grade	7th grade	8th grade	9th grade	10th grade	11th grade	12th grade
Queer boys	0.91	0.69	0.86	1.26	0.73	1.47	1.50
Straight boys	1.27	1.35	1.72	1.76	1.99	2.01	1.88
Queer girls	1.44	1.67	2.05	2.11	2.33	1.68	1.78
Straight girls	0.53	0.67	1.02	1.22	1.25	1.41	1.19

(QB: $\mu = 0.86$; SB: $\mu = 1.72$) and 10th grades (QB: $\mu = 0.73$; SB: $\mu = 1.99$) compared with straight boys. At the same time, queer girls had statistically more ($p < 0.001$) delinquent acts than straight girls at all grades except 11th grade ($p < 0.05$ at grade 12). However, as shown in Figure 13.1, even when there were no statistically significant differences within gender, the patterns demonstrate distinctly different patterns of delinquent involvement than would be anticipated given mainstream criminology's assertion that men and boys tend to be more involved in crime and delinquency.

Friendship network patterns

Table 13.2 presents results from a series of t tests examining the relationship between sexual orientation and gender on various network outcomes. First, we can see that queer boys were less likely to receive friendship nominations across time compared with straight boys. However, there were only statistically significant differences during 6th (QB: $\mu = 2.7$; SB: $\mu = 4.1$) and 7th grades (QB: $\mu = 3.2$; SB: $\mu = 4.3$). Conversely, queer girls received statistically significant fewer ($p < 0.05$) nominations across all grades in middle school and in 9th (QG: $\mu = 3.2$ SG: $\mu = 4.3$) through 11th grade compared with straight girls (QG: $\mu = 3.2$; SG: $\mu = 4.3$).

For outdegree, boys were less likely to send friendship nominations compared with their straight peers, with statistically significant differences at 10th (QB: $\mu = 2.3$; SB: $\mu = 3.2$) and 11th grades only (QB: $\mu = 1.8$; SB: $\mu = 2.8$). Queer girls were consistently found to send statistically significant fewer ($p < 0.01$) friendship nominations from 6th through 10th grade compared with their straight peers. When examining differences in social isolation (zero incoming or outgoing friendship nominations), queer boys were more socially isolated across all years, although the difference was only statistically significant ($p < 0.01$) during 11th grade (QB: $p = 0.20$ SB: $p = 0.07$). Similarly, queer girls were more likely to experience social isolation, with statistically significant ($p < 0.05$) differences in 6th, 7th, and 10th grades.

Finally, I explored differences in the friendship composition measure examining the proportion of same-gender friends that a respondent had in their grade. Across the entirety of adolescence, queer boys were much more likely to report having friends who were girls compared with straight boys in the same grade. This finding was highly statistically significant ($p < 0.001$) across all grades. At the same time, queer girls had much more similar patterns of same-gender friendships compared with straight girls in their same grade. However, queer girls were statistically less likely ($p < 0.05$) to have a greater proportion of friends who were girls in 8th grade compared with their straight girl peers (QG: $p = 0.85$ SB: $p = 0.89$).

Table 13.2: Differences in network characteristics

	Straight boys	Queer boys	Straight girls	Queer girls
Indegree				
6th grade	4.1	2.7★★	4.9	3.4★★★
7th grade	4.3	3.2★	5.1	4.2★
8th grade	4.1	3.3	5.0	3.9★★★
9th grade	3.7	2.9	4.4	3.3★★★
10th grade	3.3	3.2	3.8	3.2★
11th grade	2.9	2.4	3.3	2.6★
12th grade	2.7	2.4	2.8	2.3
Outdegree				
6th grade	3.9	3.7	4.7	3.7★★★
7th grade	4.0	3.6	5.0	4.0★★★
8th grade	4.1	3.4	4.9	4.1★★★
9th grade	3.5	3.3	4.4	3.6★★
10th grade	3.2	2.3★	3.8	3.1★★
11th grade	2.8	1.8★★	3.4	2.8
12th grade	2.6	2.3	2.0	2.3
Social Isolation (%)				
6th grade	2	3	0	4★★
7th grade	2	3	0	5★★★
8th grade	2	6	0	0
9th grade	3	9	0	3
10th grade	5	13	2	6★
11th grade	7	20★★	3	5
12th grade	8	12	6	10
Proportion of Same-Gender Friends (%)				
6th grade	93	80★★★	93	91
7th grade	91	68★★★	92	88
8th grade	90	68★★★	89	85★
9th grade	88	59★★★	89	87
10th grade	88	53★★★	88	90
11th grade	86	46★★★	86	86
12th grade	85	42★★★	86	88

Notes: ★★★ p < 0.001, ★★ p < 0.01, ★ p < 0.05.

Effect of network characteristics on adolescent delinquency

Table 13.3 presents results from the clustered negative binomial regression models examining the relationship between sexual orientation, gender, and delinquency. Models 1 through 4 examined the relationship between sexual orientation, gender, and the network characteristics on delinquent involvement. I was unable to include social isolation as a variable because of

Table 13.3: Negative binomial regression models predicting delinquent involvement

	Model 1: Sexual Orientation and Gender		Model 2: Add Interaction Term		Model 3: Add Network Characteristics		Model 4: Add Control Variables		Model 5: Girls Full Model		Model 6: Boys Full Model	
	b	RSE	b	RSE	b	RSE	b	RSE	b	RSE	b	RSE
Sexual Orientation and Gender												
Sexual orientation (ref. heterosexual)	0.32	0.12**	0.60	0.13***	0.58	0.14***	0.31	0.13*	0.31	0.13*	-0.52	0.17**
Gender (ref. girls)	0.45	0.06***	0.50	0.06***	0.44	0.06***	0.25	0.05***				
Interaction												
Sexual orientation X Gender			-1.09	0.21***	-1.36	0.24***	-0.86	0.21***				
Network Characteristics												
Indegree					0.01	0.01	0.02	0.01*	0.02	0.13	0.02	0.01
Outdegree					-0.09	0.01***	-0.03	0.01*	-0.05	0.01**	-0.01	0.01
Proportion of same-gender friends					-0.54	0.12***	-0.25	0.11*	-0.29	0.02	-0.12	0.16
Control Variables												
School grades							-0.04	0.03	-0.02	0.04	-0.06	0.04
Family relations							-0.66	0.05***	-0.75	0.07***	-0.55	0.08***
School adjustment and bonding							-0.34	0.04***	-0.38	0.05***	-0.30	0.05***
Risk and sensation seeking							0.52	0.02***	0.50	0.03***	0.52	0.03***
White							-0.22	0.08***	-0.27	0.12*	-0.20	0.10
Two-parent household							-0.09	0.06**	-0.10	0.07	-0.08	0.08
Free and reduced lunch							0.02	0.02	0.01	0.02	0.04	0.02
Average of friends' delinquency							0.18	0.01***	0.24	0.02***	0.13	0.02***
Intercept	0.05	0.05	0.02	0.05	0.82	0.12***	0.24	0.23	0.41	0.35	0.37	0.29
N	11,049		11,049		10,197		9,533		5,272		4,261	

Notes: *** p < 0.001, ** p < 0.01, * p < 0.05. RSE = robust standard errors.

collinearity with the centrality measures, indegree, and outdegree. Models 4 and 5 examine these relationships within gender.

In Model 1, I examined the effect of sexual orientation and gender on delinquent involvement. Sexual orientation was statistically significant, with queer youth having greater delinquent involvement compared with their heterosexual peers ($b = 0.21$, $p < 0.01$). Unsurprisingly, boys were statistically more likely to be involved in delinquency compared with girls ($b = 0.45$, $p < 0.001$). In Model 2, I added an interaction term between sexual orientation and gender. The interaction term was statistically significant, pointing toward the importance of examining within-gender differences ($b = -1.09$, $p < 0.001$).

In Model 3, I added the network characteristics to the regression model. Sexual orientation ($b = 0.58$, $p < 0.001$), gender ($b = 0.44$, $p < 0.001$), and the interaction term ($b = -1.36$, $p < 0.001$) remained significant. Of the three network characteristics, only outdegree ($b = -0.09$, $p < 0.001$) and the proportion of same-gender friends ($b = -0.54$, $p < 0.001$) were statistically significant. As respondents' outdegree increased, their delinquent involvement decreased as well. Similarly, as the proportion of respondents' same-gender friends increased, their delinquent involvement decreased. The effect size and statistical significance of sexual orientation did not change when the network characteristics were introduced in Model 3.

Model 4 presents the results when all the covariates were introduced. Sexual orientation ($b = 0.31$, $p < 0.05$), gender ($b = 0.25$, $p < 0.001$), and the interaction term ($b = -0.86$, $p < 0.001$) remained statistically significant when the control variables were added. However, the size and statistical significance of the sexual orientation term were attenuated with the introduction of the control variables. For the control variables, family relations ($b = -0.66$, $p < 0.001$), school adjustment and bonding ($b = -0.34$, $p < 0.001$), risk and sensation seeking ($b = 0.52$, $p < 0.001$), white ($b = -0.22$, $p < 0.001$), two-parent household ($b = -0.09$, $p < 0.01$), and the average of respondents' friends' delinquency ($b = 0.18$, $p < 0.001$) were all statistically significant predictors of delinquent involvement.

Finally, the results for Model 5 reflect within-gender differences in the relationships being examined among girls, while Model 6 reflects within-gender differences among boys. For girls, queer girls were more likely to engage in delinquency compared with their heterosexual peers ($b = 0.31$, $p < 0.05$). Conversely, queer boys were less likely to be involved in delinquency compared with heterosexual boys ($b = -0.52$, $p < 0.01$). The only statistically significant network characteristic was outdegree for girls ($b = -0.05$, $p < 0.01$): as girls' outdegree increased, their likelihood of delinquent involvement decreased.

Figure 13.2 presents the predicted number of delinquent activities by sexual orientation and gender for ease of interpretation. After controlling

Figure 13.2: Predicted number of delinquent acts

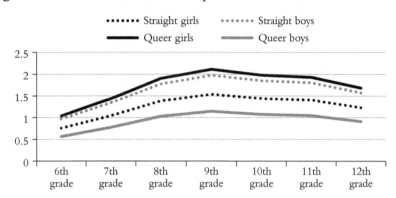

for network characteristics and the covariates, I found a similar pattern to the one demonstrated in Figure 13.1. Queer boys were the least likely group to be involved in delinquency while queer girls were the most likely to be involved in delinquency.

Discussion

Few studies have explored the relationship between sexual orientation, gender, and adolescent delinquency (Himmelstein & Brückner, 2011; Conover-Williams, 2014; Koeppel, 2015; Beaver et al., 2016). The studies that have examined this relationship have been limited by the availability of data as well as adolescent misreporting of same-sex attraction (Savin-Williams & Joyner, 2013). Given the dearth of research on the topic, results from this chapter are among the first to investigate how friendship network characteristics affect queer youths' involvement in delinquency. To my knowledge, no other studies have used longitudinal social network data capturing the full length of adolescence while also avoiding issues related to measuring sexual orientation during adolescence by using young adult sexual-identity data. I assessed whether these network characteristics affected the relationship between sexual orientation, gender, and delinquency.

Several findings from this chapter merit discussion. First, I find support that sexual orientation and gender interact to create different paths of delinquent involvement among youth. Queer boys were found to be less delinquent than their heterosexual male peers while queer girls were found to be consistently more delinquent than their female peers. The lack of evidence for mediation by the network characteristics suggests that gendered opportunities for crime may be more important than where queer youth are positioned in their school's social network (Steffensmeier & Allan, 1996; Kruttschnitt, 2013).

I did not find evidence of a significant relationship between adolescents' proportion of same-gender friends and delinquency. These findings do not appear to support social learning theory's expectation that friendship composition, or who adolescents are friends with, matters for their exposure to delinquency. In opposition to strain theory, poor social integration was not found to be strongly associated with greater delinquency for all queer youth. Instead, queer girls were more likely to engage in the externalizing behaviors compared with heterosexual girls, while queer boys were less likely to be delinquent. These findings suggest that strain, as related to individuals' social integration, does not necessarily lead to greater delinquency even though all queer youth, regardless of gender, were found to be not well integrated within their in-school friendship networks. If anything, strain at home and at school may help explain some of the differences found between queer girls and their heterosexual peers given the significant effects of the covariates.

Policy implications

Beyond expanding our understanding of the social world of queer adolescents, the results from this chapter provide multiple avenues for interventions and policies related to integrating queer youth at school, including by queering curriculum and increasing feelings of school belongingness through supportive programming.

There are also multiple approaches that schools can employ to increase queer youth's social integration. First, school districts could include queer content as part of the curriculum to increase the general population's understanding of issues related to queer people (Snapp et al., 2015). For instance, history classes could include lessons about contributions from queer individuals, such as Harvey Milk or Sylvia Rivera, language arts classes could include stories about queer characters, or health classes could instruct students on issues related to queer health. These kinds of micro-interventions at the local level have the potential to change norms and expectations, leading to possible adoption of such policies at larger levels when successfully implemented. Prior work has shown that inclusive curricula are associated with greater feelings of safety at school and reduced instances of bullying (Snapp et al., 2015). Coupled with existing programs designed for adolescents, including components that address issues related to queer youth's experiences, would enhance efforts designed to promote positive youth development. Additionally, because such interventions tend to include parents as part of the programming, more inclusive curricula would potentially also improve queer youth's home lives.

Efforts to increase feelings of school belongingness and support are also important because prior work has found that approximately 40–50 percent of queer students reported hearing anti-queer language by school staff since 2001, showing the significant prevalence of such language in schools (Kosciw et al., 2016). It would not be surprising if such biased language is even more common in rural communities such as the ones examined in this chapter. Prior work has shown that positive school climates and reduced instances of homophobic victimization reduce poor outcomes among queer youth (Birkett et al., 2009; Martin-Storey et al., 2015). Of particular importance has been the success of gay–straight alliances (GSAs) in improving queer youth's outcomes and feelings of acceptance within schools (Russell et al., 2009; Walls et al., 2010, Poteat et al., 2017). Schools should continue to consider efforts that improve queer youth's feelings of belongingness and support at school.

Limitations

There are a few limitations that should be noted. Although the network characteristics did not mediate the relationship between sexual orientation, gender, and delinquency, it may instead be the case that the network characteristics interact with sexual orientation and gender to create different patterns through adolescence. Given the extent to which the findings differ by gender, it is likely that interactions between the network characteristics and sexual orientation could help explain the patterns of delinquency.

In addition, it is crucial to recognize the challenges of using the retrospective sexual identity coding to identify queer youth. First, there is no guarantee that individuals who self-identified as queer during young adulthood would have done so during adolescence or even thought of themselves as non-heterosexual at the time. Similarly, a substantial body of literature (for example, Diamond, 2008) points to the increasing prevalence of sexual fluidity, or how individuals change their sexual orientation across the life course. An openness to change one's sexual orientation or to disregard traditional labels associated with sexual orientation or gender identity appear to be a hallmark of younger generations (Savin-Williams, 2009), which has important implications for the social lives of modern queer youth. Nevertheless, few studies have collected data related to sexual orientation during adolescence, limiting researchers' ability to examine directly how sexual orientation affects adolescent behavior. Instead, by leveraging retrospective identity coding, we are able to approach a better understanding of how queer youth fit within their school's social networks.

Conclusion

Results from this chapter reinforce the importance of examining the impact of sexual orientation on adolescents' social lives. Adolescence is a critical developmental period in individuals' lives, yet as this chapter has shown, individuals experience adolescence differently. I found substantial evidence that the friendship networks of queer youth differ substantially from those of their heterosexual peers and that the specific differences depend on gender. Moreover, these configurations of sexual orientation and gender also lead to different patterns of delinquent behaviors. Although I found limited evidence of friendship network characteristics mediating these relationships, adolescents' experiences with their peers and at school are important factors to consider when developing programming aimed at improving queer adolescents' well-being. Moreover, schools and researchers should take into consideration the evolving nature of sexual orientation and gender identity labels among adolescents today to ensure that programming is relevant. Tailored interventions that improve queer youth's self-esteem and feelings of social support, and strategies to reduce risky behaviors, are fruitful avenues for prevention.

Through these efforts we can queer criminology in both theory and praxis, first by improving how our existing criminological theories explain the experiences of queer individuals with crime and delinquency, and, equally as important, by using research findings to improve the experiences of queer youth within schools.

References

Agnew, R. (1992) 'Foundation for a general strain theory of crime and delinquency', *Criminology*, 30(1): 47–88. https://doi.org/10.1111/j.1745-9125.1992.tb01093.x

Beaver, K.M., Connolly, E.J., Schwartz, J.A., Boutwell, B.B., Barnes, J.C., & Nedelec, J.L. (2016) 'Sexual orientation and involvement in nonviolent and violent delinquent behaviors: findings from the National Longitudinal Study of Adolescent to Adult Health', *Archives of Sexual Behavior*, 45(7): 1759–1769. https://doi.org/10.1007/s10508-016-0717-3

Birkett, M., Espelage, D.L., & Koenig, B. (2009) 'LGB and questioning students in schools: the moderating effects of homophobic bullying and school climate on negative outcomes', *Journal of Youth and Adolescence*, 38(7): 989–1000. https://doi.org/10.1007/s10964-008-9389-1

Broidy, L. & Agnew, R. (1997) 'Gender and crime: a general strain theory perspective', *Journal of Research in Crime and Delinquency*, 34(3): 275–306. https://doi.org/10.1177/0022427897034003001

Burgess, R.L. & Akers, R.L. (1966) 'A differential association-reinforcement theory of criminal behavior', *Social Problems*, 14(2): 128–147.

Conover-Williams, M. (2014) 'The queer delinquent: impacts of risk and protective factors on sexual minority juvenile offending in the U.S.', in D. Peterson & R.V. Panfil (eds.), *Handbook of LGBT Communities, Crime, and Justice*, New York: Springer, pp. 449–472. http://dx.doi.org/10.1007/978-1-4614-9188-0_21

Diamond, L. (2008) *Sexual Fluidity*, Cambridge, MA: Harvard University Press.

Dijkstra, J.K., Cillessen, A.H.N., Lindenberg, S., & Veenstra, R. (2010) 'Basking in reflected glory and its limits: why adolescents hang out with popular peers', *Journal of Research on Adolescence*, 20(4): 942–958. https://doi.org/10.1111/j.1532-7795.2010.00671.x

Durso, L.E. & Gates, G.J. (2013) 'Best practices: collecting and analyzing data on sexual minorities', in A.K. Baumle (ed.), *International Handbook on the Demography of Sexuality*, Dordrecht: Springer, pp. 21–42. http://link.springer.com/chapter/10.1007/978-94-007-5512-3_3

Fan, X., Miller, B.C., Park, K.-E., Winward, B.W., Christensen, M., Grotevant, H.D., & Tai, R.H. (2006) 'An exploratory study about inaccuracy and invalidity in adolescent self-report surveys', *Field Methods*, 18(3): 223–244. https://doi.org/10.1177/152822X06289161

Gottfredson, M.R. & Hirschi, T. (1990) *A General Theory of Crime*, Stanford, CA: Stanford University Press.

Himmelstein, K.E.W. & Brückner, H. (2011) 'Criminal-justice and school sanctions against nonheterosexual youth: a national longitudinal study', *Pediatrics*, 127(1): 49–57. https://doi.org/10.1542/peds.2009-2306

Kann, L., Olsen, E.O., McManus, T., Harris, W.A., Shanklin, S.L., Flint, K.H., Queen, B., Lowry, R., Chyen, D., Whittle, L., Thornton, J., Lim, C., Yamakawa, Y., Brener, N., & Zaza, S. (2016) 'Sexual identity, sex of sexual contacts, and health-related behaviors among students in grades 9–12: United States and selected sites, 2015', *MMWR. Surveillance Summaries*, 65(9): 1–202. https://doi.org/10.15585/mmwr.ss6509a1

Koeppel, M.D.H. (2015) 'Assessing the association between self-control and self-reported criminal behaviors between sexual orientation groups', *Criminal Justice Review*, 40(2): 117–130. https://doi.org/10.1177/0734016814549236

Kosciw, J.G., Greytak, E.A., Giga, N.M., Villenas, C., & Danischewski, D.J. (2016) 'The 2015 National School Climate Survey: the experiences of lesbian, gay, bisexual, transgender, and queer youth in our nation's schools', Gay, Lesbian and Straight Education Network (GLSEN). https://eric.ed.gov/?id=ED574780

Kreager, D.A. & Haynie, D.L. (2011) 'Dangerous liaisons? Dating and drinking diffusion in adolescent peer networks', *American Sociological Review*, 76(5): 737–763. https://doi.org/10.1177/0003122411416934

Kruttschnitt, C. (2013) 'Gender and crime', *Annual Review of Sociology*, 39(1): 291–308. https://doi.org/10.1146/annurev-soc-071312-145605

Martin-Storey, A., Cheadle, J.E., Skalamera, J., & Crosnoe, R. (2015) 'Exploring the social integration of sexual minority youth across high school contexts', *Child Development*, 86(3): 965–975. https://doi.org/10.1111/cdev.12352

Poteat, V.P., Yoshikawa, H., Calzo, J.P., Russell, S.T., & Horn, S. (2017) 'Gay–straight alliances as settings for youth inclusion and development: future conceptual and methodological directions for research on these and other student groups in schools', *Educational Researcher*, 46(9): 508–516. https://doi.org/10.3102/0013189X17738760

Robinson, J.P. & Espelage, D.L. (2011) 'Inequities in educational and psychological outcomes between LGBTQ and straight students in middle and high school', *Educational Researcher*, 40(7): 315–330. https://doi.org/10.3102/0013189X11422112

Russell, S.T., Muraco, A., Subramaniam, A., & Laub, C. (2009) 'Youth empowerment and high school gay–straight alliances', *Journal of Youth and Adolescence*, 38(7): 891–903. https://doi.org/10.1007/s10964-008-9382-8

Savin-Williams, R.C. (2009) *The New Gay Teenager*, Cambridge, MA: Harvard University Press.

Savin-Williams, R.C. & Joyner, K. (2014) 'The dubious assessment of gay, lesbian, and bisexual adolescents of add health', *Archives of Sexual Behavior*, 43(3): 413–422. https://doi.org/10.1007/s10508-013-0219-5

Snapp, S.D., McGuire, J.K., Sinclair, K.O., Gabrion, K., & Russell, S.T. (2015) 'LGBTQ-inclusive curricula: why supportive curricula matter', *Sex Education*, 15(6): 580–596. https://doi.org/10.1080/14681811.2015.1042573

Steffensmeier, D. & Allan, E. (1996) 'Gender and crime: toward a gendered theory of female offending', *Annual Review of Sociology*, 22(1): 459–487. https://doi.org/10.1146/annurev.soc.22.1.459

Sutherland, E. (1939) 'Differential association', in E.H. Sutherland and D.R. Cressey (eds.), *Principles of Criminology*, Lanham, MD: Rowman & Littlefield, pp. 4–7.

Sweeten, G. (2012) 'Scaling criminal offending', *Journal of Quantitative Criminology*, 28(3): 533–557. https://doi.org/10.1007/s10940-011-9160-8

Walls, N.E., Kane, S.B., & Wisneski, H. (2010) 'Gay–straight alliances and school experiences of sexual minority youth', *Youth & Society*, 41(3): 307–332. https://doi.org/10.1177/0044118X09334957

Warr, M. (1993) 'Age, peers, and delinquency', *Criminology*, 31(1): 17–40. https://doi.org/10.1111/j.1745-9125.1993.tb01120.x

Zuckerman, M. (1994) *Behavioral Expressions and Biosocial Bases of Sensation Seeking*, Cambridge: Cambridge University Press.

14

'At the Very Least': Politics and Praxis of Bail Fund Organizers and the Potential for Queer Liberation

Luca Suede Connolly and Rose M. Buckelew

Introduction

The Uprisings for Black Liberation, the hundreds of nationwide protests ignited by the police murder of George Floyd beginning in May 2020, heightened the visibility of community organizations already on the ground working to address the brutalities of policing and incarceration. Some of that attention was directed toward bail funds, leading to a waterfall of donations mostly from individuals. Among those most notable was the Minnesota Freedom Fund, which fundraised $30 million in less than a month (Bromwich, 2020; Condon, 2020). While bail funds captured the attention of a new audience, the subject has yet to hold the interest of researchers as there is little academic scholarship on the politics or praxis of bail fund organizers.

The primary work of bail funds is collecting donations and posting cash bail for individuals held in pre-trial detention. The cash bail system requires an individual charged with a crime to pay a sort of security deposit, which is then refundable upon their completion of court proceedings or the dismissal of the charge. In each case, the judge determines if bail is applicable and if so, the amount, which is then determined by a host of factors, including severity of the alleged crime; the individual's criminal record, employment history, and community ties; amount of evidence; and likelihood of conviction. Based on these factors and the discretion of the judge, a bail amount can range from a few hundred dollars to hundreds of thousands of dollars. To secure their freedom from having to await trial in jail, an individual can pay the bail amount in full or pay a fee to a commercial bond company to post bail on their behalf (most often 10 percent of the bail amount).

There has long been concern about how the cash bail system works to penalize and criminalize poor people. While held in jail, individuals are at risk of losing their jobs, housing, and custody of their children. Further, there is concern that pre-trial detention pressures detainees to plead guilty to lower charges rather than spend more time locked up (Eisen & Chettiar, 2018). In addition to this, detention itself proves to be a dangerous, even lethal experience, as evidenced in the murder of Layleen Xtravaganza Cubilette-Polanco. Cubilette-Polanco, an Afro-Latinx trans woman, died following an epileptic seizure. At the time of her death, Cubilette-Polanco was being held in solitary confinement at the Rikers Island Jail Complex, a site known for heinous human rights abuses, on a $500 bond (Feller et al., 2020). Although a psychiatrist had refused to clear Cubilette-Polanco for solitary confinement due to her history of seizures, the jail placed her in isolation, claiming she had conflicts with individuals in the Transgender Housing Unit dorms and because Department of Corrections policy does not permit housing trans women with the general population of cis women. Video recordings from the day of Cubilette-Polanco's murder show that officers failed to follow orders and did not check on her every 15 minutes. The same recordings also show officers laughing as they open Cubilette-Polanco's cell and find her unresponsive (Sosin, 2020). And, even after her death, New York City Department of Investigations continued the transphobia, misgendering her on Twitter and deadnaming her in a press release (NYC DOI, 2020).

The problem of pre-trial detention is manifold. Scholars and organizers have drawn attention to the rapid increase in the pre-trial detained population and the disproportionate detention of Black, Latinx, and Native people. Although the Department of Justice has failed to provide national data since 2002, local data suggests that Black, Latinx, and Native men are more likely to be detained pre-trial, to receive financial conditions for release, and to be issued higher bond amounts (Sawyer, 2019). And, while cash bail disproportionately affects people of color, queer, trans, and gender nonconforming (Q/T/GNC henceforth) people are also uniquely impacted by the criminal punishment system.

In 2015, Black and Pink, a national prison abolitionist organization working to liberate lesbian, gay, bisexual, transgender, queer, intersex, asexual, Two-Spirit, plus (LGBTQIA2S+) people and those living with HIV/AIDS, conducted a survey of over a thousand LGBTQ identified prisoners across the United States. In 'Coming out of the concrete closet', they shared that nearly three-quarters of respondents reported being held in jail prior to conviction and of those who experienced pre-trial detention, more than half reported being detained for more than a year (Black and Pink, 2015). Additionally, a survey by the National Center for Transgender Equality (2012) reports that roughly a quarter of transgender women have experienced incarceration, while nearly half of Black transgender Americans have been incarcerated in their lifetime.

The problems of pre-trial detention and the particular vulnerability of Q/T/GNC people has only increased during the COVID-19 pandemic. As the pandemic rages with no clear end, there is increased concern about the risk of infection for those held in jail as research indicates that incarcerated people are at much higher risk of infection than the public (Jimenez et al., 2020).

This project is situated within the context of the COVID-19 pandemic, the national Uprisings for Black Liberation, and ongoing movements for bail reform and abolition. This chapter will examine the day in and day out work of bail fund organizers, how bail fund organizers understand their work and define their goals, and the potential of bail funds as an important tool for the liberation of Q/T/GNC people.

The historical and contemporary landscape of bail funds

While there is considerable scholarship on bail, bail legislation, bail reform, and bail as a mechanism reproducing racial and economic inequalities, little academic attention has been paid to bail funds, bail fund organizers, or how bail funds can disrupt the criminalization of Q/T/GNC people. Despite bail fund organizing having at least a century-long history in the US, there are no readily available studies on bail fund organizers, although Steinberg et al. (2018) has written the most recognized history of bail funds, which is summarized here and expanded to include a history of queer bail funds.

Bail funds have been organized for diverse purposes, functioning as part of and apart from social movements. While there is a long tradition in America of families, communities, and churches 'passing that hat' or pooling together resources to buy the freedom of loved ones and strangers, the earliest form of an organized bail fund can be found in the 1920s. Steinberg et al. (2018) found multiple periods of bail fund organizing: following World War I, the American Civil Liberties Union organized the first large-scale fund to bail out labor organizers, anarchists, and suspected Communists; in the 1950s, the Civil Rights Congress organized bail funds to support African American organizers; and in the 1960s, bail funds continued as a practice by groups such as the Student Non-Violent Coordinating Committee and the National Association for the Advancement of Colored People. In the 1970s the practice of bail funds as an organizing tactic was adopted by queer organizers who crowd-sourced money from their communities to pay bonds for queer people. Abolitionist community organizer and legal scholar Dean Spade (2020) reminds us:

> Queer and trans activists have a long history of protesting against police violence. In fact, annual Pride celebrations mark the anniversary of the Stonewall Rebellion: In June 1969, at a bar called the Stonewall Inn in New York City, queer and trans people fought back against the ongoing violence they faced at the hands of the police. (para 2)

Less than a year after Stonewall, in 1970, an early iteration of a bail fund emerged from the Gay Liberation Front (GLF), an organization inspired by 'the women's liberation front, the Black Panthers, and the Young Lords' (Mogul et al., 2011). GLF organized in response to police brutality, anti-queer criminalization, and state surveillance of queer communities in New York. In the organization's communiqué 'Gay Flames', sandwiched between an events calendar and an erotic poem, the GLF calls on readers and members to donate to support 'your Sisters and Brothers that are being brutalized and arrested', explaining GLF needed funds to support 16 'homosexuals' arrested after 'the police rioted' in Greenwich Village. The fundraising language specified that 'every penny received will go into this bail fund and will be used to assist ALL homosexual men and women. Gay Power to the Gay People!' (Gay Liberation Front, 1970).

Following in the ancestral footsteps of the GLF, the Emergency Release Fund (ERF), located in New York City, emerged after the cofounder learned of Cubilette-Polanco's murder (Baume, 2019). According to their website, ERF's mission is to 'ensure that no trans person at risk in New York City jails remains in detention before trial. If cash bail is set for a trans person in New York City and no bars to release are in place, bail will be paid by the Emergency Release Fund' (Emergency Release Fund, 2020). The ERF website further positions their all-volunteer work inside a broader analysis of state violence against transgender people:

> Trans people face dramatically elevated risk of harm or death in pre-trial detention. Because of systemic discrimination and criminalization that pushes them to the margins of society, trans people are less eligible for pre-trial release under existing programs. They are more likely to be assaulted in jail and less likely to get out, a lethal combination.

The ERF is one of many bail funds affiliated with the National Bail Fund Network (NBFN), the only coalition of its kind for bail workers nationally. The NBFN maintains an emphasis on connecting and supporting bail funds utilizing an abolitionist framework in their organizing. To understand bail funds today, it is helpful to be familiar with both NBFN and the Bail Project (TBP). The NBFN is a project of the Community Justice Exchange, an explicitly abolitionist organization that works toward 'a world without prisons, policing, prosecution, surveillance or any form of detention or supervision' and draws upon the abolitionist frameworks established by Critical Resistance to ground their abolitionism in strategy and tactics (Community Justice Exchange, n.d.). The NBFN grew out of the Brooklyn Community Bail Fund, a revolving fund that also closed in early 2020, and now has over 80 affiliates. As a network, the organization provides affiliates with mentorship, guidance, monthly calls to troubleshoot and strategize, as well as fundraising support.

The Bail Project is a national nonprofit organization that employs and trains 'bail disruptors', who in turn operate 22 bail funds across the country. The organization grew out of the Bronx Freedom Fund, a revolving bail fund that closed in early 2020 when New York state eliminated most cash bail for non-violent felonies and misdemeanors (The Bail Project, n.d.). As per their mission statement, the organization works toward the goal of 'a more just and equitable pretrial system, one that is truly grounded in the presumption of innocence for *all*, regardless of race, economic status, or accusation' (The Bail Project, n.d.) and aims to end the cash bail system by demonstrating the efficacy of their Community Release with Support Model, a program that releases people on their own recognizance and provides court notifications. 'Charge agnostic', the organization does not use type of charge to determine who they bail out but employs a 'soft cap' of $10,000, which can eliminate more serious crimes. In determining eligibility, TBP evaluates bail amount, their assessment of the reliability of the person's contact information and track record of prior court appearances, as well as an 'individual needs assessment to determine whether [they] can adequately support the person through [their] network of community partners and social service providers' (The Bail Project, n.d.). What becomes clear is that TBP is committed to making a more equitable pre-trial system and abolishing cash bail, which stands in radical contrast to the NBFN. While not all bail funds are associated with TBP or the NBFN, understanding their differing approaches is helpful in situating this project.

Methods

We drew on recent news coverage of bail fund organizing and conducted interviews with four bail fund organizers in the Southern United States. The interviews examined here represent an emerging data set. We estimate there are roughly 100 bail funds nationally, and we chose to narrow in on Southern bail funds, which created more points of comparison, as these bail funds were operating within comparable political and legal conditions.

Two interview participants were recruited through already established networks. Luca, a Southern, gender nonconforming white trans woman, knew two of the bail fund organizers through her own experience organizing. The other two participants were identified from appearing in news accounts and recruited via email. Luca interviewed those organizers she held connections with, and Rose interviewed the others. Although the interview schedule was consistent across interviews, Luca was able to draw from her experience and position as a local bail fund organizer to develop rapport and establish trust. Rose, a cis Chicana, coming from outside community organizing but within a university, was able to use her title as a professor to gain respectability with participants. What resulted was rich, in-depth interviews where participants were seemingly forthright in sharing the details of their bail funds and experiences.

Interviews were conducted in mid- to late summer 2020 by phone or Zoom, as per Institutional Review Board (IRB) protocols. Interviews lasted 50 to 90 minutes and involved a range of questions where participants were asked to describe the history of their organizations, their everyday work, and their understanding of why bail funds are important. Further, participants were asked to describe how they do or do not communicate or interact with local government and to reflect on how the uprisings impacted their work. Through these interviews we were able to gather firsthand accounts of the mechanical, logistical, and financial work of bail funds, as well as organizers' political analysis of bail funds. Pseudonyms have been used in reporting the interviews and quoted materials have been trimmed of distractions (for example, like, um).

Results

Descriptive analysis

From our interviews with bail fund organizers we were able to gain insight into their everyday work and how they understand it, addressing an existing gap in the literature. The four bail fund organizers we interviewed shared an understanding that cash bail was a harmful and unfair system. In addition, they described their bail funds as primarily functioning to pay bail through fundraised money. In conducting interviews, we asked organizers to articulate their politics and through this, hoped to better understand how bail funds could be used to disrupt the criminalization of Q/T/GNC people, whether intended or not. What emerged were differing constructions of worthiness and innocence, and varying engagements with abolitionist frameworks, which may shape how bail funds support Q/T/GNC people.

Jacob, a white cis man, cofounded the Centerville Bail Fund in 2016, after returning from college where he interned with a well-known bail fund and participated in a prison abolitionist student coalition.[1] Upon returning to Centerville, Jacob connected with a handful of other local abolitionist organizers to establish the bail fund and quickly affiliated with the NBFN. What stands out as important to Centerville's origin story, when compared with the others, is that the bail fund was established with explicitly abolitionist politics. When asked to explain the importance of bail fund work, he said:

> I think the only reason it is inherently important to organize a bail fund is to get people out of jail. I think it can be important for lots of other reasons. And I think it is important to me for a lot of other reasons.

Beyond paying for bail, Centerville Bail Fund provides post-release support (transportation to court, connections to resources, cash support) and has developed a court watch program. But for Jacob, bail fund work was important because it 'strengthened abolitionist movement work, first and foremost', which explains his attention to educating the local community on abolitionist politics. Centerville Bail Fund has a robust social media presence, with Twitter and Instagram accounts that present political theory and statistics in easy-to-understand language and graphics. That Jacob was a student and practitioner of abolition may explain why Centerville Bail Fund emphasized community education, as he sees the bail fund as just one abolitionist practice. For the first three years, Centerville Bail Fund paid approximately 60 bails, but since COVID-19 and the Uprising for Black Liberation it has paid an additional 300 bails. The bail fund received a waterfall in donations during the uprising, but before this, the bail fund would fundraise as needed, usually maintaining a cash reserve of a few thousand dollars. In early fall of 2020, Centerville Bail Fund had increased that reserve to $1.4 million.

In Centerville Bail Fund's volunteer training, the organizers describe the bail fund as a 'queer and trans powered abolitionist organization striving for Black liberation'. Jacob identified their team as 'almost all visibly queer and or gender non-conforming'. Centerville volunteers have articulated to Jacob their ongoing experiences with misgendering from clients and state officials, as well as deadnaming from magistrates who use official documents in the bail posting process. Volunteers have also experienced some clients even commenting on, questioning, or sexualizing volunteers' gender presentation. In response to these aggressions, some volunteers commented on editing their everyday presentation to present as less visibly queer or gender nonconforming. We see this as Q/T/GNC volunteers choosing to minimize queer expression as a praxis of solidarity with incarcerated people via reducing potential obstacles in the process of decarceration. In this spirit, Centerville wants to center formerly incarcerated people in their organization and actively recruits former clients to volunteer. This desire creates some anxiety for current volunteers as some former clients may 'not share the same commitment' to a 'space totally free of anti-queer and anti-trans violence'. To address this anxiety, Centerville explicitly names their pro Q/T/GNC and abolitionist politics during volunteer training, hoping to encourage individuals to self-select out of volunteering with the fund if they do not hold or are not open to these values.

In contrast, Fairview Bail Fund was developed by members of a predominately Black Baptist church working to address social and economic issues impacting their community and without explicit politics critiquing the state. Mildred, a Black cis woman and the codirector of the Fairview Bail Fund, when asked to explain the beginning of the organization, said: 'It's really simple. It was the pastor's idea.' Through conversations with her pastor and church members, Mildred explains how she came to realize the harms of pre-trial detention:

> We realized that people get arrested, but they aren't necessarily guilty. They may be, but they, if you can afford to pay bail, you get your day in court whenever that day is. But if you can't afford it, you may stay locked up until you get to go to court. And then in that time period, you may end up losing your house. Or if you rent, you may end up losing your rental property. You may end up losing your job. So it affects more than just you were arrested. And they say, you're innocent until proven guilty.

Inspired by the National Bail Out, Mildred and her group organized a Mother's Day fundraiser. Although Mildred thought of the fundraiser as a 'one-time thing', the event was successful and donations from the community continued to come in. In describing the early stages of developing the bail fund, Mildred called herself 'naive'. As she explains, '[w]e thought you could just say, okay, whoever you [the police] have arrested on this day, can we bail them out? And it doesn't work like that.' Realizing she needed support, Mildred turned to a member of the congregation, a local sheriff, who in turn connected her with a group of local bondsmen. The bondsmen group agreed to an arrangement where the Fairview Bail Fund would provide the 10 percent needed to pay the bond and the bondsmen would assume all liability. When the person is released, the bondsmen group provides Mildred with their contact information and she in turn calls them to connect them with local 'wraparound services': drug counseling, parenting classes, job placement and training, and housing assistance. Mildred understood the goal of Fairview Bail Fund as helping people become 'productive citizen[s]' and move to the 'next stage of their life'. She estimated that from 2017 to 2020 her organization had paid 50 bails a year, although her work stopped suddenly during the uprisings; as she explained, 'nobody's asked us, nobody's reached out to us'.

When Fairview's bailouts stopped at the start of the pandemic, the Mountain Bail Fund was established. Robin, a white cis woman and cofounder of Mountain Bail Fund, explained why she and a handful of other law students started the organization:

> It definitely started with the protests. Honestly at the beginning of the pandemic, you know, I've been reading a lot about COVID in jails and prisons and public health and in prisons in general has always been kind of a concern of mine. And we went, you know, online for the rest of the semester. And I think that a lot of us found that we had extra time starting around March. And it had been something that I had been thinking about ... this fear about prisons and jails handling COVID and people being held in pretrial and also in enclosed spaces.

Robin made brief connections with other bail funds and with both TBP and NBFN, and she leaned on a friend for support who was running a bail fund in the Northeast. In doing her research she quickly learned there was 'very little cash bail' in her city and redirected her attention to a neighboring county. At first, she struggled to get their 'name out there' and found the public defender's office to be a useful source of referrals. For Robin and her team, establishing and publicizing the bail fund has involved learning by mistakes. She describes her first attempts at establishing a presence at the jail:

> I've tried to give flyers to all of them [jails], but they won't accept flyers. I've recently got business cards, cause I know bail bondsmen are allowed to have business cards in these jails, but they still haven't been accepted in one place. So, we actually are having a lot of trouble in terms of just access to the jails themselves, in terms of, you know, people there knowing that we are there to help.

At the time of the interview, the bail fund was only two months old and had already bailed out 16 people. After release, Robin and her team offer no-cost rides to support individuals to return for court appearances. But other than transportation support, Mountain Bail Fund does not provide or connect people to other services, relying mostly on the public defender's office to do that work. Although she had reached out to both the NBFN and TBP, she chose only to discuss her relationship with TBP, which she described as 'unbelievably helpful' in that 'they [TBP] have the same philosophy as us'.

Although TBP had provided the Mountain Bail Fund with guidance, it was responsible for establishing the Franklin Bail Fund. Melvin, one of the bail fund's organizers, a Latinx cis man, explained that a local attorney had made a request to TBP to establish the bail fund about three years earlier. Melvin was hired within a few months of the bail fund opening, recommended for the position from a local political organizer. Melvin was a well-known community organizer, having advocated for immigration-related issues for about a decade. It is important to note that initially the bail fund was located in the public defender's office.

Moreover, Melvin was a paid employee of TBP; in contrast, all other bail funds were organized by unpaid volunteers. He enjoyed working for TBP, especially because of the staff training, which he described as in-depth, focusing on issues of diversity and equity, and led by people of color and trans people. He also shared that he appreciated TBP for teaching him how to better serve LGBTQ clients, for example finding the best language to inquire if a client would benefit from LGBTQ-specific resources. The Bail Project also provided the bail fund with money, which meant the organizers were not tasked with collecting donations. When asked how they fundraise, Melvin explained: 'Oh, we don't. We were told to not put much focus on fundraising here, that they'll [TBP] take care of it nationally.' And when asked to explain his motivation for doing bail fund work, Melvin's response echoed Mildred's from Fairview Bail Fund:

> Bail funds are important because we're able to provide the person the opportunity to go back to their house, to make sure they don't lose their job, to [provide a] reference [for] them. As simple as a thing of calling a rehab center and just initiating the conversation goes a long way for a person who doesn't even know how to do that, you know?

Aside from paying bail, Melvin's work involves connecting released people with resources to help find employment and secure drug and mental health support, as well as arrange transportation for future court appearances. Referrals come to Melvin through TBP, the public defender's office, and social media, but unlike any of the other bail funds, Franklin Bail Fund receives a daily roster from a local county jail providing information on any person detained on a bond of $10,000 or less. The roster was facilitated through a relationship with the county sheriff, which Melvin described as 'great'. He explained, 'I mean, publicly, he's done nothing but praise us. And in times of uncertainty, like he's always supported us publicly.' At time of the interview, the Franklin Bail Fund reported posting 300 bails in the last year. When asked why he did bail work, Melvin explained that he didn't think bail was 'effective' and that it punished the poor.

The interviews revealed that while the bail funds operated similarly, they practiced different politics. Some imagined their work as an effort toward helping individuals, abolishing cash bail, or motivating the abolition of the carceral state. In comparing their objectives and strategies, what mattered was how the bail funds grounded their work and how they perceived the state. When imagining the potential of bail funds as a liberative tool for Q/T/GNC people, it was clear that Centerville and Franklin were more explicit in their practice, although still varying in their engagement with abolitionist politics.

Abolitionist values and strategies: what defines abolitionist work?

Of our participants, Jacob, from Centerville, identified their entire organization as abolitionist, and Robin, from Mountain, reported they personally identified as an abolitionist but chose not to identify their organization as an entirely abolitionist one. Neither of our other participants at the Fairview or Franklin bail funds identified themselves or their organizations as holding abolition as a framework in their community work.

Though many of these community organizations do not directly attack the prison industrial complex as a system, at the very least they reduce the harm of incarceration. All four participants spoke to the importance of getting people out of cages. Ruth Wilson Gilmore reminds us that 'it's obvious that these systems won't disappear overnight, no abolitionist thinks that is the case' (Kushner, 2019). Robin, of the Mountain Bail Fund, spoke to the role that bail funds can play:

> We can, at the very least make sure that those who cannot afford their secured bond are not sitting in jail, waiting for their trial. We want as an organization to dismantle all of these oppressive systems, but I think that we're recognizing that we're just doing a small thing that we feel capable of right now.

National Bail Fund Network organizers note that 'as a tool of abolitionist organizers with a clear analysis about pretrial freedom, community bail funds are well-positioned to intervene at the point of release, free people from incarceration, and serve as organizing tools to end incarceration altogether' (Davidson et al., 2020). For Jacob, from Centerville, political education surrounding abolition is a major tenet for how bail funds further the abolitionist vision and can do the work of 'strengthening abolitionist movement work'. Jacob also cited inspiration from Jackie Wang's (2018) essay 'Against innocence', from her book *Carceral Capitalism*, in arguing that bail funds that post bond for anyone regardless of the charges or history of the person challenge the logic of the prison industrial complex. Jacob reported that bail funds have been 'dangerous to abolitionist movement work' when they have promoted a message that 'this issue only matters because it's happening to legally innocent people'. Jacob argued that the approach of bailing out anyone who needs the service 'can force people to confront the idea that people who are accused of terrible things don't deserve what the state gives them'. He also reported that Centerville has bailed out one individual on a 'murder charge'.

Mildred, of the Fairview Bail Fund, noted that though her organization once bailed out someone with a 'kidnap charge', her organization explicitly does not serve individuals with charges such as rape or murder, stating that there are some clients with certain charges 'we don't want to touch'. In sharing another story, Mildred described a teenager who was stopped by police for 'joyriding in a stolen car'. He was hesitant to tell Mildred his story, but she reassured him she wouldn't judge, saying 'all of us have made a poor choice at 15 years old'. She then explained, it is only for the 'grace of God that we all aren't locked up for it'. For Mildred, her work is grounded in a Christian notion of 'forgiveness'. When placed alongside her refusal to consider bailing out people on rape and murder charges, yet with her history of bailing out a person on 'kidnapping' charges, there appears a complicated and possibly inconsistent understanding of who should be caged, and one is left wondering if Q/T/GNC would deserve grace or be untouchable.

Robin, of Mountain Bail Fund, utilized innocence when asked about whether or not her organization would post a bond for a rape or murder charge, saying, 'the problem with this is that nobody has been convicted of a crime, you know?' Robin further found solace in the courts' authority, noting that if the legal system thinks someone is deserving of a bond, they must be safe to bail out. Robin finds relief in judges and magistrates holding responsibility, noting that 'then we're not the ones making the risk assessment'. Here, we see Robin articulating that she does not feel individual bail funds are accountable for who they bail out but instead trust the courts to determine who is and isn't eligible for bond. What is left out is how Robin would account for a carceral system that disproportionately targets, surveils, criminalizes, and punishes Q/T/GNC people, people judges find more 'at risk'. As Leslie Feinberg (1999) writes, '[e]ven where the laws are not written down, police are empowered to carry out merciless punishment for sex and gender difference' (p. 11).

Though both Mildred and Robin said their organization would have posted bail for protesters, neither organization received any protest-related requests. The Centerville Bail Fund was the only fund that served as a 'protest bail fund' for individuals experiencing state repression as a result of their alleged participation in the Uprisings for Black Liberation in the spring and summer of 2020.

Moving forward in tension with the state and toward queer liberation

Jacob offered a clear distinction between the work of his organization and 'actual abolitionists', because for him, activists 'in the streets' are the ones 'actually trying to achieve abolition'. In comparing Jacob's position to that of other organizers, one learns an abolitionist approach is not held universally by bail fund organizers. Melvin did not share any conceptions of abolition outside of 'abolishing bail'. Mildred related to abolition by saying 'I'm not going to say do away with the system, do away with policing or police funding'. She further identified her work as emerging from a 'restorative justice' framework, suggesting 'the justice system as a whole can use some tweaking'. When asked if all bail funds are abolitionist, Robin quickly responded 'yes'. When asked for elaboration, she explained, 'the work is inherently pushing towards one thing, which is the elimination of the system, therefore it is both political and abolitionist'. Jacob elaborated that he believes a bail fund is abolitionist when he sees certain procedures in the mechanization of the revolving bail fund, as well as efforts outside this function. He believes an abolitionist bail fund is one where bail is posted for anyone, regardless of charge, and there is no cap on the bail amount unless the organization has an extremely small pool of money. In Jacob's opinion, a bail fund is not abolitionist if it is not offering political education around the importance of abolition or supporting protests that resist state violence and the carceral system. Some active NBFN organizers believe bail funds are an abolitionist tool in how they reduce state power: 'As we chip away at the power of the criminal legal system to incarcerate, surveil, and monitor people during the pretrial period, we weaken the system's overall reach' (Davidson et al., 2020). And as Spade (2020) reminds us, queer and trans people have been 'leading activists for police and prison abolition', illuminating Q/T/GNC people both as abolitionist leaders and as groups needing the liberation abolition can bring.

Critical Resistance can provide us further insight. Formed in 1997 and including many queer and trans scholars and activists working for the abolition of the prison industrial complex, today the organization is widely understood to be a leader in abolition (Critical Resistance, n.d.a). Critical Resistance's argument that abolition is 'not to improve the system' (Critical Resistance, n.d.b) gives perspective to TBP's Arkansas chapter, which was invited to establish itself in the region to assist the local sheriff with jail overcrowding (Gilker, 2019). Here we see the bail fund acting as a pressure valve for the state rather than forcing the police to arrest fewer or release more people. Pilar Weiss, the director of the NBFN, shared that 'for a bail fund to be pushing towards abolition, they must exist in tension with the state' (P. Weiss, personal communication, October 11, 2020). As we have uncovered, many bail fund organizations and the individuals who lead them do not exist in tension with the state but rather find partnership with the state as an effective way to do their work. This leads us back to our initial research question: why do bail fund organizers do this work? At the very least, all our participants reported finding the purpose of their work to free some people caged in pre-trial incarceration. Though Jacob placed emphasis on providing bail for everyone, no matter the context, our research leaves us questioning how an abolitionist framework asks us to prioritize Q/T/GNC and other more vulnerable folks in liberating people from cages.

Conclusion

In our research, we have found that community bail funds are a deeply overlooked topic, and we hope this study will inspire others to examine the politics and praxis of community organizations working against the criminal punishment system. We also hope this study will be a helpful resource to community bail organizers, as we believe that some of these organizations and their workers serve a vision for an abolitionist future without prisons and jails. We are left with many questions: how do these organizations work to eliminate pre-trial incarceration, rather than act as a pressure valve for the carceral state, supporting and reinforcing the functions of the criminal punishment system? How do the data and stories gathered by community bail funds provide support for efforts to eliminate pre-trial incarceration and to prevent state murders of trans folks such as Cubilette-Polanco? Cubilette-Polanco's murder was not caused by the lack of transgender-specific prisons or by her presence in solitary confinement, but by her incarceration and interaction with the carceral state. The praxis of bail fund work shows that freeing people from cages can at the very least disrupt state violence.

As Spade (2020) reminds us, '[q]ueer and trans liberation is inextricable from other leftist liberation movements'. To understand this entanglement, we again look to data collected by the National Center for Transgender Equality (2012), indicating that nearly half of Black trans folks in the US have been incarcerated at least once in their lifetime. When state violence via policing, criminalization, and incarceration so clearly disproportionately affects the Black transgender community, carceral abolition is essential for queer liberation. Unfortunately, much contemporary scholarship paints queer liberation as a conversation of gendered bathrooms, adoption rights, bullying, and health insurance battles centering thin, white, able-bodied LGBT people of the professional class. Too often, conversations of criminalization focus narrowly on the experiences of poor Black cishetero men (Ritchie, 2017). Though all these people and battles are necessary for collective liberation, the harmful differentiation of queer liberation and carceral abolition erases the most vulnerable members of the queer and trans community, who the data show must be centered. State-sanctioned killings such as the murder of Layleen Polanco are not abstract possibilities but confirm that queer liberation and prison industrial complex abolition are inextricable in politics and praxis.

Note

1 All names of participants and bail funds represent pseudonyms.

References

The Bail Project (n.d.) 'FAQ', The Bail Project. https://bailproject.org/faq/

Baume, M. (2019) 'New Yorkers establish bail fund to rescue trans women from jail', *Out Magazine*, September 6. https://www.out.com/transgender/2019/9/06/new-yorkers-establish-bail-fund-rescue-trans-women-jail

Black and Pink (2015) 'Coming out of concrete closets: a report on Black and Pink's National LGBTQ Prisoner Survey'. https://www.issuelab.org/resources/23129/23129.pdf

Bromwich, J.E. (2020) 'How a Minnesota bail fund raised $20 million', *The New York Times*, June 1. https://www.nytimes.com/2020/06/01/style/minnesota-freedom-fund-bail-george-floyd-protests.html

Community Justice Exchange (n.d.) 'About us', Community Justice Exchange. https://www.communityjusticeexchange.org/en/about-us

Condon, P. (2020) 'Small Minnesota bail nonprofit pulled into presidential politics, draws Trump criticism', *Star Tribune*, June 4. https://www.startribune.com/small-minnesota-bail-nonprofit-pulled-into-presidential-politics-draws-trump-criticism/570980942/

Critical Resistance (n.d.a) 'History', Critical Resistance. http://criticalresistance.org/about/history/

Critical Resistance (n.d.b) 'About', Critical Resistance. http://criticalresistance.org/about/

Davidson, B., Epps, E., Grace, S., and Rich-Shea, A. (2020) 'Community bail funds as a tool for prison abolition', Law and political economy project, February 13. https://lpeproject.org/blog/community-bail-funds-as-a-tool-for-prison-abolition/

Eisen, L.B. & Chettiar, I. (2018) 'Criminal justice: an election agenda for candidates, activists, and legislators', Brennan Center for Justice. https://www.brennancenter.org/sites/default/files/publications/Criminal_Justice_An_Election_Agenda_for_Candidates_Activists_and_Legislators%20.pdf

Emergency Release Fund (2020) 'About', Emergency Release Fund. https://emergencyreleasefund.com/about/

Feinberg, L. (1999) *Trans Liberation: Beyond Pink or Blue*, Boston, MA: Beacon Press.

Feller, M., Walsh, S., & Weaver, H. (2020) 'Activists demand justice and cash bail reform for Layleen Polanco a year after her death in solitary confinement', *Elle*, August 31. https://www.elle.com/culture/career-politics/a27921290/who-is-layleen-polanco-transgender-woman-died-solitary-confinement/

Gay Liberation Front (1970) 'Money needed for bail', Gay Flames, October 1. JSTOR. https://www.jstor.org/stable/10.2307/community.28037174

Gilker, K. (2019) 'Nonprofit pays bonds for inmates at Washington County detention center', September 18. https://www.5newsonline.com/article/news/local/outreach/back-to-school/non-profit-pays-bonds-for-inmates-at-washington-county-detention-center/527-d7954c72-1eb4-4cbb-a15f-aec4405d006c

Jimenez, M.C., Cowger, T.L., Simon, L.E., Behn, M. Cassarino, & N. Bassett, M.T. (2020) 'Epidemiology of COVID-19 among incarcerated individuals and staff in Massachusetts jails and prisons', *JAMA Network Open*, 3(8): e2018851. doi:10.1001/jamanetworkopen.2020.18851

Kushner, R. (2019) 'Is prison necessary? Ruth Wilson Gilmore might change your mind', *The New York Times*, April 17. https://www.nytimes.com/2019/04/17/magazine/prison-abolition-ruth-wilson-gilmore.html

Mogul, J.L., Ritchie, A.J., & Whitlock, K. (2011) *Queer (In)Justice: The Criminalization of LGBT People in the United States*, Boston, MA: Beacon Press.

National Center for Transgender Equality (2012) 'Prison and detention reform', Transequality.org. https://www.transequality.org/sites/default/files/docs/resources/NCTE_Blueprint_for_Equality2012_Prison_Reform.pdf

NYC DOI (New York Department of Investigations) (2020) Out of respect, we are not relinking to the referral letter, where Layleen Polanco's birth name still unfortunately appears. We apologize for our insensitivity [Tweet], June 5. https://twitter.com/NYC_DOI/status/1269070613165072384?s=20

Ritchie, A. (2017) *Invisible No More: Police Violence Against Black Women and Women of Color*, Boston, MA: Beacon Press.

Sawyer, W. (2019) 'How race impacts who is detained pretrial', Policy Prison Initiative, October 9. https://www.prisonpolicy.org/blog/2019/10/09/pretrial_race/

Sosin, K. (2020) 'New video reveals Layleen Polanco's death at Rikers was preventable, family says', *NBC News*, June 13. https://www.nbcnews.com/feature/nbc-out/new-video-reveals-layleen-polanco-s-death-rikers-was-preventable-n1230951

Spade, D. (2020) 'The queer and trans fight for liberation – and abolition', *Medium*, October 13. https://level.medium.com/amp/p/caec82374018

Steinberg, R., Kalish, L., & Ritchin, E. (2018) 'Freedom should be free: a brief history of bail funds in the United States', *UCLA Criminal Justice Law Review*, 2(1): 79–104.

Wang, J. (2018) *Carceral Capitalism*, Los Angeles, CA: Semiotexte Publishing.

15

A Conspiracy

Lucilla R. Harrell and S. Page Dukes

QAF

Women's prisons are epicenters of intersectionality. More than any other slice of society, these swelling institutions (Sawyer, 2018) contain multitudes of marginalized identities. Included is the trinity of 'concentrated disadvantage' (Richie, 2004) – race, gender, and class – but also people with disabilities, sex workers, immigrants, trans women and men, survivors punished. Every condemned combination and their literal mother is living there, one on top of another, 'such a profound concentration of the most vicious forms of economic marginalization, institutionalized racism, and victimization that it can almost seem intentional or mundane' (Richie, 2004, p. 438). Our invisibility, or rather the imagined soulless landscape in the back of every American psyche, lends credence to our dehumanity. We are called junkies, murderers, and violent offenders. 'Labels on anyone can be notoriously misleading and unforgiving things', said our friend Kelly Gissendaner (McBride, 2017, p. 32). In her wisdom and grace, she called us 'real human beings in the real world' (p. 31) –loving defiantly, as queer people once did, in closets.

In other words, women's prisons are queer as fuck.

As queer people have been throughout history, those of us imprisoned are forever and uniquely othered by the stigma of deviance. We are disenfranchised and discounted, an invisible substratum. In our pre-prison lives, some of us were criminalized by our queerness. As Stanley (2015) put it, 'trans/gender-non-conforming and queer people, along with many others, are born into webs of surveillance ... Inheriting a long history of being made suspect' (p. 13). Heteronormativity is both policed and perpetuated when people are placed, quite literally, into one box or another. (People in men's prisons, for instance, face a different kind of brutally toxic environment to which we cannot speak. Ashley Diamond won the rights of trans people in Georgia prisons in 2015, only for them to be violated without oversight in the years since; Ashley Diamond v. Timothy Ward, et al., n.d.) Once inside, however, where we are desocialized, stripped of our street clothes and freeworld gender roles, there is 'a natural evolution of gender fluidity' (N. Herren, personal communication, November 17, 2020). Everyone is queered. Even those who work there escape the constant discerning gaze of gender assignment. One friend, who began transitioning while teaching college classes in the prison, said he felt more comfortable there than anywhere else:

> I was struggling with my own dual thinking, raised with an either/ or mentality … with where I fit in the world as a person who didn't identify as female but also wasn't presenting as recognizably male, yet … For some reason, being in the prison felt like one of the only safe spaces for me … I could locate myself in the walls of the prison, on a spectrum of gender; in the outside world I had to fit into one box or the other. (N. Herren, personal communication, November 17, 2020)

Where everyone is assumed to have the same biological sex, we escape the police scanner learned in childhood – 'Are you a boy or a girl?' – which 'places many in the panopticon long before they enter a prison' (Stanley, 2015, p. 13). People are sometimes policed for performing gender – wearing too much make-up or altering the shapeless, state-issued clothing to fit or flatter their bodies. Ironically, Butler's (1990) discussion of gender performativity includes the analysis of a heavy history of 'cultural inscriptions' written on the bodies of those imprisoned (p. 130). Laws and labels approved by society are vacuously ascribed to our persons, our uniforms literally stamped 'state property'. Stripped of autonomy, we are supposedly no longer able to consent. All love is queer; all love is illegal. In this chapter, we will explore the hardships and victories that make our love resilient, profound, and – by state standards – criminal.

Inspired by the strength of Damien Echols

Luci: The love of my life is greatly inspired by the strength of Damien Echols. Well before the events that prescribed my or Page's individual journey to prison, we were separately appalled by the injustice incurred by the West Memphis Three, and Damien's story particularly. In our first conversation we talked about him and also about our friend Kelly (R.I.P.), who'd been sentenced to death, too. But I had never read any of his writing until 2015, when Page suggested we read *Yours for Eternity: A Love Story on Death Row* (Echols & Davis, 2015), which Damien and his wife Lorri Davis co-authored. My life prize and I read aloud together, a comforting practice. Doing so was reflexively inspiring and an apt testament to the nonlinear nature of time and our perceptions of it. Lorri and Damien were more powerful, more focused, than the fearsome biopolitical force that aspired to execute him. Their resilience, their transcendence, inspired ours. The two of us would go on to endure years of separation, too – Page working hard at the road to freedom but never really reaping its rewards because I remained unfree.

Page: I spent ten years in maximum security women's prisons, my twenties a penance that never repaired or atoned for a thing. Luci and I share similarly harsh and senseless sentences, juxtaposed with the privilege of being cis, white, educated, and supported. While many people in prison have support from family and friends, many others have none. We were both fortunate to have a lot. When we were together physically, I was taking college courses in sociology the one way I could, at a snail's pace, through archaic distance learning. My grandfather footed my tuition (R.I.P. Opa; as promised I am staying clean). I had yet to learn about intersectionality in a more cerebral sense. Much later I would read Crenshaw and Frye in a feminist philosophy class and learn about the wires of the cage into which I'd been released.

It may be true that all queer people navigate internalized homophobia (Meyer & Dean, 1998, as cited in Forbes & Ueno, 2020). Meyer (2012, as cited in Forbes & Ueno, 2020) goes on to note that 'those who possess other disadvantaged identities have to consider their queerness within the context of a matrix of domination (Collins, 2000) and combat the entire system of disadvantage and not just one spoke in the wheel' (p. 163). This is especially true for queer people in prison. Barreto (2006) talked about 'prisonization', or the way that people are molded by the institutional environment during incarceration and after release (p. 583). That ever-evolving process represents the way those of us who have experienced incarceration navigate internalized disenfranchisement. For us (and many others), the two identities – being criminalized and being queer – intersect naturally, though that intersection may not be naturally recognized in academia or in the criminal legal world.

Luci: Forbes and Ueno's (2020) research focused on queer allies. Perhaps, as a queer community, fortifying allegiances isn't done in the same way it was when I was a teenager in the 1990s.

Growing up gay in a Christian family in a small South Georgia town left me constantly grappling for allies. Each one I made I held onto tightly. I also clamped down on music and literature, hope for social support that filled the gap where my physical community was largely missing. Those pockets of support guided and nurtured me when I felt forcibly repressed. Though I have never *not* felt loved and supported by my relatives, their surgery in differentiating between the parts of me that were acceptable, hence lovable, and the part that was not (the gay part), created an inter and intra divide. Too much interaction between my true self and their response to her bore natural cracks from time to time; these transpired covertly, subconsciously, like little mini deaths, fossilizing into the multilayered rock that family makes, unearthed only when we dig. I couldn't, and sometimes still cannot, reconcile the idea that those who love me the most might not love the whole of me. As a person I am, after all, indivisible.

Like people who have been ostracized and ousted because of their sexuality or gender identity, solidarity is vital in our struggle against the prison industrial complex (PIC). In our experience of being criminalized, though, supporters do not always announce their allyship. And, as is true for many queer teens, supporters often struggle with accepting the person versus accepting the marginalized category to which she or he belongs. A good example of this would be spiritual supporters who support those imprisoned while simultaneously supporting what they believe to be a fair 'criminal justice system'. Due to personal conflicts or political ones, many allies choose to support quietly.

The love of my life in prison

'The theories I'm interested in are not divorced – they can't be – from political questions about how we live' (Greenwood & Fateman, 2015). Greenwood's reflections of her own, and others', contributions to queer-feminist cultural history exemplify how we identify as queer artists and people. They also speak profoundly to the choices we make about how we live, even as people imprisoned. Queer criminology, too, includes 'projects that chart the experiences of queer populations within criminal justice institutions' and, most often, lead to 'critiques of mainstream criminology, further theoretical reflection, and political projects that seek to address injustice and inequality' (Ball et al., 2014, p. 2). So that we're not overlooked, we engage in such projects, contributing to a framework that is naturally queer in its intention of broadening the narrative of what goes on in criminal systems. We do not suggest that our experiences or views are majority, conclusive, or normative. In fact, we believe *queering* criminology involves erasing those sorts of institutional restrictions.

Queering is a refusal to accept the world as it is. Damien and Lorri are a heterosexual couple, yes, but undeniably queer. As we read their book together we realized it was showing, not telling. The story of their joined-at-a-distance lives provided a critical example of a love built upon the pillar of creative expression, something required of any pair conflicted by incarceration. Lorri, especially when she moved from New York City to Arkansas to be closer to Damien (Echols & Davis, 2015), was closeted in her love. This stigma is felt by countless people whose love is bound by the state. When a criminal system interferes in the most intimate, private bonds of our lives, typical social constructs of identity (that is, being straight or gay) pale to the unnatural claim on our bodies. Our action of queering is rejecting this lie.

Page: I never expected to find the love of my life in prison. One year later, I'd leave her there.

We met in the chaplaincy of Georgia's largest women's prison. There we had guitars and a Motif production synthesizer we named the 'hip-hop machine'. Luci programmed drum tracks and played keys and guitar; I played bass. We both sang. It worked. In more ways than one. I fell head-first into the deepest kind of love I can fathom, contraband love, the kind that eats away bars (Shakur, 1987, p. 145). Living together incarcerated was the freest year of our lives.

That summer we sat outside in the sun, joyfully discussing political possibilities through a chain link fence. We'd been separated the first of three times. It was the day in late June 2015 that the United States Supreme Court decided marriage is a constitutional right. I jokingly asked if she'd marry me, but it felt like a sincere proposal. The M word (monogamy, monotony, mediocrity, mommyhood) was no less an alien and undesirable institution, now that the gates of this ultimate heteronorm had reluctantly cracked open to us gays. But in that dizzy moment I knew I would spend the rest of my life with her, if I was lucky.

A few weeks earlier, Luci had been ordered, along with several others, to pack up her property. They were being moved to another dorm. She packed her things, but 'bucked' the move. I watched helplessly as they put her in handcuffs and took her to solitary. She had done nothing wrong; she'd simply refused to accept this arbitrary upheaval. She was known as a 'model prisoner'. We both were. We knew better than to 'give them bullets to shoot us with', as our friend Melissa Burgeson (R.I.P.)

would say. That was, in fact, why Luci was among those chosen to move – they were least likely to resist orders. But she asserted our right to be together for the first time that day.

More of a risk

What does *Obergefell* really mean for people in prison? For us, it was more of a risk than a right.

We do not champion gay marriage. It is, and has always been, symbolic. For millennia, marriage symbolized and stabilized patriarchy, the literal bondage and trade of women subject to rape, violence, and servitude. Gay marriage, too, enforces norms that are inherently anti-queer, privileging certain hetero-mimicking, nuclear relationships, and denying important rights such as next-of-kinship to those who do not desire to enter into such a contract. Feminist philosopher Clare Chambers (2017), who argues for a marriage-free state, acknowledges that 'the right to marry is both intrinsically valuable and sometimes illegitimately denied' (p. 30).

Page: The equality same-sex marriage represents is symbolic in the way that the right to vote I recently reclaimed is symbolic. Every vote doesn't count in the purely democratic sense, and casting a ballot is not enough to change the systemic racism that pervades every aspect of our society. I was halfway free when half of free America chose to make America hate again. Unjust laws relegate certain swaths of the citizenry to lower rungs of representation, less deserving of life, liberty, and happy pursuit. This includes laws that disenfranchise and enslave people in prison, and those which continue to inhibit queer people from living their chosen lives with the same rights and freedoms as the straights. We will take our equality seriously, where we find it.

In 2015 in the United Kingdom, Mikhail Gallatinov and Marc Goodwin were legally married in prison (Pidd & Allison, 2015). To be clear, the two men were incarcerated at the same facility. After submitting their application for marriage, the men were split up and housed in different locations. The fear of retaliatory separation deterred us from trying to get married while we were both inside. We made the decision that, unless getting married would offer us some sort of security, a right to be together, we would wait until we were both free.

It's the same in the UK as it is here. There are two legal mechanisms that *should* allow people incarcerated together to marry: (1) the constitutional right to marry (*Turner v. Safley*, 1987) and (2) the common law right to marry someone of the same sex (*Obergefell v. Hodges*, 2015). Unfortunately,

Gallatinov and Goodwin's ability to marry, which came the year after gay marriage became legal in the UK, might not be as simple an option for queer people in American prisons.

Less than a month after the *Obergefell* decision, the Arizona Department of Corrections (DOC) changed its marriage policy to reflect the change in law but maintained the stance that 'prisoners cannot wed other prisoners' (Brodheim, 2015). Civil rights attorneys believe such a policy is challengeable. In practice, it's plausible that we won't see more gay marriages in prison until people are more willing to take on the risks involved in legalizing their love.

It's also plausible that the slim possibility of queer people in prison getting married could disappear completely if *Obergefell* were to be overturned. Recently, in what Blake (2020) called 'an unusually political speech' to the Federalist Society, US Supreme Court Justice Samuel Alito harped on his *Obergefell* dissent (para. 2). Blaming the high court's decision to acknowledge marriage as everyone's right, Alito decried the pressing fear that people who publicly express judgmental hatred toward homosexual folks might be labeled bigots as a result (Blake, 2020). If the 'vast majority of Americans' (Blake, 2020), to use Alito's lingo, are no longer free to rescind the civil rights of those they despise, what kind of society are we living in exactly? Religious liberty, to Alito – and to newly appointed Justice Amy Coney Barrett and others – seems much more about individuals curtailing the rights of others than exercising religious freedoms within the scope of their own lives. That puts not only *Obergefell* at risk, but *Roe v. Wade* as well, another protection that is largely theoretical in prison. In Justice Ruth Bader Ginsburg's final dissent, she wrote that the US Supreme Court 'has taken a balanced approach, one that does not allow the religious beliefs of some to overwhelm the rights and interests of others who do not share those beliefs' (*Little Sisters v. Pennsylvania*, 2020, p. 2400).

Kyger (2017) made the argument that getting married is a civil right that should apply to people incarcerated together but then noted, '[t]he United States relies on a theory of retributive correction and places *sufficient* emphasis on punishment' (p. 272, emphasis added). Richie (2004) basically instructed the PIC to strip butt-naked when she said that 'the contemporary shift away from rehabilitation to a more repressive politics of punishment in this country is evidenced by renewed support for the death penalty and racial profiling', our rhetoric, and the never-ending war on drugs (p. 439). So many of today's junked-up social dilemmas – for example, whether and how those who now have the right to marry are able to do so in practice – subsist on these direct intentions to destroy, which is exactly how each of them was purposefully crafted.

In 2013, Texas banned marriage by proxy (one or both of the individuals being married are not present) but, considering that the law was meant to protect all state citizens from fraud and not to expressly restrict the rights of those incarcerated, a revised prison policy lifted the ban in 2015 (Prison Legal News, 2016). Unfortunately for gay couples, the new policy also banned marriage between two people imprisoned, which seemed to be the easy way for any individual state to discriminate accordingly (Prison Legal News, 2016; McCotter, n.d.). Long before *Obergefell*, California prisons also had a policy that prohibited marriage by proxy. When the state legalized gay marriage in 2008, people saw the issue of whether those in prison could marry each other as more of a 'problem' that officials had to 'figure out' than a right – since gay couples often live together in prison, the proxy rule was no longer a good defense for marriage application denials (Mullane, 2008). After Hawaii legalized gay marriage in 2013, prison officials saw no legal reason to prohibit those incarcerated together from getting hitched. Just a year later, Terann Pavao and Totie Tauala were married inside the Women's Community Correctional Center in Kailua (Lincoln, 2014). Unlike in Texas, the Hawaiian couple was allowed to exchange and keep wedding rings (Lincoln, 2014; Prison Legal News, 2016). Local media touted Pavao and Tauala's union as the first in the state, but, in fact, it could very well be the first – and only – in the nation.

It's not just when both people are in prison that access to marriage for queer folks becomes an issue. After waiting more than six months for the prison to stop blocking their request, North Carolinians Sandy Dowell (incarcerated) and Amanda Marriner (not incarcerated) were married in 2019. According to a letter threatening suit by Dowell's attorney, the facility where she was housed had been blocking the marriage simply because the couple is same-sex (Billman, 2019). While Dowell and Marriner's story is inspiring, we wonder whether they had to get married in order to see each other. Where the prison might be criticized for denying visitation privileges based solely on the fact that a couple is gay, it can easily do so if the visitor is on probation.

Even with marriage a legal option, queer people who have also been criminalized face innumerable, arbitrary blockades in tying the knot. Following suit with the usual abhorrent journalistic convention, completely unrelated conviction information and dehumanizing language were included in reports of what were otherwise calls for celebration for both the Pavao/Tauala and Dowell/Marriner unions (Lincoln, 2014; Billman, 2019). In 2020, the first gay couple married in prison in Cyprus was separated by deportation, even though their union – just as it does in most countries – lawfully allows for permanent residency (Bitar, 2020; Michael, 2020). As queer people who have experienced incarceration together, we understand the hatred and jealousy that come into play to try to drive couples apart. One so-called gay marriage supporter said she believed that the men who got married in the UK should subsequently be separated 'so as not to give them a privilege heterosexual prisoners cannot enjoy' (Pidd & Allison, 2015). In what world, exactly, do LGBTQ people have more privileges than heterosexual folks?

Model status

Luci: In May 2016, Page was transferred to a state transitional center, physically a part of the prison complex where I remained but sequestered from the general population. For the year she was there, we saw each other in brief moments through the chain link fence. Seven months after Page's release, on my 36th birthday, the warden approved for us to see each other as a 'special visit'. Again, none of this would've been possible had we both not been 'model prisoners'. In no small way, that day I distinctly remember feeling empowered and overwhelmed by the fact that we were, for the first time ever, *allowed* to kiss and hug. It was a different kind of freedom, as if we were in a protected bubble, surrounded by a mix of curious supporters and enemies. I remember some officers being happy to see her back, a few even happy for us to be visiting with each other, while others stared as if our love offended them. Certainly, our lawful right to visit must have. It kept them from being able to separate us for those measly six hours, but not from shooting daggers with their eyes.

Page: Our status as 'model prisoners' was what Owen et al. (2017) referred to as 'capital' (p. 1). The staff for whom we worked for free trusted and respected us, as much as they allowed themselves. We both worked in the school teaching English. I taught adult GED classes; Luci taught high-school English to the children at night in the same classroom. My boss, Mrs. Greene, was a white, white-haired intellectual type. She was generally pleasant and polite, until one day she found a page left in the printer tray by accident. It was a piece Luci had penned about gender fluidity, an open love letter to my androgyny.

          'Is this about you?' she asked. Luci had not named me, but described me, in the piece, and it was most obvious. She held the page away from me, over my head, like her moral superiority. I tried to explain, even though it was none of her business. It was 'her' printer in 'her' room, and we were writing subversive content about illicit queerness. It was not a secret that Luci and I were together – however, it was overlooked, ignored, and, in that sense, accepted. How dare we write openly about it? How dare we be 'Out'? Mrs. Greene had to decide whether or not to report us.

We were the specific 'type' she liked – white, well behaved, educated, non-threatening. She relied on me, to give lectures and grade tests, work one on one with students, explain the rhetorical devices. But I could always be replaced, and she held our life together in her hands. She could have had us locked down so easily. I watched as she weighed her power over our lives.

Ultimately, Ms. Greene leaked the page to the education director, who thankfully didn't share her homophobic sentiments. She hadn't known until that day we were an item, but she didn't care. She waved it off. It was the first of many moments of grace, where the capital of being relied upon and well liked meant our bubble was left intact. Later, after I had gone, Luci talked openly with the director about me, after the threat of separation had passed, fulfilled.

I was giving a lecture in that same classroom on the day I was transferred, Out of the blue, an abrupt chasm torn in our life together that has gaped open ever since. My name was called over the school officer's radio. I walked outside and looked up, shielding my eyes against the sun, to where Luci was working on the roof at her daytime detail, building maintenance – literally keeping the place running. I shouted up to her, still in denial. We had known this day was coming. We just didn't expect it so soon.

This same capital later allowed us to assert our right to go to school – to push the limits of what sort of a life one could live behind bars. With the confidence of women once entitled to every opportunity, we refused to settle for what we supposedly deserved. We believed in and asserted our right to define our own lives. We dealt with the hateful pushback as it came, but we never gave them what they wanted – violence, outward displays of rage, insubordination, anything they could use to discredit our 'model' status. This is why I was finally approved on her visitation list – with a letter from my probation officer, a shining review from the man I had to ask for permission to see my person.

Love overrides

For the past four years we've straddled the razor wire (ouch). We've navigated letter-writing, phone-calling, reentry, visitation, parole, college, research, activism. No matter the restrictions or mechanisms required for survival, being in love overrides being incarcerated. This was our ethos, even amid internal struggles over the bliss of being together and the risk of getting caught.

Beyond our romantic relationships and the sociopolitical realities of being abolitionists trapped inside the criminal system, perhaps there is a cultural queerness to the intersection of love and incarceration that makes people more and more interested in it. Mass incarceration's effects become more widespread over time. Despite the empty promises of reform, the US prison industry disappeared an additional million people over the past two decades (Beck & Harrison, 2001; Sawyer & Wagner, 2020). Sentence lengths dramatically increased for those of us convicted of 'violent crimes', who now comprise more than half of our state prison populations – even though we're the least likely, by a long shot, to ever be recriminalized (Sawyer & Wagner, 2020). Americans now go to jail at a rate of 10.6 million times per year (Sawyer & Wagner, 2020). Statistically speaking, for everyone in our society, it's become much easier to find yourself in prison and much harder to get Out.

Luci: I remember reading Meili Cady's *Smoke* at the prison and thinking, *this* is what people think happens? Serving time with friends who had 30-year sentences for drug trafficking made Cady's 30-day prison experience seem like a joke. Not to downplay anyone's carceral experience, I think the glamour of federal prison in popular culture is simply incongruent to what people tucked away in state facilities suffer, especially in terms of racism, overpopulation, ill-equipped staff, negligent and deadly medical 'care', and the trauma of obscure and tyrannical parole practices.

   I felt similarly skeptical about *Orange Is the New Black* (Kerman, 2011), which I'd read when I first got to prison. My friends at home had already been glued to the show, which, ironically, allowed for more exploration of real-life situations. When I was finally transferred to the transitional center and reconnected to technology, it was surreal for us to watch a lot of the show's scenarios play out because we had lived them: retaliation, shakedowns, middle-of-the-night transfers, going to lockdown, mayhem over a missing tool, living with bad bunkies. Other details – like those imprisoned driving or answering phones – were obviously fictional.

Watching the last season together, a way to be together that has caught on with the rest of the world in the COVID-19 era, we suddenly realized the narrative had become the life we were living. Piper was Out and Alex wasn't. Reentry was difficult. The separation was exhausting. While the world streamed *Orange* for entertainment value, it was nonfiction for us.

COVID-19 behind bars

COVID-19 has brought many overlooked intersectional issues to the surface, including the disproportionate toll of those who have died from COVID-19 behind bars. This pandemic has provided dark days in which our most exacting domestic war machine, the PIC, has further isolated those in prison while aiding and abetting their illness and death. As Kauffman and Stinebrickner-Kauffman (2020) explained, the COVID-related deaths of people incarcerated has not been incidental but rather 'the result of deliberate and informed choices to allow a despised subgroup to sicken and die when other choices could have been made to save them' (Kauffman & Stinebrickner-Kauffman, 2020, Our leaders' failure section, para. 5).

Luci: This horrific disregard for human life is an issue we understand quite well. For one, living in a state transitional center where social distancing is impossible and mask-wearing unenforceable has been a daily struggle. Social consideration for each other's well-being hasn't exactly been a shared concept among those around me. Toward the beginning of the pandemic I attributed my fellow residents' unconcern to a lack of basic knowledge – like that provided publicly by the Centers for Disease Control and Prevention – and even to a conditioned mode of complacency. We all experience this. Of institutionalization, Haney (2001) rightly noted that the psychological mechanisms a person in prison must employ in order to adjust and survive become internalized over time. We agree. However, we challenge his statement that 'persons gradually become more accustomed to the restrictions that institutional life imposes' (p. 80). You just don't ever get used to some things.

    When a system never places any priority on health, that compounded negligence rains down over time. The unhealthy food, manual labor, untreated injuries, exposure to pathogens and toxins, cost and hassle of attempting to see a doctor, and the burden and degradation of having to 'prove' that something is wrong with your body or mind lead to insanely disproportionate rates of stress, depression, diabetes, heart disease, cancer, mental illness, addiction, and suicide. It's no wonder that each year in prison takes two years off a person's life expectancy (Widra, 2017). Like the federal poverty line, prison sentences can't be measured at face value.

    In addition to being queered and criminalized, the pandemic brought a new brand of ostracization and marginalization. The anxiety of not being able to visit with Page or the rest of my family was compounded by the DOC's hypocrisy. Large groups of people were continually transferred in and sent Out into the community to work minimum wage jobs, putting all of us at risk while the DOC collected weekly room and board. For a brief period of time in March, this reckless exploitation was halted when people at the center first began getting sick. This solidified the state's disregard for the health of those of us who live and work inside, which was suddenly juxtaposed against a narrative of public perception that we might, in turn, infect outsiders.

In August 2020 I began as a juris doctor student at Atlanta's John Marshall Law School. Early on I (virtually) attended a special lecture headed by Professor Jonathan Rapping. Rapping founded the transformative public defense movement Gideon's Promise. Ever the champion of constitutional rights, he keenly noted that the pandemic has brought the horrors of our criminal-legal system to an undeniable forefront of public awareness (Rapping, 2020), which rekindled that abolitionist hope in me. The backdrop to this optimism was a summer filled with deadly police violence and civil unrest. Page's work at the Southern Center for Human Rights was heavier than usual. Two of their clients, both of whom we'd been in prison with, Shauntrice 'Tricie' Murry and Miss Mozel Anderson, passed away as the parole board ignored numerous pleas for their release. Earlier that year we'd helped launch Mourning Our Losses, and all through the summer we'd tracked the rising national death toll of COVID-19 deaths in jails, prisons, and detention centers.

Haney (2001) warned that the challenges of prison and reentry in the US had intensified with each passing year, and that we had moved from a society that once 'justified putting people in prison' to one that uses prison to inflict pain, disable people, or 'to keep them far away from the rest of society' (p. 78). In other words, those who are criminalized are excised from mainstream society, much as queer people have been, for decades.

For us, rejecting the way criminal systems treat people is embedded – it's a *lifestyle*, we might say, of struggling against oppression. A process. An unending action. As nontraditional students of Angela Davis and Ruth Wilson Gilmore, who have taught abolition and solidarity through decades of personal action, we understand this struggle as an intersectional endeavor at its core. Yet now, more than ever, our societal grief demands a new, more intimated form of intersectionality. Solidarity has become our mental health. Our grief over the loss of our own time and togetherness has been umbrellaed by the collective grief of our families and communities. We help ourselves by helping each other, even when we feel like there's nothing we can do.

Conclusion: contraband love

Our love is contraband because it subverts the disorienting degradation of the PIC, insists upon our right to exist Outside of it. We zero in on the one thing that keeps us intact, reinforces the will to survive and thrive, to find freedom in the least likely of places. In our bubble, eyes focused on one another, we're shielded from the oppressive environment around us. We made a commitment to each other but also to our people. We will not let this break us down, no matter how long we have to endure. We are lifers, in this together. Not one of us is free until everyone is free (Hamer, 2011, p. xxi).

Abolition is the solidarity of two that multiplies, a creative contagion. It refuses to be bound, despite the confines, despite the boundaries of hard time. This is what freedom looks like, even while we cannot yet see its fruition. We constructed a life for ourselves, out of pure love and determination, one we will not relinquish. We will win, odds stacked against us. When our friends inside call us a power couple, they mean we empower them. We reach back through the bars to pull each other Out of despair and defy their disappearance. We see them, we know them, we are them. Continuing the work of abolition together, each step forward on either side of the fence, is powerful in a way the PIC is not. It is an opposite, equally powerful, biopolitical force. It is relationship-building, solidarity work in the face of chaos and enmity. It is connection and community made illegal by policies against maintaining relationships with those we leave inside. A bird has two wings (Wilson, 2019), a hacksaw two blades (Shakur, 1987). This is biopower on our own humanizing terms. The terminology is important. Do not call us inmates, offenders, or convicts. We are friends, lovers, comrades. We are siblings in arms. And we cannot be owned by the state if we give ourselves fully to one another.

References

Ashley Diamond v. Timothy Ward, et al. (n.d.) Southern Poverty Law Center. https://www.splcenter.org/seeking-justice/case-docket/ashley-diamond-v-timothy-ward-et-al

Ball, M., Buist, C.L., & Woods, J.B. (2014) 'Introduction to the special issue on queer/ing criminology: new directions and frameworks', *Critical Criminology*, 22: 1–4. https://link.springer.com/article/10.1007/s10612-013-9231-2

Barreto, M.L.S. (2006) 'Depois das grades: um Reflexo da cultura prisional em indivíduos libertos', *Psicologia: Ciencia e Profissao*, 26(4): 582–593. DOI: 10.34117/bjdv7n9-053

Beck, A.J. & Harrison, P.M. (2001) 'Prisoners in 2000', *Bureau of Justice Statistics*. https://bjs.ojp.gov/content/pub/pdf/p00.pdf

Billman, J.C. (2019) 'Same-sex couple allowed to marry in N.C. prison after all', *Indy Week*, May 22. https://indyweek.com/news/northcarolina/same-sex-couple-allowed-to-marry-in-n-c-prison-after-all/

Bitar, M. (2020) 'First gay couple married in prison to be separated by way of deportation', *In-Cyprus*, August 7. https://in-cyprus.philenews.com/first-gay-couple-in-prison-to-be-separated-by-way-of-deportation/

Blake, A. (2020) 'Samuel Alito's provocative, unusual political speech', *The Washington Post*, November 13. https://www.washingtonpost.com/politics/2020/11/13/samuel-alitos-provocative-unusually-political-speech/

Brodheim, M. (2015) 'Arizona Department of Corrections adopts same-sex marriage policy', *Prison Legal News*, July 7. https://www.prisonlegalnews.org/news/2015/jul/7/arizona-department-corrections-adopts-same-sex-marriage-policy/

Butler, J. (1990) *Gender Trouble: Feminism and the Subversion of Identity*, Abingdon: Routledge, Chapman & Hall.

Chambers, C. (2017) *Against Marriage: An Egalitarian Defence of the Marriage-Free State*, Oxford: Oxford University Press.

Collins, P.H. (2000) *Black Feminist Thought: Knowledge, Consciousness, and the Politics of Empowerment* (2nd ed.), New York: Routledge.

Echols, D. & Davis, L. (2015) *Yours for Eternity: A Love Story on Death Row*, New York: Penguin.

Forbes, T.D. & Ueno, K. (2020) 'Post-gay, political, and pieced together: queer expectations of straight allies', *Interpersonal Relationships and Social Networks Formation*, 63(1): 159–176. https://doi.org/10.1177/0731121419885353

Greenwood, W. & Fateman, J. (2015) 'Exploding plastics inevitable', *Artforum*, November 23. https://www.artforum.com/slant/wynne-greenwood-speaks-with-johanna-fateman-about-tracy-the-plastics-56168

Hamer, F.L. (2011) *The Speeches of Fannie Lou Hamer: To Tell It Like It Is*, edited by D.W. Houck & M.P. Brooks, Jackson: University Press of Mississippi.

Haney, C. (2001) 'The psychological impact of incarceration: implications for post-prison adjustment', Office of the Assistant Secretary for Planning and Evaluation, US Department of Health & Human Services. http://webarchive.urban.org/UploadedPDF/410624_PyschologicalImpact.pdf

Kauffman, K. & Stinebrickner-Kauffman, T. (2020) 'When mass incarceration becomes mass murder', *Medium*, April 6. https://medium.com/@TarenSK/when-mass-incarceration-becomes-mass-murder-e089e852d61e

Kerman, P. (2011) *Orange Is the New Black: My Year in a Women's Prison*, New York: Random House.

Kyger, M.H. (2017) 'Inmates, incarcerated and in love: predicting how the United States would respond to marriages between inmates by evaluating case law and the United Kingdom's decision', *University of Baltimore Journal of International Law*, 5(2): 269–296. https://scholarworks.law.ubalt.edu/cgi/viewcontent.cgi?article=1060&context=ubjil

Lincoln, M. (2014) 'Hawaii's first same-sex marriage in prison', *Hawaii News Now*, December 20. https://www.hawaiinewsnow.com/story/27675516/hawaiis-first-same-sex-marriage-in-prison/

Little Sisters of the Poor Saints Peter & Paul Home v. Pennsylvania, 140 S. Ct. 2367. Supreme Court of the United States (2020).

McBride, J.M. (2017) *Radical Discipleship: A Liturgical Politics of the Gospel*, Philadelphia: Fortress Press.

McCotter, T. (n.d.) 'Inmate marriage: the 'I dos' and don'ts of sound policy', National Institute for Jail Operations. https://jailtraining.org/inmate-marriage-the-i-dos-and-donts-of-sound-policy/

Meyer, D. (2012) 'An intersectional analysis of lesbian, gay, bisexual, and transgender (LGBT) people's evaluations of anti-queer violence', *Gender & Society*, 26(6): 849–873. https://doi.org/10.1177/0891243212461299

Meyer, I.H. & Dean, L. (1998) 'Internalized homophobia, intimacy, and sexual behavior among gay and bisexual men', in G.M. Herek (ed.), *Stigma and Sexual Orientation: Understanding Prejudice Against Lesbians, Gay Men, and Bisexuals*, Thousand Oaks, CA: Sage Publications, pp. 160–186. https://doi.org/10.4135/9781452243818.n8

Michael, P. (2020) 'Brazilian man deported after jail release despite civil partnership', *Cyprus Mail*, September 7. https://cyprus-mail.com/2020/09/07/brazilian-man-deported-after-jail-release-despite-civil-partnership/?utm_source=ground.news&utm_medium=referral

Mullane, N. (2008) 'Does same-sex marriage law apply to prisoners?', NPR, July 28. https://www.npr.org/templates/story/story.php?storyId=92993519

Obergefell v. Hodges, 576 U.S. 644. Supreme Court of the United States (2015).

Owen, B., Wells, J., & Pollock, J. (2017) *In Search of Safety: Confronting Inequality in Women's Imprisonment*, Berkeley: University of California Press.

Pidd, H. & Allison, E. (2015) 'Gay couple serving life sentences to marry in prison', *The Guardian*, February 20. https://www.theguardian.com/society/2015/feb/20/gay-couple-serving-life-sentences-marry-prison-marriage-full-sutton

Rapping, J.A. (2020) 'The role of a lawyer in promoting social justice', Webinar, August 19, Atlanta's John Marshall Law School.

Richie, B.E. (2004) 'Feminist ethnographies of women in prison', *Feminist Studies*, 30(2): 438–450. doi: 10.2307/20458973

Sawyer, W. (2018) 'The gender divide: Tracking women's state prison growth', Prison Policy Initiative, January 9. https://www.prisonpolicy.org/reports/women_overtime.html

Sawyer, W. & Wagner, P. (2020) 'Mass incarceration: the whole pie 2020', Prison Policy Initiative, March 24. https://www.prisonpolicy.org/reports/pie2020.html

Shakur, A. (1987) *Assata: An Autobiography*, London: Zed Books.

Stanley, E.A. (2015) 'Fugitive flesh: gender self-determination, queer abolition, and trans resistance', in E.A. Stanley & Nat Smith (eds.), *Captive Genders: Trans Embodiment and the Prison Industrial Complex* (2nd ed.), Chico, CA: AK Press, pp. 7–17.

Prison Legal News (2016) 'Texas prisons to allow in-person wedding ceremonies after prohibition on proxy marriages', February 2. https://www.prisonlegalnews.org/news/2016/feb/2/texas-prisons-allow-person-wedding-ceremonies-after-prohibition-proxy-marriages/

Turner v. Safley, 482 U.S. 78. Supreme Court of the United States (1987).

Widra, E. (2017) 'Incarceration shortens life expectancy', Prison Policy Initiative, June 26._https://www.prisonpolicy.org/blog/2017/06/26/life_expectancy/

Wilson, S. (2019) 'Prison organizing: a personal genealogy', Making and Unmaking Mass Incarceration Conference [Symposium], December 5, University of Mississippi, Oxford, MS. https://www.facebook.com/MUMIConference/videos/1503228036501654

LGBTQ+ Homelessness: Resource Obtainment and Issues with Shelters

Trye Mica Price and Tusty ten Bensel

Homelessness is a prevalent issue in the United States.[1] In 2018, Morten et al. reported that there were approximately 3.48 million individuals between the ages of 13 and 25 years old who were homeless nationwide (Morten et al., 2018). Homelessness is especially problematic among those who identify as lesbian, gay, bisexual, transgender, and queer/questioning (LGBTQ+). In fact, previous research has found that 8–37 percent of LGBTQ+ youths and 5–30 percent of LGBTQ+ adults are homeless in the US (Ecker, 2016; Ecker et al., 2019). In general, LGBTQ+ individuals are four to 13 times more likely to be homeless than their heterosexual counterparts (Corliss et al., 2011).

There are a number of reasons why LGBTQ+ individuals become homeless, which can include parental rejection of their sexual orientation or gender identity (Cochran et al., 2002; Whitbeck et al., 2004; Rew et al., 2005; Corliss et al., 2011; Choi et al., 2015; Forge et al., 2018; Rhoades et al., 2018; Côté & Blais, 2019), negative relationships with family members (Cochran et al., 2002; Ryan et al., 2009; Choi et al., 2015; Ecker, 2016; Schmitz & Tyler, 2018), and various types of abuse at home (Cochran et al., 2002; Ryan et al., 2009; Rosario et al., 2012b; Rhoades et al., 2018; Ecker et al., 2019). LGBTQ+ individuals who disclose their sexual orientation and/or gender identity may face backlash from their family, peers, and society (Cochran et al., 2002; Whitbeck et al., 2004; Rosario et al., 2012a, 2012b; Rhoades et al., 2018). For example, familial rejection can stem from the parent's inability to understand or accept their child's sexual orientation/ gender identity (Whitbeck et al., 2004; Mottet & Ohle, 2006). At times, family members not only reject their child's sexual orientation/gender identity but also lash out through verbal and physical victimization (Cochran et al., 2002; Whitbeck et al., 2004; Rosario et al., 2012a, 2012b; Irvine & Canfield, 2016; Forge et al., 2018; Rhoades et al., 2018), which forces many LGBTQ to voluntarily leave their home to avoid conflict and abuse (Cochran et al., 2002; Whitbeck et al., 2004; Rosario et al., 2012a, 2012b; Rhoades et al., 2018). Individuals who identify as transgender have reported higher frequencies of homelessness compared with other sexual minorities because family members often have a harder time accepting a change in gender orientation than same-sex relationships (Mottet & Ohle, 2006; Choi et al., 2015; Rhoades et al., 2018).

When LGTBQ+ individuals are rejected by members of their family, they often experience negative health consequences such as depression, suicidal ideation, and post-traumatic stress disorder (PTSD) (Ryan et al., 2009; Rhoades et al., 2018), which often go untreated. Many LGBTQ+ individuals have also reported experiencing discrimination, stigmatization, and physical/sexual victimization while homeless (Cochran et al., 2002; Whitbeck et al., 2004; Milburn et al., 2006; Sakamoto et al., 2009; Rosario et al., 2012b; Coolhart & Brown, 2017; Ecker et al., 2019). Homeless LGBTQ+ individuals between the ages of 13 and 21 are more likely to experience physical violence compared with their heterosexual counterparts (Cochran et al., 2002). Sexual victimization is also more prevalent for homeless LGBTQ+ individuals compared with heterosexual individuals (Cochran et al., 2002). Sexual victimization is especially prevalent among LGBTQ+ individuals who must resort to survival sex (Whitbeck et al., 2004; Boyer et al., 2017). To survive while homeless, they often have to resort to panhandling, dumpster diving, or prostitution, which also increases the likelihood of discrimination and victimization (Whitbeck et al., 2004; Boyer et al., 2017). These issues are only exacerbated the longer individuals live on the street.

In addition, some will engage in substance abuse and risky sexual behaviors to survive on the streets (Whitbeck et al., 2004; Clatts et al., 2005; Van Leeuwen et al., 2006; Reback et al., 2007; Rosario et al., 2012a, 2012b; Rhoades et al., 2018). Survival sex, for example, increases health risks and the likelihood of contracting a sexually transmitted disease due to the frequency of partners (Greene et al., 1999; Whitbeck et al., 2004; Wilson et al., 2009; Boyer et al., 2017).[2] In addition, survival sex can lead to victimization among homeless LGBTQ+ individuals because they interact with multiple sexual partners who may take advantage of them both physically or sexually during their sexual encounters. Homeless LGBTQ+ individuals may put themselves in compromising positions where they are unable to escape from their attacker to seek help. After being victimized, individuals may not report their victimization out of fear of secondary victimization or persecution for conducting sex work.

To escape homelessness, LGBTQ+ individuals need resources from agencies (that is, drop-in resource centers) and shelters that ensure safety and provide appropriate accommodations for the LGBTQ+ population. These services include, but are not limited to, private showers, gender-neutral restrooms, separate rooms, medical referrals, and group-specific counseling (Mottet & Ohle, 2006; Hunter, 2008; Prock & Kennedy, 2017; Shelton et al., 2018). Unfortunately, not all resource centers provide adequate resources for LGBTQ+ individuals and some have little to no specific provisions for homeless LGBTQ+ people (Mottet & Ohle, 2006; Abramovich, 2016, 2017; Prock & Kennedy, 2017). In this chapter, we will discuss previous research on homeless LGBTQ+ resource obtainment and availability within shelters, focusing specifically on pathways into homelessness, resource availability, and issues with and while obtaining resources. We will conclude with a discussion on policy and practical implications and provide recommendations for future research.

Resources and experiences with shelters

Research has found that to exit homelessness LGBTQ+ individuals need resources such as focus groups, gender-neutral facilities, counseling, separate living quarters, referral to medical care, and support to successfully exit homelessness (Mottet & Ohle, 2006; Prock & Kennedy, 2017). Since LGBTQ+ individuals are likely to become homeless due to familial rejection (Cochran et al., 2002; Whitbeck et al., 2004; Rew et al., 2005; Corliss et al., 2011; Choi et al., 2015; Forge et al., 2018; Rhoades et al., 2018; Côté & Blais, 2019), individuals enter homelessness with little to no social support or resources (Schmitz & Tyler, 2018). Additionally, the prevalence of street-level victimization makes homeless LGBTQ+ individuals likely to succumb to issues with mental and physical health (Cochran et al., 2002; Whitbeck et al., 2004; Milburn et al., 2006; Sakamoto et al., 2009; Rosario et al., 2012b; Coolhart & Brown, 2017; Ecker et al., 2019). Although there has been limited research on resource availability and necessity, Prock and Kennedy (2017) examined the types of services provided at transitional-living programs funded by the Family and Youth Services Bureau. This study found that the most common LGBTQ-specific services offered included support groups, affirming therapy, gender-neutral facilities (for example, bedrooms, bathrooms), referral to medical treatments (for example, hormone replacement therapy), and advocacy from the community. Of the 124 transitional-living programs that participated in this study, less than half of the agencies offered LGBTQ-specific services and resources. Additionally, only ten of these agencies noted being LGBTQ-specific. Agencies that did offer LGBTQ-specific resources were generally found to be located either on the West Coast or in the Northeast of the US.

Previous research has shown that shelters can be negative environments for homeless LGBTQ+ people (Mottet & Ohle, 2006; Sakamoto et al., 2009; Abramovich, 2017; Coolhart & Brown, 2017; Côté & Blais, 2019), due to homophobia and transphobia among other residents and employees (Abramovich, 2017; Coolhart & Brown, 2017). Coolhart and Brown (2017) conducted interviews with service providers and LGBTQ+ youth and found that shelters may not be LGBTQ+ inclusive with available services and gender placements. Present issues with homophobia and transphobia can cause gender segregation and isolation of LGBTQ+ individuals (Sakamoto et al., 2009; Coolhart & Brown, 2017) and may even cause LGBTQ+ individuals to endure victimization in order to utilize the services provided (Côté & Blais, 2019). Additional research has noted that homeless LGBTQ+ individuals may choose not to take advantage of resources because they fear victimization from other residents or employees (Abramovich, 2016; Côté & Blais, 2019).

Staff and employees at shelters can perpetuate an unsafe environment for homeless LGBTQ+ people seeking resources (Mottet & Ohle, 2006; Sakamoto et al., 2009; Irvine & Canfield, 2016; Abramovich, 2017; Coolhart & Brown, 2017; Forge et al., 2018; Côté & Blais, 2019). Shelter employees can create an unsafe environment for this population because they may either promote or fail to intervene in acts of homophobia and transphobia (Abramovich, 2017; Coolhart & Brown, 2017; Côté & Blais, 2019). When a staff member mistreats an LGBTQ+ individual, it generally stems from personal beliefs or lack of understanding about a person's sexual orientation/gender identity and/or religious beliefs (Coolhart & Brown, 2017). Research has also noted that other homeless individuals utilizing resources victimize homeless LGBTQ+ individuals verbally, physically, and sexually (Abramovich, 2017; Coolhart & Brown, 2017; Côté & Blais, 2019).

Types of victimizations from shelter employees and other residents include discrimination, emotional abuse, and verbal and physical victimization (Abramovich, 2017; Coolhart & Brown, 2017; Côté & Blais, 2019). Based on these issues, many LGBTQ+ individuals are likely to hide their identity or choose to stay on the streets (Abramovich, 2017; Côté & Blais, 2019). In addition, shelters often segregate people based on their biological gender rather than their gender identity (Mottet & Ohle, 2006; Sakamoto et al., 2009; Abramovich, 2016; Coolhart & Brown, 2017). Gender classification based on biology over identity can cause issues with psychological distress and anxiety (Mottet & Ohle, 2006; Coolhart & Brown, 2017). For instance, individuals segregated based on sex rather than gender identity may experience emotional injury because they are not able to stay where they feel most comfortable (Mottet & Ohle, 2006). Homeless transgender individuals who are placed based on biology are vulnerable to discrimination and victimization from staff and other residents who stay at shelters (Mottet & Ohle, 2006; Sakamoto et al., 2009; Coolhart & Brown, 2017; Côté & Blais, 2019). These issues stem from individuals' perceptions of a person's sexual orientation and/or gender identity (Mottet & Ohle, 2006; Sakamoto et al., 2009; Coolhart & Brown, 2017; Côté & Blais, 2019). Service providers can marginalize transgender people because of institutional prejudice or inability to accommodate this population (Mottet & Ohle, 2006; Coolhart & Brown, 2017; Sakamoto et al., 2009).

Institutional erasure is apparent when agencies and shelters enact rules and regulations on gender conformity (Namaste, 2000; Abramovich, 2016, 2017; Shelton et al., 2018). It involves formerly set institutions' failure to acknowledge the lives of transgender people by excluding individuals from services and denying their experiences as homeless LGBTQ+ persons (Namaste, 2000). Due to institutional erasure, homeless transgender individuals may be turned away due to institutional rules, difficulties with accommodations, or prejudice (Mottet & Ohle, 2006; Sakamoto et al., 2009; Ecker et al., 2019). Abramovich (2016) discussed a cycle where staff at agencies and shelters were unable to intervene on issues of homophobia and transphobia due to lack of knowledge. The cycle starts with homeless shelters having no formal training with handling LGBTQ+ populations. Since staff have no formal training, the employees at the shelter either do not intervene or are unprepared to intervene when instances of homophobia/transphobia happen, thus increasing the likelihood of homophobic/transphobic acts. The staff's inability to intervene in homophobic/transphobic acts relates to LGBTQ+ individuals having unmet needs. LGBTQ+ individuals then choose to avoid the shelter to reduce the chances of being victimized. The cycle continues with shelter employees not having any knowledge on the LGBTQ+ population and having no formal training. Homeless LGBTQ+ individuals may choose not to take advantage of services because staff are unable to intervene in homophobia and transphobia (Abramovich, 2016). Due to lack of proper training that may result in victimization and refusal of services, LGBTQ+ individuals are vulnerable to street-level violent victimization (Sakamoto et al., 2009; Spicer, 2010; Abramovich, 2016; Côté & Blais, 2019; Ecker et al., 2019).

Research has found that shelters often do not provide proper training for workers to address the needs of LGBTQ+ homeless individuals (Abramovich, 2016, 2017). Inadequate knowledge of how to assist this population can relate to staff mistreatment and a lack of intervention in instances of homophobia or transphobia within the shelter (Abramovich, 2016). Due to these issues, LGBTQ+ individuals may hide their sexual orientation and/or gender identity status to reduce the likelihood of victimization (Coolhart & Brown, 2017). Additionally, individuals may not pursue resources because they are fearful of victimization (Abramovich, 2016; Côté & Blais, 2019). Therefore, homeless LGBTQ+ people are vulnerable to victimization within the street setting (Abramovich, 2016; Côté & Blais, 2019). As indicated earlier, the homeless LGBTQ+ population faces a number of different challenges due to their gender identity and sexual orientation. These challenges are further exacerbated while living on the streets and there are limited resources available for homeless individuals who have specific needs such as the LGBTQ+. In the following section, we provide some discussion on various ways to improve services and assist this population, especially in regard to exiting homelessness.

Practical implications

Although our knowledge is limited on exiting homelessness, an exploratory study conducted by Ecker and associates (2019) found that there are a variety of risk factors for exiting homelessness. These factors include substance abuse and mental disorders, short durations of homeless episodes, social support, and the ability to gain assistance with income, employment, and resources (Ecker et al., 2019). Many need resources such as therapy referrals, counseling, medication, and educational information on how to get assistance, which is often unavailable to them (Mottet & Ohle, 2006; Prock & Kennedy, 2017). Housing and employment can be difficult to obtain without the proper paperwork such as a social security card, birth certificate, or a permanent address (Mottet & Ohle, 2006; Prock & Kennedy, 2017). Those who are homeless, especially individuals who were kicked out of their homes by their family members, may not have ready access to these documents. To obtain new documents, they would have to pay an agency to provide them copies, which may be difficult to do given that they may not have the funds to purchase the necessary copies.

Programs such as transitional living, however, can assist in securing these services, as well as teaching LGBTQ+ individuals how to live independently through career training, educational attainment, and securing employment. They can also help with therapy referral, accessing the necessary medications, and obtaining safe places for them to live. These programs, however, are limited in resources and availability. Furthermore, programs that aid homeless individuals may have little to no specific resources for LGBTQ+ individuals (Prock & Kennedy, 2017). These programs also had a weak media presence regarding their LGBTQ+ services and policies on their websites and Facebook pages (Prock & Kennedy, 2017). These limitations make it difficult for homeless LGBTQ+ individuals to locate and access these programs. There should be a wider set of locations across the US that offer LGBTQ-specific resources. When creating these places, websites and social media pages must ensure that their services are advertised properly so that individuals are able to find and understand what is available at each location. The creation of these service providers can assist in intervening on more cases of LGBTQ+ homelessness and encourage individuals to make use of more services without the fear of homophobic and transphobic victimization.

Although agencies and shelters can be a great resource for LGBTQ+ homeless individuals, research has found that this population is often discriminated against by those who work at these types of locations, which hinders their access to resources (Sakamoto et al., 2009; Coolhart & Brown, 2017; Prock & Kennedy, 2017; Côté & Blais, 2019). Homeless LGBTQ+ individuals are often hesitant to trust and obtain resources from agencies and shelters where they feel discriminated against or harassed by the staff or residents. Educational pursuits should be placed in the curriculum of employment training for agencies and shelters that work with the LGBTQ+ homeless population. These training initiatives can educate staff and prepare them to work with homeless LGBTQ+ individuals that may seek out resources. Other service providers, such as law enforcement officers, public school employees/teachers, and medical staff, should also receive similar training to identify and intervene to assist homeless LGBTQ+ adults. Individuals such as public school employees may promote discrimination against LGBTQ+ students (Snapp et al., 2015). For instance, Snapp and associates (2015) discovered in their qualitative study of LGBTQ+ youth and adult advocates that youths are likely to be punished for self-expression and public displays of affection. Additionally, LGBTQ+ individuals were likely to receive punishment or be singled out due to their identity by faculty and staff, thus promoting the school-to-prison pipeline. These issues were influenced by stigmatization in school, familial rejection, and homelessness. Further education on LGBTQ+ terminology, personal development, and prevalent issues faced by LGBTQ+ individuals may assist in providing a more inclusive place that could reduce victimization and intervene on problems with homelessness.

Past victimization and familial rejection of gender identity and sexual orientation can lead to depression, anxiousness, hostility, paranoia, antisocial personality disorder, hopelessness, PTSD, obsessive-compulsive disorder, and suicide ideation (Whitbeck et al., 2004; Reback et al., 2007; Rosario et al., 2012a, 2012b; Rhoades et al., 2018). These issues are further exacerbated among homeless individuals the longer they live on the streets (Whitbeck et al., 2004; Rosario et al., 2012a, 2012b; Rhoades et al., 2018). The lack of shelter, resources, support, and the ability to satisfy basic human needs coupled with various emotional and mental issues can create a cumulative effect in which homeless LGBTQ+ individuals find themselves lacking the ability to exit homelessness. To date, there have been few to no publications that have inquired about LGBTQ+ individuals who have successfully exited homelessness (Ecker et al., 2019). We have little understanding of how some LGBTQ+ homeless individuals have overcome these obstacles and exited homelessness; therefore, research is needed to understand the lived experiences of homelessness LGBTQ+ individuals, focusing specifically on exit outcomes and strategies. Research on how individuals exit homelessness can pinpoint ways to assist the LGBTQ+ population through intervention, advertisement of resources, and education for those who work in schools, agencies, and shelters.

Conclusion

In this chapter, we discussed some of the pathways to homelessness for LGBTQ+ individuals, experiences while homeless, and the resources these individuals are likely to need to escape homelessness. In addition, we focused on research that has found that agencies and shelters can be a negative environment for LGBTQ+ individuals due to homophobia and transphobia perpetuated by staff and other shelter residents. Lastly, research, policy, and practical implications were presented, discussing ways that scholars, policymakers, and practitioners in the field can provide further elaboration on the problematic issue of LGBTQ+ homelessness. The research recommendations discussed in this chapter can contribute to the literature by having criminology scholars recognize that LGBTQ+ homelessness is a prevalent issue that needs further attention. Additionally, providing education for shelter employees, law enforcement officers, public school teachers, and medical staff can promote inclusiveness and a measure of safety for homeless LGBTQ+ individuals who are in desperate need of services and help. Lastly, the addition of more LGBTQ+-specific resources and shelters can help in providing important resources for LGBTQ+ individuals across the US in an effort to end LGBTQ+ homelessness.

Notes

[1] Homeless is defined as 'a person who lacks a fixed, regular, and adequate nighttime residence' (Henry et al., 2018, p. 2). Sheltered homelessness 'refers to people who are staying in emergency shelters, transitional housing programs, or safe havens' (Henry et al., 2018, p. 2). Unsheltered homelessness 'refers to people whose primary nighttime location is a public or private place not designated for, or ordinarily used as, a regular sleeping accommodation for people (for example, the streets, vehicles, or parks)' (Henry et al., 2018, p. 3).

[2] Survival sex is the act of exchanging sex for resources (for example, food, money, drugs, shelter) (Greene et al., 1999; Reback et al., 2007; Marshall et al., 2010; Walls & Bell, 2011; Boyer et al., 2017).

References

Abramovich, A. (2016) 'Preventing, reducing, and ending LGBTQ2S youth homelessness: the need for targeted strategies', *Social Inclusion*, 4(4): 86–96.

Abramovich, A. (2017) 'Understanding how policy and culture create oppressive conditions for LGBTQ2s youth in the shelter system', *Journal of Homosexuality*, 64(11): 1484–1501.

Boyer, C.B., Greenberg, L., Chutuape, K., Walker, B., Monte, D., Kirk, J., & The Adolescent Medicine Trials Network (2017) 'Exchange of sex for drugs or money in adolescents and young adults: an examination of sociodemographic factors, HIV-related risk, and community context', *Journal of Community Health*, 42(1): 90–100.

Choi, S.K., Wilson, B.D.M, Shelton, J., & Gates, G. (2015) 'Serving our youth 2015: the needs and experiences of lesbian, gay, bisexual, transgender, and questioning youth experiencing homelessness', Los Angeles: The Williams Institute with True Colors Fund.

Clatts, M.C., Goldsamt, L., Yi, H., & Gwadz, M.V. (2005) 'Homelessness and drug abuse among men who have sex with men in New York City: a preliminary epidemiological trajectory', *Journal of Adolescence*, 28(2): 201–214.

Cochran, B.N., Stewart, A.J., Ginzler, J.A., & Cauce, A.M. (2002) 'Challenges faced by homeless sexual minorities: comparison of gay, lesbian, bisexual, and transgender homeless adolescents with their heterosexual counterparts', *American Journal of Public Health*, 92(5): 773–777.

Coolhart, D. & Brown, M.T. (2017) 'The need for safe spaces: exploring the experiences of homeless LGBTQ youth in shelters', *Children and Youth Services Review*, 82(1): 230–238.

Corliss, H.L., Goodenow, C.S., Nichols, L., & Austin, S.B. (2011) 'High burden of homelessness among sexual-minority adolescents: findings from a representative Massachusetts high school sample', *American Journal of Public Health*, 101(9): 1683–1689.

Côté, P. & Blais, M. (2019) 'Between resignation, resistance and recognition: a qualitative analysis of LGBTQ+ youth profiles of homelessness agencies utilization', *Children and Youth Services Review*, 100, 437–443.

Ecker, J. (2016) 'Queer, young, and homeless: a review of the literature', *Child & Youth Services*, 37(4): 325–361.

Ecker, J., Aubry, T., & Sylvestre, J. (2019) 'A review of the literature on LGBTQ adults who experience homelessness', *Journal of Homosexuality*, 66(3): 297–323.

Forge, N., Hartinger-Saunders, R., Wright, E., & Ruel, E. (2018) 'Out of the system and onto the streets: LGBTQ-identified youth experiencing homelessness with past child welfare system involvement', *Child Welfare*, 96(2): 47–74.

Greene, J.M., Ennett, S.T., & Ringwalt, C.L. (1999) 'Prevalence and correlates of survival sex among runaway and homeless youth', *American Journal of Public Health*, 89(9): 1406–1409.

Henry, M., Mahathey, A., Morrill, T., Robinson, A., Shivji, A., & Watt, R. (2018) 'The 2018 annual homeless assessment report (AHAR) to congress, part 1: point-in-time estimates of homelessness', Washington, DC: US Department of Housing and Urban Development.

Hunter, E. (2008) 'What's good for the gays is good for the gander: making homeless youth housing safer for lesbian, gay, bisexual, and transgender youth', *Family Court Review*, 46(3): 543–557.

Irvine, A. & Canfield, A. (2016) 'The overrepresentation of lesbian, gay, bisexual, questioning, gender nonconforming and transgender youth within the child welfare to juvenile justice crossover population', *Social Policy*, 24(2): 1–19.

Marshall, B.D., Shannon, K., Kerr, T., Zhang, R., & Wood, E. (2010) 'Survival sex work and increased HIV risk among sexual minority street-involved youth', *Journal of Acquired Immune Deficiency Syndromes*, *53*(5): 661–664.

Milburn, N.G., Ayala, G., Rice, E., Batterham, P., & Rotheram-Borus, M.J. (2006) 'Discrimination and exiting homelessness among homeless adolescents', *Cultural Diversity & Ethnic Minority Psychology*, 12(4): 658–672.

Morten, M.H., Dworsky, A., Matjasko, J.L., Curry, S.R., Schlueter, D., Chávez, R., & Farrell, A.F. (2018) 'Prevalence and correlates of youth homelessness in the United States', *Journal of Adolescent Health*, 62(1): 14–21.

Mottet, L. & Ohle, J. (2006) 'Transitioning our shelters: making homeless shelters safe for transgender people', *Journal of Poverty*, 10(2): 77–101.

Namaste, V.K. (2000) *Invisible Lives: The Erasure of Transsexual and Transgendered People*, Chicago, IL: University of Chicago Press.

Prock, K.A. & Kennedy, A.C. (2017) 'Federally-funded transitional living programs and services for LGBTQ-identified homeless youth: a profile in unmet need', *Children and Youth Services Review*, 83(1): 17–24.

Reback, C.J., Kamien, J.B., & Amass, L. (2007) 'Characteristics and HIV risk behaviors of homeless, substance-using men who have sex with men', *Addictive Behaviors*, 32(3): 647–654.

Rew, L., Whittaker, T.A., Taylor-Seehafer, M.A., & Smith, L.R. (2005) 'Sexual health risks and protective resources in gay, lesbian, bisexual, and heterosexual homeless youth', *Journal for Specialists in Pediatric Nursing*, 10(1): 11–19.

Rhoades, H., Rusow, J.A., Bond, D., Lanteigne, A., Fulginiti, A., & Goldbach, J.T. (2018) 'Homelessness, mental health, and suicidality among LGBTQ youth accessing crisis services', *Child Psychiatry & Human Development*, 49(4): 643–651.

Rosario, M., Schrimshaw, E.W., & Hunter, J. (2012a) 'Homelessness among lesbian, gay, and bisexual youth: implications for subsequent internalizing and externalizing symptoms', *Journal of Youth and Adolescence*, 41(5): 544–560.

Rosario, M., Schrimshaw, E.W., & Hunter, J. (2012b) 'Risk factors for homelessness among lesbian, gay, and bisexual youths: a developmental milestone approach', *Children and Youth Services Review*, 34(1): 186–193.

Ryan, C., Huebner, D., Diaz, R.M., & Sanchez, J. (2009) 'Family rejection as a predictor of negative health outcomes in white and Latino lesbian, gay, and bisexual young adults', *Pediatrics*, 123(1): 346–352.

Sakamoto, I., Chin, M., Chapra, A., & Ricciardi, J. (2009) 'A "normative" homeless woman? Marginalization, emotional injury and social support of transwomen experiencing homelessness', *Gay & Lesbian Issues and Psychology Review*, 5(1): 2–19.

Schmitz, R.M. & Tyler, K.A. (2018) 'The complexity of family reactions to identity among homeless and college lesbian, gay, bisexual, transgender, and queer young adults', *Archives of Sexual Behavior*, 47(4): 1195–1207.

Shelton, J., Poirier, J.M., Wheeler, C., & Abramovich, A. (2018) 'Reversing erasure of youth and young adults who are LGBTQ and access homelessness services: asking about sexual orientation, gender identity, and pronouns', *Child Welfare*, 96(2): 1–28.

Snapp, S.D., Hoenig, J.M., Fields, A., & Russell, S.T. (2015) 'Messy, butch, and queer: LGBTQ youth and the school-to-prison pipeline', *Journal of Adolescent Research*, 30(1): 57–82.

Spicer, S.S. (2010) 'Healthcare needs of the transgender homeless population', *Journal of Gay & Lesbian Mental Health*, 14(4): 320–339.

Van Leeuwen, J.M., Boyle, S., Salomonsen-Sautel, S., Baker D.N., Garcia, J.T., Hoffman, A., & Hopfer, C.J. (2006) 'Lesbian, gay, and bisexual homeless youth: an eight-city public health perspective', *Child Welfare*, 85(2): 151–170.

Walls, N.E. & Bell, S. (2011) 'Correlates of engaging in survival sex among homeless youth and young adults', *Journal of Sex Research*, 48(5): 423–436.

Whitbeck, L.B., Chen, X., Hoyt, D.R., Tyler, K.A., & Johnson, K.D. (2004) 'Mental disorder, subsistence strategies, and victimization among gay, lesbian, and bisexual homeless and runaway adolescents', *Journal of Sex Research*, 41(4): 329–342.

Wilson, E.C., Garofalo, R., Harris, R.D., Herrick, A., Martinez, M., Martinez, J., Belzer, M., The Transgender Advisory Committee, & Adolescent Medicine Trials Network for HIV/AIDS Interventions (2009) 'Transgender female youth and sex work: HIV risk and a comparison of life factors related to engagement in sex work', *AIDS and Behavior*, 13(5): 902–913.

17

The Color of Queer Theory in Social Work and Criminology Practice: A World without Empathy

Rebecca S. Katz

Social justice goals and objectives necessitate rethinking the systems of criminal injustices both toward the LGBTQAI+ population and the LGBTQAI+ population that includes people of color. For example, while two of the founders of Black Lives Matter are also LGBTQ folks, this has been omitted from most of the queering criminology literature. By extension, social control through criminalization mirrors social control as exhibited by the social welfare system in both its inherent racism and classism when it removes children from poor Black single mothers and when it ceases to offer assistance to the wide swath of homeless LGBTQ persons. Queer criminology must open the interdisciplinary door to social work practice and theory both to illuminate these methods of social control and to create a theory of social justice that may lead to the replacement of both systems of social control. This chapter will compare and contrast the author's experience in the institutions of prison work and social work to build a new theory of social justice and new systems of human sustenance and development that does not rely on punitive policies and practices.

Personal reflections

This author's work as a mental health counselor in prisons, psychiatric hospitals, community agencies, and substance abuse treatment facilities facilitated a path to academia and back again after 25 years of being immersed in pedagogy and research. In the early 1990s when this author's academic career began, both orthodox and critical criminology were dominated by the voices of white heterosexual males who ignored the patriarchal, white, gendered binary and class-based existence of individual lives as well as the constraints of those social structures (Agnew, 1992). While some initial criminological work took early childhood experiences into account, most ignored and continue to ignore the plethora of data on mental health, substance abuse, and early trauma in the field of psychology and social work. (Most of the clients whom I have served endured severe trauma in early childhood resulting from abusive and/or neglectful parents, and a racist, xenophobic, heterosexist, and classist child welfare system.)

I recall writing a paper taking into account early childhood traumatic experiences[1] and their influence on the development of later violence, substance use, and other types of crimes, and the professor being surprised and excited and explaining that this would take a lifetime of research. Well, I have spent an academic career doing just this kind of research, beginning with my dissertation investigating the effects of early harsh discipline (code words for abusive parents) and early infant insecure attachment's effects on the absence of the development of empathy and subsequent effects on criminal behavior. Historically and contemporaneously, I continue to encounter traumatized people like this as a mental health counselor. My clients have been transgender, brown and white, nonbinary, bisexual, heterosexual, poor and middle class. They have been emotionally abused, neglected, sexually abused, abandoned, with incarcerated parents, and parents with alcohol and drug use disorders. When I began my career as a criminologist there was no reckoning that these problems existed. My dissertation addressed the late Travis Hirschi's control theory, which borrowed from John Bowlby's work on early parent–child attachment that demonstrated the early childhood trauma across 44 male thieves' lives. Unfortunately, John Bowlby's work continues to be ignored by criminology just as much as we white queers have ignored Black and brown queers. Thus, queer criminology has positioned itself in an intellectual and epistemological barricade. This author attempts to offer a new antiracist, compassionate, and trauma-informed queer criminology that embraces Black and brown lives and the central goal of all social work, *social justice*, that aims to end economic inequality, end the oppression of all religious, ethnic and racial, and sexual minority groups, and end racial profiling and mass incarceration.

Black Lives Matter (BLM)

The murder of Trayvon Martin by a want-to-be cop gave rise to a new social movement called Black Lives Matter. Black Lives Matter was developed as a Black feminist, environmental, human rights, and queer organization (Saltzman, 2020), as it was founded by three women of color, two of whom were queer women. The subsequent police killings of Breonna Taylor, Michael Brown, Tamir Rice, George Floyd, and countless others including disproportionate murders of Black and brown trans women should be teaching us how to become activists or to develop a criminological praxis. Black Lives Matter has principles or ethical commitments to improve society; social work similarly has principles and challenges that are committed to transforming mass incarceration and ending poverty, childhood suffering, and homelessness, as well as ending the domination and subordination of all oppressed groups. It clearly acknowledges, rather than debating as criminology has done for decades, that Black, brown, Latinx, and LGBTQ groups, and all religious minority groups, are oppressed. Criminology does none of these things and is not operating from a trauma-informed perspective like social work has with its investment in social justice and trauma-informed praxis. Black Lives Matter is invested in social justice. Black Lives Matter's commitments to social transformation are provided here from 'What We Believe':

1. Every day, we recommit to healing ourselves and each other, and to co-creating alongside comrades, allies, and family a culture where each person feels seen, heard, and supported.
2. We acknowledge, respect, and celebrate differences and commonalities.
3. We work vigorously for freedom and justice for Black people and, by extension, all people.
4. We intentionally build and nurture a beloved community that is bonded together through a beautiful struggle that is restorative, not depleting.
5. We are unapologetically Black in our positioning. In affirming that Black Lives Matter, we need not qualify our position. To love and desire freedom and justice for ourselves is a prerequisite for wanting the same for others.
6. We see ourselves as part of the global Black family, and we are aware of the different ways we are impacted or privileged as Black people who exist in different parts of the world.
7. We are guided by the fact that all Black lives matter, regardless of actual or perceived sexual identity, gender identity, gender expression, economic status, ability, disability, religious beliefs or disbeliefs, immigration status, or location.
8. We make space for transgender brothers and sisters to participate and lead.
9. We are self-reflexive and do the work required to dismantle cisgender privilege and uplift Black trans folk, especially Black trans women who continue to be disproportionately impacted by trans-antagonistic violence.

10. We build a space that affirms Black women and is free from sexism, misogyny, and environments in which men are centered.
11. We practice empathy. We engage comrades with the intent to learn about and connect with their contexts. (Black Lives Matter, 2017)

Unfortunately, a variety of complaints were made about these commitments, alleging that these were too 'socialist', and they have since been redacted from the BLM website and replaced with what is now called 'Campaign Zero' (2020), which includes ten policy recommendations more focused on criminal justice system changes:

1. end broken windows policing;
2. develop community oversight for police departments;
3. limit the use of police force;
4. independently investigate and prosecute police behavior;
5. develop community representation within police departments;
6. utilize body cams and other methods to film police;
7. improve police training;
8. end for-profit policing;
9. demilitarize police; and
10. develop fair police union contracts.

Black Lives Matter and criminological ethics

Enquiring about social justice in criminology for LGBTQ+ individuals necessitates the utilization of a developmental, sociopolitical, and historical familial lens that analyzes what it's like to grow up being told you are less than, that you do not measure up to heterosexual white hyper-feminine or hyper-masculine standards, and thus feeling like or being told 'I wish you had never been born' or 'you are too young to know you are gay' or 'you are too young to know what it is to be Black in a white world'. The absence of ethics in raising queer children of color or queer white children is mirrored by the absence of an ethical framework within criminology. An ethical framework is a necessary prerequisite of doing social justice in both criminological research and teaching. By extension, criminology continues to avoid becoming interdisciplinary by embracing other ethical disciplines that have a practice component such as social work. In this time and place, where trans people are denied civil rights, where being queer or a trans woman, nonbinary, or Black, Indigenous, or an immigrant results in police murder, detention, and child abuse and neglect, ethics must become as embedded in criminology practice as it is in social work practice. Black Lives Matter has been giving criminologists lessons on ethics through its attempts to address police murders including those of George Floyd, Breonna Taylor,

Michael Brown, and many others as the 45th president flaunted an absence of any sort of ethical consciousness, as thousands of people continued to die due to his denial of a public health pandemic and efforts to dehumanize immigrants and LGBTQ+ people who are Black, brown, and white. Black Lives Matters represents ethical queer thought and practice all by itself.

Adverse childhood experiences (ACES)

Some children are sexually abused within their families, often by their father, grandfather, or brother, less often by their mother, sister, or babysitter (Katz, 2000; Seto et al., 2015; NCANDS, 2020). The short-term consequences of this abuse include substance abuse, acting out physically, depression, anxiety, anger, and rage, and they face long-term physical consequences as well as they age (Felitti et al., 1998; Zarse et al., 2019). These are adverse childhood experiences that restructure the brain of the child by reducing the neurological capacity for emotional and behavioral regulation. During abuse, the body's cortisol response increases – this is our flight, fight, or freeze response to danger. These increased levels change the structure of the brain just as neurochemical changes impact the immune system, making the individual highly susceptible to chronic diseases such as diabetes, heart disease, and cancer (Felitti et al., 1998; Zarse et al., 2019; Palmer-Bacon et al., 2020).

In 1998, a groundbreaking study investigating the etiology of early mortality in the United States found that the best predictors of a number of disease processes were a variety of traumagenic early childhood events ranging from having an incarcerated parent to a variety of different types of child abuse (Felitti et al., 1998). The higher the number of these so-called adverse childhood experiences (ACES) an individual suffers, the greater likelihood of early mortality as the result of chronic diseases and mental health problems as well as involvement in crime and being diagnosed with a substance abuse disorder. The original sample was a predominantly white middle-class group of more than 13,000 adults who were being treated in a large HMO group (Felitti et al., 1998). These ACES are not more common in Black families or white families or wealthy or poor, but many of the men and women in our prisons and juvenile justice institutions across the country have extremely high levels of ACES. These findings have been replicated on numerous occasions (Zarse et al., 2019).

The following is a replication of the adverse childhood experiences assessment instrument that should also inform all our future research in criminology.

1. Did a parent or other adult in the household often or very often …
    Swear at you, insult you, put you down, or humiliate you? or Act in a
    way that made you afraid that you might be physically hurt?

2. Did a parent or other adult in the household often or very often ... Push, grab, slap, or throw something at you? or Ever hit you so hard that you had marks or were injured?
3. Did an adult or person at least 5 years older than you ever ... Touch or fondle you or have you touch their body in a sexual way? or Attempt or actually have oral, anal, or vaginal intercourse with you?
4. Did you often or very often feel that ... No one in your family loved you or thought you were important or special? or Your family didn't look out for each other, feel close to each other, or support each other?
5. Did you often or very often feel that ... You didn't have enough to eat, had to wear dirty clothes, and had no one to protect you? or Your parents were too drunk or high to take care of you or take you to the doctor if you needed it?
6. Were your parents ever separated or divorced?
7. Was your mother or stepmother: Often or very often pushed, grabbed, slapped, or had something thrown at her? or Sometimes, often, or very often kicked, bitten, hit with a fist, or hit with something hard? or Ever repeatedly hit over at least a few minutes or threatened with a gun or knife?
8. Did you live with anyone who was a problem drinker or alcoholic, or who used street drugs?
9. Was a household member depressed or mentally ill, or did a household member attempt suicide?
10. Did a household member go to prison? (Felitti et al., 1998)

In addition to being LGBTQ and a racial or ethnic minority with a high ACE score, religious coercion, commonly called 'conversion therapy', increases the level of trauma (Blosnich et al., 2020). Moreover, other research also illustrates that for trans men or trans women adults and youth, familial and/or religious non-acceptance results in high rates of self-harm as well (Ryan, 2010; Herman et al., 2019).

Specifically, in 2016 the New Mexico Sentencing Commission studied 220 juveniles incarcerated (committed) to the Children and Youth Families Department and found that a majority of the juveniles encountered at least one adverse childhood experience (only having a parent with a mental illness was omitted) as well as other traumas, had multiple foster care placements, and witnessed a murder or death. They found that all the females experienced childhood physical neglect, as had 93 percent of the males (Cannon et al., 2016). Sixty-three percent of the females and 21 percent of the males were sexually abused as children (Cannon et al., 2016). Seventy-four percent of the males had experienced five or more ACES compared with 86 percent of the females (Cannon et al., 2016). This validates my own experiences working with adults and juveniles in prisons, group homes, substance abuse treatment facilities, mental health agencies, and psychiatric units. Moreover, some contemporary criminologists have revealed similar findings, but this work has been ignored in mainstream criminology. For example, Cathy Widom and Maxfield's research long supported the link between early childhood abuse and later involvement in crime (Widom & Maxfield, 2001). Specifically, they found a link between early childhood abuse and neglect and later adult and juvenile crime. Their work followed more than 1,500 cases from childhood through adolescence and adulthood using arrest records from 1988 through 1994, and while no SOGIE (sexual orientation, gender identity, and expression) data were collected, 41 percent of adults involved in criminal behavior were in the abuse and neglected group compared with only 32 percent in a comparison group of offenders. However, 18 percent of abused and neglected children were later convicted of violent crimes compared with only 14 percent of the control group. Unfortunately, ACES were not used to analyze the data.

A more recent study of 400 women in parenting classes in three separate jails found that 80 percent of the women had four or more ACES (Wooten, 2015). Sixty percent reported six or more ACES. Unfortunately, again no SOGIE data were collected. Similarly, a recent study of 22 South African individuals incarcerated for murdering their own children (SOGIE status was unexamined) revealed that all had a number of ACES themselves including sexual abuse, parental abandonment, physical abuse, neglect, and insecure attachments (Dekel et al., 2019). Fortunately, more recent work is illustrating similar findings among LGBTQ folks.

Research on ACES among lesbian, gay, and bisexual (LGB) individuals as well as heterosexuals in a joint North Carolina and Washington study found that LGB individuals had 1.3–4.1 greater odds of a higher prevalence rate for all ten ACES studied than straight individuals (Austin et al., 2016). This portended significantly poorer health outcomes among the LGB individuals. The same study found a higher level of psychological distress and higher levels of binge drinking as adults among the LGB group. Their review of the extant literature also revealed a greater proportion of LGB adults reporting physical, sexual, and emotional childhood abuse than heterosexual adults. They also found only five previous studies that examined these types of childhood traumas among SOGIE populations. Thirteen percent of the LGB individuals were Black and 9 percent identified as 'other' with regard to race. LGB individuals were also significantly more likely than the straight respondents to report sexual abuse, adult mental illness in the household, and having a parent in prison. Black and brown queer women and/or trans women are often more likely to have suffered early childhood sexual abuse and adult sexual assault.

Patrick Johnson completed oral history interviews with 79 queer Black women in 2013 and reported that 66 had experienced some form of sexual abuse in their lifetime at the hands of male relatives including rape, molestation, and/or fondling (Johnson, 2018). Only one these victims was molested by a female (an aunt). The same individual also experienced another victimization by a male friend of the family. Generational sexual abuse was common among both parents in some cases. It is important to note here that sexual abuse or rape by a male does not cause same-sex-desire; the women he interviewed made it quite clear that their sexual orientation existed outside the traumatic abuse (Johnson, 2018).

Research since this time has included a focus on being a LGTBQAI+ child and having one's identity diminished, devalued, or dismissed, or being coerced into 'conversion therapy' by one's parents (Blosnich et al., 2020). Experiences with racism, xenophobia, or nativism have also been addressed. Further, being an LGTBQAI+ person of color who may experience racialized heterosexist discrimination by heterosexist people of color is trauma-inducing (Vargus et al., 2020). Social workers are recognizing that LGBTQ children and nonbinary children are at increased risk of ACES. One study found that non-performance of binary gender representations often resulted in formal or informal sanctioning (Conron & Wilson, 2019). Sexual minority youth, particularly those who are also ethnic and racial minorities, were significantly more likely to suffer from social and family stigma, rejection, and violent, sexual, and emotional victimization, and to contract sexual transmitted infections and HIV. Other research illustrates that a higher rate of child mistreatment occurs among LGBTQ children, at almost 13 percent versus almost 6 percent of non-LGBTQ youth (Wilson et al., 2014).

The Trevor Project's 2020 survey of more than 40,000 LGBTQ youth ages 13 to 24 found a substantial degree of trauma among these young people. LGBTQ youth of color were well represented in their survey. They found that among SOGIE youth, one in three LGBTQAI+ children had been physically abused within their families. Moreover, 68 percent of these children developed generalized anxiety disorders, 48 percent tried to harm themselves or attempted suicide, while among trans youth of color this percentage reached 60 percent. Similarly, 78 percent of trans youth of color were forced to participate in conversion therapy. These microaggressions may explain why 15 percent of queer SOGIE youth attempt suicide, and why 41 percent of trans youth had done so (The Trevor Project, 2020). Another recent study examined ACES and found that they predicted suicidal ideation and suicide attempts among more than 1,500 non-transgender sexual minority adults (Blosnich et al., 2020). They also found that 7 percent of respondents reported experiencing efforts at sexual orientation change (SOCE), and 80 percent of those attempts were initiated by religious leaders. These sexual minorities exposed to SOCE had twice the lifetime odds of suicidal ideation, 75 percent odds of planning to attempt suicide, and an

88 percent increased likelihood of a suicide attempt. Moreover, among the sample as a whole the average number of ACES among those experiencing SOCE was four, including witnessing parental violence as a child and emotional, physical, and sexual abuse as a child.

Queer, bisexual, and trans children, adolescents, and young adults have been shuffled from poverty-stricken families and sometimes abusive or neglectful families into abysmal foster care systems and then racist, traumatizing, and dehumanizing juvenile justice systems. One study of the population of all children in the care of the Los Angeles child welfare department found that 19 percent of all children aged 12–21 in foster care were LGBTQ children (Wilson et al., 2014). LGBTQ+ youth were more likely to have multiple foster care placements, more likely to end up in group homes, and more likely to have been hospitalized for mental health issues (Wilson et al., 2014). Across the entire city, almost 55 percent of these LGBTQ youth were Latino and 29 percent were Black or African American; 10 percent were foreign born and 32 percent had at least one parent who was foreign born, while only 6 percent were white. Twelve percent of their sample reported experiencing discrimination as the result of their gender expression, and slightly under 1 percent reported experiencing discrimination because of their trans identity (Wilson et al., 2014). LGBTQ+ foster care children are also more likely to be placed in out-of-home care (Annie Casey Foundation, 2016; Field, 2018) and more likely to be mistreated by child welfare workers, peers, and their foster parents (Mountz et al., 2019).

This work is supported by a 2019 report from the Williams Institute that found Black LGBTQ+ children were disproportionately represented in the child welfare system as well as in the juvenile justice system (Conron & Wilson, 2019). The Williams Institute study found that 13 percent of foster care youth in Los Angeles were LGBTQ+ and among that group, 55 percent were Latinx and 24 percent were Black (Wilson et al., 2014).

The Williams Institute's findings reveal a pattern and practice that involves more pervasive discrimination for LGBTQ+ children of color including some of the following:

- historic and contemporary stigma, forced assimilation, and discrimination resulting in racial segregation and poverty among American Indian LGBTQ youth;
- school-based disparity in disciplinary practices against LGBTQ youth of color;
- police targeting of LGBTQ youth of color and more likely to end up in the school-to-prison pipeline;
- socially constructing youth of color and promoting views of them as more threatening by child welfare rather than deserving of protection;
- homelessness and commission of survival crimes;

- LGBTQ youth of color remain in child welfare and juvenile justice systems longer and are more likely to be victimized; and
- multiple traumatic experiences as the result of the above and absence of recognition by community agencies. (Conron & Wilson, 2019)

Criminologists must begin collecting data on sexual orientation, gender identity, sex assigned at birth, and gender expression as well as race and ethnic data to better alleviate LGBTQ children's mistreatment by systems and structures of oppression and repression (Greif-Hackett & Gallagher, 2018; Conron & Wilson, 2019). Therefore, queer criminologists must collect data on whether or not LGBTQ+ and nonbinary children have been in foster care as well as measuring their adverse childhood experiences.

Conclusion

Social work praxis is trauma- and empathy-informed, and it is now time for a trauma- and empathy-informed compassionate queer criminology. We must explore the traumatic childhood and adult histories of every person in jail or prison and the traumatizing institutions that have historically and contemporaneously continued to do harm, including the foster care system and the child welfare system (Javier et al., 2020). Neurological findings consistently illustrate both the damage of developmental trauma on the child's brain and the reduction in the ability to trust, connect emotionally to others, and self-regulate emotions and behavior (Dana & Porges, 2018; Kain & Terrell, 2018). We must advocate for change, not simply sit in our ivory towers pontificating about the etiology of crime. This means advocating for the end of regimes of power that represent straight, white, heterosexist, and wealthy elitists' campaigns of social control.

Three years of prison work as a mental health counselor, ten years in mental health counseling with survivors of parental abuse and maltreatment, four years working with victims of battering and queer parents caught up in the child welfare system, as well as four semesters teaching a university class in a prison setting have shown me the failures of an inherently white supremacist and heterosexist Department of Human Services as well as homophobic, transphobic, and cisgendered punitive racist federal and state correctional systems. We must become trauma- and empathy-informed rather than informed only by quantitative methodologies and alleged scientific objectivity that simply masks our inherent biases.

This theory of social justice begins by examining the development of secure or insecure infant-childhood attachments, the development of sexual orientation and trans and gender nonconforming identity, as well as the development of racial, religious, and ethnic identity in toddlerhood, early and middle childhood, and adolescence (Bowlby, 1946). Moreover, it is necessary to observe and examine parental empathy and compassion toward the infant, child, and teenager as developmental milestones are achieved. Research observations of early parental interactions with infants and toddlers outside a laboratory setting is not likely without substantive funding, consent, and legal documentation. Therefore, researchers must attempt to answer these questions of parents and caretakers retrospectively. Utilizing the ACES questionnaire with youth and adults will make criminology trauma-informed while also taking into account experiences with microaggressions or experiencing heterosexist homophobic, trans, and nonbinary phobia as well as experiences with discrimination, xenophobia, and racism at home, work, and school. We know that LGBTQ+ children and youth who grow up in affirming homes are better adjusted and thus this must also be accounted for in future research (Kuvalanka et al., 2017).

References

Agnew, R. (1992) 'Foundation for a general strain theory of crime and delinquency', *Criminology*, 30: 47–87.

Annie Casey Foundation (2016) 'LGTQ in child welfare: a systematic review of the literature', Public Research and Education Services.

Austin, A., Herrick, H., & Proescholdbell, S. (2016) 'Adverse childhood experiences related to poor adult health among lesbian, gay and bisexual individuals', *American Journal of Public Health*, 106(2): 314–320.

Black Lives Matter (2017) 'Guiding principles'. http://blacklivesmatter.com/guiding-principles/

Blosnich, J.R., Henderson, E.R., Coulter, R.W.S., Goldbach, J.T., & Meyer, I.H. (2020) 'Sexual orientation change efforts, adverse childhood experiences and suicide ideation and attempt among sexual minority adults, United States, 2016–2018', *The American Journal of Public Health Surveillance*, 110(7): 1024–1030.

Bowlby, J. (1946) *Forty-four Juvenile Thieves: Their Characters and Home Life*, London: Baillière, Tindall & Cox.

Campaign Zero (2020) 'Campaign Zero'. https://www.joincampaignzero.org/#vision

Cannon, Y., Davis, G., Hsi, A., & Bochte, A. (2016) 'Adverse childhood experiences in the New Mexico juvenile justice population', *Georgetown Law Faculty Publications and Other Works*. 2191. https://scholarship.law.georgetown.edu/facpub/2191

Conron, K.J. & Wilson, B.D.M. (2019) 'LGBTQ youth of color impacted by the child welfare and juvenile justice systems: a research agenda', June, Williams Institute School of Law, UCLA.

Dana, D. & Porges, S.W. (2018) *The Polyvagal Theory in Therapy: Engaging the Rhythm of Regulation*, Norton Series on Interpersonal Neurobiology, London: W. W. Norton.

Dekel, B., Abrahams, N., & Andipatin, M. (2018) 'Exploring adverse parent-child relationships from the perspective of convicted child murderers: a South African qualitative study', *PLoS ONE*, 13(5): 1–21. DOI: 10.1371/journal.pone.0196772

Felitti, V.J., Anda, R.F., Nordenberg, D.F., Williamson, A.M., Spitz, A.M., Edwards, V., Koss, M.P., & Marks, J.S. (1998) 'Relationship of childhood abuse and household dysfunction to many of the leading causes of death in adults: the Adverse Childhood Experiences (ACE) study', *American Journal of Preventative Medicine*, 14: 245–258.

Field, T. (2018) 'It is time to start counting kids who are LGBTQ in child welfare', *Child Welfare*, 96(1): xii–xx.

Greif-Hackett, M.L. & Gallagher, S. (2018) 'Creating safer places for youth who are LGBTQ in Broward County Florida: collecting SOGIE data for life-coaching services', *Child Welfare*, 96(1): 27–51.

Herman, J.L., Brown, T.N.T., & Haas, A.P. (2019) 'Suicide thoughts and attempts among transgender adults: findings from the 2015 U.S. Transgender Survey', UCLA Williams Institute.

Javier, R.A., Owen, E.A., & Maddux, J.A. (eds.) (2020) *Assessing Trauma in Forensic Contexts*, Cham: Springer.

Johnson, E.P. (2018) *Black. Queer. Southern. Women. An Oral History*, Carolina: The University of North Carolina Press.

Kain, K.L. & Terrell, S.J. (2018) *Nurturing Resilience: Helping Clients Move Forward From Developmental Trauma*, Berkeley, CA: North Atlantic Books.

Katz, R.S. (2000) 'Explaining girls' and women's crime and desistance in the context of their women's experiences. A developmental test of revised strain theory and the life-course perspective', *Violence Against Women*, 6(6): 633–660.

Kuvalanka, K.A., Weiner, J.L., Munroe, C., Goldberg, A.E., & Garner, M. (2017) 'Trans and gender-nonconforming children and their caregivers: gender presentations, peer relations and well-being at baseline', *Journal of Family Psychology*, 31(7): 889–899.

Mountz, S., Capous-Desyllas, M., & Perez, N. (2019) 'Speaking back to the system: recommendations for practice and policy from the perspectives of youth formerly in foster care who are LGBTQ', *Child Welfare*, 97(5): 117–140.

NCANDS (National Child Abuse and Neglect Data System) (2020) 'Child Maltreatment 2018. U.S. Department of Health and Human Services administration for children and families', Washington, D.C: Children's Bureau.

Palmer-Bacon, J., Willis-Esqueda, C., Spaulding, W.D., McLeigh, J.D., & Spaulding, W. (2020) 'Stress, trauma, racial/ethnic group membership, and HPA function: utility of hair cortisol', *American Journal of Orthopsychiatry*, 90(2): 193–200. https://doi.org/10.1037/ort0000424

Ryan, C. (2010) 'Engaging families to support lesbian, gay, bisexual and transgender youth. The Family Acceptance Project', *The Prevention Researcher*, 17(4): 11–13.

Saltzman, S. (2020) 'From the start, Black Lives Matter has been about LGBTQ lives. Two of the three Black Lives Matter founders identify as queer', ABC News, June 21. https://abcnews.go.com/US/start-black-lives-matter-lgbtq-lives/story?id=71320450

Seto, M.C., Babchishin, K.M., Pullman, L.E., & McPhail, I.V. (2015). 'The puzzle of intrafamilial and extrafamilial offenders with child victims', *Clinical Psychology Review*, 39: 42–57.

The Trevor Project (2020) 'The Trevor Project National Survey on LGBTQ Youth Mental Health'. https://www.thetrevorproject.org/survey-2020/?section

Vargus, S.M., Huey, S.J., & Miranda, J. (2020) 'A critical review of current evidence on multiple types of discrimination and mental health', *American Journal of Orthopsychiatry*, 90(3): 374–390. http://dx.doi.org/10.1037/ort0000441

Widom, C.S. & Maxfield, M.G. (2001) 'An update on the "Cycle of Violence"', U.S. Department of Justice. Office of Justice Programs. National Institute of Justice Research in Brief. NCJ 184894. http://www.ojp.usdoj.gov/nij

Wilson, B.D.M., Cooper, K., Kastanis, A., & Nezhad, S. (2014) 'Sexual and gender minority youth in foster care: assessing disproportionality and disparities in Los Angeles', UCLA Williams Institute.

Wooten, A.B. (2015) 'The impact of ACES on health care costs-how parenting classes at a Tennessee prison are breaking the cycle', *Corrections Today*, September–October, 42–48.

Zarse, E.M., Neff, M.R., Yoder, R., Hulvershorn, L., Chambers, J.E., & Changers, R.A. (2019) 'The adverse childhood experiences questionnaire: two decades of research on childhood trauma as a primary cause of adult mental illness, addiction, and medical diseases', *Cogent Medicine, Psychiatry Review Article*, 6: 1–24.

18

Camouflaged: Tackling the Invisibility of LGBTQ+ Veterans When Accessing Care

Shanna N. Felix and Chrystina Y. Hoffman

There is an extensive history of LGBTQ+ invisibility in the United States military. For instance, although official regulations banning the enlistment of sexual minorities such as lesbian, gay, and bisexual people can be traced back to the 1920s (Bérubé, 2010), the more recent (and notorious) 'don't ask, don't tell' (DADT) policy was implemented in 1993 and later repealed in 2011 (Kerrigan, 2012; Proctor & Krusen, 2017). While the DADT policy prohibited the military from directly asking a service member about their sexual orientation, service personnel were still able to be discharged if their sexual orientation became known through credible information or voluntary disclosure (where credible information might include ambiguous references to sexuality on medical records; see Howe, 2018). Indeed, 1,046 service personnel were discharged in 1999 alone for 'conduct unbecoming' related to sexual orientation (Sobel et al., 2001), and more than 13,000 service members have been discharged as a result of the DADT policy (McDermott, 2016).

While the repeal of DADT has been heralded as a victory for LGBTQ+ rights, the policy did not apply to transgender service members (Kerrigan, 2012). Trans people were unable to enlist and serve in the armed forces until the Department of Defense lifted the ban in 2016 under the Obama administration, which would have allowed transgender military personnel not only to openly serve their country but also to receive gender-affirming surgery previously excluded by the Veterans Health Administration

(VHA) starting in January 2018 (Zucker, 2018, p. 329). However, this 2016 decision was reversed by the Trump administration in 2017 through a series of memorandums issued by President Trump, the second of which states that 'transgender persons with a history or diagnosis of gender dysphoria ... are disqualified from military service except under certain limited circumstances', with the justification that the medical treatment for gender dysphoria is 'substantial', including medications and surgery (cited in Manuel, 2020, p. 82). In 2019, the Supreme Court 'stayed the preliminary injunctions while the lower courts continued to hear arguments, allowing the transgender military ban to go into effect' (Manuel, 2020, p. 88). This is not the same as the Supreme Court directly upholding these restrictions, for which there are still several lower court cases pending in multiple states at the time of writing this chapter (Manuel, 2020).

As Proctor and Krusen (2017) note, policies such as DADT and the ban on transgender service members (since overturned by the Biden administration) have resulted in entire generations of thousands of veterans who were unable to come out or seek social support from the LGBTQ+ community. According to the 2015 Department of Defense Health Related Behaviors Survey (HRBS), 6.1 percent of their sample of nearly 16,700 service members identified as LGBT (Meadows et al., 2018). Further, the estimated prevalence of transgender individuals serving in the US military is substantially higher than in the general public (Blosnich et al., 2014; James et al., 2016; Zucker, 2018). Yet gender and sexual minority veterans remain an underserved subgroup of the military population.

LGBTQ+ veterans are at a heightened risk for homelessness, victimization (Dardis et al., 2017), poor mental health (Cochran et al., 2013; Brown & Jones, 2016), poor physical health (Blosnich et al., 2013), death (Blosnich et al., 2014), and other negative outcomes (Harrison-Quintana & Herman, 2012; Meadows et al., 2018). Further, they may have unique service needs or may face different barriers when attempting to access services via the VHA compared with their heterosexual and cisgender veteran counterparts (Bryant & Schilt, 2008; Simpson et al., 2013; Chen et al., 2017). In this chapter, we outline some of these unique needs of LGBTQ+ military veterans, followed by the common barriers LGBTQ+ people may face when attempting to utilize services to address those needs. We close by making recommendations to improve the accessibility and utilization of services for this population.

The needs of LGBTQ+ veterans

Relative to the general population, American military veterans face disproportionate amounts of homelessness (Khadduri & Culhane, 2010; Fargo et al., 2012), poverty (Fargo et al., 2012), suicide (US Department of Veterans Affairs, 2020), and mental illness (Pemberton et al., 2016). LGBTQ+ veterans, however, are at particularly high risk for experiencing these and other issues. For example, LGBTQ+ veterans are more likely to experience adverse mental health outcomes compared with gender and sexual minorities in the general population, as well as compared with their heterosexual and cisgender veteran peers (Blosnich et al., 2013; Cochran et al., 2013; Meadows et al., 2018). As evidence, Blosnich et al. (2013) found that, compared with sexual minority females in the general population, lesbian and bisexual female veterans were more than twice as likely to experience frequent mental distress. Compared with their heterosexual female veteran peers, sexual minority female veterans had approximately three times the odds of experiencing frequent mental distress and of reporting low satisfaction with life (Blosnich et al., 2013). Further, according to a study conducted by Cochran et al. (2013), LGB veterans were more likely to screen positive for post-traumatic stress disorder (PTSD), depression, and alcohol misuse compared with an existing sample of veterans pulled from the Veteran Integrated Service Network (VISN) 20 Data Warehouse. Lastly, a study conducted by the RAND Corporation revealed that LGBT military personnel were more likely than their non–LGBT counterparts to have a history of severe depression, self-injury, suicidal ideation, and suicide attempts (Meadows et al., 2018).

In addition to poor mental health outcomes, LGBTQ+ veterans also have poor physical health outcomes (Blosnich et al., 2013; Anderson-Carpenter & Rutledge, 2020). Compared with gender and sexual minority females in the general population, lesbian and bisexual female veterans are more likely to smoke cigarettes and to lack adequate sleep (Blosnich et al., 2013). Additionally, compared with heterosexual veterans, bisexual veterans were at greater risk of misusing prescription opioids (Anderson-Carpenter & Rutledge, 2020). Lastly, LGBTQ+ veterans experience high rates of victimization. Indeed, Dardis et al. (2017) found that lesbian, bisexual, and questioning female veterans were more likely than cisgender female veterans to experience sexual, physical, and emotional intimate partner violence, including stalking. Mattocks et al. (2012) revealed in their study that LGB veterans were more likely to experience military sexual trauma compared with their heterosexual veteran counterparts. Similarly, Meadows et al. (2018) found LGBT service members were more likely to report experiencing physical abuse and nonconsensual sexual contact than non-LGBT military personnel.

Previous research has also focused on transgender populations specifically (Harrison-Quintana & Herman, 2012; Brown & Jones, 2014, 2015, 2016; Blosnich et al., 2015). Not only are transgender service members less likely to be open about their gender identity than trans people in the general population (Harrison-Quintana & Herman, 2012), but they are also at a disproportionately higher risk for a variety of negative outcomes. Using data from the National Transgender Discrimination Survey (NTDS), Harrison-Quintana and Herman (2012, p. 47) noted that transgender veterans were three times more likely than the general population to be homeless and that experiencing discrimination was common. Indeed, 14 percent of transgender veterans said that they had been evicted from a home or apartment and nearly one in four reported being refused medical treatment due to bias (Harrison-Quintana & Herman, 2012). In an extensive study of 5,135 transgender veterans, Brown and Jones (2016, p. 127) found that they are more likely to experience serious health issues such as heart disease, renal disease, diabetes, eating disorders, traumatic brain injuries, PTSD, depression, and suicidal ideation (see also Tucker et al., 2019), among many other physical and mental health concerns. Further, Blosnich et al. (2014) found that transgender veterans were more likely to die as a result of their physical and mental health disorders. Additionally, transgender veterans were twice as likely as cisgender veterans to be involved with the criminal justice system and to experience military sexual trauma (Brown & Jones, 2015).

Barriers to utilizing services for LGBTQ+ veterans

All the aforementioned factors combined result in a high need for services. Indeed, cisgender and heterosexual veterans in the general population already experience great disparity in access to care for their needs (for example, see Kehle et al., 2011), but the disparity is far greater for LGBTQ+ veterans. Existing research indicates that VHA services are underutilized by gender and sexual minority veterans. As evidence, Simpson et al. (2013) found that only 45.8 percent of their sample of 356 LGB veterans reported lifetime VHA healthcare utilization and only 28.7 percent had used VHA services in the past year. Likewise, Chen et al. (2017) found that more than one-third of their sample of 201 transgender veterans reported never accessing healthcare services through Veterans Affairs (VA).

It is important to highlight that regardless of what policies are currently in place, many LGBTQ+ veterans may not ever actively seek out certain services related to their gender identity or sexual orientation due to the possibility of being forcefully discharged or experiencing other repercussions at a later date because these policies are susceptible to shifting political climates. Similarly, another salient barrier to utilizing services for LGBTQ+ veterans is fear of or past experiences with discrimination either in the military or outside the military (Bryant & Schilt, 2008; Shipherd et al., 2012; Simpson et al., 2013; Rosentel et al., 2016; Chen et al., 2017). Just over 25 percent of LGB veterans in Simpson et al.'s (2013) study reported avoiding VHA services due to concerns about stigmatization. Similarly, approximately one in five transgender veterans reported that they previously experienced discriminatory treatment by a doctor when seeking or receiving care through the VHA (Bryant & Schilt, 2008). Discriminatory treatment can involve the failure to use pronouns that aligned with their gender identity or the denial of services (Kerrigan, 2012; Rosentel et al., 2016). Additionally, transgender veterans reported concerns regarding lack of privacy and safety when accessing VA facilities (Chen et al., 2017; Dietert et al., 2017). These negative experiences have the potential to influence whether or not LGBTQ+ veterans actively seek care, as well as whether or not they will continue with ongoing treatment.

Transgender veterans can also be impacted by other exclusionary behaviors. In a qualitative analysis of 201 transgender veterans' experiences, Chen et al. (2017) noted a pattern of discrimination in veteran support groups. For instance, although women's support groups for military sexual trauma exist (Mattocks et al., 2012), one participant in Chen et al.'s (2017) study noted that she was specifically excluded from cisgender women's spaces. Indeed, prior research on both trans people and LGB people in the general population has highlighted exclusionary practices as a common barrier to accessing shelter services (Carlson, 2016). According to the National Coalition of Anti-Violence Programs (Waters, 2016), 61.6 percent of LGBTQ victims who sought help from a shelter were denied services due to their sexual orientation or gender identity. Relatedly, the United States Transgender Survey (USTS) found that 29 percent of transgender individuals who sought assistance from a shelter were turned away due to their gender presentation, and nearly one in ten were thrown out of the shelter once staff learned that they were transgender (James et al., 2016). Transgender women specifically are viewed as invaders when attempting to access women-centered shelter services and are often denied access to these services unless they are able to pass as female (Ard & Makadon, 2011; Goodmark, 2013). More frequently, trans women are referred to men's homeless shelters where they are forced to present as male (Goodmark, 2013). The USTS also found that 70 percent of trans people that stayed in a shelter reported some form of mistreatment due to their gender identity (James et al., 2016). For veterans, these types of exclusionary practices are especially concerning given the high rates of homelessness found among veterans who are also LGBTQ+, particularly transgender people who only have access to 'gendered' shelters (Harrison-Quintana & Herman, 2012).

Transgender veterans may also face further difficulty when attempting to receive transition-specific care through the VHA, such as hormone replacement therapy (HRT) or gender-affirming surgeries. As evidence, in a study conducted by Rosentel et al. (2016), transgender veteran patients often reported delays in receiving care through the VHA due to lack of provider knowledge and the need to be referred to more knowledgeable medical professionals. Further, transgender veteran patients reported physician hesitancy in authorizing hormone therapy and poor promotion of transition-related care (Rosentel et al., 2016). Many transgender veterans may also face unique administrative barriers because incorrect paperwork (that is, their name and gender not matching formal government documents) can cause issues when accessing VA care and other service benefits, such as the G.I. Bill (Chen et al., 2017). Although it is possible for a transgender patient's name and gender to be modified on military medical records by submitting a letter from their physician attesting to the fact that they identify as a gender that differs from their service records, this is a costly and time-consuming hurdle that also requires legal documentation (such as a birth certificate or passport) reflecting that their name and gender have been legally amended (Dietert et al., 2017).

Recommendations for improving accessibility and utilization of services for LGBTQ+ veterans

Informed by the literature, we suggest the following to improve the accessibility and utilization of services for LGBTQ+ veterans: (1) culturally competent care, (2) effective staff education and reviews, (3) fostering strong social support networks, and (4) macro-level structural changes. Each of these recommendations is discussed in further detail.

Veterans Services Officers (VSOs) often describe using a 'one size fits all' approach to veterans' services because 'a veteran is a veteran' (Ahlin & Douds, 2018, p. 3173). While it is a commendable aspiration to treat every veteran equally, this perspective erases the unique needs gender and sexual minority veterans have and, thus, limits access to culturally competent care. Culturally competent care refers to the ability of healthcare practitioners and organizations to provide adequate care to patients with diverse backgrounds, values, beliefs, and behaviors while also adapting services to meet patients' unique service needs (Ricca et al., 2018; Kahle & Rosenbaum, 2020). Therefore, culturally competent treatment for LGBTQ+ people should be a priority in the VHA (Shipherd et al., 2012; Ahlin & Douds, 2018). Beginning in 2016, the VHA has required the assignment of a clinical staff member as an LGBT patient advocate at each facility through the LGBT Veteran Care Coordinator (VCC) program (Henrickson, 2019; Valentine et al., 2019). Most LGBT VCCs report high self-efficacy in fulfilling the responsibilities associated with their role, with 65 percent reporting that their facilities had launched websites detailing LGBT-relevant services along with applicable VHA policies (Valentine et al., 2019). Further, all LGBT VCCs included in Valentine et al.'s (2019) report used items such as lapel pins, rainbow lanyards, and posters to create warm and welcoming environments (Valentine et al., 2019). Service providers should also post non-discrimination policies in visible locations, use inclusive outreach materials that depict images of LGBTQ+ veterans, and use gender-neutral or patient-preferred terminology. While subtle, these strategies signal and affirm that LGBTQ+ veterans are welcome.

Further, effective staff education on LGBTQ+-relevant services has the potential to increase the number of LGBTQ+ veterans that seek care, which has the potential to lead to better care among this population that can ultimately promote good health and prevent disease (Henrickson, 2019). LGBT VCCs could be a valuable resource for providing this kind of continuing education to staff in-house. Still, service providers should not only be educated but take actionable steps to make their services accessible to LGBTQ+ veterans. For example, Kauth and colleagues (2019) note that following the repeal of DADT, although VA medical services have educational programs in place to increase cultural sensitivity toward LGBTQ+ veterans, only a minority of LGBTQ+ reported that the VA is actually welcoming (see also Mark et al., 2019, p. 88). Therefore, LGBT VCC programs might consider conducting internal reviews to address issues as they come up.

There is a wealth of literature that suggests a strong social support network is greatly beneficial for LGBTQ+ people's mental health and for their ability to cope with stressors (for example, see Meyer, 2003; Budge et al., 2013). More specifically, various scholars have recognized the benefits of having support groups (Lutwak et al., 2014; Sherman et al., 2014; Chen et al., 2017; Drebring et al., 2018). For example, Chen et al. (2017, p. 70) concluded that knowing other transgender veterans (through online and offline support groups as well as other advocacy groups) was associated with a positive self-image. As such, the VHA should encourage the development of support groups for LGBTQ+ veterans at all medical facilities. It could also be beneficial if VA housing assistance could identify LGBTQ-friendly and inclusive housing options not only to address the disparity in homelessness, but also to help foster stronger social support networks (Proctor & Krusen, 2017).

There are also structural issues that are worth considering, even if macro-level change is slow to occur. For example, Evans (2015) noted that one of the greatest challenges faced by female LGB service members is a lack of support from military leadership, military peers, and military-affiliated organizations. Since DADT has been repealed, and because LGBTQ+ service members experience disproportionate levels of negative experiences, military groups as a whole would greatly benefit from diversity and inclusion training to ensure that all veterans can coexist in welcoming environments and are able to adequately access services. Further, on the issue of adequate access to medical care, such as HRT and gender-affirming surgeries, there is a strong argument to be made that it would be more unethical to *not* provide this type of care for armed services veterans (and, arguably, existing servicemembers) because of the significant positive impact on both their mental and physical health (Kuzon et al., 2018).

Conclusion

Although DADT has been repealed, the recent reinstatement of exclusionary policies toward transgender service members demonstrates that the political climate can sometimes have an impact on the experiences of LGBTQ+ people in the military (because, as was implied to be the case when DADT was in effect, just because LGBTQ+ service members are 'banned' does not mean that they will not exist in the military). Therefore, the VA and other veterans' advocacy associations have a strong incentive to be more inclusive of LGBTQ+ veterans, who have a high need for services. Despite all the challenges and significant barriers to care, existing research does show that LGBTQ+ veterans have high resilience, possibly as a result of trauma and other challenges that may have existed prior to military service (Chen et al., 2017; Ramirez & Bloeser, 2018). Furthermore, as noted by Howe (2018, p. 163), the military has the unique capability of quickly enforcing new policies and procedures once they are in place – these organizations need only take steps toward providing 'the highest medical and ethical standards of care'.

References

Ahlin, E.M. & Douds, A.S. (2018) 'Many shades of green: assessing awareness of differences in mental health care needs among subpopulations of military veterans', *International Journal of Offender Therapy and Comparative Criminology*, 62(10): 3168–3184.

Anderson-Carpenter, K.D. & Rutledge, J.D. (2020) 'Prescription opioid misuse among heterosexual versus lesbian, gay, and bisexual military veterans: evidence from the 2015–2017 National Survey of Drug Use and Health', *Drug and Alcohol Dependence*, 207(1): 1–5. https://doi.org/10.1016/j.drugalcdep.2019.107794

Ard, K.L. & Makadon, H.J. (2011) 'Addressing intimate partner violence in lesbian, gay bisexual, and transgender patients', *Journal of General Internal Medicine*, 26(8): 930–933.

Bérubé, A. (2010) *Coming Out Under Fire: The History of Gay Men and Women in World War II: Twentieth Anniversary Edition*, Chapel Hill: University of North Carolina Press.

Blosnich, J.R., Foynes, M.M., & Shipherd, J.C. (2013) 'Health disparities among sexual minority women veterans', *Journal of Women's Health*, 22(7): 631–636.

Blosnich, J.R., Brown, G.R., Wojcio, S., Jones, K.T., & Bossarte, R.M. (2014) 'Mortality among veterans with transgender-related diagnoses in the Veterans Health Administration, FY2000–2009', *LGBT Health*, 1(4): 269–276.

Blosnich, J.R., Gordon, A.J., & Fine, M.J. (2015) 'Associations of sexual and gender minority status with health indicators, health risk factors, and social stressors in a national sample of young adults with military experience', *Annals of Epidemiology*, 25(9): 661–667.

Brown, G.R. & Jones, K.T. (2014) 'Racial health disparities in a cohort of 5,135 transgender veterans', *Journal of Racial and Ethnic Health Disparities*, 1(4): 257–266.

Brown, G.R. & Jones, K.T. (2015) 'Health correlates of criminal justice involvement in 4,793 transgender veterans', *LGBT Health*, 2(4): 297–305.

Brown, G.R. & Jones, K.T. (2016) 'Mental health and medical health disparities in 5135 transgender veterans receiving healthcare in the Veterans' Health Administration: a case-control study', *LGBT Health*, 3(2): 122–131.

Bryant, K. & Schilt, K. (2008) 'Transgender people in the U.S. military: summary and analysis of the 2008 Transgender American Veterans Association Survey', The Palm Center. https://www.palmcenter.org/wp-content/uploads/2017/12/TGPeopleUSMilitary.pdf

Budge, S.L., Adelson, J.L., & Howard, K.A.S. (2013) 'Anxiety and depression in transgender individuals: the roles of transition status, loss, social support, and coping', *Journal of Counseling and Clinical Psychology*, 81(3): 545–557.

Carlson, R. (2016) 'Shelter response to intimate partner violence in the lesbian, gay, bisexual, and transgender community', Master of Social Work Clinical Research Paper, University of St. Thomas/St. Catherine University, St. Paul, Minnesota. https://sophia.stkate.edu/cgi/viewcontent.cgi?article=1566&context=msw_papers

Chen, J.A., Granato, H., Shipherd, J.C., Simpson, T., & Lehavot, K. (2017) 'A qualitative analysis of transgender veterans' lived experiences', *Psychology of Sexual Orientation and Gender Diversity*, 4(1): 63–74.

Cochran, B.N., Balsam, K.F., Flentje, A., Malte, C.A., & Simpson, T. (2013) 'Mental health characteristics of sexual minority veterans', *Journal of Homosexuality*, 60(2–3): 419–435.

Dardis, C.M., Shipherd, J.C., & Iverson, K.M. (2017) 'Intimate partner violence among women veterans by sexual orientation', *Women & Health*, 57(7): 775–791.

Dietert, M., Dentice, D., & Keig, Z. (2017) 'Addressing the needs of transgender military veterans: better access and more comprehensive care', *Transgender Health*, 2(1): 35–44.

Drebring, C.E., Reilly, E., Henze, K.T., Kelly, M., Russo, A., Smolinsky, J., Gorman, J., & Penk, W.E. (2018) 'Using peer support groups to enhance community integration of veterans in transition', *Psychological Services*, 15(2): 135–145.

Evans, J. (2015) 'Does identification with the LGBTQ community impact reintegration experiences? Female service members' perspectives', Clinical Research Project, St. Catherine University/University of St. Thomas, St. Paul, Minnesota.

Fargo, J., Metraux, S., Byrne, T., Munley, E., Montgomery, A.E., Jones, H., Sheldon, G., Kane, V., & Culhane, D. (2012) 'Prevalence and risk of homelessness among US veterans', *Preventing Chronic Disease*, 9(45): 1–9.

Goodmark, L. (2013) 'Transgender, intimate partner abuse, and the legal system', *Harvard Civil Rights-Civil Liberties Law Review*, 48(1): 51–104.

Harrison-Quintana, J. & Herman, J.L. (2012) 'Still serving in silence: transgender service members and veterans in the National Transgender Discrimination Survey', *LGBTQ Policy Journal*, 3: 39–52.

Henrickson, S.C. (2019) 'Improving care for transgender veterans through staff education', dissertation, Walden University.

Howe, E.G., III (2018) 'Ethical issues regarding LGBT and intersex service members', in E.C. Ritchie, J.E. Wise, & B. Pyle (eds.), *Gay Mental Healthcare Providers and Patients in the Military*, Cham: Springer, pp. 153–164.

James, S.E., Herman, J.L., Rankin, S.R., Keisling, M., Mottet, L.A., & Anafi, M.A. (2016) 'The report of the 2015 U.S. Transgender Survey'. https://transequality.org/sites/default/files/docs/usts/USTS-Full-Report-Dec17.pdf

Kahle, L. & Rosenbaum, J. (2020) 'What staff need to know: using elements of gender-responsive programming to create safer environments for system-involved LGBTQ girls and women', *Criminal Justice Studies*, 34(1): 1–15.

Kauth, M.R., Barrera, T.L., & Latini, D.M. (2019) 'Lesbian, gay, and transgender veterans' experiences in the Veterans Health Administration: positive signs and room for improvement', *Psychological Services*, 16(2): 346–351.

Kehle, S.M., Greer, N., Rutks, I., & Wilt, T. (2011) 'Interventions to improve veterans' access to care: a systematic review of the literature', *Journal of General Internal Medicine*, 26(2): 689–696.

Kerrigan, M.F. (2012) 'Transgender discrimination in the military: the new don't ask, don't tell', *Psychology, Public Policy, and Law*, 18(3): 500–518.

Khadduri, J. & Culhane, D. (2010) 'Veteran homelesness: a supplemental report to the 2010 Annual Homeless Assessment Report to Congress'. https://www.va.gov/HOMELESS/docs/Center/AHAR_Veterans_Report_2010.pdf

Kuzon, W.M., Sluiter, E., & Gast, K. (2018) 'Second thoughts: exclusion of medically necessary gender-affirming surgery for America's armed service veterans', *AMA Journal of Ethics*, 20(4): 403–413.

Lutwak, N., Byne, W., Erickson-Schroth, L., Keig, Z., Shipherd, J.C., Mattocks, K.M., & Kauth, M.R. (2014) 'Transgender veterans are inadequately understood by health care providers', *Military Medicine*, 179(5): 483–485.

McDermott, J. (2016) 'Few vets expelled under "don't ask" seek remedy', *Military Times*, June 24. https://www.militarytimes.com/veterans/2016/06/24/few-vets-expelled-under-don-t-ask-seek-remedy/

Manuel, V. (2020) 'Trump's transgender military ban: policy, law, and litigation', *Tulane Journal of Law & Sexuality*, 29, 75–91.

Mark, K.M., McNamara, K.A., Gribble, R., Rhead, R., Sharp, M.-L., Stevelink, S.A.M., Schwartz, A., Castro, C., & Fear, N.T. (2019) 'The health and well-being of LGBTQ serving and ex-serving personnel: a narrative review', *International Review of Psychiatry*, 31(1): 75–94.

Mattocks, K.M., Haskell, S.G., Krebs, E.E., Justice, A.C., Yano, E.M., & Brandt, C. (2012) 'Women at war: understanding how women veterans cope with combat and military sexual trauma', *Social Science & Medicine*, 74, 537–545.

Meadows, S.O., Engel, C.C., Collins, R.L., Beckman, R., Cefalu, M., Hawes-Dawson, J., Doyle, M., Kress, A.M., Sontag-Padilla, L., Ramchand, R., & Williams, K.M. (2018) '2015 Department of Defense health-related behaviors survey'. R. Corporation.

Meyer, I.H. (2003) 'Prejudice, social stress, and mental health in lesbian, gay, and bisexual populations: conceptual issues and research evidence', *Psychological Bulletin*, 129(5): 674–697.

Pemberton, M.R., Forman-Hoffman, V.L., Lipari, R.N., Ashley, O.S., Heller, D.C., & Williams, M.R. (2016) 'Prevalence of past year substance use and mental illness by veteran status in a nationally representative sample', *CBHSQ Data Review*, November. https://www.samhsa.gov/data/sites/default/files/NSDUH-DR-VeteranTrends-2016/NSDUH-DR-VeteranTrends-2016.pdf

Proctor, A.R. & Krusen, N.E. (2017) 'Time to ask and tell: voices of older gay and bisexual male veterans regarding community services', *Journal of Gay & Lesbian Studies*, 29(4): 415–425.

Ramirez, H. & Bloeser, K. (2018) 'Creating safe spaces: best practices for clinicians working with sexual and gender minority military service members and veterans', in E.C. Ritchie, J.E. Wise, & B. Pyle (eds.), *Gay Mental Healthcare Providers and Patients in the Military*, Cham: Springer, pp. 105–123.

Ricca, P., Wahlskog, C., & Bergren, M.D. (2018) 'Enhancing cultural sensitivity in a community health care setting for LGBTQ patients', *Journal of Community Health Nursing*, 35(4): 165–178.

Rosentel, K., Hill, B.J., Lu, C., & Barnett, J.T. (2016) 'Transgender veterans and the Veterans Health Administration: exploring the experiences of transgender veterans in the Veterans Affairs healthcare system', *Transgender Health*, 1(1): 108–116.

Sherman, M.D., Kauth, M.R., Shipherd, J.C., & Street, R.L., Jr. (2014) 'Communication between VA providers and sexual and gender minority veterans: a pilot study', *Psychological Services*, 11(2): 235–242.

Shipherd, J.C., Mizock, L., Maguen, S., & Green, K.E. (2012) 'Male-to-female transgender veterans and VA health care utilization', *International Journal of Sexual Health*, 24, 78–87.

Simpson, T.L., Balsam, K.F., Cochran, B.N., Lehavot, K., & Gold, S.D. (2013) 'Veterans Administration health care utilization among sexual minority veterans', *Psychological Services*, 10(2): 223–232.

Sobel, S., Cleghorn, J.M., & Osburn, C.D. (2001) 'Conduct unbecoming: the fifth annual report on "Don't Ask, Don't Tell, Don't Pursue"', S. L. D. Network.

Tucker, R.P., Pardue-Bourgeois, S., Snow, A., Bradstreet, M., & Cerel, J. (2019) 'The relationship between suicide-related exposure and personal history of suicidal behavior in transgender and gender-diverse veterans', *LGBT Health*, 6(7): 335–341.

US Department of Veterans Affairs (2020) '2020 National Veteran Suicide Prevention Annual Report'. https://www.mentalhealth.va.gov/docs/data-sheets/2020/2020-National-Veteran-Suicide-Prevention-Annual-Report-11-2020-508.pdf

Valentine, S.E., Shipherd, J.C., Smith, A.M., & Kauth, M.R. (2019) 'Improving affirming care for sexual and gender minority veterans', *Psychological Services*, advance online publication. https://doi.org/10.1037/ser0000378

Waters, E. (2016) 'Lesbian, gay, bisexual, transgender, queer, and HIV-affected intimate partner violence in 2015', National Coalition of Anti-Violence Programs. https://avp.org/wp-content/uploads/2017/04/2015_ncavp_lgbtqipvreport.pdf

Zucker, B. (2018) 'Transcending limitations: obstacles to benefits for transgender veterans', *Federal Circuit Bar Journal*, 27(3): 321–347.

19

Barriers to Reporting, Barriers to Services: Challenges for Transgender Survivors of Intimate Partner Violence and Sexual Victimization

Danielle C. Slakoff and Jaclyn A. Siegel

On July 30, 2019, 22-year-old Tracy Williams was found stabbed to death in Houston, Texas. Shortly after, her boyfriend was charged in connection with her murder (Tripathi, 2020). According to her friends, Tracy was an artistic woman who was experiencing homelessness at the time of her death. Tracy's tragic story is just one of countless examples of intimate partner violence (IPV) and sexual violence perpetrated against members of the transgender community. In this chapter, we provide a non-exhaustive overview of the barriers transgender individuals face when seeking help for IPV and sexual violence. We also address the importance of including transgender women in initiatives to protect and support survivors.

Sexual violence is defined as 'sexual abuse occurring at any time in the life span, including instances of sexual harassment' (Gentlewarrior, 2009, p. 1). While violence does substantial short- and long-term damage to survivors' physical and mental well-being (WHO, n.d., para. 1), trans survivors of physical and/or sexual victimization are significantly more likely to report attempting suicide, sometimes multiple times (Testa et al., 2012). Relatedly, IPV can be defined as 'physical violence, sexual violence, stalking, or psychological harm by a current or former partner or spouse' and is a worldwide public health issue (CDC, 2018, para. 1). Survivors may experience physical injury, physical health issues, and mental health issues such as depression as a result of victimization (CDC, 2019). Survivors of IPV also pay a high economic price for their victimization: due to abuse, survivors often work less, and they may spend money in order to receive mental and physical healthcare (Peterson et al., 2018). Importantly, for people experiencing IPV and/or sexual abuse, the decision to leave the situation can be dangerous and difficult. Intimate partner homicide victims are most likely to be killed as they attempt to flee (National Coalition Against Domestic Violence, n.d.), and many IPV survivors return to their abusers several times before severing ties completely (National Domestic Violence Hotline, 2013).

For the purposes of this chapter, we define transgender (trans) individuals as 'people whose gender identity and/or expression is different from cultural expectations based on the sex they were assigned at birth' (HRC, n.d., para. 5). We also include nonbinary individuals under the 'transgender umbrella' (see Davidson, 2007). Although some entities define transgender people as those who have undergone gender confirmation surgery or those who have begun taking hormone medications, we make no such distinction. Indeed, not all trans folx want surgery or hormone therapy (Israel & Tarver, 1997) and many trans folx do not have access to them (Dubov & Fraenkel, 2018). We define cisgender individuals as those whose gender identity matches their sex at birth (Cava, 2016).

Prevalence of IPV and sexual abuse in the trans community

Research on the prevalence of IPV and sexual violence victimization for trans people is sparse, as large-scale surveys generally focus on the experiences of cisgender survivors (Calton et al., 2015). However, extant research indicates transgender people are at an increased risk for IPV and sexual violence (Stotzer, 2009). Indeed, in their survey of gay, lesbian, bisexual, and transgender youth in the United States, Dank et al. (2014) found transgender youth 'reported some of the highest victimization rates of physical dating violence, psychological dating abuse, cyber dating abuse, and sexual coercion' compared with the other groups (p. 852). In another study, Langenderfer-Magruder et al. (2016) found trans people had a significantly higher rate of IPV victimization than cisgender people. Similarly, Hooley (1996) found a significant portion of trans folx had experienced assaults publicly or within the home; specifically, 59 percent of trans folx had experienced assault, and nearly 55 percent had been sexually assaulted (as cited in Moran & Sharpe, 2002).

There are various reasons why transgender individuals in abusive relationships may struggle to flee their situations. First, they may struggle with financial or emotional dependence on an abuser (McGee, 2004).

Indeed, trans folx are chronically underemployed, so trans survivors may be especially susceptible to financial abuse (Greenberg, 2012). Abusers may use emotional and/or financial dependence to coerce their survivors into staying with them; moreover, they may threaten to 'out' them as transgender if they try to leave (Messinger, 2020).

Sexual victimization is another pressing issue within the trans community. In the National Transgender Discrimination Survey, 64 percent of trans respondents reported being survivors of sexual assault (Grant et al., 2011). Moreover, Fernández-Rouco et al. (2017) found transgender people in Spain had high rates of sexual violence victimization during their childhoods as well as a high rate of sexual violence victimization later in their lives. Moreover, Gender PAC's (1997) First National Survey of Transgender Violence found that nearly 60 percent of trans respondents were survivors of harassment or violence at some point in their lives, and many reported incidents within the past year.

Taken together, these findings show that transgender people are at high risk for IPV and sexual victimization and may face heightened barriers to exiting their abusive situations. Clearly, equitable and inclusive programming is needed to help all survivors, including trans folx (Slakoff & Lopez, 2021). However, existing supports do not provide adequate safety and security for transgender women.

Hotline support available to survivors of IPV and sexual violence

In general, survivors of IPV and sexual assault can receive confidential services and support via phone or internet-based hotlines. In the US, IPV survivors can call the National Domestic Violence Hotline for help, and they can find contact information for state-based (and other nationwide) hotlines on the National Domestic Violence (2020a) website. When a victim calls the National Domestic Violence Hotline, they can speak with an advocate to receive general support, discuss healthy aspects of a relationship, or receive information about resources available to them (National Domestic Violence Hotline, 2020b). Importantly, although trans IPV survivors can call the National Domestic Violence hotline and speak with an advocate, there are hotlines listed on the National Domestic Violence (2020a) website that specialize in advocacy for LGBT survivors. Some of the LGBT-friendly organizations listed include FORGE-Forward, the LGBT National Hotline, and the Trans Lifeline (National Domestic Violence Hotline, 2020a).

Similarly, the US-based National Sexual Assault Hotline, run by the Rape, Abuse, & Incest National Network (RAINN), provides a place where all survivors of sexual assault in the US can call for confidential information and be connected to local resources (RAINN, 2020a). If you search for

'LGBTQ' on the RAINN (2020b) website, there is information about extra barriers LGBTQ survivors may face when disclosing sexual assault, such as fears of being 'outed' or concerns that faith-based community centers will not offer support. Like the National Domestic Violence (2020a) website, the RAINN (2020b) website provides additional resources for LGBTQ survivors to call for support.

Undoubtedly, these hotlines are a vital resource for all survivors of IPV and sexual assault and can provide a safe avenue to receive initial support and information. However, hotlines provide only emotional support, and not direct protection from violence. Therefore, it is important to understand the numerous barriers to reporting and services trans survivors face when looking to report or leave unsafe situations. In the section that follows, we delineate barriers to reporting and services for trans survivors, and we explain some of the situational factors that disproportionately impact trans survivors' abilities to seek help and support safely.

Barriers to reporting and barriers to service for trans survivors

'Legal limbo'

It is not uncommon for trans folx to live in 'legal limbo', in which their identification papers have a gender marker on them that does not match their own experience of their gender (Greenberg, 2012). It can be tremendously burdensome for a trans person to change their gender markers on their identification, and some states in the US require certification from a medical professional for a change to occur on identification papers (Movement Advancement Project, 2020). As of this writing, in nine states within the US, a person must show proof of surgery, a court order, or an amended birth certificate to change their gender marker on their driver's license (Movement Advancement Project, 2020). The focus on completed gender confirmation surgery is especially problematic when one considers that it can cost over $70,000 (Mottet & Ohle, 2006). Simply put, the process of changing gender markers can be costly and difficult (see Mottet, 2013).

Updated identification papers are important because police, when called for service, may ask for them, and those whose legal identifiers do not match their experienced gender may be at risk for being misgendered or deadnamed. Moreover, access to services and benefits may be decided based on the gender marker on a person's identification papers/cards (Greenberg, 2012). If a trans victim of IPV or sexual violence is in 'legal limbo', they may be unable to access the life-saving services survivors need or they may only have access to services designed for survivors of their sex at birth, as described in more detail in the section 'Barriers to seeking shelter services'.

Police and correctional staff interactions

For all survivors of IPV and sexual violence, reporting their victimization to law enforcement agents may present challenges: survivors may be worried that their concerns will be dismissed, or they may feel revictimized by a less than understanding police force (Maier, 2008). Indeed, in a recent US Transgender Survey, 58 percent of transgender respondents who had experiences with law enforcement reported 'harassment, abuse, or other mistreatment by the police' (National Center for Transgender Equality, 2018). These negative experiences range from insensitivity and trivialization to blatant dismissal of reports. Transgender women from minoritized racial backgrounds may face additional concerns about police brutality and insensitivity.

There are numerous stories of police insensitivity toward the trans community. For example, one transgender man – who is only referred to in reports by his pseudonym, Tom – reported an instance of stranger sexual assault to the police. The police allegedly asked invasive questions such as '[When did the assailant] realize that you didn't have a dick?' and failed to support him in completing a rape kit (Sullivan, 2019). In another incident, a transgender person named Atif Siddiqi went on a date with a person they met online and was raped and robbed. When they reported it to the police, the police allegedly failed to take the report seriously, going so far as to laugh at their distress (Krishnan, 2018). In another incident, Brandon Teena, a transgender man, was ridiculed after his rape; reports stated that the sheriff referred to Brandon as 'it' and 'ask[ed] him if he put a sock in his pants and pretended to be a boy' (as described by Buist & Stone, 2014, p. 41). Brandon was later murdered by his attackers when they discovered he had reported the rape to police. Put simply, the trivialization of transgender people's experiences has both psychological and material consequences for those victimized by IPV and sexual violence.

Notably, transgender women housed in men's prisons are 13 times more likely than cisgender men to be sexually assaulted while incarcerated (National Center for Transgender Equality, 2018). These experiences often go unreported; however, several lawsuits have been filed against prisons for the sexual violence gender-nonconforming and trans people have faced. As an example, in 2020, a trans woman named C. Jay Smith filed a federal lawsuit against the California Department of Corrections and Rehabilitation. She alleges that the prison staff failed to investigate after she reported being sexually abused and that staff members retaliated against her for reporting, potentially adding up to ten years to her sentence for speaking out (Lang & Sosin, 2020). At the time of this writing, the case is ongoing. Further attention is needed on transgender people's sexual victimization while incarcerated.

Lack of social support and the challenges of leaving

Due to factors such as prejudice and discrimination, trans people may have lower levels of social support than cisgender people and are at heightened risk for family rejection (Aparicio-García et al., 2018). This potential lack of social support is important because IPV survivors often disclose their victimization experiences to at least one informal supporter, such as a friend, family member, or coworker, and survivors often feel the emotional support given by that person is helpful to their healing process (Sylaska & Edwards, 2014). And, although not all sexual assault survivors disclose what occurred to others, the ones that do may endure further adverse mental health consequences if the person to whom they disclose reacts negatively (Jacques-Tiura et al., 2010).

While some IPV survivors may rely on family support, transgender IPV survivors may not have the same support in place (Guadalupe-Diaz & Jasinski, 2017), limiting their options for safe escape from abuse. Indeed, transgender survivors of IPV or sexual violence may feel forced to stay in unsafe situations out of fear of experiencing homelessness or being rejected by family members. People within the homeless population have a higher rate of victimization than people who are not experiencing homelessness (Fitzpatrick et al., 1993). Moreover, many homeless shelters classify people's sleeping arrangements based on their sex at birth (Shelton, 2015), so transgender survivors of abuse who have left their homes may find themselves in an extremely distressing situation. (We discuss challenges unique to accessing shelters in more detail in the next section.)

Homelessness, in turn, is a significant predictor of engaging in sex work (Wilson et al., 2009). While people engage in sex work for a variety of reasons (Murphy, 2010), those who do so are at a high risk of sexual victimization while working (Sanders & Campbell, 2007). Moreover, due to sex work's illegality in some locations, a transgender person who is victimized while engaging in sex work may be arrested if they call police for help. As described above, trans people face a heightened risk of sexual violence in jail or prison settings (Bromdal et al., 2019), so shelters undoubtedly provide safer spaces for sex workers to heal without police involvement. Taken together, these findings suggest that failing to provide safe and supportive housing to transgender women may ultimately put them at higher risk of experiencing further harm.

Barriers to seeking shelter services

In 2020, the Trump–Pence administration's Department of Housing and Urban Development proposed a rule that would eliminate several non-discrimination protections currently provided by the Equal Access Rule

(EAR). The EAR, proposed by the Obama administration in 2012 and updated in 2016, prohibits discrimination in government-funded housing based on sexual orientation and gender identity (effectively providing federal protections for transgender survivors). The Trump–Pence proposal would provide shelters with a list of reasons to deny services to certain community members. At the time of this writing, it is unclear whether this rule will pass (Meyer, 2020).

However, at the present time, the EAR is still in effect, and survivors of IPV or sexual violence who need secure housing cannot legally be denied access on the basis of their 'sexual orientation, gender identity, or marital status' (Housing and Urban Development Department, 2016). Despite legal protection, trans survivors may still experience (illegal) discrimination or perceive shelter services to be 'unavailable' or 'unwelcoming' (Messinger, 2020, p. 121). Indeed, research suggests that survivors of IPV or sexual violence rarely consider shelters as an option (Guadalupe-Diaz & Jasinski, 2017).

Unfortunately, despite the protections in place, many shelter spaces are still discriminating against trans people (Shelton, 2015; Apsani, 2018). For example, some trans women seeking safety in domestic violence shelters are denied service (Apsani, 2018). Similarly, only a fraction of shelters for unhoused people accommodated trans women appropriately (Rooney et al., 2016). Homeless shelters in the US are often divided on biological sex lines, meaning that trans folx may face psychological distress in these settings because they are forced to categorize themselves with people who share their sex assigned at birth (Mottet & Ohle, 2006). Shelter programs that accept trans survivors may not be sensitive to the unique needs of transgender service users (Seelman, 2015), and trans people may experience transphobia from staff and other patrons (Mottet & Ohle, 2006).

Responding to concerns about trans women in shelter spaces

There is some debate regarding the appropriateness of transgender survivors in domestic violence shelters, which often serve as '[cisgender] women-only safe spaces' for those victimized by IPV and sexual violence to explore 'female empowerment … and find a "sisterhood" of support' (Apsani, 2018, p. 1692). This setup has been criticized by intersectional feminists and LGBT+ activists as centering the experiences of heterosexual women and failing to recognize the unique ways that IPV and domestic violence influence the lives of women who are not cisgender, wealthy, or white (Apsani, 2018). Nevertheless, some cisgender women who utilize shelter services may feel unsafe in spaces where what they perceive to be 'male bodies' are present, regardless of that person's gender identity and expression (Apsani, 2018). As described by Mottet and Ohle (2006), 'shelters fear that a transgender woman ... may sexually or physically assault another resident, or that such a possibility will trigger fears for residents who have been traumatized by abuse and sexual assault' (p. 87). In our personal and professional opinions, these fears are largely unfounded, as 'transgender women are no more dangerous than other women' (Mottet & Ohle, 2006, p. 87). Indeed, transgender people are more at risk of being victimized within shelters than of perpetrating violence (Mottet & Ohle, 2006).

For staff, it may seem daunting to navigate people's fears surrounding the presence of trans folx in shared shelter spaces, but staff can take steps to ensure the safety and comfort of all by engaging in educational conversations (Mottet & Ohle, 2006). An important first step in this conversation may be to ensure concerned patrons that no men are allowed within the shelter, and that trans women are women and need support just like they do (a 'conversation starter' described by Mottet & Ohle, 2006). Moreover, staff can reiterate their policies surrounding violence within the shelter space and explain that the policies cover every woman in the facility (Mottet & Ohle, 2006).

Put simply, by excluding transgender women from these spaces, the safety and well-being of cisgender women is privileged over the safety and well-being of transgender women (Apsani, 2018). Transgender women are more vulnerable to harm and have fewer resources for coping. If transgender women have nowhere to go, they risk additional harms at the hands of police, as well as an increased likelihood of homelessness and intimate partner and sexual violence.

Conclusion: recommendations for the future and the need for queer criminology

Given the high rate of sexual and intimate partner violence victimization trans people face, it is clear that safe, inclusive spaces and programming for trans survivors are sorely needed (Slakoff & Lopez, 2021). Many trans survivors avoid shelter services due to concerns of being misgendered or discriminated against by other survivors or staff (Guadalupe-Diaz & Jasinski, 2017). While LGBTQ-specific shelters and programs are viewed by trans survivors as helpful (Messinger, 2020), there are far fewer of these shelters. These shelters also receive less funding and attention and may therefore become overburdened. Indeed, a better step toward inclusive programming for trans survivors is a focus on training workers within intimate partner and sexual violence shelters, with a purposeful focus on giving trans survivors privacy, respect, and protection while they heal (Mottet & Ohle, 2006).

Improvements to the reporting and service experiences of transgender survivors must occur at every level of support. To that end, we recommend that diversity and inclusion trainings for police, hotline workers, and shelter staff integrate information about the unique vulnerabilities facing transgender individuals. Shelter staff should welcome transgender women within their spaces and have transparent policies for assisting survivors with their emotional and physical needs while they receive shelter support. Having at least one transgender service provider on staff could also increase the perceived safety and accessibility of that space for trans survivors.

Intersectional feminist thinkers posit that scholars, activists, and practitioners should consider that various oppressions – such as sexism, racism, and transphobia – simultaneously impact women as they experience their lives and interact with others (Bowleg, 2012). To date, little research has been conducted to differentiate the experiences of transgender women along racial lines. However, we anticipate that transgender women of color (such as Black and/or Indigenous women), as well as women with physical or psychological disabilities, may face additional hardships while seeking assistance after victimization. We encourage exploration into these and other intersectional issues when conducting future research.

Indeed, we believe a pointed focus on trans women's experiences within (and adjacent to) the criminal justice system is needed to fully understand – and rectify – the issues within the system. These efforts should center the experiences of women whose identities and experiences place them at various axes of oppression, in order to ensure that all people's experiences are accounted for. More to the point, queer criminology – in its focus on queer experiences within the system (Buist & Lenning, 2016) – is a guiding framework for a more inclusive study of the field of criminology and criminal justice.

References

Aparicio-García, M.E., Diaz-Ramiro, E.M., Rubio-Valdehita, S., Lopez-Nunez, M.I., & Garcia-Nieto, I. (2018) 'Health and well-being of cisgender, transgender, and non-binary young people', *International Journal of Environmental Research and Public Health*, 15(10): 1–11.

Apsani, R. (2018) 'Are women's spaces transgender spaces: single sex domestic violence shelters, transgender inclusion, and the equal protection clause', *California Law Review*, 106(5): 1689–1754. http://www.californialawreview.org/print/6-are-womens-spaces-transgender-spaces-single-sex-domestic-violence-shelters-transgender-inclusion-and-the-equal-protection-clause/

Bowleg, L. (2012) 'The problem with the phrase women and minorities: intersectionality—an important theoretical framework for public health', *American Journal of Public Health*, 102(7): 1267–1273.

Bromdal, A., Mullens, A.B., Phillips, T.M., & Gowd, J. (2019) 'Experiences of transgender prisoners and their knowledge, attitudes, and practices regarding sexual behaviors and HIV/STIs: a systematic review', *International Journal of Transgenderism*, 20(1): 4–20.

Buist, C.L. & Lenning, E. (2016) *Queer Criminology*, Abingdon: Routledge.

Buist, C.L. & Stone, C. (2014) 'Transgender survivors and offenders: failures of the United States criminal justice system and the necessity of queer criminology', *Critical Criminology*, 22: 35–47. https://doi.org/10.1007/s10612-013-9224-1

Calton, J., Cattaneo, L.B., & Gebhar, K.T. (2015) 'Barriers to help seeking for lesbian, gay, bisexual, transgender, and queer survivors of intimate partner violence', *Trauma, Violence, and Abuse*, 17(5): 585–600. https://doi.org/10.1177/1524838015585318

Cava, P. (2016) 'Cisgender and cissexual', in N.A. Naples (ed.), *The Wiley Blackwell Encyclopedia of Gender and Sexuality Studies* (1st ed.). https://doi.org/10.1002/9781118663219.wbegss131

CDC (Centers for Disease Control and Prevention) (2018) 'Intimate partner violence'. https://www.cdc.gov/violenceprevention/intimatepartnerviolence/index.html

CDC (Centers for Disease Control and Prevention) (2019) 'Fast facts'. https://www.cdc.gov/violenceprevention/intimatepartnerviolence/fastfact.html

Dank, M., Lachman, P., Zweig, J.M., & Yahner, J. (2014) 'Dating violence experiences of lesbian, gay, bisexual, and transgender youth', *Journal of Youth and Adolescence*, 43(5): 846–857. https://doi.org/10.1007/s10964-013-9975-8

Davidson, M. (2007) 'Seeking refuge under the umbrella: inclusion, exclusion, and organizing within the category *transgender*', *Sexuality Research & Social Policy*, 4(4): 60–80. https://doi.org/10.1525/srsp.2007.4.4.60

Dubov, A. & Fraenkel, L. (2018) 'Facial feminization surgery: the ethics of gatekeeping in transgender health', *American Journal of Bioethics*, 18(12): 3–9. https://doi.org/10.1080/15265161.2018.1531159

Fernández-Rouco, N., Fernández-Fuertes, A.A., Carcedo, R.J., Lázaro-Visa, S., & Gómez-Pérez, E. (2017) 'Sexual violence history and welfare in transgender people', *Journal of Interpersonal Violence*, 32(19): 2885–2907. https://doi.org/10.1177/0886260516657911

Fitzpatrick, K.M., La Gory, M.E., & Ritchey, F.J. (1993) 'Criminal victimization among the homeless', *Justice Quarterly*, 10(3): 353–368. https://doi.org/10.1080/07418829300091881

Gender PAC (1997) 'The First National Survey of Transgender Violence'. http://box5926.temp.domains/~cttransa/genderpac-first-national-survey-of-transgender-violence-1997/

Gentlewarrior, S. (2009) 'Culturally competent service provision to lesbian, gay, bisexual, and transgender survivors of sexual violence', VAWnet. https://vawnet.org/sites/default/files/materials/files/2016-09/AR_LGBTSexualViolence.pdf

Grant, J., Mottet, L., Tanis, J., Harrison, J., Herman, J.L., & Keislin, M. (2011) 'Injustice at every turn: A report of the national transgender discrimination survey', Washington, DC: National Center for Transgender Equality and National Gay and Lesbian Task Force. http://transequality. org/PDFs/NTDS_Report.pdf

Greenberg, K. (2012) 'Still hidden in the closet: trans women and domestic violence', *Berkeley Journal of Gender, Law, and Justice*, 27(2): 198–251.

Guadalupe-Diaz, X.L. & Jasinski, J. (2017) '"I wasn't a priority, I wasn't a victim": Challenges in help seeking for transgender survivors of intimate partner violence', *Violence Against Women*, 23(6): 772–792. https://doi. org/10.1177/1077801216650288

Hooley, J. (1996) 'The Transgender Project', Central Sydney Area Health Authority, Sydney.

Housing and Urban Development Department (2016) 'Equal access in accordance with an individual's gender identity in community planning and development programs'. https://www.federalregister.gov/ documents/2016/09/21/2016-22589/equal-access-in-accordance-with-an-individuals-gender-identity-in-community-planning-and-development

HRC (Human Rights Campaign) (n.d.) 'Sexual orientation and gender identity definitions'. https://www.hrc.org/resources/sexual-orientation-and-gender-identity-terminology-and-definitions

Israel, G.E. & Tarver, D.E. (1997) *Transgender Care: Recommended Guidelines, Practical Information, and Personal Accounts*, Philadelphia, PA: Temple University Press.

Jacques-Tiura, A.J., Tkatch, R., Abbey, A., & Wegner, R. (2010) 'Disclosure of sexual assault: characteristics and implications for posttraumatic stress symptoms among African American and Caucasian survivors', *Journal of Trauma and Dissociation*, 11(2): 174–192. https://doi. org/10.1080/15299730903502938

Krishnan, S. (2018) 'Transgender Montrealer says police laughed at allegations of sexual assault, robbery', CBC, April 13. https://www.cbc.ca/news/ canada/montreal/transgender-robbed-police-discrimination-1.4619785

Lang, N. & Sosin, K. (2020) 'Lawyers say transgender prisoner was "set up" after making #MeToo complaint', NBC News, July 7. https://www. nbcnews.com/feature/nbc-out/lawyers-say-transgender-inmate-was-set-after-making-metoo-complaint-n1233000

Langenderfer-Magruder, L., Whitfield, D.L., Walls, N.E., Kattari, S.K., & Ramos, D. (2016) 'Experiences of intimate partner violence and subsequent police reporting among lesbian, gay, bisexual, transgender, and queer adults in Colorado: comparing rates of cisgender and transgender victimization', *Journal of Interpersonal Violence*, 31(5): 855–871. https://doi. org/10.1177/0886260514556767

McGee, S.G.S. (2004) '20 reasons why she stays: a guide for those who want to help battered women'. http://stopviolence.com/domviol/WhySheSometimesStays.pdf

Maier, S.L. (2008) '"I have heard horrible stories ...": rape victim advocates' perceptions of the revictimization of rape survivors by the police and medical system', *Violence Against Women*, 14(7): 786–808. https://doi.org/10.1177/1077801208320245

Messinger, A.M. (2020) *LGBTQ Intimate Partner Violence: Lessons for Policy, Practice, and Research*, Berkeley: University of California Press.

Meyer, E.M. (2020) 'Advocating for transgender, intersex, and gender nonconforming people's equal access to homeless shelters', *The National Law Review*, 10(281). https://www.natlawreview.com/article/advocating-transgender-intersex-and-gender-nonconforming-people-s-equal-access-to

Moran, L.J. & Sharpe, A.N. (2002) 'Policing the transgender/violence relation', *Current Issues in Criminal Justice*, 13(3): 269–285. https://doi.org/10.1080/10345329.2002.12036234

Mottet, L. (2013) 'Modernizing state vital statistics statutes and policies to ensure accurate gender markers on birth certificates: a good government approach to recognizing the lives of transgender people', *Michigan Journal of Gender & Law*, 19(2): 373–409.

Mottet, L. & Ohle, J. (2006) 'Transitioning our shelters: Making homeless shelters safe for transgender people', *Journal of Poverty*, 10(2): 77–101. https://doi.org/10.1300/J134v10n02_05

Movement Advancement Project (2020) 'Identity document laws and policies'. https://www.lgbtmap.org/equality-maps/identity_document_laws

Murphy, L.S. (2010) 'Understanding the social and economic contexts surrounding women engaged in street-level prostitution', *Issues in Mental Health Nursing*, 31(12): 775–784. https://doi.org/10.3109/01612840.2010.524345

National Center for Transgender Equality (2018) 'Ending abuse of transgender prisoners: a guide for advocates on winning policy change in jails and prisons'. https://transequality.org/endingabuseoftransprisoners

National Coalition Against Domestic Violence (n.d.) 'Why do victims stay?' https://ncadv.org/why-do-victims-stay

National Domestic Violence Hotline (2013) '50 obstacles to leaving: 1–10'. https://www.thehotline.org/2013/06/10/50-obstacles-to-leaving-1-10

National Domestic Violence Hotline (2020a) 'Reporting agency? That's not what we are'. https://www.thehotline.org/resources/reporting-agency-thats-not-what-we-are/

National Domestic Violence Hotline (2020b) 'What to expect when you contact us'. https://www.thehotline.org/help/what-to-expect-when-you-contact-the-hotline/

Peterson, C., Kearns, M.C., McIntosh, W.L., Estefan, L.F., Nicolaidis, C., McCollister, K.E., Gordon, A., & Florence, C. (2018) 'Lifetime economic burden of intimate partner violence among U.S. adults', *American Journal of Preventative Medicine*, 55(4): 433–444. https://doi.org/10.1016/j.amepre.2018.04.049

RAINN (Rape, Abuse, & Incest National Network) (2020a) 'About the national sexual assault hotline'. https://www.rainn.org/about-national-sexual-assault-telephone-hotline

RAINN (Rape, Abuse, & Incest National Network) (2020b) 'LGBTQ survivors of sexual violence'. https://www.rainn.org/articles/lgbtq-survivors-sexual-violence

Rooney, C., Durso, L.E., & Gruberg, S. (2016) 'Discrimination against transgender women seeking access to homeless shelters', Center for American Progress. https://cdn.americanprogress.org/wp-content/uploads/2016/01/06113001/HomelessTransgender.pdf

Sanders, T. & Campbell, R. (2007) 'Designing out vulnerability, building in respect: violence, safety, and sex work policy', *The British Journal of Sociology*, 58(1): 1–19. https://doi.org/10.1111/j.1468-4446.2007.00136.x

Seelman, K.L. (2015) 'Unequal treatment of transgender individuals in domestic violence and rape crisis programs', *Journal of Social Service Research*, 41, 207–325. https://doi.org/10.1080/01488376.2014.987943

Shelton, J. (2015) 'Transgender youth homelessness: understanding programmatic barriers through the lens of cisgenderism', *Children and Youth Services Review*, 59(1): 10–18. https://doi.org/10.1016/j.childyouth.2015.10.006

Slakoff, D.C. & Lopez, V. (2021) 'Inclusivity and equity in criminal justice programming and practices across genders', in L.M. Carter, C.D. Marcum, & C. Blankenship (eds.), *Punishing Gender Past and Present: Examining the Criminal Justice System Across Gendered Experiences*, San Diego, CA: Cognella Publishing.

Stotzer, R.L. (2009) 'Violence against transgender people: a review of United States data', *Aggression and Violent Behavior*, 14(3): 170–179. https://doi.org/10.1016/j.avb.2009.01.006

Sullivan, N. (2019) 'Cape Breton man upset by police questions, actions while reporting sexual assault', *The Cape Breton Post*, November 4. https://www.capebretonpost.com/news/local/special-report-cape-breton-man-upset-by-police-questions-actions-while-reporting-sexual-assault-371961/

Sylaska, K.M. & Edwards, K.M. (2014) 'Disclosure of intimate partner violence to informal social support network members: a review of the literature', *Trauma, Violence, Abuse*, 15(3): 3–21. https://doi.org/10.1177/1524838013496335

Testa, R.J., Sciacca, L.M., Wang, F., Hendricks, M.L., Goldblum, P., Bradford, J., & Bongar, B. (2012) 'Effects of violence on transgender people', *Professional Psychology: Research and Practice*, 43(5): 452–459. https://doi.org/10.1037/a0029604

Tripathi, N. (2020) 'Man who stabbed transgender girlfriend multiple times and dumped her body at gas station parking lot arrested', MEAWW, April 8. https://meaww.com/texas-man-stabbed-transgender-girlfriend-dumped-body-joshua-dominic-bourgeois-tracy-williams

Wilson, E.C., Garofalo, R., Harris, R.D., Herrick, A., Martinez, M., Martinez, J., Belzer, M., & The Transgender Advisory Committee and the Adolescent Medicine Trial Network for HIV/AIDS Intervention (2009) 'Transgender female youth and sex work: HIV risk and a comparison of life factors related to engagement in sex work', *AIDS and Behavior*, 13, 902–913. https://doi.org/10.1007/s10461-008-9508-8

WHO (World Health Organization) (n.d.) 'Sexual violence'. https://www.who.int/reproductivehealth/topics/violence/sexual_violence/en/

Conclusion:
What Does It Mean to Do Justice?
Current and Future Directions
in Queer Criminological
Research and Practice

Lindsay Kahle Semprevivo and Carrie L. Buist

Often times, those of us doing queer criminological work come to the (politically relevant) conclusion that our institutions, communities, interactions, and even psyche must be reconstructed – or deconstructed all together – in order to effectively include the intersections of queer people. A major purpose for this volume was to put queer theoretical and empirical insights into *practice*, something that is often left as a supplementary question to be dealt with in future research. Merging theory and practice as it relates to the criminal legal system touches on a critical need less attended to in queer criminology: reimagining and *doing* justice for queer people.

What does it mean to *do* justice?

This may be a fairly common phrase used among critical scholars, activists, service-oriented professionals, and anyone interested in social justice and inclusion, but what does it really mean to *do* justice to something, whether a common goal, person, or group of people? At its most basic level, the term insinuates treatment in a way that is 'as good as it should be' (Merriam-Webster, 2021). The definition alone denotes an inherent commitment to fairness, accuracy, inclusion, and overall distribution of equality. Barrett and Lynch (2015) suggest that social justice is contingent on the notion that equality is a valued social norm and societies are just when 'they facilitate equality, and unjust when they hamper equality' (p. 386). Unfortunately, the treatment of LGBTQ+ people, people of color – and LGBTQ+ people of color – by the criminal legal system and society at large is far from the depiction of fair, just, or equal.[1] Readers may notice the subversive use of criminal 'legal' system throughout the book, which reflects similar logic as that outlined by Mogul et al. (2011), which demonstrates a focused resistance to the idea that the system treats all people – especially those most likely to be swept up by it – fairly, justly, or equally.

While this volume embraces queer as a marker of identity and community, the volume also embraces its use as a verb or a set of actions that seek to defy, deconstruct (Jakobsen, 1998; Dwyer et al., 2016), and reconstruct our current conceptualizations of applied and service-oriented work in the criminal legal system and beyond. Our hope for this volume was to provide both theoretical and practice-based recommendations that may lead to more fair and equitable treatment of LGBTQ+ folx involved in the criminal legal system. We hope that in doing so, the authors (and anyone who puts their recommendations into practice) will be making a collective step forward in *doing* justice for LGBTQ+ folx.

Major themes that emerged throughout the book

The interdisciplinarity of this book shines through, not only as a reflection of our own objective purposes for the volume but also as a testament to the collective effort that is needed in truly *doing* queer-oriented justice work in the criminal legal system. The book touched on a wide variety of topics across different aspects of the criminal legal system, including advancing theoretical paradigms, LGBTQ+ criminal legal professionals, transforming the system for trans folx, intimate partner violence, juvenile populations, courts, corrections, and the law, social work, and victims services. While each chapter highlights its own theoretical and/or practical applications, several collective themes emerged that reach across all levels of society. In no particular order of importance, the themes are: cultural competency; training, education, and research; trauma-informed care; attending to intersectionality; reducing state harm; and theoretical considerations. It is important to note that many of the authors had significant overlap among these themes and thus they may have been mentioned several times throughout. May that speak not only to the importance of this moment, but also to the vast possibilities that lie ahead if we unite across disciplinary boundaries to confront these issues.

What you may also notice across these themes is the inherent nature of queer criminology to be both identity-driven and deconstructionist in the ways that we queer criminological praxis in order to undo these harms. The discomfort that is felt not only in the existing tension of queer criminology's disciplinary boundaries, but also with working inside and outside a system that disproportionately harms queer, trans, and people of color, should also be embraced. If we have a criminal legal system, how can we work within it to better the lives of LGBTQ+ folx? How do we provide appropriate resources for folx seeking formal help? How do we invest in our communities and local resources in order to deliver services, so that folx don't have to seek formal resources (that may potentially harm them)? All these questions are relevant in our journey forward to making the world a safer place for LGBTQ+ folx. We also recognize that the book itself is not laden with queer criminological theorizing but rather highlights the concepts more broadly in the application of theory. Although theory is discussed and developed, the policy recommendations, the observations, and the lived experiences and/or narratives are presented in this volume with many goals and themes. Here we begin the discussion of those topics with cultural competency.

Cultural competency

Cultural competency is 'the ability to understand, appreciate, and interact with people from cultures or belief systems different from one's own' (DeAngelis, 2015). It includes attitudes, behaviors, and policies that work effectively across cultural settings (Kahle & Rosenbaum, 2020). At face value, researchers and practitioners should see that it is impossible to offer effective care devoid of one's lived experience – which must be recognized differently than one's intake history. Far too often, however, we see one-size-fits-all models of care and services, because there seems to be a sizeable disconnect between 'understanding' and 'appreciating' the role that social inequality plays in our lived experiences. As research and practice moves forward, cultural competency must be a requirement, not an option, and certainly not something that can be dictated within the private/public funding sphere.

Cultural competency is one of the primary recommendations made in Carrillo's case study of Naomi, a 53-year-old Black trans woman who was incarcerated in two separate Virginia facilities. Carrillo notes that correctional staff significantly lacked knowledge of the issues facing trans folx and, as Naomi summarized, were 'unsure of how to handle trans PCIs [people currently incarcerated]'. Carrillo suggests that this clearly needs to be addressed by better training that increases cultural competency among correctional staff. Carrillo recommends that this, combined with standardized enforcement of Prison Rape Elimination Act guidelines and protections, will greatly reduce the vulnerability for mistreatment among trans PCIs. In turn, Felix and Hoffman speak directly against the 'one size fits all' model that veterans' services providers tend to implement, which, they state, erases the unique needs of LGBTQ+ veterans. They claim that culturally competent care for LGBTQ+ veterans must be a priority, and they highlight the work that some facilities are doing, including coordinating LGBT patient advocates, websites outlining LGBT-relevant services and applicable Veterans Health Administration policies, and techniques that facilitate welcome environments for LGBTQ veterans. Felix and Hoffman go on to highlight that service providers must also post non-discrimination policies, have LGBTQ+ veterans depicted in outreach material, and be sensitive to gender-neutral or patient-preferred terminology. As these authors highlight, the need for cultural competency among anyone who comes into contact with LGBTQ+ folx is non-negotiable. People and institutions must be attuned to the unique needs of LGBTQ+ folx and be equipped to facilitate healing and change, not perpetuate harm and mistreatment.

Training, education, and research

Culturally competent care is achieved through better and more in-depth education, training, and research. Education and training that pushes people and institutions to understand LGBTQ+ people's lived experience and how their needs can be met is crucial. Regardless of the chapter's focus, several authors called for better education and training for service providers, staff, police officers, other criminal legal professionals, social workers, and beyond.

Three chapters discussed the need for training service providers that address LGBTQ+ homelessness, intimate partner violence (IPV), and sexual violence shelters. Price and Bensel discuss how homeless LGBTQ+ individuals are often hesitant to trust, and consequently to obtain resources from, agencies and shelters where they may feel discriminated against or fear harassment from staff and/or residents. They claim that educational pursuits should be a part of the employment training curriculum for agencies and shelters that work with LGBTQ+ homeless populations, as well as other service providers, such as law enforcement, public school employees and teachers, and medical staff. With regard to LGBTQ+ IPV and sexual violence, Evans and Denysschen state that the absence of diversity infrastructures among officers and service providers can create barriers and increase safety risks for survivors. Administering trainings that focus on inclusive approaches and evidence-based interventions can strengthen survivors' sense of safety, acceptance, and trust. Similarly, Slakoff and Siegel suggest that a better step toward inclusive programing for trans survivors is to focus on training IPV and sexual violence shelter workers. They go on to note that improvements to service experiences must happen across all levels that offer support. Therefore, they recommend diversity and inclusion training that integrates information 'about the unique vulnerabilities facing transgender individuals' across the board, for police, hotline workers, and shelter staff.

Turning the focus toward youth, at least three chapters discuss the importance of education and training with regard to juvenile justice and LGBTQ+ youth more broadly. Garcia, Badiey, Chavez, and Still note the importance of ongoing training among staff to help guide them in supporting transgender, gender nonconforming, and intersex (TGNCI) youth in juvenile detention facilities. One of the key insights from their study is that staff training is a 'continuous process' that requires constant reinforcement of the department's outlined policies and procedures (and their updates), as well as support for staff whose social and cultural norms may not align with policy changes they are expected to implement. In a broader focus on institutional harm against trans youth, one of Panfil and Wooda's ten recommendations to address this harm is the need to implement comprehensive sex education that affirms LGBTQ+ identity and promotes better understanding of bodily autonomy, sexual rights, and consent. They note that a comprehensive model such as this will reduce the vulnerability to sexual abuse that LGBTQ+ youth may face. Finally, Ramirez discusses interventions for queer youth within school systems, with specific regard to integration via school curriculum and school belongingness. Ramirez notes that districts should include queer content as part of the curriculum and strive to increase feelings of school belongingness and support (that is, gay–straight alliances), because these types of interventions have the potential to shift cultural norms and expectations at both the micro and institutional levels and in turn create safer learning environments for queer youth.

While queer criminology has developed exponentially over the last 20 years, the call is particularly pertinent for critical research that makes clear the need for more culturally competent models of care. Regardless of the topic, scholars and practitioners alike call for more in-depth and vigorous research. This is also a signal to institutions that funding must prioritize LGBTQ-related studies and work, rather than relegating it back to the margins filed under 'too specific' and 'not objective enough'. Dwyer and Colvin suggest that despite institutional improvements among LGBTQ+ criminal processing system workers, harassment and discrimination still persists. As a result, there must be more specifically targeted empirical research focusing on sexuality, gender, and sex diversity in criminal processing system workers.

They note that more frequent and deeper research, accompanied by 'robust, challenging conversations' about creating safer spaces, would improve their workplace experiences and conditions worldwide. Garcia, Badiey, Chavez, and Still stress the importance of building a data-driven foundation, with research policies that carefully protect the privacy and safety of youth. They found that this is a key component to improving services and tracking outcomes among TGNCI youth in juvenile detention facilities. In addition, Evans and Denysschen suggest that more longitudinal research, larger sample sizes, and intersectional studies are needed to understand LGBTQ+ experiences over time and how that may affect service obtainment. Finally, Price and Bensel also state that more research is needed that highlights the experiences of homelessness LGBTQ+ individuals, focusing specifically on exit outcomes and strategies. It is most evident that training, education, and data-driven research must be a priority of all organizations and their funders.

Trauma-informed care

A foundational principle of gendered theories of crime and victimization – specifically, gender-responsive programming (Bloom & Covington, 1998) – is the awareness that trauma is a major underlying factor in both offending and victimization. The research here, as well as several other studies, demonstrates that trauma is a significant catalyst in LGBTQ+ lives (not just system involvement and victimization). As a result, another critical component of LGBTQ+ care is acknowledging and attending to underlying trauma. Trauma-informed models seek to 'understand the causes and consequences of trauma, and promote healing and resilience ...' (National Resource Center for Mental Health Promotion and Youth Violence Prevention, n.d., p. 1). This approach encapsulates seven key principles: understand trauma and its impact; believe that healing happens in relationships; ensure physical and emotional safety; support choice, control, and empowerment; strive for cultural competence; view youth holistically; and use a collaborative approach.

Several chapters highlight the critical need for trauma-informed care among service providers. In relation to transgender IPV, Kurdyla, Messinger, and Guadalupe-Diaz discuss at length the need for a holistic service approach that addresses transgender-specific adverse health conditions (AHCs), which are exacerbated by IPV survival. Their study outlines that service providers must be prepared to address a broad range of AHCs and underlying trauma linked to IPV and that, in addition to screening for AHCs, intervention efforts must be multilayered and tailored to address multiple forms of violence as they relate to a wide range of health covariates. In a similar vein, Katz notes that traumatic childhood and adult histories have to be examined among all folx under state and federal supervision and advocates for more prevalent use of the adverse childhood experiences scale (ACES) in the field. Finally, Momen notes that with trans people being so significantly overrepresented in the criminal legal system, there is a vital need for gender- and trauma-responsive services as part of community supervision and re-entry. In sum, we see that regardless of the services being sought, or the stage of criminal legal system involvement – intake, current supervision, or post-supervision – anyone offering services to LGBTQ folx (and everyone more broadly) must be trauma-informed in their approach.

Attending to intersectionality

For many scholars, the purpose of our work is to ensure that marginalized voices and positions are not only heard but brought to the center of focus empirically and politically. Unfortunately, much to the dismay of both historical and contemporary social movements, it is far too easy to fall into single-axis frameworks (Crenshaw, 1989) of analysis that ignore the complexities of identity in the name of pushing a primary status forward. We must acknowledge the deep, intersectional entanglements of identities within and among all marginalized groups. Otherwise, we perpetuate injustice and harm. Irvine-Baker, Canfield, and Reyes highlight that social and systemic responses (or reactions) to forms of Black femininity and masculinity are driving more Black, gender-diverse youth into the criminal legal system. As a result, they recommend that two major intersectional measures be taken. The first recommendation encourages the youth justice field to develop a deeper understanding and practice of intersectionality, which encourages those working in the field (and society at large) to deconstruct both the protective veil of white femininity and the dehumanization of Black bodies. This means moving toward ways of protecting Black, gender-diverse youth from the court system, not punishing others at higher rates. Their second recommendation, to develop intersectional youth programs that allow for gender fluidity and affirm race and gender, states that the field must implement gender and race affirming services, such as the EBP+ Collaborative. With regard to transgender IPV and sexual violence, Slakoff and Siegel state that the exploration of intersectional concerns within the criminal legal system is needed in order to fully understand and repair the ongoing issues within the system. They go on to note that this work can ensure that all people's experiences are accounted for by centering the intersectional identities of women who occupy various axes of oppression. In sum, intersectional work not only brings all voices and experiences to the table, but also serves to dismantle systems of oppression and helps to create safer environments both inside and outside the criminal legal system.

Reducing state harm

Overcoming the systemic harm done to LGBTQ+ people is not unidirectional; relationships must be transformed throughout every level of society, not just between one another. It is a viable assumption that incorporating each of the latter themes undeniably moves us in that direction. Three chapters, however, expound on additional systemic changes that move toward humanizing LGBTQ+ system-involved folx within laws, courts, and corrections.

QUEERING CRIMINOLOGY IN THEORY AND PRAXIS

Connolly and Buckelew examine the issue of pre-trial detention across four different bail fund organizations. They found that, despite each organization's differing perceptions of their relationship (working with or in tension with) the state, all four felt that they were working toward an inherently abolitionist goal of reducing the harm of incarceration by 'getting people out of cages'. Connolly and Buckelew leave readers with the powerful point that the practice of bail fund work demonstrates ways in which these organizations disrupt state violence. In turn, Rosenstadt's analysis deconstructs the legal language of bills and laws and demonstrates how legislation is often exclusionary because it fails to represent sex and gender diversity. As a result, legislation literally writes out droves of people from societal and legal existence. Rosenstadt notes that institutional language must be interrogated and improved in ways that highlight greater understanding and acceptance 'in order to prevent the delimiting of personhood, humanity, and potential for legal recognition for those who face disproportionate risks'. Regardless of their focus, both of these pieces illustrate important mechanisms to reduce state and institutional harm, and how important that is in overcoming the dehumanizing processes that these systems tend to perpetuate.

This collection of work features an autobiographical account that brings to life the irrefutable need for reducing and abolishing state harm and violence. In their piece, Harrell and Dukes demonstrate how their love and lives, entangled through both sides of the bars, doesn't just survive in solidarity, but actively resists and rejects the ways in which the state controls every essence of what it means to be human. For Harrell and Dukes, abolition is:

> [t]he solidarity of two that multiplies, a creative contagion. It refuses to be bound, despite the confines, despite the boundaries of hard time. This is what freedom looks like, even while we cannot yet see its fruition. We constructed a life for ourselves, out of pure love and determination, one we will not relinquish. We will win, odds stacked against us. When our friends inside call us a power couple, they mean we empower them. We reach back through the bars to pull each other Out of despair and defy their disappearance. We see them, we know them, we are them. Continuing the work of abolition together, each step forward on either side of the fence, is powerful in a way the PIC is not. It is an opposite, equally powerful, biopolitical force.

Queering is active resistance, and Harrell and Dukes represent how the system is continuously being queered from the inside out.

Theoretical considerations

As mentioned, while the bulk of the chapters discuss theory as it relates to practical application and recommendations, we must reiterate what queer criminology is. Queer criminological inquiry can be both identity-driven and deconstructionist (Buist & Lenning, 2016), and in doing so it exposes the importance of making broader connections between queer theory and criminology (Ball, 2014a, 2014b). The authors here demonstrate how queer theoretical insight can be used in different ways to make space for queer recognition and inclusion.

While vastly different in their theoretical orientations, several authors used Foucault, pathways theory, and norm-centered stigma theory to deconstruct and expand contemporary conceptualizations of queer lives. McDonald uses a Foucauldian framework to exemplify how queer criminology can greatly benefit from a theoretically comprehensive approach that attempts to critique and deconstruct our understandings of harm and violence. Winters conceptualizes a 'queer' pathways approach to LGBTQ+ offending by outlining how pathways to crime (that is, victimization and trauma, developmental influences, and roles of relationships) differ for LGBTQ+ folx. Winters notes that queering pathways theory can help develop more precise policy implications for addressing and preventing future offending among LGBTQ+ folx. Worthen examines cultural responses to violations of hetero-cis-normativity through the lens of norm-centered stigma theory (Worthen, 2020). This framework analyzes LGBTQ+ negativity (that is, in the form of gendered and sexualized violence), showing the socially organizational power dynamics inherent in the relationship between the two. Worthen highlights the inevitable importance of 'norm-centered conversations' when theorizing LGBTQ+ violence and victimization. Despite their differences, all three approaches use some form of identity-driven or deconstructionist perspectives in order to expand conceptualizations of the complexities of queer lived experience, particularly as it relates to harm, violence, victimization, and offending.

Conclusion

In addition to these six themes, some other areas highlighted by authors in the volume include advocacy, mutual aid, harm reduction, abolition, inclusive healthcare, protective policies, social support networks, safer housing and transitional living options, assistance with employment training, documentation, and legal aid. Where might we situate all these themes and topics? We cannot ignore the restorative and transformative nature that many of these concepts align with. While restorative justice seeks to repair harm by holding 'offenders' accountable (Daly, 2011), a transformative model seeks to transform the conditions that facilitate abuse outside the system (Coker, 2002 as cited in Decker et al., 2020). In calling for the inclusion of LGBTQ+ needs, understanding and addressing the complexities in LGBTQ+ lived experience in models of care, and holding accountable the individuals, communities, and institutions responsible for our 'well-being', we are demanding the facilitation of equity, or social justice, via non-retributive means and care.

While there is no doubt that funding and resources are slim, at least within the current capitalist models, the need for theory, empiricism, and praxis that centers LGBTQ+ (and our intersectional) needs is critical. Perhaps it comes at no better time than when discussions of defunding the police state and reallocating resources are dominating activist and academic spaces. An op-ed from the American Civil Liberties Union states that the goal of defunding the police is to reallocate the billions of dollars spent on law enforcement to more helpful services, 'like jobs, counseling, and violence-prevention programs' (Fernandez, 2020). The practical applications of queer criminology draw to the surface this undeniable need for the redistribution of resources in order to create more equitable treatment for LGBTQ+ people, and what it means to *do* justice in ways that promote humanization and agency.

As discussed in the introduction and highlighted throughout the individual chapters and the emerging themes, structure and agency as well as the humanization of marginalized populations is something that is an integral observation within the experiences of queer folx in the criminal legal system. We have asked readers to take stock of the influence of structure on agency and how structure and agency are influenced by power. The criminal legal system as a whole, and its particular branches and ancillaries, are powerful actors who have a major influence over how their organizations are represented in the larger society. What we see is that minority populations continue to feel disenfranchised by and within the criminal legal system's police, courts, and corrections. This has a lasting impact outside the system itself, however, and it can affect the ways in which individuals operate (and live) in the world. Living in constant fear of victimization from citizens and those who are supposed to protect us leads to immense emotional pain and often physical pain as well. The potential loss of freedom hanging over one's head, the distrust and suspicion, again, felt within society as a whole, but also within a variety of institutions (education, family, religion, government, economy), prohibits people from achieving agency. Imagine for a moment what that would feel like – sadly, many of us don't need to imagine it. In order to move forward with the intention of equity and justice, we must embrace what one of our authors, Rebecca Katz, states: 'it is now time for a trauma- and empathy-informed compassionate queer criminology', both inside and outside the criminal legal system.

Note

1 While we argue for the inclusion of LGBTQ+ folx broadly, we want to create constant accountability for the need for intersectionality and thus encourage readers to consistently think about and include people of color and LGBTQ+ people of color, specifically, when we see the acronym.

References

Ball, M. (2014a) 'Queer criminology, critique, and the "art of not being governed"', *Critical Criminology*, 22(1): 21–34.

Ball, M. (2014b) 'What's queer about queer criminology?', in D. Peterson & V. Panfil (eds.), *Handbook of LGBT Communities, Crime, and Justice*, New York: Springer, pp. 531–556.

Barrett, K.L. & Lynch, M.J. (2015) 'Social justice and criminal justice', in J.D. Wright (ed.), *International Encyclopedia of the Social & Behavioral Sciences* (2nd ed.), Amsterdam: Elsevier, pp. 386–391.

Bloom, B.E. & Covington, S.S. (1998) 'Gender-specific programming for female offenders: what is it and why is it important?', Paper presented at the American Society of Criminology, Washington, DC.

Buist, C.L. & Lenning, E. (2016) *Queer Criminology*, New York: Routledge.

Coker, D.K. (2002) 'Transformative justice: anti-subordination processes in cases of domestic violence', in H. Strang & J Braithwaite (eds.), *Restorative Justice and Family Violence*, Cambridge: Cambridge University Press, pp. 128–152.

Crenshaw, K. (1989) 'Demarginalizing the intersection of race and sex', *University of Chicago Legal Forum*, 139–168.

Daly, K. (2011) 'Conventional and innovative justice responses to sexual violence', *ACSSA Issues*, 12. https://aifs.gov.au/sites/default/files/publication-documents/i12.pdf

DeAngelis, T. (2015) 'In search of cultural competence', American Psychological Association. https://www.apa.org/monitor/2015/03/cultural-competence

Decker, M.R., Holliday, C.N., Hameeduddin, Z., Shah, R., Miller, J., Dantzler, J., & Goodmark, L. (2020) 'Defining justice: restorative and retributive justice goals among intimate partner violence survivors', *Journal of Interpersonal Violence*, 1–24. https://doi.org/10.1177/0886260520943728

Dwyer, A., Ball, M., & Crofts, T. (2016) 'Queering criminologies', in A. Dwyer, M. Ball, & T. Crofts (eds.), *Queering Criminology*, New York: Palgrave Macmillan, pp. 1–11.

Fernandez, P. (2020) 'Defunding the police will actually make us safer', ACLU, June 11. https://www.aclu.org/news/criminal-law-reform/defunding-the-police-will-actually-make-us-safer/

Jakobsen, J.R. (1998) 'Queer is? Queer does? Normativity and the problem of resistance', *GLQ: A Journal of Gay and Lesbian Studies*, 4(4): 511–536.

Kahle, L.L. & Rosenbaum, J. (2020) 'What staff need to know: using elements of gender responsive programming to create safer environments for system-involved LGBTQ girls and women', *Criminal Justice Studies*, 34(1): 1–14. https://doi.org/10.1080/1478601X.2020.1786281

Merriam-Webster (2021) 'Do justice to'. https://www.merriam-webster.com/dictionary/do%20justice%20to

Mogul, J.L., Ritchie, A.J., & Whitlock, K. (2011) *Queer (In)Justice: The Criminalization of LGBT People in the United States*, Boston, MA: Beacon Press.

National Resource Center for Mental Health Promotion and Youth Violence Prevention (n.d.) 'Adopting a trauma-informed approach for LGBTQ youth'. https://healthysafechildren.org/sites/default/files/Trauma_Informed_Approach_LGBTQ_Youth_1.pdf

Worthen, M.G.F. (2020) *Queers, Bis, and Straight Lies: An Investigation of LGBTQ Stigma*, New York: Routledge.

Index

Note: References to figures appear in *italic* type; those in **bold** type refer to tables.